Linux

Clearly Explained

Linux
Clearly Explained

Bryan Pfaffenberger
University of Virginia

Morgan
Kaufmann

AN IMPRINT OF ACADEMIC PRESS
A HARCOURT SCIENCE AND TECHNOLOGY COMPANY

San Diego   San Francisco   New York   Boston
London   Sydney   Tokyo

ACADEMIC PRESS
A Harcourt Science and Technology Company
525B Street, Suite 1900, San Diego, CA 92101-4495 USA
http://www.academicpress.com

Academic Press
24-48 Oval Road, London NW1 7DX United Kingdom
http://www.hbuk.co.uk/ap/

Morgan Kaufmann Publishers
340 Pine Street, Sixth Floor, San Francisco, CA 94104-3205
http://www.mkp.com

Library of Congress Catalog Card Number: 99-63441
International Standard Book Number: 0-12-553169-9

Printed in the United States of America
99 00 01 02 03 IP 9 8 7 6 5 4 3 2 1

For Suzanne, always

Contents

Acknowledgments   xv

Introduction   xvii
   What's the Goal of This Book?   xvii
   Stop Paying for Software!   xix
   Why All the Excitement About Linux?   xix
   Who Should Read This Book?   xx
   What's So Special about This Book?   xxi
   Which Version of Linux Does This Book Cover?   xxi
   How This Book Is Organized   xxii
   What's On the CD-ROM?   xxv
   A Word from the Author   xxvi

vii

Part I   **Introducing Linux**   **1**

   1   **The Unix Heritage**   **3**
        Introducing Operating Systems   4
        A Brief History of Unix   5
        The Nature of Unix   18
        The Open Source Model   22
        From Here   25
        References and Further Reading   25

   2   **The Linux Phenomenon**   **29**
        What Is Linux?   29
        A Brief History of Linux   32
        Linux Strengths   34
        Shortcomings of Linux   40
        Getting Support for Linux   48
        Keeping Up with Linux   55
        Linux and Year 2000 (Y2K) Issues   56
        From Here   56
        References and Further Reading   57

   3   **The User Interface Challenge**   **59**
        Exploring X's History   60
        Understanding Basic X Concepts   62
        Exploring Window Managers   67
        Introducing the Desktop Alternative   70
        User Interface Horizons   77
        From Here   79
        References and Selected Reading   79

Part II   **Installing Red Hat Linux**   **81**

   4   **Preparing to Install Red Hat Linux**   **83**
        Understanding the Need to Prepare   84
        Understanding Linux System Requirements   85
        Making a System Inventory   94
        Understanding the Linux Filesystem   96
        Choosing Your Installation Class   102
        Preparing Your System for a Two-OS Installation   104
        Device Configuration Horizons   111
        From Here   113
        References and Further Reading   113

5   Starting the Installation   **115**
      Making Room for Red Hat Linux   115
      Deciding How to Boot Your System   116
      Starting Linux for the First Time   118
      Starting the Installation   119
      Running Disk Druid   124
      From Here   141
      References and Further Reading   141

6   Completing the Installation   **143**
      Configuring Your Mouse   143
      Configuring Networking   145
      Configuring the Timezone   149
      Choosing Services to Start on Reboot   149
      Configuring a Printer   155
      Choosing a Root Password   161
      Making a Bootdisk   161
      Installing LILO   162
      Configuring XFree86   165
      Reinstalling Linux   169
      From Here   170
      References and Further Reading   170

Part III   Running GNOME   **171**

7   System Configuration Essentials   **173**
      Booting with LILO   174
      Understanding the Boot Process   174
      Logging In   176
      Understanding the Root User Concept   178
      Creating a User Account   179
      Enabling User Access to Disk Drives   182
      Configuring Your Sound Card   185
      Logging Out   187
      From Here   189

8   Exploring GNOME   **191**
      Introducing GNOME   192
      Using the X Window System   194
      Exploring GNOME's On-Screen Features   197

Getting Help 201
Using Windows 203
Using Session Management 208
Using Keyboard Shortcuts 209
From Here 210
References and Further Reading 210

9 Managing Files **211**
Introducing the File Manager 212
Changing Views in the Directory Window 217
Selecting Files and Directories 221
Managing Files and Directories 222
Finding Out What's in a File 231
Finding Files 243
Creating Symbolic Links 247
Associating File Types with Applications 248
Choosing File Manager Preferences 250
Understanding File Ownership and Permissions 251
Switching to Superuser Status 256
Accessing Disk Drives 257
From Here 257

10 Personalizing GNOME **259**
Understanding GNOME Customization 260
Top Customization Options 261
Decorating Your Desktop 269
Enabling Sound within GNOME 279
Adding Applets to GNOME Panels 283
Adding Drawers to GNOME Panels 286
Choosing Edge or Corner Panels 287
Positioning Panels 288
Adding More Panels 288
Changing Your Panel's Appearance 289
Choosing Pager Options 290
Customizing the Main Menu 291
Starting Programs Automatically 294
Configuring Enlightenment 298
From Here 303
References and Further Reading 303

11   Running Applications with GNOME   305
        Introducing the GNOME Desktop Accessories   306
        Exploring GNOME Applications   310
        Running KDE Applications with GNOME   315
        Running X Applications with GNOME   318
        Running Windows Software on Linux Systems   323
        From Here   324

12   Keeping Your System Running Smoothly   325
        Mounting Disks and Filesystems   326
        Formatting a Floppy Disk   329
        Determining the Amount of Free Disk Space   331
        Installing and Upgrading Software   333
        Working with Compressed Files and Archives   339
        Changing Your Password   343
        Setting the System Time and Date   344
        From Here   345
        References and Further Reading   345

Part IV   Getting Connected to the Internet   347

13   Connecting with PPP   349
        Getting the Information You'll Need   350
        Configuring Your Modem   352
        Testing Your Modem   353
        Troubleshooting Modem Problems   356
        Configuring Your PPP Connection   357
        Determining Whether Your Connection Is Working   365
        Activating and Deactivating Connections   365
        Troubleshooting Your Connection   366
        Using Other Connection Methods   367
        From Here   370
        References and Further Reading   370

14   Using Internet Applications   373
        Configuring Netscape Helper Applications   375
        Configuring Netscape Messenger for E-Mail and Newsgroups 380
        Accessing FTP Sites with File Manager   385
        Exploring Additional Internet Applications   387
        From Here   389

Part V   Learning Command Prompt Essentials   391

15   Using the Shell and File Utilities   393
Understanding Shells   394
Creating User Accounts   398
Understanding Linux Directories   401
Displaying Directory Contents   403
Finding Files   405
Reading Files   408
Renaming Files and Directories   409
Copying Files   411
Deleting Files   412
Creating and Removing Directories   413
Using Command-Line Editing Shortcuts   415
Running Programs in the Background   417
Changing File Ownership and Permissions   419
Linking Files   428
Exploring Advanced Shell Capabilities   431
From Here   433
References and Further Reading   433

16   Mastering System Administration   435
Mounting Disks and Filesystems   436
Formatting a Floppy Disk   442
Maintaining Disks   443
Creating and Extracting Archives   446
Creating a Backup Routine   449
Compressing and Decompressing Files   454
Managing User Accounts   455
From Here   460
References and Further Reading   460

17   Using Midnight Commander   463
Running Midnight Commander   464
Sorting and Filtering the File List   470
Finding Files   472
Viewing Files   475
Renaming Files and Directories   478
Tagging Files   480
Copying Files and Directories   482

Moving Files and Directories   485
Deleting Files and Directories   487
Editing Files   489
Setting Permissions   493
Creating Links   494
Using Keyboard Shortcuts   495
From Here   496
References and Further Reading   497

Afterword   **499**

Index   **501**

Acknowledgments

A book like this one isn't a solitary job; many talented people helped bring it to you. Special thanks go to Tom Stone, whose dedication to UNIX and Unix-like operating systems proved inspirational when the going got rough, and to acquisition editor Thomas Park, whose patience I must have tested time and again. I've worked with just about every publisher in the business, and these folks are tops.

A glitch-free book is about as common as a glitch-free computer program, but we've worked hard to exterminate the bugs. Technical editor and Linux guru Phil Varner did a superb job; thanks to Felix Tan, too, for help and encouragement at every step of the way. Production editor Vanessa Gerhard helped me through the production of camera-ready copy, which—for once—was *almost* fun. Julia Pfaffenberger prepared this book's index.

As always, I'd like to thank my literary agent, Carole McClendon of Waterside Productions, for linking me up with Academic Press, for putting up with my occasional snits, and most of all, for her friendship and humor.

I'd like to reserve my warmest thanks to the great people who create open source software. Many of them donate their time freely to open source projects, expecting no financial gain. Their payoff? The satisfaction of knowing that people just like you can run this great operating system on inexpensive, Intel-based hardware. Fire up that PC, and let's get started!

Introduction

Welcome to Linux Clearly Explained, your guide to mastery of Red Hat Linux 6.0. In the pages to follow, you'll find everything you need to join the ranks of Linux converts, including a CD-ROM disc containing Red Hat Linux 6.0. As you'll learn in this book, this CD-ROM contains everything you need to get started with Linux, including GNOME, the beautiful new desktop system that finally makes Linux easy to use. What's more, you'll find a free evaluation copy of Corel WordPerfect 8.0 for Linux. Able to read and write Microsoft Word files, WordPerfect is a full-featured word processing program that runs beautifully in the Linux environment. In fact, this book's CD-ROM contains just about all the software that the average person needs to perform the computing tasks they do most often. And this book shows you how to install this software and keep it humming.

What's the Goal of This Book?

Simple: To show you how to break your dependence on Microsoft Windows.

Until now, Linux has had its greatest success as an alternative to Windows NT, Microsoft's enterprise operating system, thanks to Linux's built-in networking capabilities. Thanks to the GNOME desktop (shown below), Linux is now poised to make serious inroads into the desktop operating system market as well.

The GNOME desktop combines the best of Mac OS and Windows.

This book shows you how to create a Red Hat Linux 6.0 system *right now* that may take care of all of your computing needs. If you're like most PC users, you use your system for word processing, and you may occasionally run a few other productivity applications. You connect to the Internet by means of a dial-up modem connection; while you're online, you use e-mail, you browse the Web, and you chat with other computer users with such services as Internet Relay Chat (IRC) or "buddy list" systems such as ICQ.

By reading this book, you can create a Linux system that includes all of these computer uses. The software is outstanding. (It's so efficient that it will make an older PC run as fast as the latest, priciest Windows systems.) The interface is elegant, a joy to use, and very cool. And the price is right: Free.

Stop Paying for Software!

Think about the money you've plowed into pricey, commercial programs that are full of work-destroying bugs. As you discover Linux, you'll be pleased to discover a world of free programs that often exceed the quality of commercial offerings. And all the while, you'll be saving money. This book could pay off handsomely, should you succeed in breaking your Windows habit!

Why All the Excitement About Linux?

Linux is an *operating system* for computers—notably, IBM PC-compatible computers that use Intel processors. (Linux is also available for Power PCs and certain other computers, but the IBM PC/Intel version is the one that's causing all fuss.) It's a version of the powerful Unix operating systems that have powered much larger computers for years. It's exceptionally well programmed and remarkably free from system-freezing bugs. Although Linux is copyrighted, it is distributed under the terms of a license that enables anyone to distribute the software freely, provided that they include the underlying source code and a copy of the license itself.

Free Software: Worth Only What You Pay?

Not necessarily, as millions of Linux users will readily agree. With built-in support for networking, Internet access, multiple users, and industrial-strength security, Linux rivals and may even surpass Microsoft Corporations flagship operating system, Windows NT. What's more, many people are tired of forking over so much money to Microsoft every time a new version of the Windows operating system appears. The constant cycle of upgrades forces people to purchase ever-more-powerful computers, and they must upgrade their applications, too.

The Goal: World Domination

As already mentioned, Linux has already made significant inroads into the NT market; Linux is winning acclaim as a *server* operating system for networks large and small. (A server is a computer configured to dish out information to other computers, on demand.) However, Linux is just starting its assault on the much larger user market, currently dominated by Microsoft Windows 98. The reason is simply that, until recently, Linux was just too hard to learn and use.

Thanks to the GNOME desktop, that's no longer true. When you install this book's CD-ROM and restart your system, you'll be treated to an easy-to-use interface that disguises the underlying complexity of Linux. If you've already learned Mac OS or Microsoft Windows, you can use the skills you've already learned, and you'll be up and running in no time at all.

Who Should Read This Book?

This book is for anyone who has previously used a Macintosh or Windows system, and would like to try using Linux.

You don't have to make a major investment here; as this book explains, Linux is so efficient that it can bring a disused 486 computer back to life. If you have a relatively large hard disk (say, 8GB or more), you can install Linux within the free space remaining on your hard disk. At start-up, you can choose whether to run Linux or Microsoft Windows. There's little to lose here; if you try Linux and decide it isn't for you, the 486 can go back in the closet, or you can reformat the Linux part of your disk so that it's useful to Windows again. But I'll bet you keep Linux around.

What's So Special about This Book?

GNOME makes Linux easier to use, but GNOME's pretty face cannot hide all of the underlying complexities of Linux. Some of Linux's underlying quirks show up in GNOME, too. GNOME looks a lot like Mac OS or Windows, but you'll need to understand some fundamental Linux concepts in order to use GNOME productively. A book that tells you little more than where to click within GNOME won't help you understand Linux fully, and you won't know what to do when you encounter GNOME's limits.

Linux Clearly Explained teaches the *concepts* as well as the *procedures* of Linux usage. After you've read this book, you'll possess the understanding that will enable you to make the most of GNOME.

Which Version of Linux Does This Book Cover?

This book focuses squarely on Red Hat Linux 6.0, the version of Linux you'll find on the included CD-ROM.

Although this book may prove of value to users of earlier Red Hat versions, and of other versions of Linux, I do not attempt to discuss the differences between these various "flavors" of Linux. It's not that I hold the other versions in low regard; rather, I want to get you up and running with a powerful, useful Linux system. It makes good sense, therefore, to focus on the software that's included on this book's CD-ROM. If you've messed about with other Linux versions unsuccessfully, install this book's software, and learn Red Hat Linux 6.0. Once you've mastered the fundamentals of Linux and GNOME usage, you won't have any trouble switching to a different version of Linux, should you be so inclined.

How This Book Is Organized

Unlike most of the Linux books on the market, this book was written from scratch to teach the concepts and usage of Red Hat Linux 6.0, which defaults to the GNOME desktop. Accordingly, it's organized to do the best possible job of getting you up and running with Red Hat Linux 6.0. What's more, this book is written from a "Mac-and-Windows-up" perspective, rather than a "Unix-down" perspective. I will not drag you through dozens of pages of outmoded Linux commands just because doing so is "good for you." If you can accomplish something the easy way, that's the way you learn.

Part I: Introducing Linux

To grasp Linux and use it well, it's important to understand Linux's background. In these three chapters, you'll learn how to put Linux into perspective. Chapter 1 introduces the Unix family of operating systems, and explains why Unix has dominated in every computer market except personal computers. In Chapter 2, you'll learn how Linux came to be, thanks to the efforts of a young Finnish programmer named Linus Torvalds. Chapter 3 chronicles the struggle, culminating in GNOME, to make Linux easy to use.

Part II: Installing Red Hat Linux 6.0

Contrary to what you've heard, Linux isn't much more difficult to install than other operating systems, and that's especially true when you're talking about Red Hat Linux 6.0. Still, it's nice to have a guide. In Chapter 4, you'll learn how to perform a system inventory, so you'll know whether your system is suitable for Red Hat Linux (and how you should answer certain questions that come up when the installation is underway). In Chapter 5, you'll get started with the installation, and in Chapter 6, you complete it. At the end of Part II, you'll restart your system, and you'll see for yourself just how impressive Red Hat Linux 6.0 and GNOME look on-screen.

Part III: Running GNOME

Other Linux books get to GNOME toward the end of the book, in keeping with long-standing Linux prejudices that the command-line (text) interface is "good for you." It's time to put such notions aside. In Part III, you'll learn how to make full use of GNOME for virtually everything you'll do with your computer.

Chapter 7 shows you how to configure your system so that you can use it safely; you'll learn how to set up a user account for yourself, and why it's so dangerous to run Linux as the root user. (Don't worry if these concepts don't mean much right now; they're easy to learn.) You'll learn how to get GNOME's beautiful sound system running.

In Chapter 8, you explore the GNOME desktop, which combines the best features of Mac OS and Microsoft Windows. You'll learn about some underlying quirky characteristics of Linux that could give you fits if you didn't understand them. By the time you've finished Chapter 8, you'll learn how to work around these quirks and you'll quickly gain confidence in the GNOME desktop environment.

Chapter 9 introduces the GNOME File Manager (also called GNU Midnight Commander, or GMC), which—for the first time—enables Linux users to manage files without having to learn complex commands.

Chapter 10 shows you how to personalize GNOME, creating an interface that's alive with your aesthetic sensibilities. And in Chapter 11, you'll learn how to run applications with GNOME, including WordPerfect 8.0 for Linux, which is included on this book's CD-ROM. Chapter 12 shows you how to use GNOME utilities to perform basic system administration tasks, such as formatting disks and checking the amount of free disk space.

Part IV: Getting Connected to the Internet

Now that you've mastered the fundamentals of GNOME, it's time to get connected to the Internet. Chapter 13 shows you how to create a dialup modem connection to your Internet service provider (ISP). In Chapter 14, you'll explore the world of Internet applications for Linux, including Netscape Communicator (included with this book's CD-ROM) and the new GNOME Internet utilities.

Part V: Learning Command Prompt Essentials

As you've learned, the complexity of Linux lurks beneath GNOME's good-looking exterior. And sometimes, it makes good sense to leave GNOME aside and go *mano-a-mano* with the Linux command-line interface. Some jobs are actually accomplished more easily at the *Linux prompt*, a symbol that tells you that Linux is waiting for you to type something. And sometimes there's no other way to install new software than to follow the instructions detailing what to type at the command prompt. Accordingly, Part V teaches the fundamentals of command prompt usage.

In Chapter 15, you'll learn how to use the default Red Hat *shell*, the program that provides a text-based interface to Linux. You'll also learn how to use the file utilities that come with Red Hat Linux. You don't have to memorize the information in this chapter, but it may come in very handy for reference purposes.

In Chapter 16, you'll learn how to perform system administration tasks with the command prompt interface. As you'll learn, there are still certain operations that can only be performed using the command-prompt approach, whereas others are more conveniently performed at the command prompt.

Chapter 17 fully teaches the use of Midnight Commander, the text-based version of the GNOME File Manager. With more features than the GNOME version, Midnight Commander is the utility of choice for quick, effective system administration. With Midnight Commander, you can safely perform powerful system maintenance operations and increase your understanding of Linux.

What's On the CD-ROM?

This book's CD-ROM includes Red Hat Linux 6.0 and Word-Perfect 8.0 for Linux. In this section, you'll learn how to install this software on your computer.

Installing Red Hat Linux 6.0

To install Red Hat 6.0 on your system using this book's CD, please follow the instructions in Chapters 4, 5, and 6.

Installing WordPerfect 8.0 for Linux

After you've installed Red Hat Linux 6.0, you can install WordPerfect for Linux 8.0. I'd suggest that you work through Chapters 7 through 9 before you attempt to install WordPerfect.

> **CAUTION** Do not install WordPerfect for Linux 8.0 as the root user. Doing so could create a security hole that intruders could exploit. Please install the software after logging in to your user account. To create a user account, see Chapter 7. In addition, you will need to configure your system so that you can access your CD-ROM drive from your user account. For more information, see Chapter 7.

To install WordPerfect for Linux 8.0, do the following:

1. **Important:** Log in to GNOME with your user login name and password. Do not install WordPerfect from the root user account.

2. Insert this book's CD-ROM in your CD-ROM drive.

3. On the GNOME desktop, point to the CD-ROM icon, click the right mouse button, and choose Mount.

4. Double-click the CD-ROM icon. You'll see a File Manager window showing the CD-ROM's contents.

5. Double-click the /wp directory. You'll see the file in this directory (GUILG00.GZ).

6. In the Tree View, display your home directory.

7. In the GNOME File Manager, click File, point to New, and choose Directory. In the Create a New Directory window, type **temp** and click OK.

8. Hold down the Shift key, and drag GUILG00.GZ to your temp directory you just created.

9. Click the Main Menu button, point to Utilities, and choose GNOME Terminal.

10. In the GNOME Terminal window, type **cd temp** and press Enter.

11. In the GNOME Terminal window, carefully type the following: **gunzip GUILG00.GZ** and press Enter. Note that you must type the capital letters as shown here. Those are zeros in the file name, not the letter O.

12. In the GNOME Terminal window, type **tar -xvf GUILG00** and press Enter.

13. In the GNOME Terminal window, type **./Runme** and press Enter. Don't forget the dot and forward slash. Also, note that you must type a capital R.

14. You'll see the message, "Did you unzip and untar the files you downloaded?" Type y and press Enter. The script will continue extracting the archives, and you'll see the Install Configuration dialog box.

15. Now you'll see the WordPerfect installation program, which is an X Window System application. Click one of the license options to confirm your acceptance of the WordPerfect license and select your default language, and click OK to continue.

16. You'll see the license text. Please read this carefully. If you accept, click Accept.

17. In the Installation Directory dialog box, type **/usr/local/wp** and click OK.

18. In the Installation Size dialog box, select the installation size you prefer (Full, Medium, or Minimal). The default setting (Full) is best if you have sufficient disk space (70MB). Click OK to confirm.

19. In the next two dialog boxes (Existing Application and Edit /etc/magic), just click OK to accept the defaults.

20. In the Selection of Languages to Install dialog box, select your language preference, and click OK.

21. In the Select WordPerfect Printer Drivers dialog box, highlight your printer and click Select. If you're using a PostScript printer that isn't on the list, choose Apple Laserwriter. Click OK to confirm your printer choice.

22. In the Assign Printer Drivers to Printer Destinations dialog box, select your printer, if necessary, and click Assign. In the Destinations dialog box, select lp, and click OK. Click OK to confirm.

23. In the Optional Installation Features dialog box, just click OK to accept the default.

24. You'll see the Installation Review List. To review your installation choices, select any of the options, and click OK. To continue the installation using the choices you've made, click OK without selecting anything.

    The installation software installs the files on your computer. This will take a few minutes.

25. Click Done to exit the installation program.

Note that WordPerfect for Linux is a copyrighted commercial program. You are free to use the software for a period of 90 days before you must register the product. For personal and educational uses, you can continue to use the product for free. For more information, see http://linux.corel.com.

Running WordPerfect for Linux 8.0

To run WordPerfect for Linux 8.0, click the Main Menu button in GNOME, and choose Run Program. In the Run Program dialog box, type **/usr/local/wp/wpbin/xwp** and click Run.

TIP To start WordPerfect without having to type the lengthy path-name, add an application launcher to your GNOME Panel. Learn how in Chapter 10.

A Word from the Author

I believe that Linux will soon dominate the user operating system market. Microsoft Windows has done an excellent job of making Bill Gates rich (not to mention Microsoft stockholders), but it hasn't accomplished all that it should have for users: Windows seems too buggy to many users, and Windows applications are too expensive. What's more, computing now stands at a crucial moment, historically. If non-computer users in developed and developing countries are to have a chance to join the computer revolution, they need an operating system and applications that do not force them into a cycle of repeated, expensive upgrades. Linux and GNOME represent the leading points of a revolution, in which users are taking computing back from the hands of huge, wealthy corporations.

It's time to join them, and that's why I've written this book. I hope it lives up to its name, and explains Linux in the clearest possible terms. Please bear in mind, though, that Linux in general—and GNOME in particular—are undergoing very rapid development. Already slated is a 1.1 release of GNOME, which will enable new features. To learn Linux and GNOME, you'll be wise to install this book's software so you can follow this book's presentation, but be aware that new versions of GNOME will sport new features that this book can't discuss.

Also, please remember that I can't provide technical support for Linux or GNOME. Here in my Charlottesville home, it's just me, my two kids, my wife, and the cat. Surely you'll see that I can't deal with 20,000 people sending me e-mail about various problems they're experiencing. The answer's out there; you just need to learn how to get it, as Chapter 2 explains. If you've a *specific* question or suggestion concerning *this* book, or if you've found a glitch in the text somewhere, by all means let me know (bp@virginia.edu). Due to the huge volume of mail I get, please don't get your feelings hurt if you don't get a reply right away.

Bryan Pfaffenberger
Charlottesville, Virginia

Part One

Introducing Linux

1

The Unix Heritage

To grasp the Linux phenomenon, it's helpful to begin with its progenitor and inspiration, the operating system called Unix. Created by a small group of researchers at Bell Laboratories starting in 1969, Unix is unquestionably the most influential operating system ever developed; it has influenced virtually every subsequent operating system, including MS-DOS, Mac OS, Sun's Solaris, and many more.

In this chapter, you'll learn what operating systems do, how Unix developed, and why many experts believe Unix to be the best operating system ever created. You'll also learn about the struggle to create a free version of Unix. This background will enable you to grasp the significance of Linux, a version of

Unix that has been developed for a wide variety of computing platforms (including PCs with Intel processors).

NOTE In this chapter, I use the term "Unix"—with an initial capital letter and lowercase letters following—to refer to the family of operating systems that derive directly or indirectly from the code originally developed at AT&T's Bell Laboratories, including Unix clones (such as Linux) that mimic Unix but do not incorporate any of the code developing from AT&T's versions of Unix or code subsequently developed by companies that held the rights to AT&T's code. When I use the term "UNIX"—all capital letters—I'm referring only to the copyrighted code that derives directly from the AT&T code. The rights to UNIX are currently held by X/Open, Inc.

Introducing Operating Systems

An *operating system* (Tanenbaum 1987) is a type of computer system software that is loaded automatically at the beginning of an operating session. In today's computers, operating systems are devoted to the following essential tasks:

- Handling input and output operations from peripherals, such as hard disks, printers, and modems, so that these operations do not conflict with each other or interfere with the execution of programs.
- Managing the computer's memory so that two or more programs can use memory without interfering with each other.
- Managing processor usage so that each application is given a turn in an efficient way.
- Interacting with the user (by means of a user interface) so that the user can initiate operations and deal with errors.

In the beginning of the computer era, operating systems did not exist. A computer was programmed to process data in a rigid, four-step operation: input, storage, processing, and output. Called *batch processing*, this technique is extremely inefficient because the processing unit is idle most of the time.

In the 1960s, IBM began work on a massive new operating system, System/360, that would run on all of its new computers. To make more efficient use of the processor, System/360 introduced a number of innovations, including *multiprogramming* and *time-sharing*. In multiprogramming (also called *multitasking*), the operating system allows two or more applications to take turns gaining access to the processor. In time-sharing, two or more users can operate the computer independently, and each of them is given the illusion of having sole control of the computer.

In collaboration with General Electric and Massachusetts Institute of Technology (MIT), AT&T's Bell Labs also initiated work on an equally massive operating system, called Multics, that could support hundreds of simultaneous time-sharing users. However, the Multics project ran into difficulties, and by the late 1960s it had become apparent that the "bigger is better" philosophy of operating system development posed enormous risks. IBM eventually delivered System/360, but only after encountering massive cost overruns and lengthy delays.

A Brief History of Unix

Unix developed in the aftermath of the Multics fiasco (Ceruzzi 1998, Salus 1994). If bigger wasn't necessarily better, there was another way: "Small is beautiful," a saying popularized by ecologist E.F. Schumaker in a widely read 1960s best-seller by the same name.

"The Little-Used Machine in a Corner"

After Bell Labs pulled out of the Multics project, two Multics veterans—Ken Thompson and Dennis Ritchie—were hoping to find a computer they could use to play a game they had developed, called Space Travel. They found a disused PDP-7 minicomputer (a "little-used machine in a corner"), and soon succeeded in porting a miniaturized version of Multics to this computer (as well as Space Travel). Because their reduced version of the giant operating system could support only one user at a time, they called it "Unix," a pun on Multics.

As they experimented with the machine, Thompson and Ritchie developed a multi-user file system so that they could avoid interfering with each other's files. Soon, the two realized that they had the germ of an effective operating system—one founded on principles of simplicity and economy—and the Unix philosophy began to take shape: keep programs small and simple, and combine programs to do complicated tasks.

To develop the nascent operating system, Thompson and Ritchie needed a better computer. However, they knew they could not persuade the Bell Labs to purchase such a computer to support operating system development. So they developed a proposal to create a text-processing system, and wound up with a brand-new PDP-11 minicomputer. This is the reason you'll find so many text-processing programs included with a standard Unix distribution.

From its beginnings, Unix was developed as a platform for programming as well as an operating system. Thompson and Ritchie developed the C programming language, so named because it was the successor to the B language, and rewrote much of the core of Unix (called the *kernel*) in C.

The Unix Philosophy

Thompson and Ritchie developed not only an operating system and a programming language; they also developed a coherent philosophy of software design, and did an excellent job of conveying this philosophy to their colleagues in colleges and universities.

As outlined by Mike Gancarz in his *Unix Philosophy* (Digital Press, 1995) and by others, the essential tenets of the Unix philosophy can be summarized as follows:

- **Keep programs small; each should accomplish just one task well.** Small programs are easy to create, debug, and reuse. You should focus on creating small programs that function perfectly; only then should you put them together to do more complicated things.
- **Portability is better than efficiency.** You can write operating system software in assembly code for maximum efficiency, but assembly language is difficult to maintain and cannot be translated to function on new hardware. For this reason, it's best to write code—even operating system code—in high-level programming languages, which can be translated easily from one computing platform to another. Any losses in efficiency will be compensated by gains in the speed of the next generation of computer hardware.
- **Enable programs to transfer data to each other.** Instead of designing programs so that they process data and write results to a file, you should enable programs to pass data to other programs as a data stream that does not require interim storage. In this way several simple programs can be grouped in a series to perform complex operations.

- **Don't reinvent the wheel.** Program code should be openly shared so that programmers can gain leverage from each others' efforts.
- **Get a prototype running as soon as possible, and use it.** The only real testing is real-world testing.
- **Make the operating system as small as possible.** This tenet is yet another variant on the "small is beautiful" theme. Small operating systems are much more likely to be stable. In Unix, the core operating system components are called the *kernel*. If complexity is needed, it can be added at a higher level of abstraction.
- **Permit users to choose their own shell.** The *shell*, or user interface, should be completely separate from the kernel. Users should be able to choose their own shell or switch between shells transparently, as needs arise.
- **Store configuration data in ASCII text files.** Doing so makes it easy to edit and process these files using text-manipulation software.
- **Use a simple, overarching metaphor.** In Unix, everything the computer does is conceptualized as a stream of data that can be grouped and understood as a file —and this includes peripherals, such as CD-ROM drives, floppy disks, and more. This is one of the most confusing things about Unix for first-time users.

The Unix philosophy can be summarized by the phrase "worse is better." This phrase implies that technology that incorporates working compromises is more likely to gain market acceptance than technology that tries to excel in all areas.

The "worse is better" philosophy is, admittedly, far from universally admired. At universities such as MIT and Stanford, some computer scientists recoil in the face of Unix's willingness to compromise; for example, Unix sacrifices efficiency for portability. Here, Thompson and Ritchie's working environment (a private-sector research lab) undoubtedly freed them to make such compromises; had they worked in a university, they would have been under considerable pressure to create systems that met high standards of coherence and logicity. (It's interesting to note that much of the hostility directed toward Unix stems from university researchers who specialize in LISP, an elegant and beautifully logical language originally developed for artificial intelligence research. The university researchers' esteem for LISP is not shared by outside world, which has shown very little interest in LISP-based operating systems and applications.)

Unix Escapes from the Lab

Unix first came to the attention of the computer science community in 1973, when Thompson and Ritchie gave a paper at a symposium on operating system principles. The paper was subsequently published in the influential *Communications of the ACM*, the flagship journal of the Association for Computing Machinery. In response to a flood of requests from colleagues in computer science departments, Thompson and Ritchie began to distribute computer tapes containing the operating system code.

Despite the excitement created by Unix, AT&T couldn't sell the nascent operating system. Before the court-mandated breakup of AT&T in 1981, the company was under a court order that prohibited its involvement in the commercial computing market. In exchange, the company retained its lucrative telephone service monopoly throughout the United States.

These restrictions did not prevent Bell Labs from distributing Unix to colleges and universities, however. For a nominal fee, AT&T made Unix available to computer science departments at colleges and universities, which found the offer very attractive. Unix appealed for the following reasons:

- Because most of Unix was written in the C programming language, the operating system could be compiled and installed on any computer that had a C compiler.
- Unlike commercial OS vendors, AT&T had little interest in protecting the integrity of the Unix source code. As a result, university students and faculty were free to modify Unix so that the OS could work with specific peripherals, such as disks and printers. This work provided excellent training for students.

The circumstances under which Unix was released favored the development of an active, collaborating community of users. AT&T's policies concerning Unix forbade the system's originators from providing support, documentation, or bug fixes. This policy virtually forced Unix users to collaborate in order to solve problems and configure the system to work with new peripherals and new platforms. A Unix User's Group first met in 1974; the organization later became the Usenix Association (www.usenix.org), which is today the largest organization of Unix users worldwide.

The Berkeley Software Distribution (BSD)

Although the number of Unix installations grew steadily during the mid- to late-1970s, the operating system gained a reputation for being extremely difficult to use. One wag called it a "guru-friendly operating system," pointing out that the cryptic commands were close to useless unless you had considerable experience with Unix.

Unix's user-unfriendliness derived, in part, from the memory limitations of the PDP-7 minicomputer that served as the original development platform. The original Unix command set is cryptic to the extreme; abbreviated commands (such as "grep" for "globally search for the regular expression and print") were the norm. In addition, a cornerstone of the Unix philosophy is that the output of one program should be useful as the input for another. For this reason, programs did not generate a lot of verbose messages, which would be useful to the user but not to the program to which the output was being piped.

During the 1970s, minicomputers steadily gained more memory and processing power, presenting an opportunity to create a more user-friendly version of Unix. At the University of California, Berkeley, a computer science graduate student named Bill Joy created a more accessible version of Unix, one designed to take advantage of CRT-based terminals. In 1978, Joy and his colleagues started offering tapes of the Berkeley Software Distribution (BSD) at a nominal cost. Soon, BSD acquired momentum as a de facto "standard" version of Unix. For the next 15 years, Berkeley's Computer Systems Research Group (CSRG), which emerged from Joy's efforts, released a series of influential BSD distributions that served to define the nature and capabilities of Unix.

In creating the BSD distribution model, CSRG achieved more than an improved version of Unix, one that is today considered by many to be one of the best ever created. Joy and his colleagues also created a powerful model for effective, noncommercial software development. With each BSD release, programmers worldwide would receive the latest versions of the Unix kernel and associated software; if they improved an existing module or created a new one, they sent it to Berkeley, and it would be included in the next distribution. The only incentive offered to participating programmers was to receive credit for their work—and, if the software turned out to be excellent, the esteem of their colleagues. This incentive proved

sufficient to encourage thousands of programmers to contribute to the rapidly developing system.

The TCP/IP Factor

At Berkeley, Unix joined paths with another phenomenon of
the computing industry: the Internet protocols, called TCP/IP.
Developed under funding from the U.S. Advanced Research
Projects Agency (ARPA), TCP/IP enables computers of differing makes or models to network efficiently over a wide variety
of transmission media. Inherently a multiplatform networking
technology, TCP/IP would seem to have a natural affinity to
Unix—and at Berkeley, the two crossed paths, thanks to an
ARPA grant in support of BSD software development. Version
4.2 BSD included TCP/IP support for this first time, and its
widespread acceptance at colleges and universities launched
the Internet on its spectacular upward trajectory.

UNIX Goes Commercial

With Unix installations proliferating like wildfire, AT&T's
management soon realized that its research labs had created
technology that could prove lucrative if the U.S. government
freed AT&T from entering the computer and software markets. The company awarded the rights to UNIX to the Unix
Systems Laboratories (USL), which—unlike AT&T—was free
to pursue commercial development. USL developed UNIX System V, a commercial product that could cost a corporate buyer
up to $100,000 in software licensing fees (Martin 1993).

For more than a decade, USL tolerated the Berkeley Software
Distribution, presumably because the distribution seemed to
pose no threat to USL's lucrative corporate sales. However,
when Berkeley faculty formed a startup firm called Berkeley
Software Design, Inc. (BSDI), and proposed to market the BSD
distribution, USL filed suit. But AT&T sold the UNIX System

V rights to Novell, which subsequently decided to pull out of the UNIX market (Bozman 1995). Novell dropped the lawsuits and sold the UNIX trademark to X/Open, Inc.

The efforts to establish UNIX as a proprietary (and pricey) operating system were not received warmly by the Unix community. Unix users and programmers were accustomed to the free Berkeley software distributions, and resented not only the high cost of commercial UNIX software, but also the UNIX licensing restrictions that prevented them from incorporating the AT&T code into their programs. Resentment over efforts to transform UNIX into a commercial product led to the emergence of the Free Software Foundation and the GNU Project, an essential predecessor of Linux.

A Unix Chronology

1965	Bell Laboratories joins MIT and General Electric in bid to create a multi-user operating system called Multics
1969	AT&T drops out of Multics project; Thompson and Ritchie create first versions of Unix on a disused PDP-7 microcomputer.
1973	Unix rewritten in C, a new high-level programming language.
1974	Unix philosophy explained in widely read article.
1977	AT&T released UNIX System 7, and announces fees for use of UNIX source code.
1979	Berkeley Software Distribution (BSD Unix) begins.
1983	AT&T releases UNIX System V; Berkeley releases the influential BSD 4.2, including support for TCP/IP.
1984	AT&T divestiture; AT&T free to compete in computer marketplace.
1991	Linus Torvalds creates Linux kernel as part of a master's thesis in Finland.
1992	AT&T sues BSDI for copyright infringement, but sells UNIX to Novell; Berkeley's Computer Systems Research Group closes down; Microsoft announces Windows NT.
1994	Novell sells "UNIX" trademark to X/Open, Inc.

The GNU Project and the General Public License (GPL)

In 1984, Richard Stallman, then a professor of computer science at MIT, resigned his position to found a new, nonprofit organization called the Free Software Foundation (FSF). Its goal is to develop a new, copyright-free version of the Unix operating system, called GNU's Not UNIX (Free Software Foundation 1999, Fraser 1990). Harnessing the efforts of hundreds of volunteer programmers, the GNU Project has created copyright-free code that emulates much of the Unix operating system. They have also created an important new concept of intellectual property, often called *open source software* (FSF prefers the term "free software").

TIP Open source software isn't necessarily free; companies can and do charge money for open source software. What's free about open source software is the source code, the programming that underlies a product's functionality. A software company can charge money for compiled open source software, but they must make the source code freely available to others.

The GNU Project releases software under the terms of the GNU General Public License (GPL), which specifies a form of intellectual ownership that FSF calls *copyleft*. In brief, GPL gives software licensees the right to use, copy, and redistribute the software. It also gives users the right to view and modify the *source code*, the programming code that underlies the software's functioning.

What GPL expressly forbids, however, is the inclusion of any GPL-licensed code in a commercial software product that does not come with open, modifiable source code. In other words, if you obtain GPL-licensed code, and wish to distribute it to others, you must give others the same rights you were initially given; you can't incorporate GPL-licensed code in a product and then deny others the GPL-mandated right to your source code. According to FSF, the General Public License directly addresses the deficiencies of the BSD license, which did not forbid licensees from incorporating the code into commercial products that denied access to the underlying code.

TIP Note that GPL terms do not prohibit software developers from receiving money for their efforts; open source software isn't necessarily free in a monetary sense. Open source developers can and do receive payment for their work, but they must allow those who obtain their programs to get the source code too, and they must also permit licensees to modify and redistribute the source code. In practice, all or most open source software can be obtained without charge, but it's often more convenient to pay a small fee to obtain the software in an easy-to-install collation called a distribution. You'll learn more about distributions in Chapter 2.

The GNU Project did not succeed in its goal to create a complete Unix clone. Although Stallman succeeded in creating copyright-free versions of most of the associated software, he was sidelined by an incapacitating repetitive strain injury and never finished the Unix kernel, the core of the operating system (Mann 1999).

The Need for Standardization

The legal wrangling over Unix has ended, but no single, standard version of Unix has emerged in the marketplace. Most current versions of Unix are influenced by either AT&T's System V or Berkeley BSD, but the derivatives are numerous. According to one estimate, more than 200 versions (or "flavors") of Unix exist, each with its own, sometimes idiosyncratic command set.

In the commercial UNIX marketplace, several commercial versions vie for the enterprise computing marketplace, but the lack of standardization—especially user interface standardiza-tion—has created a tremendous market opportunity for Microsoft Windows NT. Offering the familiar and easy-to-use Windows interface, NT is targeted directly at the client/server networks where Unix current predominates.

In an effort to standardize UNIX so that it can fend off the NT threat, commercial UNIX vendors have rallied around the Open Group, an industry consortium formed in 1996 by merging the Open Software Foundation (OSF) and the X/Open Company. The Open Group promotes the Single UNIX Specification, which specifies a common application programming interface (API) for UNIX operating systems. By conforming to this interface, a programmer can be confident that an application will run on any UNIX system that also conforms to these guidelines. Conforming operating systems and applications can apply for, and use, the UNIX trademark under license from the Open Group. In addition, the Open Group promotes and supports the Common Desktop Environ-ment (CDE), a desktop/windowing interface for UNIX com-puters. Although official Linux organizations cannot refer to the Open Group standards without paying licensing fees, Linux conforms to these standards (Irwin 1998).

Standardization is proceeding along another, compatible avenue, thanks to the Portable Operating System Interface for Unix (POSIX) standard, jointly developed by the Institute for Electrical and Electronic Engineering (IEEE) and the Interna-tional Organization for Standardization (ISO, which isn't an acronym but rather the Greek word *iso*, which means "equal"). POSIX defines a standard application programming interface (API) for Unix operating systems, thus giving pro-grammers some assurance that their programs, when compiled on a POSIX-compliant platform, will run properly. Linux is a POSIX-compatible version of Unix.

Unix in the Enterprise

In spite of these standardization efforts, the various versions or flavors of Unix continue to differ, and Unix still has an unenviable reputation of being difficult to learn and use.

Unix continues to win adherents in corporate information systems (IS) departments, where Unix possesses an excellent reputation for *scalability* (the capacity to cope with a rapid growth in the number of users). To free themselves from expensive mainframes, corporations developed Unix-powered *client/server networks*. In a client/server network, powerful computers called *servers* dish out data and applications to networked *workstations*, where users run programs called *clients* to tap into the central data repository. Because Windows NT is essentially restricted to PCs running Intel hardware, Unix will continue to prevail in the high-end server market (Babcock 1995). Unix also prevails in the technical workstation market, but Windows NT is making inroads, particularly on smaller networks that don't need Unix's industrial-strength server capability (Greenfield 1997). As the next chapter explains, Linux is also moving into this niche.

Despite the rapid growth of Windows NT, you shouldn't write off Unix in the enterprise just yet. In 1999, the Unix market will generate an estimated $23 billion in sales, as against $12.8 billion for its closest competition, Windows NT. According to a recent report, Unix is widening its lead against Windows NT in the server market (Patrizio 1998); the Unix share of the server market grew from 36 percent to nearly 43 percent from 1996 to 1998, and NT's share grew from nearly 10 percent to 16.2 percent (half Unix's rate). Linux will accelerate this trend by bringing Unix capabilities to inexpensive Intel-based processors.

The Nature of Unix

Unix's popularity is simply explained: It is arguably the most sophisticated, robust, scalable, and stable operating system ever developed. In this section, you learn more about the technical design and capabilities of today's Unix operating systems.

The Three Levels of Unix

To understand Unix's design philosophy, it's useful to think of Unix as being composed of three independent levels:

- **Kernel** This is the operating system in the strict sense, the core of the code that manages the computer's resources, handles input/output operations, and allocates access to the memory and processor.
- **File system** More than just a way of organizing files, the Unix file system provides the overarching metaphor for conceptualizing all aspects of the computer system, including peripherals (which are represented as if they were files). Founded on a concept of the file system as a hierarchy of objects (with directories and subdirectories), the Unix file system model profoundly influenced subsequent operating system development (for example, MS-DOS directories and subdirectories are modeled expressly on Unix file system concepts).
- **Shell** Completely separate from the operating system proper, the shell accepts user input and displays messages from the system. Because the shell is totally independent from both the file system and the kernel, users can use the shell of their choice.

This "divide and conquer" approach enables system programmers to focus on keeping each component as small and manageable as possible.

The Unix design philosophy contrasts sharply with Microsoft's recent efforts to incorporate more features into the inner workings of its operating systems. In Windows 98, for example, the shell is irretrievably tied to the kernel and file system—users have no choice of shells—and the company seems bent on incorporating applications as well, such as the Internet Explorer web browser.

Viewed from the perspective of Unix design philosophy, Microsoft's strategy embodies a serious and potentially fatal technical design mistake. Trying to weave so many components into the operating system could lead to a bloated, unstable, bug-ridden monstrosity that can't be delivered on time and on budget (like Multics).

According to Microsoft's critics (among them the U.S. Department of Justice), Microsoft has pursued this approach, not on its technical merits, but rather in the hope of putting competitors out of business. In response, Microsoft argues that its customers want features such as browsers to be included as tightly integrated components of the operating system. Unix, in contrast, goes to the other extreme, giving users almost total freedom to define their operating environment—so much freedom that there is less consistency from one Unix workstation to the next than one finds in the Windows or Macintosh worlds.

The Achievements of Unix

Simply put, Unix defines what a high-quality operating system should do. One by one, competing systems (such as Microsoft Windows) have been upgraded so that they match a feature set that Unix achieved more than a decade ago. These features include the following:

- **Multitasking** Unix can run two or more programs at the same time. When running, these programs are called *processes*. They can communicate with each other. Some processes, called *daemons*, are configured to run occasionally, or at regular times.

- **Preemptive multitasking** Unix controls multitasking processes so that an abnormal process can be terminated ("killed") without crashing the computer.
- **Symmetric multiprocessing** Unix can work with computers that have more than one processing unit (CPU).
- **Time-sharing** Two or more users can use the system independently, with each of them having the illusion of being the sole users of the system.
- **Virtual memory** By using part of the computer's hard disk, Unix can make the computer's RAM memory seem larger than it is. The portion of disk space used for this purpose is called the *swap file*.
- **Built-in TCP/IP and Ethernet support** Unix supports the Internet protocols (TCP/IP) and Ethernet networking at the operating system level, making the system ideal for Internet and local area network (LAN) use.
- **Portability** Because Unix is written mostly in C, a high-level programming language, it can be easily ported (translated) to many computer platforms. Today, Unix runs on more different types of computers than any other operating system.

The Shortcomings of Unix

Despite the technical achievements of Unix, the system's design philosophy pushes the shell out of the operating system proper. This design philosophy makes good technical sense, and as you'll learn in the next chapter, it opens up important possibilities for shell configuration that stretch most people's understanding of what a user interface is about.

From the user's perspective, however, the shell's second-fiddle, independent status, coupled with the proliferation of varying Unix flavors, means that there's no single, universal skill set for Unix use. As you'll learn in the next chapter, universities and vendors have developed graphical user interfaces (GUIs) for Unix computers, but they vary considerably from one interface to the next. For example, the now-defunct but brilliant NeXT workstation and Sun SPARCStations both run Unix, but their user interfaces are as different, arguably, as the difference between Mac OS and Microsoft Windows.

For most users, though, the worst of Unix lies in the near-impossibility of avoiding command-line shells, which requires users to type commands such as the following:

```
mv GUILG00.bin GUILG00.tar.gz; gunzip
GUILG00.tar.gz; tar -xvf GUILG00.tar
```

This is the command used to install a downloaded copy of Corel WordPerfect for Linux. Do you think that current Windows or Macintosh users would appreciate having to type such a command?

Looking at Unix, we see not only the technically powerful operating system, but also the various accumulated strata of its historical development: the wealth of infrequently-used text processing commands left over from Unix's earl justification as a text-management system; the original, cryptic commands that can be chained together, but only by a highly experienced user; and the earliest Internet software, such as Telnet and the trn newsreader, with their nongraphical user interfaces and terse documentation. Unix is often taught as if learning to use these artifacts is part and parcel of Unix literacy. That may be true in a historical sense, but it flies in the face of what Unix stands to become, if it ever gains the user interface technology that it deserves.

In the next chapter, you'll find out whether the long-promised easy Unix interface is about to materialize. Without it, Unix will remain a high-end server system, and Windows will continue to dominate the desktop.

The Open Source Model

When the Unix story reaches its final chapter, historians will surely conclude that one of its greatest achievements is social rather than technical.

Open Source Software Can Excel

The Berkeley Software Distribution was the first of a long series of development projects that proved, incontrovertibly, that open source software development could produce high-quality software. That this is counter-intuitive is a major understatement: One would think that a chaotic, wide-open process, in which anyone can submit code, would lead to a buggy, unreliable, mess. But that's not necessarily the case. What Unix demonstrated is the surprising possibility that open source development could lead to software that is actually superior to commercial offerings.

Why does the open source development process work so well? Here are the key factors:

- **The Internet** Distributed with BSD 4.2 and later, the Internet makes it possible to harness the collective IQ of hundreds or even thousands of volunteer programmers.
- **Hacker culture** In the computing community, the term *hacker* does not mean "computer criminal." It refers instead to a programmer who uses considerable expertise and ingenuity to make computers perform in impressive ways (Levy 1984, Raymond 1998b). Hackers enjoy

solving problems just for the intellectual challenge of doing so, and often because they both seek and appreciate the esteem and admiration of their peers (Raymond 1998c).

- **Peer review** In contrast to closed source software, open source software is constantly subject to rigorous, probing peer review, in which highly competent professional programmers can inspect the source code and detect programming errors. What is more, these programmers are generally far closer to a program's customer base than closed source developers; the peer reviewers work for companies that ultimately will adopt the product. For this reason, open source software often offers superior security; security concerns are very high on the radar of programmers working in private-sector companies.

- **Norm development** Open source software development is susceptible to *forking*, in which the very openness of the process—the availability of source code—leads to the development of alternative versions of a program. Although forking occurs, it is inhibited by community norms that devalue forking. Out of respect for an important program's original developer, contributors submit their modifications to the original developer, who becomes the unofficial project leader, the source of software redistribution, and (generally) the final arbiter of which modifications get into a product (Raymond 1998c). Open source development works best when a respected leader assumes the role of a benevolent dictator.

To capture the significance of open source software development, Eric S. Raymond (1998) uses the metaphors of the cathedral and the bazaar:

- **The Cathedral** In this model, which was once thought to be the only way quality software could be developed, a team of expert programmers work in isolation; the product will turn out to have many vexing bugs, which take a long time to find and fix. The product isn't released until it's sufficiently stable.

- **The Bazaar** In this model, a developer publishes the very incomplete, very buggy source code for a new program, and invites assistance. As contributions come in, they're incorporated into the code and released; the releases are frequent. Participants are praised for their work and rewarded by seeing how well the product is coming along.

The Lessons of Open Source Development

Since BSD, the following facts about mature open source programs have been affirmed by experience:

- **Open source software is more reliable than commercial products**. Unlike commercially developed software, open source software is subjected to widespread peer review by competent, brilliant programmers. Bugs are quickly discovered and quickly propagate via the network; the fixes are incorporated rapidly into the next distribution.
- **Open source software offers better security**. The software is exposed to scrutiny by user/programmers who are familiar with the actual, day-to-day challenges of computer security. The open source development model is much closer to the customer.
- **Open source software is rich in features.** With so many participants contributing their "pet" ideas, open source software becomes rich in features and associated tools. BSD remains a force in the Unix marketplace precisely because it offers such a rich feature set.

Skeptical? The Unix story makes the case. When Unix tapes first found their way to university computer science departments, proprietary operating systems prevailed (including DEC's VAX/VMS, CDC's Scope, and the dominant operating system of workstation computing, Apollo's Domain). But BSD set in motion a transformation that, within 15 years, had completely wiped out virtually all competing operating systems for workstations.

Still skeptical? The software that runs the Internet was developed using the open software model. For example, a mail server program called sendmail runs an estimated 80 percent of the mail servers currently operating worldwide. BIND (Berkeley Internet Name Daemon) is the *de facto* standard name server (also called DNS server) for the Internet. Without BIND, the Internet would not function.

From Here

What's been missing in the Unix world is a *complete* Unix operating system distributed on open source principles, one that combines GNU software with a functioning, efficient kernel. Unix growth has been slowed by the fact that, outside colleges and universities, anyone who wished to run Unix had to go to one of the commercial vendors for an expensive, functioning kernel.

Enter Linux, introduced in the next chapter.

References and Further Reading

Babcock, Charles. 1995. "Unix Dominates High-End Servers," *Computerworld* (March 27, 1995).

Bozman, Jean. 1995. "Novell Drops Unix, Blindsides Users," *Computerworld* (September 25, 1995).

Ceruzzi, Paul. 1998. *A History of Modern Computing*. Cambridge, MA: MIT Press.

Gancarz, Mike. 1995. *The Unix Philosophy*. Digital Press.

Fiamingo, Frank, Linda DeBula, and Linda Condron. 1996. "Introduction to Unix." Available online at http://www.wks.uts.ohio-state.edu/unix_course/intro-2.html.

Fraser, Jay. 1990. "Keeper of the Faith: Richard Stallman is Leading a Crusade to Preserve Your Programming Freedom," *Electronic Data News* (October 1, 1990), pp. 174–179.

Free Software Foundation, "Categories of Free and Non-Free Software." Available online at http://www.gnu.ai.mit.edu/philosophy/categories.html.

Free Software Foundation. "Richard Stallman." Available online at http://www.gnu.ai.mit.edu/people/rms.html.

Fulton, Sean. 1997. "OS Holy Wars," *Internet Week* (September 1, 1997), pp. 87–94.

Greenfield, Norton. 1997. "Unix Industry Issues," *Unix Review* (May, 1997).

Irwin, Roger. 1998. "The Linux FUD Factor FAQ," available online at http:// www.geocities.com/ SiliconValley/ Hills/ 9267/fud2.html.

Levy, Steven. 1984. *Hackers: Heroes of the Computer Revolution*. New York: Anchor Press/Doubleday.

Mann, Charles C. 1999. "Programs to the People," *Technology Review* (January/February, 1999).

Martin, John. 1993. "UC Berkeley Embroiled in Computer Software Lawsuit," *Science* 259:5093 (Jan. 15, 1993), pp. 304–306.

Patrizio, Andy. 1998. "Unix Growth Still Outpaces Win NT." Available online at http://www.nytimes.com/techweb/ TW_Unix_Growth_Still_Outpaces_Win_NT.html.

Raymond, Eric. 1998a. "The Cathedral and the Bazaar." Available online at http://www.tuxedo.org/ ~esr/writings/cathedral-bazaar/cathedral-bazaar.html.

Raymond, Eric. 1998b. "A Brief History of Hackerdom," Available online at http://www.tuxedo.org/~esr/faqs/hacker-history.html.

Salus, Peter. 1994. *A Quarter Century of Unix*. Reading, MA: Addison-Wesley.

Tanembaum, Andrew S. 1992. *Modern Operating Systems*. Englewood Cliffs, NJ: Prentice Hall.

Quarterman, John. 1993. *Unix, Posix, and Open Systems: The Open Standards Puzzle*. Reading, MA: Addison-Wesley.

The Linux Phenomenon

With an estimated 16 million installations at the time of this book's writing, Linux is the fastest-growing operating system in today's computer marketplace. In this chapter, you'll learn what Linux is, how it developed, and examine its strengths and weaknesses. You'll also learn how to harness the rich Linux support resources that you'll find on the Internet.

What Is Linux?

Linux (pronounced LIH-nucks) is the *kernel* of a Unix-like operating system that is distributed on open source principles. A kernel alone doesn't make a complete operating system. Linux could not have succeeded without the availability of many open source utilities, including support for TCP/IP networking and the file utilities created by the GNU project. To give proper credit to GNU, some prefer the term GNU/Linux when referring to the complete operating system rather than just the kernel.

Linux is not the only open source Unix kernel. Also available are offshoots of the Berkeley Software Distribution (BSD), such as FreeBSD. Although these competing systems have their adherents, Linux has the lion's share of the market and attracts the greatest number of volunteer programmers.

Linux Distributions

To transform the Linux kernel into a complete operating system, you need to supplement the kernel with hundreds of system programs and utilities. You also need to prepare your system with the proper disk format and directory structure. Because these tasks are beyond the expertise level of most potential Linux users, companies such as Red Hat, Inc. create *Linux distributions*. A distribution typically includes the latest version of the Linux kernel plus all the additional system software and utilities needed for a successful installation. Distributions also include installation software, which guides the user through installation and configuration tasks.

In keeping with open source principles, the companies that sell Linux distributions make them available for free downloading via the Internet. However, most users find it more convenient to purchase a CD-ROM containing the complete distribution. This book focuses on the leading Linux distribution, Red Hat Linux 6.0.

Not Just for Intel-Powered PCs

Offering all the advanced features of Unix (summarized in Chapter 1), Linux is best known as a version of Unix for PCs running Intel hardware, but this characterization is inaccurate; although initially developed for Intel hardware, Linux (in line with the Unix philosophy, explained in Chapter 1) is written mostly in a high-level programming language, and is therefore easily ported to other computer platforms. Versions of Linux are now available for a wide variety of computers, including Sun, Digital, and Silicon Graphics workstations and the Power PC. Projects are under way to port Linux to many additional computer platforms. Because Linux excels in nearly every performance category, even when compared with very expensive commercial UNIX systems, some experts believe that Linux may become the most widely-used Unix-like system in the coming years.

The Respectability Factor

Any operating system created by part-time, volunteer programmers will necessarily struggle for legitimacy. At Southwestern Bell, engineers chose Linux for a mission-critical installation that monitors switches, fibers, and call centers. The legal department objected, asking who they could sue if something went wrong. The IT department also objected, calling Linux "hackerware." But the skeptics became believers when the installation cut maintenance costs by 90 percent. Clearly, Linux is winning the battle for legitimacy. Linux has been deployed in mission-critical settings with excellent results. For example, the U.S. Postal Service has been running Linux systems since 1997 to detect destination addresses.

A Brief History of Linux

The story has all the makings of a legend—and it's getting plenty of press (for example, Eisenberg 1998, Levy 1998), including a write-up in *Economist*, a periodical not noted for indulgence in fads. But then again, Linux's installed user base grew in 1998 at a 212% annual clip (Shankland 1998)—and those are precisely the kind of numbers that transformed the Internet from an obscure university and military network into the world's newest mass medium.

A "Real" Operating System

In 1991, Linus Torvalds, a computer science student at the University of Helsinki, Finland, bought a new computer—a PC powered by an Intel 386 processor—but didn't think much of the operating system that came with the machine (MS-DOS). Rather than working around the bugs in MS-DOS, Torvalds decided that he'd rather run a real operating system (in other words, Unix).

What appealed to Torvalds about Unix was its philosophy, its 25 years of history, and the reliability of its core (kernel). Unlike the patched-together operating systems for personal computers, Unix exhibits an architectural design that struck Torvalds as not only the right way to create an operating system, but deeply pleasing in an aesthetic sense. For Torvalds, nothing less would do for his new machine.

A Benevolent Dictatorship

Using his own code, the brilliant young programmer began work in earnest. But he didn't start entirely from scratch. A key inspiration was Minix, a small Unix-like system for Intel CPUs created by Andy Tanenbaum. Torvalds posted the source code on the Internet and invited other programmers to modify and expand the code. Many were attracted to the project: by the end of the first year, 100 developers were working with Torvalds, and by the end of the second year, this number had grown to 1,000. Torvalds became the central communication point for this developing effort; programmers mailed bug fixes, changes, and additions to Torvalds, who worked them into the kernel and re-released it to the growing community. Although Torvalds has since taken a job with a Silicon Valley firm, he remains the focus of Linux development efforts.

The Right Mix

Torvalds distributes the Linux kernel by means of the General Public License (GPL) discussed in Chapter 1. As a result, anyone is free to obtain the Linux source code and make modifications; however, they must release the modified code and make this code available at no cost. In theory, there's nothing to stop Microsoft from obtaining Linux, modifying the code, and releasing a version of the Linux operating system—but they'd have to release the source code too.

Although Torvalds chose to license Linux using GPL, he did not adopt the anticommercialism exhibited by some open source advocates. For example, he chose not to display hostility towards individuals and companies who attempt to make money from Linux by selling compilations of Linux software (such compilations, called *distributions*, are introduced in the next section). Torvald's moderation played a key role in winning converts to the Linux cause; programmers could engage themselves in Linux development without having to fear castigation were they to try to figure out some way to make money from their activities within the confines of GPL framework.

How Did Linux Get Its Name and Logo?

Torvalds originally named the kernel Freix (a contraction of Free Unix), but friends who ran a Finnish FTP site—the site used for Linux distributions—talked him out of it. They suggested Linux instead, drawing on Torvald's first name (Linus). Linux is pronounced "LIN-nucks." The Linux logo—a rather fat penguin—is Torvalds' choice (see Figure 2.2). It reflects, he says, the sort of contentment a penguin feels after stuffing himself with herring—and presumably, by extension, the sort of contentment you get from using Linux.

Linux Strengths

In this section, you'll learn why Linux is creating so much excitement. As an operating system, Linux offers outstanding performance, sophisticated technical features, outstanding reliability, all the benefits of open source licensing, a zero price

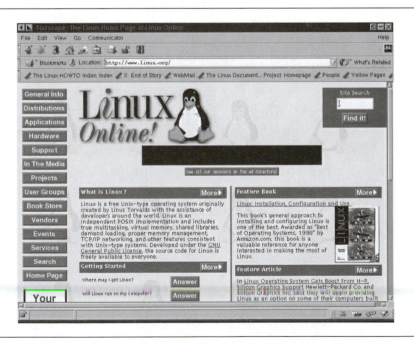

Figure 2.1 Linux sites proudly display the Linux penguin.

tag, resistance to computer viruses, and freedom from licensing hassles.

Outstanding Performance

In head-to-head tests on inexpensive Intel hardware, Linux outperforms most other versions of Unix, including expensive commercial versions, and outperforms all other versions in certain key areas. In most tests, Linux also outperforms its chief competitor, Microsoft Windows NT.

An exception was a 1999 test conducted by Mindcraft, in which NT server was found to be more than twice as fast as Linux. It was subsequently revealed that the test, funded by Microsoft, pitted an expertly configured NT workstation against a poorly configured Linux system. Microsoft's own internal tests, revealed in a memo that was leaked to the Internet (see Raymond 1998), show a contrasting picture. The memo records a test in which Linux and Windows NT were run in a head-to-head competition on identical systems; for Web browsing, Linux and Netscape Communicator 4.5 outperformed NT and Internet Explorer by a factor of 40 percent.

Benchmarking is an inexact science, at best, and test results are sometimes manipulated or inaccurately reported by interested parties. Still, the evidence shows that Linux performs as well or better than competing commercial operating systems, particularly on inexpensive Intel hardware.

Sophisticated Technical Features

Linux is a sophisticated, cutting-edge operating system that supports features that are lacking or incompletely implemented in competing systems, such as UNIX commercial systems and Windows NT. For example, Linux has been capable of working with 64-bit processors since 1995, and Linux implements symmetric multiprocessing (SMP), the capability to work with two or more processors simultaneously.

These capabilities enable advanced applications. At Digital Domain, a production studio located in Venice, CA, more than 100 networked Linux computers generated the full-motion rendering for the movie *Titanic*. The systems ran 24 hours per day, 7 days per week, with no extended downtimes (Strauss 1998). At the Los Alamos National Laboratory in New Mexico, scientists built a supercomputer out of 68 off-the-shelf processors united by Linux, and it outperformed systems costing ten times as much (Moody 1998). The Linux-powered supercomputer ran for months at a time without rebooting (Hill, Warren, and Goda 1997).

Optimized for inexpensive Intel hardware, Linux does not currently scale upward as well as commercial Unix operating systems, particularly on systems running more than four processors simultaneously. Planned upgrades to the Linux kernel should address this deficiency.

Outstanding Reliability

If you're used to rebooting Windows after the frequent crashes, Linux is sure to impress: Many users report, as did Digital Domain, that Linux computers are capable of running for months on end without problems. According to a team of University of Wisconsin researchers who performed laboratory experiments of system reliability, Linux's reliability is, on average, twice as good as the best commercial UNIX operating systems (Miller, *et al.*, 1995). Engineers and IT administrators generally believe that Linux is far more robust, bullet-proof, and reliable than competing Microsoft products, including Windows NT.

Why is Linux so stable? Part of the credit goes to the excellence of the underlying Unix design philosophy, and the rest goes to the Linux development community's sedulous efforts to find and eliminate bugs. All Linux code is subjected immediately to thorough, probing peer review, which is conducted by some of the best programmers around.

Linux vs Windows 95/98/NT

As thousands of computer users are discovering, Linux is more stable than any version of Windows. The reasons are attributable to severe deficiencies in Windows' technical design. For example, Windows enables programmers to use DLLs (Dynamic Link Libraries) to store program code that is used by two or more applications. However, Windows does nothing to track and control the DLLs. If you install a program that overwrites an existing DLL with a new version, you may inadvertently destabilize your system. Linux also uses DLLs (in Linux, they're called *shared libraries*), but the operating system automatically tracks them by version number, and links them to the applications that need them. Another example: Windows permits some programs to use the computer's memory in a way that can interfere with other running programs, and even the operating system itself. In Linux, such interference is impossible; every program runs in its own, rigorously separated memory space.

Open Source Licensing

Distributed under the terms of the GNU General Public License (GPL), the Linux kernel is under the supervision of Torvalds himself, who is regarded as the final arbiter of just what gets into the Linux kernel. Although anyone may develop code for the Linux kernel, Torvalds alone decides which contributions become part of the official kernel distributions.

The fact that the source code is available for modification is itself an attraction. Because programmers can modify the underlying code, companies can add features to the operating system that are needed for specific purposes.

For Linux critics, the fact that the source code is open to inspection poses a security risk. They say that intruders can study the code to determine how to break into Linux systems, and they prefer to purchase commercial software from vendors who regard the source code as a trade secret. Security experts discount such concerns. Linux is created and maintained by expert programmers who are working in real-world situations, in which their systems are constantly exposed to intrusive attacks. When they discover a security flaw, fixes are created quickly and distributed by means of the Internet, often within hours of a security breach.

Zero Price Tag

Linux is an attractive operating system option for technical reasons, as the preceding features have explained, but its major appeal is the price tag: $0.00.

The kernel is freely available for download from online sources, but most people obtain Linux as part of a *distribution*, a compilation consisting of the current Linux kernel combined with a host of open source shells, utilities, and applications. The voluminous distributions can be obtained online via FT for free, but it's much more convenient to purchase a CD-ROM (or a book such as this one that contains a CD-ROM). Once you've purchased the CD-ROM, you can freely copy it or share it with others.

For cash-strapped organizations, Linux's zero price tag can make all the difference. In Mexico, the government will save $124 million by using Linux instead of Microsoft operating systems in an ambitious plan to equip all of the nation's schools with computers. According to one estimate, a fully configured Microsoft NT workstation would cost nearly $5,000 to set up with all the required software, while a correspondingly equipped Linux workstation would cost only $50.

When you take support issues into account, no operating system is entirely free, and the same goes for Linux. For now, Linux users must turn to Internet resources (discussed later in this chapter) for assistance when something goes wrong. For Linux to succeed in the enterprise (and ultimately on users' desktops), support must improve. Linux service and support companies (including Red Hat, Inc.) are moving into this market with services designed to remedy Linux support deficiencies.

Resistance to Computer Viruses

Hardly a week goes by without new reports of computer viruses, such as Melissa, that spread by exploiting the tight integration between Microsoft Windows and Windows applications. Windows and Macintosh systems are also afflicted by *boot sector viruses*, which infect the portion of the hard disk used to start the computer. Computer virus victims may devastating work losses and even public embarrassment; one particularly nasty virus surreptitiously posts a user's Microsoft Word files to Internet newsgroups with the subject heading "Child pornography!"

Although no operating system provides total immunity from computer viruses and other destructive programs, Linux offers the best available protection. First, Linux applications do not integrate tightly with the operating system in the way that Windows applications do. In Windows, this tight integration gives malicious program authors many ways to create destructive programs. In addition, Linux enforces a distinction between ordinary users and the *root user*, or system administrator. When you use Linux after logging on as an ordinary user (as you should), no program can write data to the boot sector. As a result, viruses are almost completely unknown in the Linux environment. Unfortunately, this situation may change because unsophisticated new users may run Linux without taking steps to secure their systems.

Freedom from Licensing Hassles

Commercial operating systems specify severe penalties for failure to remain in compliance with licensing terms; should a company breach these terms, the result could be an expensive, time-consuming lawsuit or even criminal charges. An organization can violate commercial software licenses inadvertently; for example, some commercial Internet transaction programs specify a maximum number of concurrent transactions, but this number may be exceeded should the service experience an unexpected surge in demand. If the transgression is detected by the vendor's monitoring software, the organization could find itself threatened with hefty fee increases or a lawsuit. Commercial software licenses expose organizations to unwanted liabilities; Linux carries no such burden.

Shortcomings of Linux

Although Linux has many strengths, it has weaknesses, as well. This section summarizes the current shortcomings of Linux, including its reputation for user-unfriendliness, installation hassles, poor documentation, and a dearth of user applications.

Is Linux Too Difficult to Use?

Linux's reputation as a user-unfriendly system stems from its command-line operating mode, called the *shell*. However, the shell is only one of several available means of communicating with the Linux kernel. For example, Linux distributions typically include a free, open source version of the X Window System, called XFree86. The X Window System provides windowing services for applications. As you'll learn in Chapter 3, the X Window System has many deficiencies; unlike Microsoft Windows or Mac OS, it does not provide the desktop services that users have come to expect, such as drag-and-drop among applications, an integrated help system, and user utilities such as calendars, calculators, and to-do lists.

Recognizing that Linux needs a viable desktop interface in order to gain acceptance, programmers have been busy filling the void. Unfortunately, two desktop projects are in competition. The first, a European project called the K Desktop Environment (KDE), is the better developed of the two, but questions remain concerning licensing restrictions in KDE's underlying graphics toolkit. The second project, called GNOME (pronounced "guh-nome"), relies exclusively on tools released under the terms of the GNU Project's open source licenses.

Although neither desktop system is currently as advanced as Microsoft Windows or Mac OS, they already enable a Linux user to avoid using the command line interface (see Figure 2.2). This is the first Linux book to take this point seriously; you'll learn Red Hat Linux by exploring the GNOME interface. Use of the shell is relegated to the end of the book. As you'll discover, you can't quite skip the shell entirely. It's still convenient to use for some purposes, and for others there's no alternative.

Is Linux Too Difficult to Install?

Early versions of Linux were nothing short of a nightmare to install. For example, programs and system utilities were distributed in source code; to install them on your system, you

Figure 2.2 The GNOME desktop gives Linux a graphical user interface.

had to *compile* them. (To compile a program, you use software
called a *compiler*, which translates program instructions—also
called source code—into the *object code* that can run on your
system.) What's more, all the supporting files and utilities
required by programs had to be obtained and manually
installed in the correct directories. In addition, most programs
required a lot of manual configuration before they would run
correctly. Some charged that Linux was indeed free—but only
if your time is worth nothing.

Linux distributions are changing this picture. A Linux distribution includes all the software needed to install Linux successfully, including an installation utility that handles all the tasks
of preparing your system to run Linux. What's more, the
installation software will put all the pieces in the right places.

Typical Linux distributions include the following, in addition to the most recent Linux kernel:

- **A comprehensive development environment** For program development, program compilers, debuggers, and other programming aids are included.
- **Powerful tools for serving information on the Internet** Most distributions come with Web, FTP, and mail servers.
- **Proven technologies for networking** Most distributions fully support Ethernet, AppleTalk, and other networking protocols; some come with software (Samba) that can act like a Windows NT server, enabling companies to dispense with pricey NT Server licenses.
- **A complete desktop environment** The X Window System provides windowing services for applications; desktop systems such as KDE and GNOME provide the desktop utilities and graphics capabilities that today's users expect.
- **Freedom from license fees** Once you've obtained a Linux distribution, you are free to make as many copies of the open source software as you wish. There are no limits on the number of users, registration codes, expiration dates, or other restrictions other than those imposed by GPL and other open source licenses.

Although some users find Linux distributions quite easy to install, others find themselves struggling with problems that prevent them from completing the installation successfully. The reason lies in the bewildering variety of hardware components and accessories found in the Intel hardware environment.

In order to use a specific component, such as a video adapter or network card, the operating system must install a compatible *driver* (a configuration utility that tells the operating system how to work with a specific component). Most installation failures stem from attempts to install Linux on a system that contains *unsupported hardware* (hardware for which no driver exists).

Although the latest Linux distributions include support for thousands of popular hardware components, you may experience difficulty if your system contains very new or exotic components. In addition, the most popular Linux distribution, Red Hat Linux 6.0, does not support popular accessories such as digital cameras, scanners, and Universal Serial Bus (USB) peripherals. (As you'll learn in Chapter 4, it's possible to get these devices to work with Red Hat Linux 6.0 if you're willing to do some do-it-yourself configuration.)

To avoid installation difficulties, it's important to scrutinize your system to make sure that it contains nothing but supported hardware. You'll learn how to perform this system evaluation in Chapter 4.

Where are the Applications?

No operating system will succeed in the absence of useful applications. Although it's a commonplace to point out that Linux suffers from a dearth of applications, this claim isn't entirely true, and it's becoming less true by the day.

In the server market, Linux is experiencing rapid acceptance precisely because it offers so many powerful applications. Chief among these is Apache, the world's most popular Web server. Developed on open source principles, Apache powers more than half of the Web's servers. The sendmail utility powers an estimated 70 percent of the world's mail servers.

In the desktop market, Linux users can take advantage of thousands of X Window System applications, including Linux

Gnumeric: Untitled.gnumeric

File Edit View Insert Format Help

B4

	B	C	D	E	F	G	H	I	J
1									
2		ORAL1	Dis o#	PRE	ORAL2	bib	PROPORAL	PROP	
3		2.5		5	10				
4									
5		1.75	2	4.75	8.25	ok	15	26.4	
6		2	4	5	9	ok		15.2	
7		2.5	1	4.75	8.75	ok	14		
8		2	5	4.75		ok	10	24.6	
9		2	2	3.75	8	ok	12.5	25.7	
10		2	4	3.75	8.75	ok	13.5		
11		2	6	3.75		ok		21.5	
12		2.25	7	2.75		ok		30	
13		2	1	4	9	ok	14	29.7	
14		2.25	3	4	8.75	ok	13.5	23.3	
15		2.25	4	5	10	ok	12.5		
16		2.5	2	4	8.5	ok		28.5	
17		2	6			ok+	14	29.4	
18		1.75	3	4	9	OK+	14	26.2	
19		1.75	2	3.75	8.25	OK	15	30	
20		1.75	6	4		OK+	15	28.5	
21			5	3.75		OK+	15	16.2	
22		2	5	3		OK+		26.1	
23		1.5	7	3.75		ok			
24		2.25	3	5	9.75		12.5	25.5	
25		2.5	7	1		ok	13	26.72	
26		1.5	7	5		ok	11.5	24.3	

MW3-30 | TR11 | TR2 | MW ROLL | TR 11 ROLL | TR 2 ROLL

Sum=0

Figure 2.3 Gnumeric can read and write Microsoft Excel workbooks.

versions of leading Windows programs (such as Corel Word-Perfect for Linux, version 8.0) and commercial office suites such as StarOffice and ApplixWare. However, Linux will not convert many Windows or Mac OS users unless user applications are designed to take full advantage of the KDE or GNOME desktop systems, which provide services (such as drag-and-drop) that users expect. The KDE project leads the way with KOffice, a suite of free applications that includes a word processor, spreadsheet, and presentation graphics program. GNOME applications are also beginning to appear. These include the Gnumeric spreadsheet (Figure 2.2), which can read and write Microsoft Excel files, and AbiWord (Figure 2.3), which can read and write Microsoft Word files.

In time, Linux will offer enough applications to satisfy the needs of most computer users. Already, many Linux users

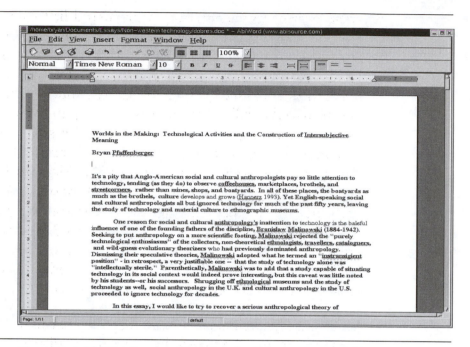

Figure 2.4 AbiWord can read and write Microsoft Word files.

report that they have successfully made the transition from Microsoft Windows or Mac OS to Linux; they find that Linux offers all the applications they need, including e-mail, Internet browsing, Internet file transfer, "buddy list" software (ICQ), Internet chatting (IRC), word processing, and spreadsheets. To make this transition now requires giving up some of the features and ease of use found in popular Windows and Mac OS applications, but it is compensated by the fact that much of the available commercial Linux software is distributed free for personal or educational use or on open source principles.

Linux Futures

Although the success of Linux as a desktop computer operating system is far from assured (Brookshaw 1999), it's instructive to compare Linux to early versions of Microsoft Windows (those prior to version 3.1). Considered little but a crude toy by many, these early versions offered little of value to users, including a paucity of integrated applications and inferior technical performance. However, version 3.1 of Microsoft Windows introduced a key technical innovation; it enabled users to take full advantage of the capabilities of Intel 386 processors. Coupled with the release of a spate of Windows-compatible applications, Windows 3.1 brought to IBM PC users much of the functionality of the Macintosh user interface, but at a considerable savings; a Windows 3.1 system cost as much as one-half the price of a comparably equipped Macintosh. Although many believe Windows 3.1 to be inferior to the Macintosh interface in terms of ease of use, it was Windows 3.1, not the Mac OS, that appeared on the screens of more than 90 percent of the desktop systems then in use.

This example is instructive. It suggests that users indeed want ease of use, but they are willing to put up with a less-than-ideal interface if they can obtain the applications they need—and most of all, if the price is right. Based on this example, it seems clear that Linux has a very bright future indeed as a desktop operating system.

Against this rosy scenario, pessimists warn of a backlash from commercial software firms. In particular, software patents could be used to hamstring open source software development. Microsoft's internal documents mention such a strategy. In addition, the GNU General Public License (GPL) has never been tested in a court of law. An adverse decision could severely undermine the entire open source software enterprise and create devastating legal liabilities for open source software developers. Only time will tell whether the open source software movement will succeed in surmounting these obstacles.

Getting Support for Linux

It's often assumed that a noncommercial operating system would not offer much technical support, but this is false. In fact, Linux is *better* supported than most commercial programs. If you're skeptical, note that Linux was the recipient of the respected trade journal *Info World*'s Best Technical Support of the Year Award in 1997 (Foster 1997). In this section, you learn the many ways you can get technical support for the Linux operating system and Linux applications.

Vendor Technical Support

If you purchase a Linux distribution, you may be able to take advantage of vendor technical support. For example, you get 90 days of free e-mail technical support concerning installation issues when you purchase a Red Hat installation.

Red Hat's web site (http://www.redhat.com) is jammed with information (see Figure 2.4) about the company's Linux distribution, including:

- Hardware compatibility lists
- Product updates, fixes, and errata
- Extensive documentation
- Links to e-mail technical support
- Bug reporting forms
- Installation guide for Red Hat Linux
- Red Hat Linux FAQs (frequently asked questions)
- Links to external information sources, including general Linux information, mailing lists, user-supported FAQs, and much more.

Program Documentation

Most of the Linux programs you'll install come with documentation, which you'll find (generally) in the /usr/doc/ directory. With Red Hat Linux, documentation is installed automatically when you install a package with RPM or the Red Hat installation software; both automatically place the documentation in the correct location. You can read the documentation on-screen using a text editor or the GNOME help system, introduced in Chapter 8.

The Linux Documentation Project (LDP)

The documentation you'll find in /usr/doc is extensive, but it's nothing compared to what you'll find online, thanks to the Linux Documentation Project (LDP), located at http:// metalab.unc.edu/ LDP. With dozens of *mirror sites* worldwide, LDP information is accessible to anyone with an Internet connection. LDP is compiling a series of HOWTOs and Mini-HOWTOs, which are designed for beginners and take you through procedures step-by-step.

> **TIP** The Linux HOWTO Search Engine (http://lagrange.la.asu.edu/ VirtualClass/LinuxOnline/index.html) enables you to search all the current Linux HOWTOs and Mini-HOWTOs.

In addition to the very valuable HOWTOs, you'll find the following book-length treatises:

- Installation and Getting Started Guide
- The Linux Kernel
- The Linux Kernel Hackers' Guide
- The Linux Kernel Module Programming Guide
- The Linux Network Administrators' Guide
- The Linux Programmer's Guide

- The Linux System Administrators' Guide
- The Linux Users' Guide

FAQs (Frequently Asked Questions)

Once you've learned the basics, FAQs—lists of frequently asked questions and answers—provide a useful resource. If you have a question, you should read the relevant FAQ before posting a question to a newsgroup, as described in the next section. Chances are, your question has already been answered. To look for FAQs, you can start with the FAQs page at Linux Online (www.linux.org/help/faq.html).

MAN Pages

MAN pages are brief reference documents that are accessible from the Linux system prompt. Although terse, they come in handy when you're trying to remember how to type a complicated command.

Newsgroups

You'll find plenty of Linux-related information on Usenet. The following are the best-known newsgroups that focus on Linux:

- **comp.os.linux.announce** Announcements concerning Linux products and events
- **comp.os.linux.setup** Discussion of Linux installation and configuration issues
- **comp.os.linux.hardware** Discussion of issues concerning getting Linux to work with specific processors and peripherals, including video adapters, modems, and other accessories
- **comp.os.linux.networking** Discussion of issues and problems associated with Linux networking (Internet and local area network)

- **comp.os.linux.x** Discussion of X Window System servers and window managers
- **comp.os.linux.development.apps** Issues and problems concerning application development for Linux
- **comp.os.linux.development.system** Issues and problems concerning Linux operating system development, including drivers for peripherals
- **comp.os.linux.advocacy** Debate concerning the merits of Linux vs. competing operating systems
- **comp.os.linux.misc** Any subject that doesn't fit into the preceding categories.

TIP For more information on Linux-related newsgroups, see "Linux USENET Newsgroups," located at http://www.linuxresources.com/online.html.

Please refrain from posting questions on any of these newsgroups that could be answered by reading the program documentation, FAQs, HOWTOs, and other resources. Also, be aware that someone has probably already asked the same question; you can search newsgroup archives, as described in the following section, and chances are you'll find your answer.

After you've made a serious, sustained effort to get your question answered by reading and searching information sources, follow these suggestions when posting:

- Begin with a brief, orienting overview of the problem you're experiencing.
- Describe your system in detail, including the Linux distribution you're using, the version number, processor type, amount of memory, etc.
- Provide any other information that could help people figure out what's wrong.

- Close with a promise to post a summary of the results you receive—and follow through on this!
- Send your message with a descriptive subject line; don't just type "Help, please!" Here's a good example: "RH Linux 6.0: Can't configure Dell onboard video."

Searchable Newsgroup Archives

Rather than scrolling through newsgroups manually looking for information about a specific problem, try searching the archives of Linux newsgroups. You can do so at DejaNews (http://www.deja.com). Other Web search engines (such as Altavista, located at http://www.altavista.com and Google, located at http://www.google.com/linux) also enable you to search archives of Usenet newsgroups.

Internet Relay Chat (IRC) Channels

For immediate assistance, Linux users often turn to Internet Relay Chat (IRC) channels. However, this method isn't recommended unless you're familiar with IRC and you've exhausted all other means of obtaining the information you need. It's not so much that the people you'll find in Linux channels are uncivil—they are, sometimes—but they're impatient with people who ask questions that could have been easily answered through other channels.

TIP To find Linux-related IRC channels, try searching Liszt's IRC Directory (http://www.liszt.com/chat/). Also try Slashdot's IRC servers (http://www.slashdot.org/slashnet/). You'll also find Web-based chat groups at Linux.com (http://www.linux.com).

Mailing Lists

Hundreds of Linux-related Internet mailing lists exist. Although they're mainly intended for developers, most are publicly accessible and may prove useful if you need advanced information about the Linux kernel, system utilities, or popular Linux applications.

Linux®

In August, 1996, Linux Journal and a number of other Linux-related publications received a letter from attorneys of a Mr. William R. Della Croce, Jr., informing them that Della Croce owned the Linux trademark and that further use of the trademark would require licensing. Della Croce reportedly attempted to collect 10% royalties from firms selling Linux products. You can imagine the Linux community's outrage.

In association with several Linux companies and Linux International, Torvalds petitioned the U.S. Patent and Trademark Office to cancel Della Corce's trademark. Assisting the petitioners was a high-powered California intellectual property law firm, Davis & Schroeder, of Monterey, CA, which handled the case at reduced fees as a service to the Linux community. In August, 1997, Della Croce settled, transferring the Linux trademark to Linus Torvalds.

Red Hat Linux users may want to subscribe to the redhat-list, which offers general discussion of issues related to Red Hat Linux. Sponsored by Red Hat software, this list is one of several that may interest you, including the following:

- **redhat-install-list** Discussion of Red Hat Linux installation issues, including getting Red Hat Linux to work with specific peripherals such as network interface cards, video cards, and modems.
- **redhat-announce-list** This is a low-traffic, moderated list that every Red Hat user should join. You'll receive important announcements about Red Hat software,

including new releases, security fixes, and other vital information.

To subscribe to any of these lists, do the following:

1.   Make sure your e-mail program is set up to send plain text mail, rather than HTML-formatted ("rich text") mail. If you're not sure how to check this setting, click Help or read your program's documentation.

2.   Start a new mail message.

3.   On the To: line, type the name of the mailing list followed by -request@redhat.com. For example, to subscribe to the main Red Hat list, type **redhat-list-request@redhat.com**.

4.   In the Subject line, type **subscribe.**

5.   Leave the rest of the message blank.

6.   Click Send.

If you would like to unsubscribe from any of the Red Hat mailing lists, do the following:

1.   Make sure your e-mail program is set up to send plain text mail, rather than HTML-formatted ("rich text") mail. If you're not sure how to check this setting, click Help or read your program's documentation.

2.   Start a new mail message.

3.   On the To: line, type the name of the mailing list followed by -request@redhat.com. For example, to subscribe to the main Red Hat list, type **redhat-list-request@redhat.com**.

4.   In the Subject line, type **unsubscribe.**

5. Leave the rest of the message blank.

6. Click Send.

Keeping Up with Linux

Linux is developing very rapidly, so you'll want to keep informed. Here's a list of Web sites that will keep you up-to-date:

- **Freshmeat** (http://www.freshmeat.net) News of the latest Linux applications.
- **GNOME** (http://www.gnome.org) The home page of the GNOME desktop system. The GNOME software map includes links to the newest GNOME applications.
- **Linux.com** (http://www.linux.com) Links to books, FAQs, newsgroups, user groups, software, and more.
- **Linux Journal** (http://www.linuxjournal.com) This monthly magazine has a Web page with feature articles, fast-breaking news, and links to Linux sites.
- **Linux Mall** (http://www.LinuxMall.com) A commercial site with fast-breaking Linux news and online ordering for Linux products (including the Linux Top 40).
- **Linux Planet** (http://www.linuxplanet.com) Another major site with news reports, reviews, tips, and discussions.
- **Linux Resources** (http://www.linuxresources.com) A well-organized site with links to Linux headlines, additional press clippings, new products, and links to online Linux journals.
- **Linux Start** (http://www.linuxstart.com) Resembling Yahoo, this directory focuses on Linux exclusively.
- **Slashdot** (http://www.slashdot.org) Oriented to Linux hackers and developers, this site is still worth visiting if you're in search of fast-breaking Linux news.

Linux and Year 2000 (Y2K) Issues

The Year 2000 (Y2K) problem dates from the early days of computing, when computer hardware designers and programmers reserved only two digits for storing dates. As a result, many computers, operating systems, and applications will not be able to distinguish between the year 2000 and the year 1900. This problem could cause havoc; imagine receiving a bill from your electrical company, for example, informing you that your bill is 100 years overdue and assessing a $688,000 penalty!

Like any Unix-like operating system, Linux is a good bet if you're worried about Year 2000 issues. In general, Unix systems track dates by using programming libraries that store dates as 32-bit integers. For Unix, time begins on January 1, 1970, and each subsequent second gets its own integer. There's enough to count all the seconds until the year 2038. Before that time, the operating system will have to be rewritten so that there are 64 bits reserved for date storage.

> **TIP** Even though Linux can handle the year 2000, this doesn't necessarily mean that Linux applications are Y2K-compliant. Check your application's documentation or Web site for information on Y2K issues pertinent to the software you're using.

From Here

As you've learned in this chapter, Linux is already making significant inroads into the market for server operating systems. What remains to be seen is its potential as a replacement for desktop operating systems such as Mac OS and Microsoft Windows. To understand that potential, you need to explore the strengths and limitations of the X Window System and the graphical desktop systems (such as KDE and GNOME) that are just now becoming available.

References and Further Reading

Brookshaw, Chris. 1999. "Next Stop, The Desktop?" *InfoWorld Electronic* (January 18, 1999). Available online at http://www.infoworld.com.

Eisenberg, Rebecca. 1998. "Free Operating System is Gaining Headway in a Windows-Dominated World," *San Francisco Examiner* (August 2, 1998).

Foster, Ed. 1998. "Best Technical Support Award: Linux User Community," *InfoWorld*. Available online at http://www.infoworld.com.

Hill, Jim, Michael Warren, and Patrick Goda, 1997. "I'm Not Going to Pay a Lot for this Supercomputer," *Linux Journal* (December, 1997). Available online at http://www.ssc.com/ lj/ issue45/2392.html.

Levy, Doug. 1999. "Linux Creator: Next Bill Gates?" *USA Today* (January 7, 1999).

Metro Detroit Linux User's Group, 1999. "What is Linux?" Presentation available online at http://www.tir.com/~sorceror/ mdlug/preso.html.

Miller, Barton P., et al., 1995. "Fuzz Revisited: A Re-Examination of the Reliability of UNIX Utilities and Services," available online at http://www.cs.wisc.edu:80/Dienst/UI/2.0/ Describe/ ncstral.uwmadison/CS-TR-95-1268.

Moody, Glyn. 1998. "The Wild Bunch," *New Scientist* (December 12, 1998).

Raymond, Eric. 1998. "The Halloween Documents," available online at http://www.opensource.org/halloween.html.

Shankland, Stephen. 1998. "Linux Shipments Up 212 Percent," *CNET News.com* (December 16, 1998). Available online at http://www.news.com/News.

Strauss, Daryll. 1998. "Linux Helps Bring *Titanic* to Life," *Linux Journal* (February, 1998). Available online at http://www.linuxjournal.com/issue46/2494.html.

The User Interface Challenge

Unix and Unix-like operating systems will really take off, we've been told, just as soon as someone finally develops a truly easy-to-use graphical user interface (GUI) that runs on Unix systems. The trouble is, we've been hearing the same thing for at least 15 years—and in the meantime, Unix has been left far behind as Microsoft Windows has all but dominated the market for desktop operating systems.

Perhaps you're saying, "Wait a minute! Unix and Linux do have a graphical user interface—the X Window System." As you'll learn in this chapter, X—as it's called—provides a graphical *windowing* environment for Unix and Unix-like operating systems, but it's a far cry from the comprehensive *desktop* operating environments that Mac OS and Microsoft Windows users enjoy. What's been missing from X is the desktop functionality that Mac OS and Windows provide, such as the ability to drag icons onto the desktop, an integrated file manager, a unified help system for applications, and utilities such as clocks, calendars, and calculators.

Once you've understood the deficiencies of X, you'll grasp the significance of GNOME, the new desktop environment that's included with Red Hat Linux 6.0. GNOME is perhaps as significant as Linux itself, in that—like Linux—it provides a comprehensive, open-source solution to the problem of bringing a Unix-like operating system to personal computer users.

Exploring X's History

So that you can fully understand the X Window System (including its minuses as well as its pluses), this chapter begins with a brief note on X's design philosophy, on which there's precious little unanimity: some believe this philosophy brilliant (e.g., see Lee 1997), others call it idiotic. (If you are of the latter persuasion, don't miss the deliciously acerbic chapter titled "The X-Windows Disaster" in *The Unix Haters Handbook* [Garfinkel, *et al.,* 1994], which calls X a "disaster," a "molten blob of pig iron," a "toxic waste dump," and a "virus.")

Like many technologies, X was shaped by the environment that produced it. As you'll see, X is a big, complex solution to a problem that isn't much of a concern for most computer users: how to display applications running on two or more computers. X's network-savvy design goal makes the system difficult to grasp and unwieldy to use, which hasn't helped its reputation. But X has something going for it that will pay off in the end: It's *inherently* a cross-platform interface, capable of running on just about any computer that can run Unix or a Unix-like operating system.

X's Beginnings

At the Massachusetts Institute of Technology (MIT), researchers working on the Argus Project were attempting to develop a programming language that could be used on a variety of computers, and they soon realized that they needed a terminal that could display the results of computations on more than one computer.

A second project, called Project Athena, involved MIT researchers with sponsorship from Digital Equipment Corporation (DEC) and IBM. Project Athena sought to create an easy-to-use user interface that would work on a variety of computers.

Argus and Athena researchers discovered their common interests, and the result was the X Window System. (It's called X because its predecessor was called W.) It's interesting to look at X's history, because it helps to explain why X is designed the way it is. As you'll see, X succeeds for both Argus and Athena; for Argus, it's a networked windowing system that really can open windows to applications running on two or more computers. For Athena, it's a graphical user interface that establishes at least some consistency for differing types of computers, provided that they're all running Unix or a Unix-like operating system. What's not clear, still, is whether X succeeds for users.

The X Window Consortium

To promote the development of X, the X Window Consortium took shape in the late 1980s. Funded by industry members, the Consortium helped to transform X into a credible windowing system for Unix computers. Currently maintained by the Open Group (http://www.x.org), the X Window standard is proprietary, but liberal licensing terms have enabled programmers to create freely redistributable emulations of X software. The current official version of X is X11R6.4. Linux systems typically run an open source clone of X called XFree86 (see http://www.xfree86.org). However, the Open Group has recently decided (wisely, I believe) to release X11R6.4 on an open source, freely redistributable basis, and it's likely that XFree86 and X11R6.4 are headed for integration.

The X Window Consortium has promoted a number of initiative to improve X, including the Inter-Client Communication Conventions Manual (ICCCM), a set of standards that specify how well-behaved X applications can communicate with each other (and with window managers). In 1989, the Motif user interface guidelines were introduced. These guidelines laid down standards (still widely accepted) for the appearance of X applications (including window managers) on-screen. In keeping with the X philosophy (see the sidebar, "The X Philosophy"), these guidelines do not enforce a specific "look-and-feel" on-screen; instead, they merely encourage programmers to follow the guidelines by providing "hooks" for the appearance of windows and other visible features.

Understanding Basic X Concepts

The X Window System distinguishes between *servers* and *clients*, but it does so in a way that fundamentally differs from the use of these concepts in other areas of computing (such as databases and the Internet). If you've used the Internet, you probably know that you run some sort of *client* program (such as an e-mail program or a Web browser) that knows how to obtain information from a remote *server*. In the X Window

System, these terms have different meanings, as the following sections explain.

X Servers and X Clients

In the X Window System, a *server* is software running on a specific type of computer, equipped with a specific video card, mouse, keyboard, and monitor. The server is configured to take advantage of this equipment. Like other types of servers, an X server is designed to act on requests from clients, discussed in the next section.

In the X Window System, a *client* is any program that requests some sort of service that the X server knows how to provide, such as redrawing the screen, moving the mouse pointer, or accepting keyboard input. Two important clients are the *window manager*, the program that enables the user to control the size and appearance of windows on the computer's display, and X *applications*, which can't display anything without the X server's help.

Here's where Argus and Athena come together, and in a very interesting way. Because the X Window System distinguishes between a workstation-based server and clients, and because it's also designed to work in a networked environment, there's no particular reason why the clients and the server have to be located on the same computer. As you're sitting in front of your workstation, you're making use of this workstation's server, but you could be running clients on several different machines located elsewhere on the network (see Zweije 1998).

"So what," you're probably saying—and rightly so, considering that you're probably setting up your Linux system as a single-user, nonnetworked workstation. I could point out that you might want to set up a network someday, and X could start to have advantages. But the reality is that X's underlying design is far from ideal for single-user, nonnetworked work-stations. X gives you a lot of complexity, and there isn't much of a compensating tradeoff; X is best thought of as a lowest-common-denominator windowing system, designed to work on a huge variety of computer systems, but very far from optimized for any one of them.

Windowing Systems vs Desktops

To grasp the limitations of X fully, it's helpful to distinguish between *windowing systems* and *desktops*. X is a windowing system—which means that it's limited to providing windowing functions for applications. X provides the services that enables applications to appear in windows on a huge variety of different computer systems; for this reason, programmers don't have to worry about the details of the window display. But that's about all it does. In a *desktop*, the user interface software provides support for copying and pasting between applications, drag-and-drop procedures, file management integration, and *interprocess communication* (the means by which one application can send instructions to another application, such as "start up and display this file"). X does a passable job as a windowing system; it's a disaster as a desktop.

Window managers do not begin to approach the capabilities of the Mac OS and Microsoft Windows desktops. A special kind of X client, they are restricted to providing very basic tools for users. With a window manager, you can manipulate windows by moving them, resizing them, minimizing them to an icon, and closing them. Some window managers enable you to choose *themes*, which give the screen a different visual appearance. Window managers are very much more limited than desktops.

The X Philosophy

Experts agree that there's a reason Microsoft Windows and the Mac OS are so popular: consistency. If you've learned Windows, for example, you can sit down at just about any Windows system, and use skills you've already learned. To be sure, Windows allows some customization, but not *that* much. X is different. With X, you've the freedom to choose from a variety of window managers, each of which gives the screen a different "look and feel." Although there are, arguably, some fundamental skills that are useful on any system running X, it's indisputable that consistency isn't one of X's strong points.

The lack of consistency is quite deliberate. It stems from the X philosophy, which is summed up by the following phrase: "mechanism, not policy." This means, "give people powerful tools—but don't force them to adopt a specific look and feel." In the X philosophy, you've a right to design your workstation just as you please, even if that means you come up with a system that even another X user would have difficulty using!

The lack of consistency may be slowing down X's market penetration, but that other philosophy we've discussed—the Unix philosophy (see Chapter 1)—holds that X is doing things the Right Way. In contrast to Windows and Mac OS, X isn't tightly coupled to the operating system; in fact, it's completely independent. With well-written code, this augers for greater system stability, and that's something that may prove more important than interface consistency for millions of users.

An X Window User's Pet Peeves List

Here are some of the shortcomings of X that prove particularly galling to most users:

- **Configuration** X is notoriously difficult to configure. For example, there's no user-friendly procedure for adding applications to menus. In Mac OS and Windows, menu items automatically appear after you install a program, but that's not the necessarily case in X. To create menu items for programs, you may have to edit configuration files.

- **Color map flashing** In Microsoft Windows and Mac OS, the desktop configuration imposes a given *color depth* (the number of bits set aside for representing colors), resulting in a fixed color palette (consisting of 16, 256, 16,536, or more than 16 million colors). All applications are displayed using the available colors, whether they like it or not. In X, there's a default *colormap* (generally 256 different colors), but applications can request that this list of 256 colors contains colors that aren't used by other applications (including the window manager). The result is a distortion called *colormap flashing*, which occurs when you move the cursor into a window that uses a different colormap. Surround windows, as well as the window background, display distorted colors and may become completely illegible. The result is a display that looks like the result of a decidedly amateur programming project.

- **Lack of support for drag and drop** Because this capability is now expected in professional applications, programmers have been implementing their own versions of it, with the result that procedures aren't consistent from one program to another (and you can't use drag and drop between applications). Thanks to efforts to establish drag and drop standards, this situation is about to change.

- **Lack of support for TrueType fonts** The X Window Systems has its own methods of specifying fonts for on-screen display, but the reality is that the rest of the world is using the TrueType font standard. TrueType support is only now finding its way into X.

In the past few years, various vendors have attempted to resolve these problems by creating proprietary extensions of the X Window System, such as the Motif window manager.

However, these solutions have not been judged appropriate by the Linux user community, which prefers open source solutions for a computer system's basic and essential software (there's more tolerance for commercial software at the application level). In the open source world, efforts to resolve X's shortcomings focus on building desktop environments such as KDE and GNOME, which are explored in the following chapter.

Exploring Window Managers

As you've already learned, window managers are just another client within the X Window System; like applications, window managers must ask the X server to redraw the screen and perform other operations. Because the client and server layers in X are completely independent, you can use any window manager you want, as long as it knows how to "talk" to the X server. The following sections explore some of the more popular window managers, including those provided with Red Hat Software's Linux distributions.

FVWM

Originally created by Robert Nation, FVWM launched a family of window managers that have long been the default window managers in Linux distributions. Compliant with the ICCCM guidelines, FVWM has been succeeded by FVWM2, recently released in a stable (nonbeta) version. In Red Hat Linux version 5.2, FVWM2 is the default window manager (see Figure 3.1). Configured to work much like Microsoft Windows 98, Red Hat's version of FVWM provides an easy migration path for Windows users.

AfterStep

Emulating the user interface of the defunct NeXT computer system, AfterStep (see Figure 3.2) is an extension of FVWM that's highly regarded by many in the Linux community. An appealing feature of AfterStep is its use of themes, which change the look and feel of the window manager in many ways. A popular feature of AfterStep is the *wharf,* a customizable toolbar that enables you to add links to your applications without doing a lot of fussing with configuration files. You can learn more about AfterStep at http://www.afterstep.org.

LessTif

Designed to emulate the commercial OSF/Motif window manager, LessTif (pronounced "less-teaf") can run most of the applications that require OSF/Motif, the commercial window

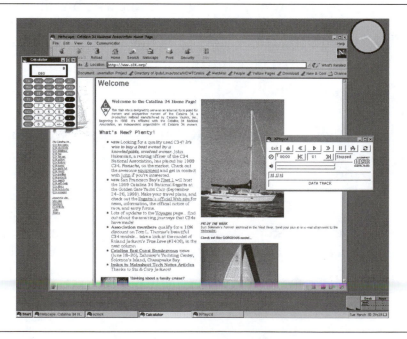

Figure 3.1 FVWM2 is the default in Red Hat Linux 5.2.

manager packaged with the Common Desktop Environment (CDE), discussed later in this chapter. The window manager is a dead ringer for Motif, but—like the other window managers we've discussed— it's constructed from FVWM. For more information about Lesstif, see http://www.lesstif.org.

Enlightenment

The default window manager with Red Hat Linux 6.0, Enlightenment takes the premise of user customization to its logical extreme; Enlightenment themes enable users to paint their desktops in visually appealing ways (see Figure 3.3). With the highest degree of GNOME compatibility among all available window managers, Enlightenment combines all the attractive features of other window managers, including After-Step's wharf feature. Written from scratch, Enlightenment isn't

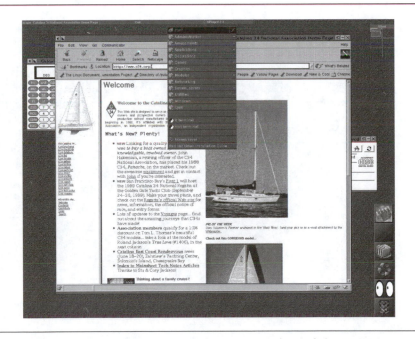

Figure 3.2 AfterStep emulates the user interface of the NeXT computer.

dependent on FVWM code, as are the other window managers discussed thus far in this section. Currently, Enlightenment is the default window manager for Red Hat Linux version 6.0.

Window Maker

Modeled after NeXT's OpenStep desktop, Window Maker (http://www.windowmaker.org) is another respected window manager that offers compability with the GNOME and KDE desktops.

Introducing the Desktop Alternative

As you've learned thus far, the X Window System does not provide the desktop features that users have come to expect, based on their experiences with Mac OS and Microsoft

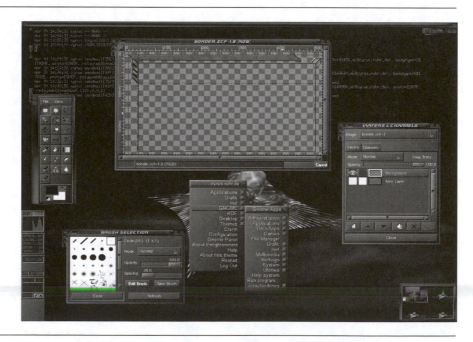

Figure 3.3 Enlightenment offers the ultimate in GUI customization.

Windows. For this reason, efforts have been underway to create desktop environments that work with X. Such efforts began with the Common Desktop Environment (CDE), created by a consortium of Unix industry vendors. A proprietary system designed to work with the Motif window manager, CDE isn't popular among Linux users, who have been waiting for an open source desktop environment. In this section, you'll learn about the two leading contenders for the Linux desktop, KDE and GNOME.

The KDE Desktop Environment

KDE—short for the K Desktop Environment—is inspired by CDE, and closely emulates its overall structure: It's designed to work with a specific window manager, and works best with compliant applications. Reading the list of KDE features, it's

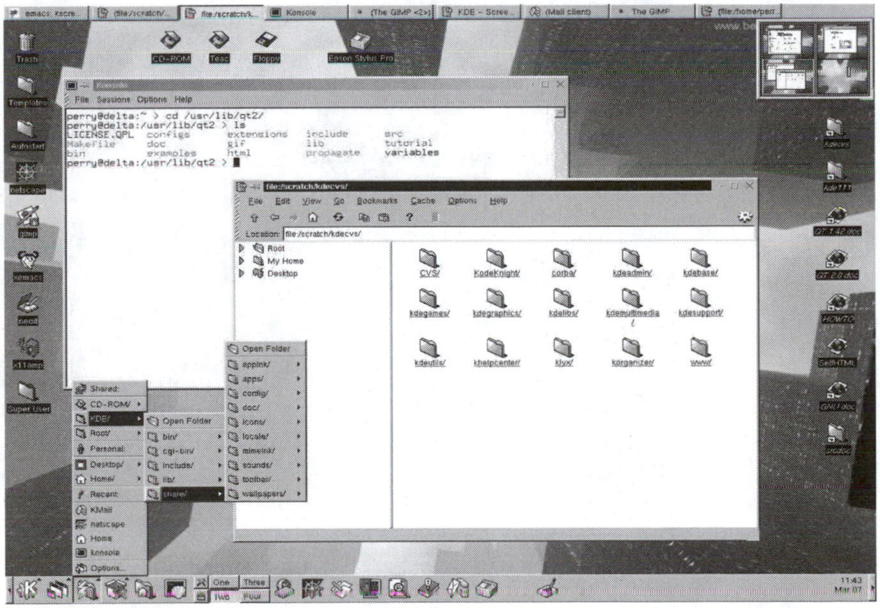

Figure 3.4 KDE provides a comprehensive desktop environment.

obvious that KDE is a cure for that which ails X: drag-and-drop, transparent desktop configuration, a unified application help system, interprocess communication, a consistent look and feel for compliant applications, standardized menus and toolbars, and a professional-looking appearance (see Figure 3.4). The KDE home page is located at http://www.kde.org.

Unlike CDE, KDE is free of charge and distributed, in the main, on open-source principles. The sticking point for many Linux users, however, has been KDE's use of the Qt toolkit, which was not released on an open source basis. This toolkit, created by a small Norwegian software firm called Troll Technologies, is a set of software tools and resources that KDE requires in order to run. This company insists on controlling the source code and places restrictions on the use of the code in commercial products. As a result, programmers are not

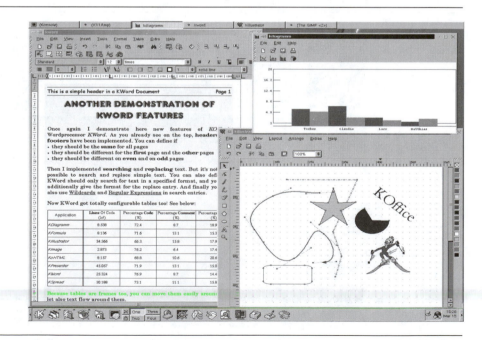

Figure 3.5 KOffice offers an open source alternative to Microsoft Office.

certain that they can write for the KDE environment without getting embroiled in a relationship or lawsuit with the Qt toolkit's authors. The license has since been modified, but many Linux users are still not satisfied with the terms of the license.

Squabbles concerning the KDE project have deeply divided the Linux community (for an example, see Perens 1999, and the various responses). The dispute led to the formation of the competing GNOME project, which will need to duplicate much of the effort that has already gone into KDE. The KDE/GNOME split illustrates one of the unfortunate phenomena of the open source movement, called *forking*. Forking occurs when open source developers break into two warring camps, dividing their effort and confusing potential adopters.

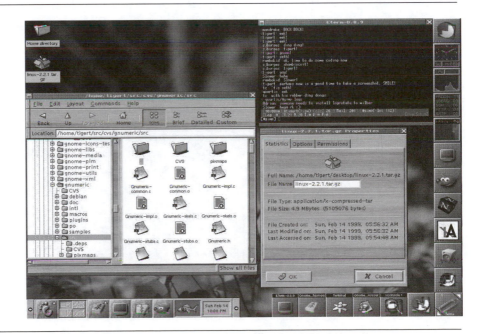

Figure 3.6 GNOME brings needed desktop tools to Linux.

Currently, KDE is further along than GNOME, particularly in the applications department. The KDE developers are at work on a suite of KDE applications, including the KDE Office Suite (see Figure 3.6). Applications currently include KSpread (spreadsheet), KPresenter (presentation graphics), KIllustrator (a vector graphics program resembling Adobe Illustrator), KWord (word processing), KDiagram (a drawing program), and KImage (an image viewer). Many more applications are on the way, and all are distributed freely.

GNOME

GNOME (pronounced "guh-nome") stands for GNU Object Model Environment. It's the newest desktop environment for Linux systems (for a technical description, see Icaza 1999). Unlike KDE, it was developed from the beginning on the

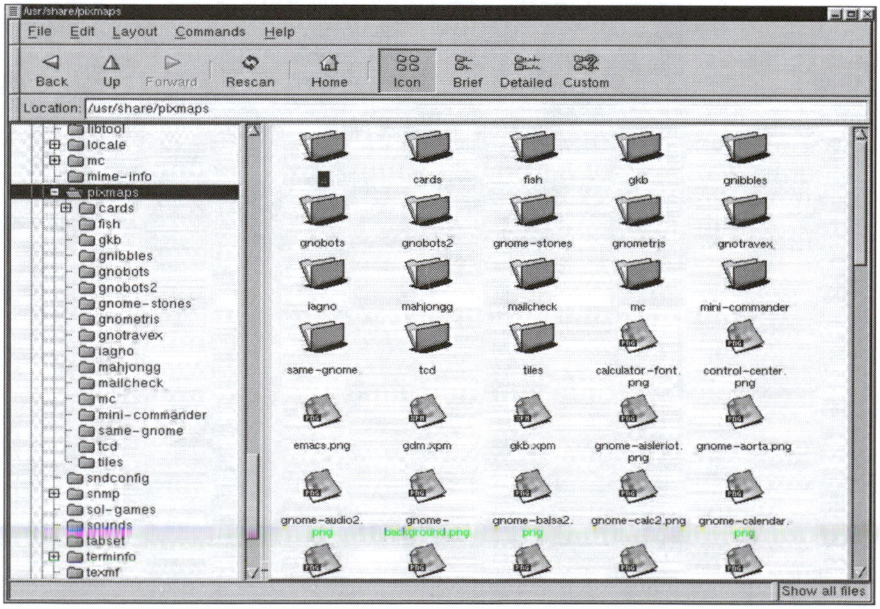

Figure 3.7 The GNOME File Manager makes it easy to manage files.

strictest open-source principles, so that developers can develop applications for GNOME without worrying about licensing problems. Instead of using a commercial software toolkit like Qt, the GNOME developers began by improving the existing GNU toolkit, now called GTK+. In January of 1998, the GNOME effort received a boost from Red Hat Software, which announced the formation of the Red Hat Advanced Development Laboratories (RHAD). A key RHAD objective is to aid the GNOME project by providing full-time programmers.

Like KDE, GNOME directly addresses the insufficiencies of the X Window System. Here's a list of some of GNOME's features:

- **Drag and Drop** Extensively implemented in GNOME, drag and drop becomes one of the fundamental ways you work with the desktop.
- **Drive Icons** For Windows and Mac OS users, accessing disk drives with Linux is a difficult and confusing procedure, but not with GNOME. Drives appear as icons on the desktop.
- **Panels** A basic GNOME feature is the Panel (see Figure 3.7), a rectangular area into which you can drag documents and applications (which transforms them into icons). As a result, you can quickly configure GNOME to run your applications without editing configuration files or scripts.
- **Integrated File Management** The GNOME File Manager (see Figure 3.7) is a graphical user interface version of the respected Midnight Commander. For the first time, it's easy to manage files on a Unix system.
- **GNOME Applications** The GNOME team is busily preparing a suite of applications designed to take full advantage of GNOME, including the Gnumeric spread-

sheet. Provided with GNOME are utilities such as the GNOME CD Player and the GNOME Calendar.

- **Integrated Session Management** If you're using a GNOME-compliant window manager, GNOME remembers which applications you were running and what you were doing with them when you logged out of GNOME. When you log in again, you'll see the same applications, showing your work where you left off. (Note: You must still save your work before exiting GNOME.)

- **Interprocess Communication** GNOME uses a new standard called CORBA (short for Common Object Request Broker Architecture) to implement interprocess communication, in which applications are able to exchange information with each other. Like the X Window System, CORBA is designed for cross-platform computing environments, in which different brands and types of computers need to work together. With CORBA, applications can request information from other programs without needing specifics about what type of computer the program is running on or what programming language was used to create the program.

Unlike other desktop environments, GNOME will work with virtually any window manager, but GNOME-compatible window managers enable you to take full advantage of all the GNOME features. Compatible window managers include Icewm and Window Maker, but the Enlightenment window manager is the only one that currently offers 100 percent compliance.

GNOME received a tremendous boost with Red Hat Software's announcement that the version 6.0 release of Red Hat Linux will default to the GNOME desktop and Enlightenment window manager. Currently the leading Linux distribution, Red Hat's preference for GNOME—not to mention the financial assistance that the company is giving the GNOME development effort—is expected to put GNOME in the lead.

Although any X application will work with GNOME, GNOME-compliant applications take full advantage of the software's desktop features. Table 3.1 lists some of the earliest GNOME applications. At this writing, some of these programs were in very early alpha (prerelease versions) and could not be reviewed here.

Table 3.1 GNOME-compliant applications (selected)

Application	Description
Abiword	A promising word processing program that can read Microsoft Word and RTF files.
gFTP	An FTP (File Transfer Protocol) client with a bevy of sophisticated features.
Gnucash	A Quicken-like personal finance program.
Gnumeric	The GNOME spreadsheet program.
GNU Photo	A graphics utility for retrieving, organizing, and publishing digital graphic images in a variety of file formats; can work with digital cameras.
gnorpm	A GNOME version of Red Hat's RPM package manager.
gnomeICU	A GNOME version of the popular ICQ "buddy list" client.
gxTar	A utility for managing the Unix standard file archive format, called tar.

User Interface Horizons

Do the X Window System and GNOME add up to a satisfactory graphical user interface for Linux systems? At this writing, GNOME is still a work in progress, and it remains to be seen whether GNOME can fully shield beginning users from the underlying complexity of the Linux environment.

In addition, some users don't understand why it's necessary to run both a window manager and a desktop. What's more, they find that some of their functions overlap. For example, the Enlightenment window manager tries to offer some desktop features (insofar as they can be implemented within the confines of X), and these duplicate certain features of GNOME. In the default Red Hat version 6.0 installation, the redundant Enlightenment features are turned off by default.

Why the overlap? It's another instance of the "mechanism, not policy" doctrine: some people will want to use Enlightenment without GNOME, so they'll want the features that emulate certain desktop functions.

Despite these shortcomings, it seems clear that the X Window System, the Enlightenment window manager, and the GNOME desktop are likely to gain acceptance as the standard graphical user interface for Linux systems. As you'll soon discover, GNOME is an exceptionally well-designed user interface, one that combines the best features of Microsoft Windows, X window managers, and the Macintosh Finder. Beneath their attractive external appearance is a technical foundation that will be regarded in the years to come as one of the most impressive technical achievements in contemporary software design.

All that's missing now are the applications needed to attract and retain users—and they're on their way. If your application needs are characterized by a high-quality word processing program, a decent spreadsheet, e-mail, and a Web browser, you'll find that Linux already offers everything you need—and everything's free, at least for personal use. (The high-quality word processing program I just mentioned is WordPerfect, a commercial program that's made available for free for noncommercial uses.)

From Here

You've got all the background you need to give Linux a try. In Part Two of this book, you'll install the Red Hat Linux version 6.0 software that's included on this book's CD-ROM disk. In short order, you'll have a chance to see for yourself why so many people are talking about Linux and GNOME.

References and Selected Reading

Bray, Hiawatha. 1999. "Linux Makeover," *Boston Globe* (March 25, 1999), p. D01.

Icaza, Miguel de. 1999. "The GNOME Project," *Linux Journal* (February, 1999). Available online at http:// www.linuxgazette.com/ issue35/ icaza.html.

Perens, Bruce. 1999. "Why KDE is Still a Bad Idea." Available online at http://slashdot.org/features/9807150935248.shtml.

Zweije, Vincent. 1998. "Remove X Apps mini-HOWTO." Available online at the Linux Documentation Project (http:// www.metalab.unc.edu/LDP).

Part Two

Installing Red Hat Linux

4

Preparing to Install Red Hat Linux

Contrary to what you've probably heard, Linux is *not* difficult to install—at least, no more than any other full-featured operating system. However, you'll find it much easier to install Linux if you do some advanced planning. In this chapter, you'll learn how to prepare for your Red Hat Linux 6.0 installation so that the whole process is trouble-free.

> **TIP** Because Linux is more efficient than Microsoft Windows, you can get excellent performance from older computers that have been lightly used or stored since a system upgrade. A Pentium system running at 166 MHz makes an excellent Linux workstation!

Understanding the Need to Prepare

To install Linux successfully, do the following:

1. **Make sure your system meets the recommended system requirements.** Most newer PCs will meet these requirements without any problem, but you may need to beef up an older system to make sure that it performs well with Linux.

2. **Decide whether you want to continue to run both Windows and Linux, or Linux alone.** If you have a very large hard drive and at least 700 MB of free space, you can run both Windows and Linux on the same computer. However, I don't recommend that you try to do this unless you have a really enormous drive—8MB or more. You'll find it much easier to install and use Linux on a disused system, or on a *separate* hard disk within a system that's also running Windows.

3. **Make an inventory of your computer's hardware.** You'll need a list of the brand and model of the various components and accessories installed on your computer, such as the CD-ROM drive, modem, network card, video card, and more. You may need to supply this information when you install Red Hat Linux.

4. **Plan your Linux filesystem.** When you install Linux, you'll need to make decisions about how to set up your Linux filesystem. Some advance planning will make this process go smoothly.

The next sections of this chapter guide you through this planning process.

Understanding Linux System Requirements

Like any operating system, Linux requires a system equipped with a supported microprocessor, a minimum amount of memory, and a minimum amount of hard disk space. However, a system that meets but does not exceed these minimums would not prove of much use.

In this section, you'll see the minimum requirements, but you'll also find my recommendations for a system that will be able to run Linux so that you can fully explore the applications discussed in this book.

The Bare-Bones Minimum

To run Red Hat Linux, the following are the *minimum* requirements:

- **An Intel 386 or later microprocessor.** Versions of Linux are available for the DEC Alpha, Sun SPARC, PowerPC, and other processors. This book focuses on the installation and use of Red Hat Linux 6.0 in the Intel environment.
- **4MB of RAM (main memory).** This is truly a bare-bones minimum. With so little RAM, you cannot run the X Window system or GNOME.
- **200 MB of free hard disk space.** Again, this is the bare-bones minimum, and would require installing just the basics of Linux.

These requirements are best ignored in favor of this book's recommendations, detailed in the next section.

The Recommended System

To run Red Hat Linux so that you can fully explore all the applications discussed in this book, your system should meet the following requirements:

- **A PC equipped with a 486 or later Intel microprocessor.** For the best performance, run Linux on a Pentium or Pentium II system. Although Red Hat Linux does run on systems powered with Cyrix and AMD processors, installation problems are more common. You'll be wise to stick with Intel processors to run Red Hat Linux 5.2.
- **At least 32MB of RAM (main) memory.** For the best performance with GNOME, equip your system with 48MB or 64MB of RAM.
- **At least 2 GB of disk space.** Although you can run Linux with as little as 200MB of free disk space, you will surely want much more to install Linux applications. To get the most out of Linux, you'll want a system with 2 GB or more of disk space. You'll need a minimum of 2.6GB if you would like to set up Linux as a file or Web server.

NOTE To install Linux on a PC using the CD-ROM packaged with this book, the computer must have MS-DOS or Microsoft Windows installed and running.

Avoid the Latest Systems and Exotic Peripherals

As you learned in the Introduction, Linux is supported by the efforts of users and volunteer programmers who develop and contribute the software necessary to work with Linux on a given computer platform. Such software includes *drivers,* instructions that tell Linux how to work with computer peripherals and accessories such as disk drives, modems, and network interface cards. If you try to install Linux on a system equipped with newly developed peripherals or accessories, or one equipped with exotic devices, you may find that Linux cannot support these devices, and you may not be able to install Linux on such a system.

In short, the best candidate for a Linux system isn't *this* year's hottest system, but the hottest system from a year ago (or a couple of years ago). What's more, such a system should be equipped with popular, well-known peripherals, such as the following:

- ATAPI (IDE) or SCSI CD-ROM drive
- ATI, Cirrus, or Matrox video card, or any video card that uses the S3 video chip
- Any modem that uses hardware rather than software for compression, error correction, and high-speed operation
- SoundBlaster (Creative Labs) or SoundBlaster-compatible sound card
- Recent Adaptec or Bus Logic SCSI adapter
- Any PostScript-compatible printer, or a popular model such as a Canon BubbleJet (BJ-10e, BJ-100, BJ-200, BJ-210, BJ-240, BJC-600, BJC-4000) or Hewlett-Packard DeskJet (400, 500, 500C, 520, 540C, 6xxC series)

TIP You can install Red Hat Linux on most notebook computers, but you may run into special problems. To find out whether Linux is compatible with your notebook, visit Linux on Laptops, at http://www.redhat.com/support/linux-info/laptop/ www.redhat.com/support/linux-info/laptop/.

Note that Red Hat Linux version 6.0 does not support any of the following out of the box:

- DVD drives
- Universal Serial Bus (USB) adapters and devices

- Scanners
- Digital cameras

Although these devices will not install automatically, you may be able to get them to work with a bit of tinkering. For more information, see "Device Configuration Horizons" at the end of this chapter.

Compatibility Levels

Red Hat extensively tests Intel hardware for compatibility with its software distributions, and rates individual components according to the following scheme:

- **Tier 1 Compatibility** Linux can detect and use these components, which are known to install and work reliably on Linux systems.
- **Tier 2 Compatibility** Although Linux should be able to detect and use these components, they are known to have some quirks that cause some users problems. Such problems can normally be resolved by doing a bit of system tweaking.
- **Tier 3 Compatibility** Linux can work successfully with many of these components. However, the drivers may be buggy or experimental, or the components may cause problems that are difficult or impossible to resolve.
- **Incompatible Hardware** These components do *not* work with Red Hat Linux.

TIP To see the current list of supported hardware, visit Red Hat's site (http://www.redhat.com), click Support, and follow the links to the Hardware Compatibility Lists.

Hardware Compatibility for Specific Components

To judge your system's compatibility, take a look at Table 4.1, which provides an overview of Red Hat's compatibility list (for specific information, see http://www.redhat.com/corp/support/hardware/Intel). Table 4.2 lists components that are known to be incompatible with Red Hat Linux.

CAUTION Be sure to check the most recent Hardware Compatibility List for information on specific brand and model numbers. Any component that is not specifically listed as compatible (Tier 1, 2, or 3) may not work with Red Hat Linux 6.0.

Table 4.1 Hardware compatibility overview

Type	Compatible hardware (selected)
CPUs	**Tier 1:** Pentium, Pentium II, Celeron, Pentium Pro, Pentium III SMP; AMD K6-2 (except the earliest chips); AMD K6-3). **Tier 2:** Cyrix 6x86, AMD K6, AMD K5, and Winship. **Tier 3:** Cyrix MediaGX.
Motherboards	**Tier 1:** All except those known to be incompatible (see Table 4.2).
Busses	**Tier 1:** CI, AGP, ISA, EISA, and VESA local bus.
IDE hard disks	**Tier 1:** All internal IDE hard disk drives. **Tier 3:** Internal IDE Zip drive.
IDE adapters	**Tier 1:** Adapters embedded onto the motherboard of Pentium or later computers. **Tier 2:** Plug-in IDE adapters.
SCSI drives	SSCI hard disks and removable drives are supported if their controllers are supported.

SCSI controllers   **Tier 1:** Most recent SCSI adapters made by Mylex (BusLogic), MultiMaster, FlashPoint, Advansys, Adaptec, and ICP. **Tier 2:** Older Adaptec controllers, and others made by Always, AM, Data Technology Corp., DTP, Quantum, Future Domain, GDT, Initio, NCR, and Tekram. **Tier 3:** Controllers made by UltraStor, Trantor, Perceptive Solutions, QLogic, Pro Audio Spectrum, Seagate, and Western Digital, as well as Adaptec 1520B and 1522B.

CD-ROM drives   **Tier 1:** All 100% ATAPI-compliant drives, including ATAPI-compliant multi-disc drives; some SoundBlaster-compatible drives made by Creative Labs, Funai, IBM, Kotobuki, Matsushita, and Teac. **Tier 2:** Proprietary CD-ROMs (such as those made by Aztec, Goldstar, Mitsumi, Optics, NEC, Sanyo, Sony, Phillips, and ISP). **Tier 3:** Certain BackPack parallel-port CD-ROMs; drives compatible with SoundBlaster Pro 16; SCSI-based multi-disc CD-ROMs (to use these drives, you must recompile the kernel).

Tape drives   **Tier 2:** Most SCSI drives. **Tier 3:** Floppy-controller tape drives; IDE tape drives; ATAPI-compliant parallel port drives.

Video adapters   **Tier 1:** Red Hat Linux ships with XFree86 version 3.3.3.1, which provides video adapter support. This version supports recent video adapters made by Actix, Ark Logic, ASUS, ATI, Avance Logic, Cardex, Chips & Technologies, Cirrus Logic, Creative Blaster, Diamond, Digital, ET, ELSA, Genoa, Hercules, LeadTek, Matrox, Miro, Number Nine, Octek, Orchid, SPEA, Spider, STB, SiS, Toshiba, Trident, VideoLogic, and WinFast.

Network adapters   **Tier 1:** Most recent adapters made by 3Com, Digital, EtherWORKS, Linksys, and Intel. **Tier 2:** Older 3Com adapters (such as EtherLink Plus and EtherLink 16), and adapters made by Allied Telesis, AMD, Apricot, AT&T, Alteon, Allied Telesis, Cabletron, Crystal LAN, Control Hostess, Compaq, AnyLan, D-Link, Fujitsu, HP, RealTek, Novell, and others. **Tier 3:** 3Com (3c501, 3c515, 3c905b), Intel EtherExpress Pro/100B, Intel EtherExpress 100/plus.

Sound cards   **Tier 2:** Acer Notebook, AdLib, Advance Logic ALS-007, Compaq Deskpro XL Sound, Crystal CS423x sound chip, Ensoniq Audio PCI 1370 (same as SoundBlaster 64/128 PCI), Creative/Ensoniq Audio PCI 1371, Ensoniq SoundScape, ESS 688 Audio Drive, ESS 1868 AudioDrive, Gravis UltraSound (including Max and PnP), Logitech, SoundMan Games, Media-Trix AudioTrix Pro, MediaVision Jazz 16, Mozart/MAD16, miroSound PCM12, Pro Audio Spectrum/Studio 16 (same as Logitech SoundMan 16), Orchid SW32 (same as Cardinal DSP16), S3 Sonic Vibes, SoundBlaster, SoundBlaster DS, SoundBlaster Pro, SoundBlaster 16/PNP, SoundBlaster 32/64 AWE, Turtle Beach MultiSound Classic/Monterey/Tahiti, Turtle Beach MultiSound Pinnacle/Fiji, Windows Sound System.

Mice   **Tier 1:** Any PS/2 mouse; serial mice (Logitech, MouseMan, early Microsoft serial mice, and Mouse Systems). **Tier 2:** bus mice (ATI XL Inport, Logitech, Microsoft. **Tier 3:** Microsoft IntelliMouse (compatible with Linux, but most applications do not support the scroll wheel); Microsoft serial mice (version 2.1A or newer).

Modems   **Tier 1:** Any external modem; Lucent Venus-based PCI modems (same as Actiontec PM-6500-LKI). Most other modems should function acceptably, although some features may not be supported (such as voice mail).

ISDN adapters	**Tier 3:** SpellCaster (Datacommute/BRI, Telecommute/BRI); any external ISDN adapter that attaches to a serial port.
Cable modems	**Tier 3:** Any cable modem that attaches to your computer by means of an Ethernet port.
Printers	**Tier 2:** Any PostScript printer, plus those supported by specific drivers (including recent printers made by Apple, Canon, DEC, Epson, HP, Imagen, Mitsubishi, NEC, Okidata, Ricoh, StarJet, Tek, tektronics, and Xerox.
Infrared devices	**Tier 3:** ACTiSYS IR-220L, Extended Systems Jet-Eye, Greenwich GIrBIL, Tekram IrMate, Sharp Universal Infrared Controller.
Joysticks	**Tier 3:** Analog (CHF/FCS), FP-Gaming Assasin 3D, Gravis GrIP, PDPI Lightning, Logitech, Microsoft SideWinder, Thrustmaster DirectConnect, TurboGraFX; console joysticks and game pads (Atari, Amstrad, Commodore, Amiga, Sega) connected to parallel port.
Radio cards	**Tier 3:** RadioTrack/Radio Reveal; Aztech; GemTek, Miro PCM20; SF16MI, Typhoon (same as EcoRadio), Zoltrix Radio Plus.
PC cards	**Tier 2:** A wide selection of recent ethernet, modem, memory, and SCSI cards are supported.

Unsupported Hardware

Table 4.2 lists the hardware components that won't work with Red Hat Linux 6.0. If you try to install Red Hat Linux on a system containing these components, the installation may fail, or the component won't work.

Table 4.2 Hardware incompatibility overview

Type	Incompatible hardware (selected)
General	Any component that is *not specifically listed* in Red Hat's Hardware Compatibility List as compatible (http:// www.redhat.com/corp/support/ hardware/ Intel) should be considered incompatible with Red Hat Linux.
CPUs	None, but avoid working with overclocked CPUs.
Motherboards	Supermicro P5MMA with BIOS earlier than 1.4; Supermicro P5MMA98; KM T5-T1; motherboards with a combined host bus interface, DRAM controller, IDE controller, PCI interface, and 2D/3D graphics controller, such as those using the SiS chipsets.
Busses	MicroChannel (MCA), Universal Serial Bus (USB), Firewire.
IDE hard disks	Removable IDE hard disks (such as those made by SyQuest).
CD-ROM drives	Parallel-port CD-ROM drives (except certain drives made by BackPack); clones of the internal LMS/Philips CD-ROM drive that use 206/cm260 interface cards.
DVD drives	These drives are not supported by Red Hat Linux, although you may be able to get the CD-ROM read capabilities of such drives to work.
Tape drives	Non-ATAPI parallel-port drives; Onstream Drive
Network adapters	Intel EtherExpress Pro/10 PCI; Xircom adapters.
Scanners	Red Hat Linux 6.0 does not offer support for scanners, but you may be able to obtain experimental drivers that will work.
Digital cameras	Red Hat Linux 6.0 does not offer support for digital cameras, but you may be able to obtain experimental drivers that will enable you to accept input from these devices.

Modems	IBM Mwave modem/soundcard; plug-and-play modems; modems that require software for compression and other functions (including SupraExpress internal 56K, SupraSonic 56K, many internal laptop modems, Multiwave Innovation CommWave V.34, U.S. Robotics WinModems, U.S. Robotics Sportster Voice/Fax X2 model 1785, Boca Research M3361, Boca Research MV34AI , Zoltrix 33.6 Win HSP, Motorola ModemSURFR, DSVD modem, Compaq 192 PCMCIA modem/serial card, New Media Winsurfer.

Making a System Inventory

Although Red Hat Linux can detect most of your system's components automatically, you may find that you'll need detailed information about one or more of them in order to complete your installation successfully. Table 4.3 lists the information you may need to install Red Hat Linux successfully. Before you install Red Hat Linux, you should obtain this information so that it's handy, in case you need it. Dig around those drawers, and find the manuals that came with system accessories such as your modem, network card, monitor, and all the other items mentioned in Table 4.3.

TIP If you're running Microsoft Windows, you can use system utilities to get much of the information you'll need. To view system information with Windows 3.1, open an MS-DOS window, type msd, and press Enter. If you're running Windows 95, you can use the System icon in the Control Panel to view information about your system. In Windows 98, click Start, point to Programs, point to Accessories, point to System Tools, and choose System Information.

Table 4.3 System inventory for a Linux Installation

Item	Record this information
Processor	**Brand** (such as Intel, Cyrix, AMD)
	Type (such as 486, Pentium, Pentium II, or Celeron)
	Clock speed (such as 333 MHz or 450 MHz)
Motherboard	**Brand** (such as Intel, Cyrix, AMD)
	Type (such as 486, Pentium, Pentium II, or Celeron)
	Clock speed (such as 333 MHz or 450 MHz)
RAM	**Amount of RAM installed** (in megabytes)
Hard drive	**Brand** (such as Quantum or Western Digital)
	Model number
	Interface type (such as IDE, ESDI, or SCSI)
	Size (in megabytes)
	Number of cylinders
SCSI adapter	**Brand** (such as Adaptec or Bus Logic)
	Model number
	IRQ (such as IRQ 9 or IRQ 11)
	I/O address (such as 0x340)
	SCSI address (such as 1 or 5)
SCSI devices	**SCSI address** (record the SCSI address, a single-digit number, for each SCSI device)
Monitor	**Brand** (Mitsumi or Panasonic)
	Model number
	Maximum horizontal refresh rate (in MHz). Multisynch monitors can work with a range of refresh rates, such as 40-150 MHz; if your monitor is a multisynch monitor, record the range.

	Maximum vertical refresh rate (in MHz). Record the range if your monitor is a multisynch monitor.
Mouse	Type (PS/2, serial, or bus). For serial mice, record the port to which it is connected (such as COM1 or COM2).
	Number of buttons (two or three)
Modem	Brand (such as U.S. Robotics or 3Com)
	Model number
	Serial port (such as COM1 or COM2)
	IRQ (such as IRQ 5 ir IRQ 9)
Network card	Type (such as Ethernet or token ring)
	Brand (such as 3Com, Digital, or Intel)
	Model number
	IRQ (such as IRQ 9 or IRQ 11)
	I/O address (such as 0x340)
Printer	Brand (such as Canon or Hewlett-Packard)
	PostScript compatibility (yes or no)
	Model number
	Brand and model numbers of printers that this printer can emulate (such as HP DeskJet 560C). Check your printer's manual to find out whether your printer can emulate another printer; many can.

Understanding the Linux Filesystem

Now that you've inventoried your system, you're almost ready to start. What you need now is a bit of conceptual orientation regarding the Linux filesystem. If you're used to MS-DOS, Microsoft Windows, or Mac OS, you'll find much that's familiar in the Linux filesystem: there's a hierarchy of directories and subdirectories (or folder and subfolders, if you prefer), and the directories are used to organize files. But there are some important differences, too (elegantly explained in Welsh, *et al.* 1992-1998: 44–47); they're summarized in this section.

Introducing Linux Directories

Let's start with concepts that do not depart radically from the knowledge you already have. As in Windows or MS-DOS, a *directory* is a named storage area that's used to group related files.

A directory can contain one or more *subdirectories*, which in turn can contain files and additional subdirectories. The directory structure is a hierarchy, with the *root directory* positioned at the top. The root directory is symbolized by a forward slash mark (/), and is analogous to the C:\ directory in MS-DOS.

Understanding Partitions

A *partition* is a portion of a disk drive that has been electronically modified so that it can be treated as a separate unit for formatting and data storage purposes.

In the Windows and MS-DOS world, the operating system gives each partition its own drive letter. For example, hard disks are often divided into two partitions, called drive C and drive D. It is not possible for a directory span two or more partitions. As a result, Windows and MS-DOS users must necessarily confront the physical realities of disk drives and partitions.

Directories and Partitions in Linux

Linux directories and partitions differ from their Windows and MS-DOS counterparts in two important ways:

- A single directory can span two or more partitions—and indeed, two or more disk drives.
- A partition doesn't appear as a separate disk drive. Instead, it can be *mounted* at any point within the overall directory structure, so that it appears to be a seamless part of this structure.

By breaking the tight link between directories and partitions, Linux enables system administrators to create seamlessly integrated filesystems that span several partitions and disk drives. Users no longer need to worry (as they must with MS-DOS and Windows) just where data is physically located. On a network, this advantage becomes even more significant. Network administrators can create seamless filesystems that span a number of separate computer systems; yet these filesystems appear to users to be a seamless whole. Without realizing, a given user might be working with a directory that is physically located on a different computer.

Mounting Partitions and Disk Drives

When you mount a partition, Linux includes the partition's directories and files within the directory tree structure that you see on-screen. The point where the partition is mounted is called the *mount point*.

Although some Linux users install Linux in one large partition on their hard drives, it's a better practice to divide the drive into several partitions. For example, it's a good practice to create separate partitions for your personal files and for any software that you install. You can then install or upgrade your system software with the assurance that your personal files and installed software will not be overwritten.

If you create more than one Linux partition on your hard drive, as this book recommends, you don't need to worry about mounting these partitions every time you use Linux. The installation software automatically configures Linux so that all the partitions on your hard drive are automatically mounted.

What about disk drives and CD-ROM drives? Like partitions, they're conceptualized as an extension of the filesystem. Instead of assigning them drive letters, as MS-DOS does, these devices are treated as if they were partitions. They're mounted within the /mnt directory. Generally, disk drives aren't automatically mounted when the system starts. In order to access the data on disk drives, you'll need to mount them, using system commands provided for this purpose.

The Filesystem Hierarchy Standard (FHS)

One obstacle to the wider acceptance of Linux is the incompatibility of filesystem structures among competing Linux versions. Recognizing that this situation is disadvantageous to everyone, a group of volunteers created the Filesystem Hierarchy Standard, currently available in version 2.0 (Quinlan 1997).

The major Linux distributors, including Red Hat and Debian, have agreed to support this standard, which is summarized in Table 4.4.

TIP Be sure to study Table 4.4 carefully and make sure you understand the organization of the Linux filesystem, as specified by the FHS standard. In particular, note that you should install new commercial programs in /opt and new, noncommercial programs in /usr/local. As you'll learn subsequently, it's very wise to assign these directories to their own partitions so that you can protect them from being overwritten when you install operating system upgrades.

Table 4.4 Structure of the standard Linux filesystem

Directory	Contents
/	This symbol stands for the root directory, the topmost directory in the Linux filesystem. The root directory must not contain any subdirectories besides the ones specified in the standard (bin, boot, dev, etc, home, lib, mnt, opt, root, sbin, tmp, usr, and var).
/bin	Short for "binaries," this directory contains many essential system utilities that need to be accessible to all users as well as the system administrator. It's not supposed to contain subdirectories.
/boot	This directory stores the files needed to start your computer.
/dev	Short for "devices," this directory contains the files that represent the peripheral devices installed on your system, such as network interface cards, modems, and your mouse.
/etc	You'll find most of the important system configuration files in this directory. This directory isn't supposed to contain any executable files (binaries).
/home	This directory is reserved for users' home directories.
/lib	This directory stores shared library files, which contain programming instructions that one or more applications use in common.
/mnt	Here's where you'll find files representing disk drives and other peripheral storage devices, such as Zip drives.
/opt	This directory is optional; it's used for installing commercial software. Ideally, this directory

should be installed on its own partition, so that you can safeguard it from being overwritten if you install a system software upgrade.

/proc   This directory's contents change depending on which programs, or processes, you're running. Each process is represented as if it were part of the filesystem. Everything's a file, remember?

/root   Don't confuse this directory with the root directory (/); it's actually just a home directory for the system administrator, who logs in with the user name "root."

/sbin   This directory includes non-vital system utility programs (the indispensable ones are stored in /bin).

/tmp   This directory is used to store temporary information needed by the programs you're using.

/usr   This read-only directory contains most of your system's software, including the executable files (binaries) and documentation. An important sub-directory is /usr/local, where you'll install the non-commercial software you add to your system. Like the /opt directory, it's wise to place the /usr/local directory in its own partition so that it's protected from being overwritten when you upgrade system software.

/var   This directory includes log files, print spooling files, and other files that typically grow in size.

Choosing Your Installation Class

When you install Red Hat Linux, you'll need to specify how you want the installation software to set up your Linux filesystem. Take a few minutes now to understand your options here.

Ordinary Users and the Superuser (Root User)

Even if you plan to install Linux on a single-user system, you should understand that Linux is a multi-user operating system. To ensure system security and efficient administration, Linux creates a distinction between the following:

- **Root user** (also called *superuser*) The root user has full access to all of the files on the entire system. In order to get root user status, you must log on to the Linux system by typing the root user's password.
- **Users** Users automatically see their own section of the filesystem, and cannot view or modify portions of the filesystem that the superuser employs in order to ensure system security. To log on as a user, you type the user's username and password.

If you're the only user of your Linux system, does this distinction matter to you? Yes, it does. When you log on as the root user, you can modify system settings—and, if you're not careful, you can do a lot of damage. You should log on to your system as the root user only when you need to make changes to the Linux system configuration. For ordinary use, you should log on as a user, so you don't do any inadvertent damage.

Deciding which Installation Class to Use

To determine how to divide your disk into Linux partitions, you need to choose between three basic types of Linux installations:

- **Workstation Class Installation** This installation automatically creates three partitions: a 32MB swap partition, a 16MB boot partition, and a root partition that uses all of the rest of the available space on the drive. To create a workstation-class installation, you need a minimum of 600MB of disk space.

- **Server-Class Installation** This is the recommended option if you are setting up a Linux system to be used as a file or Web server. This installation automatically creates three partitions: a 64MB swap partition, a 16MB boot partition, and a root partition that uses all of the rest of the available space on the drive. The root partition is an extended partition, and it is further subdivided into two 512MB partitions (a /usr partition for software and a /home partition for individual users), as well as a 256MB partition (/var) for log files. You'll need 1.6GB of disk space to create a server-class installation.

- **Custom Installation** This installation enables you to choose installation options individually. Although the custom installation option is somewhat more complex than the Workstation or Server installations, you gain by being able to specify the programs you want to run. Chapter 4 walks you through the entire Custom installation process. You'll need between 700MB and 1.6GB of disk space for a custom installation.

TIP Do not choose the server-class installation if you are planning to run two operating systems on your computer. Use the workstation-class installation instead. The workstation installation automatically installs software that enables you to choose which operating system you want to use at the beginning of an operating session.

Preparing Your System for a Two-OS Installation

This section should be read only by those who plan to create a system that enables you to choose between two operating systems (OS), Microsoft Windows and Linux. You should attempt such an installation *only* if you have a very large hard drive with a lot of free space, (I recommend at least 2 or 3 GB), or a system with two or more physical hard drives installed.

TIP Some computers with a single, large hard drive are configured with what appears to be two drives, generally called drive C and drive D. If you've haven't made much use of drive D, and if it has sufficient free space, you can use drive D for Linux.

Deciding Whether to Attempt a Two-OS System

With the software provided with Red Hat Linux, you can configure your system so that you can continue to run Microsoft Windows as well as Linux. In this way, you can continue to work with Microsoft Windows applications where necessary, and use Linux whenever you wish. In addition, you can configure your Linux system so that you can mount (access) data files within your Windows directories.

If the notion of running Linux and Windows on the same system appeals to you, bear in mind that choosing this option makes the installation process more difficult and risky. The reason lies in the fact that the two operating systems use different file storage systems. In order to run Linux, you must do one of the following:

- **Repartition an existing large drive to make room for Red Hat Linux.** You should attempt this only if you have a truly enormous hard drive with lots of free space.
- **Delete an existing *extended DOS partition* to make room for Red Hat Linux.** On many older PCs with large hard drives, there's a 2.1GB limit to the size of a DOS partition. To use all the space on the drive, the system was configured with two partitions, a primary DOS partition (the boot partition) and an extended DOS partition. These show up as drive C and drive D, but you really have only

one physical hard drive installed. If you haven't used drive D, the extended DOS partition, you can delete this partition to make room for Red Hat Linux.

- **Delete the DOS partition on a second hard drive to make room for Red Hat Linux.** If your system has two hard drives, and you haven't made much use of the second one, you can delete the DOS partition on this second drive to make room for Red Hat Linux.

Windows First, Linux Later

If you're installing Windows 95 or Windows 98 as well as Linux, start with Windows. Here's why: When you create a two-OS system, Linux will add information to your hard drive's *master boot record* that enables you to choose between two operating systems. The software that enables this choice is called LILO (Linux Loader). When you start your system, you'll see a prompt that asks you to choose the operating system you want to load (dos or linux). But here's the problem. When you install Windows 95 or Windows 98, the installation software rather cavalierly wipes out the master boot record. So install Windows first.

Because Windows wipes out the 4 upon installation, you'll run into problems should you create a two-OS installation and subsequently upgrade your Windows operating system.

TIP To prevent problems when you upgrade to a new version of Windows, you may wish to install a commercial OS switching utility, such as System Commander Deluxe (V Communications). This software also enables you to repartition your hard disk safely. If you purchase System Commander Deluxe, you won't need to run the FIPS utility, discussed in this section.

Back Up, Back Up, Back Up!

Before following the steps in the next two sections, be sure to back up all the important data in your Windows partition. Should you inadvertently press the wrong key, you could wipe out all your data.

Dividing an Existing, Large Partition

This approach is called *nondestructive repartitioning*. Choose this approach if your computer has a single physical hard drive, and this hard drive contains only one partition that occupies the entire disk.

Think twice before performing a nondestructive repartition. Do you really have enough space on your drive? You should consider that operating systems gobble up enormous amounts of disk space, and applications consume even more. If you try to install Linux and retain Windows, you may find that you run out of disk space with one or both systems. Considering future software installations and the growth of data files, you need at least 4 GB for Windows and 4 GB for Linux—and even then, you'll probably sooner or later run out of disk space for one or both systems.

In the following procedure, you'll back up your drive, defragment it, and run the FIPS utility (provided on this book's CD-ROM) to divide the existing DOS partition into two new partitions. Once you've created the new partition using FIPS, you'll need to delete it so that there's space for the Red Hat installation software to create new partitions (as discussed in the next chapter).

To prepare for a two-OS system in which Windows and Linux will share a single, large hard drive:

1. **Important:** Back up your entire hard drive before proceeding, and make sure you've made backup copies of all important data files. This operation is risky and if you're not careful, you could wipe out your Windows partition—and with it, all the programs and data stored on that partition. Do not proceed without performing a backup!

2. In the following step, you'll defragment your drive. However, most defragmenting utilities will not move the Windows swap file. Therefore, you should disable the Windows swap file. To do so in Windows 98, open the Control Panel, choose System, and click the Performance tab. Click Virtual Memory, and uncheck Disable virtual memory. Click OK to confirm. Note: After you finish the Linux installation, start Windows, and enable virtual memory again (unless you're happy with sluggish performance).

3. In Microsoft Windows, run a defragmentation utility. This is an essential step, because it will move all of your Windows data to the beginning of your drive. In Microsoft Windows 98, click Start, point to Programs, point to Accessories, point to System Tools, and choose Disk Defragmenter.

4. Insert a blank, formatted floppy disk in drive A.

5. Insert this book's CD-ROM into your CD-ROM drive, open the /dosutils directory, and select the files FIPS.EXE and ERRORS.TXT.

6. Copy these files to the floppy disk in drive A.

7. Open an MS-DOS window. With the floppy disk containing FIPS.EXE in drive A, type **sys a:** at the C:> prompt.

8. Leave the floppy disk in drive A, and restart your system so that your computer boots from the floppy disk.

9. At the DOS prompt, type **a:\fips** and press Enter.

10. Follow the on-screen instructions to let FIPS search for free space on your drive.

11. You'll see the message, "Use the cursor keys to choose the cylinder, <enter> to continue." Here, you can press the right or left arrow to change the hard drive cylinder at which the new partition will begin. On the left, you see the number of megabytes of storage in the old partition; on the right, the number in the new partition. *Be sure to leave plenty of room in the old partition for new programs and data!* When you've sized the partitions the way you want, press Enter.

12. Press **c** to continue and write the new partition to the disk.

13. Before you can install Red Hat Linux, you will need to delete the partition that has just been created. To do so, turn to the previous section, "Deleting DOS Partitions."

Using an Existing Partition on a Single, Large Drive

Because many PCs need software help to work with drives over 2.1GB in size, many PCs come configured with what appear to be two hard drives, normally called drive C and drive D. Actually, these aren't drives but two DOS partitions, each smaller than 2.1GB. If you still have space on drive C and haven't used drive D much, you can create a Linux partition in the space occupied by drive D. To do so, you must first delete the second DOS partition, which is called the *extended DOS partition*.

CAUTION Do not proceed until you have backed up all your data and moved all programs and files off drive D! If you're not careful, you could destroy all the data on your entire hard drive.

To prepare for a two-OS installation in which Red Hat Linux will be installed in a disused DOS partition, do the following:

1. In Microsoft Windows, use the Windows Explorer or My Computer to move all the Windows files off drive D.

2. Back up drive C before proceeding, and make sure you've made backup copies of all important data files.

3. In Microsoft Windows, run the Scandisk utility on drive D. Be sure to use the Thorough option to detect and lock out any bad sectors (areas of the disks containing defects). To run Scandisk, click Start, point to Programs, point to Accessories, point to System Tools, and choose Scandisk. Click Thorough, and check Automatically Fix Errors.

4. Restart your system in MS-DOS, and use the fdisk utility to delete the drive D partition. To start fdisk, type **c:\windows\command\fdisk**, and press Enter. Follow the on-screen instructions to delete the D drive letter and to delete the extended DOS partition that once occupied drive D.

Using a Second Hard Drive

If your computer has more than one hard drive, and you haven't used the second one much, you can use the second drive for Red Hat Linux. We're talking about two *physical drives* here—two separate hard disks. (If you have only one physical hard disk but see drive C and drive D in Windows, see the preceding section.) Red Hat Linux can work on the second drive of any two-drive system, including systems with two IDE drives, two SCSI drives, or one SCSI and one IDE drive.

CAUTION Do not use drive C for Red Hat Linux in a two-drive installation. Windows may not start properly if it's not installed on drive C. In a two-drive system, the second drive is probably called drive D. That's where you'll install Red Hat Linux.

To prepare for a two-OS installation in which Red Hat Linux will be installed on a second hard disk drive, do the following:

1. In Microsoft Windows, use the Windows Explorer or My Computer to move all the Windows files off the second disk drive (which is probably called drive D).

2. Back up drive C before proceeding, and make sure you've made backup copies of all important data files.

3. In Microsoft Windows, run the Scandisk utility on the second hard drive. Be sure to use the Thorough option to detect and lock out any bad sectors (areas of the disks containing defects). To run Scandisk, click Start, point to Programs, point to Accessories, point to System Tools, and choose Scandisk. Click Thorough, and check Automatically Fix Errors.

4. Restart your system in MS-DOS, and use the fdisk utility to delete all the DOS partitions on the second drive. To start fdisk, type **c:\windows\command\fdisk**, and press Enter. Select the second drive. Follow the on-screen instructions to delete the primary DOS partition on this drive, and any extended DOS partitions as well.

Device Configuration Horizons

In this chapter, you've learned how to gather the information you need to install a system containing only those components that Red Hat Linux directly supports. But many Linux users have successfully installed a whole range of devices that aren't automatically configured by Red Hat's installation software, including CD-R drives, scanners, and more. Table 4.5 shows where to learn more about a range of devices that you may wish to use.

> **TIP** If you're new to Linux, don't try to tackle installing one of these devices until you've learned all the Linux fundamentals. You'll need to know how to perform tasks such as downloading and installing software, adding new programs to menus, and other tasks that require familiarity with the Linux environment.

Table 4.5 Where to find information on unsupported devices

Device	Information source
CD-R drives	CD-Writing HOWTO, by Winfriend Trumper (http://metalab.unc.edu/LDP/HOWTO/CD-Writing-HOWTO.html). CD User-friendly X software for burning CDs includes X-CD-Roast (http://www.fh-muenchen.de/home/ze/rz/services/projects/scdroast/e_overview.html). Generally, you shouldn't have any trouble installing and working with any SCSI-based CD-R drive, and you can also use many IDE drives.
Digital cameras	Support is spotty because digital camera manufacturers are loathe to release information about how their products transmit information. Still, there's an experimental program called photopc that works with a variety of Agfa, Epson, Olympus, Sanyo, and Nikon cameras, which support in-camera JPEG picture compression (for more

	information on photopc, see http:// www.aver-age.org/ digicam/.) A graphical front end for pho-topc is phototk (http:// www.mediacity.com/ ~pwhite/Photok/ phtok.html).
Infrared devices	Linux IR HOWTO, by Werner Heuser (http://metalab.unc.edu/ LDP/ HOWTO/ IR-HOWTO.html). Experimental support is available for all infrared devices supporting the IrDA standard.
Scanners	SANE (Scanner Access Now Easy) is a public domain programming interface for a variety of raster-image devices, including scanners, cameras, and frame-grabbers. (http:/ /www.mostang.com/ sane/). XSane is a graphical front end program for scanning purposes (http:// www.wolfsburg.de/ ~rauch/sane/sane-xsane.html). Unsupported scanners include Acer scanners, many handheld scanners, and UMAX parallel port scanners. HP Scanjets and UMAX SCSI-based scanners are well supported.
TV Tuners	For a list of supported TV tuners/video capture boards and installation/configuration instructions, see Reijnan 1999. You can watch TV with xawtv (http:// www.in-berlin.de/ User/ kraxel/ xawtv.html).
UPS	A wide range of uninterruptible power supplies (UPS) are supported; see UPS HOWTO, by Harvey J. Stein (http:// metalab.unc.edu/ HOWTO/ UPS-HOWTO.html).

From Here

You're ready to install Red Hat Linux. In the next chapter, you get started with the installation. In Chapter 6, you finish running the installation software, and Chapter 7 shows you how to finalize your system configuration after you've started Linux for the first time.

References and Further Reading

Koffler, Michael. 1997. *Linux: Installation, Configuration, and Use*. Reading, PA: Addison-Wesley.

Gonzato, Guido. 1998. "From DOS/Windows to Linux HOWTO." Linux Documentation Project. Available online at http://metalab.unc.edu/LDP.

Quinlan, Daniel. 1997. *Filesystem Hierarchy Standard—Version 2.0*. Available online at http://www.pathname.com/fhs/2.0/fhs-toc.html.

Reijnen, Patrik. 1999. *Linux Hardware Compatibility HOWTO*. Available online at http://users.bart.nl/ ~patrickr/hardware-howto/Hardware-HOWTO.html.

Welsh, Matt, et al. 1992-1998. *Linux Installation and Getting Started*. Linux Documentation Project. Available online at http://metalab.unc.edu/LDP/.

Starting the Installation

If you're prepared for installing Linux as described in Chapter 4, you're ready to install the Linux operating system on your computer. This chapter walks you through the steps you follow to install Red Hat Linux 6.0 on your PC.

Making Room for Red Hat Linux

Before you run the installation software, you need to make sure that you have made room for Red Hat Linux.

You can do so in two ways:

- If you want to create a two-OS system as described in the previous chapter, you need at least 700MB of free, *unpartitioned* space on your hard drive, or a second hard drive from which you've deleted all the partitions. For more information, see "Preparing Your System for a Two-OS Installation," in Chapter 4.

- If you're creating an all-Linux system, you can use the Red Hat installation software to delete the existing DOS partition on your hard disk.

Deciding How to Boot Your System

In order to install Red Hat Linux, you must boot your system with the CD-ROM packaged with this book, or a floppy disk on which a minimal version of Linux has been installed.

Configuring Your PC to Boot from a CD-ROM

If your PC is fairly new (two years old or less), you may be able to configure your system to boot from a CD-ROM. To find out, restart your system, and press the key (usually Delete) that enables you to change your computer's BIOS settings. Page through the setting options until you find one that enables you to specify the boot disk order. (By default, most systems are set up to boot from the A drive, and then the C drive.) If you can change this setting so that the first boot drive is a CD-ROM, you can install Linux directly from the CD-ROM packaged with this book. Change the setting so that your computer will boot first from a CD-ROM.

If your computer can't boot from a CD-ROM, then you need to make a boot disk. You learn how in the next section.

Creating a Boot Disk

This section is for users whose systems can't boot directly from a CD-ROM. You'll need to create a boot disk, as explained in this section. To do so, you use the rawrite.exe program, which you'll find in the \dosutils directory. You use this program to transfer a file called boot.img (stored in the \images directory) to the floppy disk. This file transforms the floppy into a Linux boot disk.

To create the Linux boot disk:

1. Format a 3.5 inch diskette.

2. Insert the diskette in your computer's floppy disk drive (drive A).

3. Insert this book's CD-ROM into your CD-ROM drive.

4. Use Windows Explorer to view the contents of the CD-ROM disk.

5. Display the \dosutils directory.

6. Locate and double-click **rawrite.exe.** You'll see an MS-DOS application window. The program asks you to specify the name of the image file you want to copy.

7. Type **..\images\boot.img** and press Enter. (Don't forget the two initial periods.)

8. To identify the destination of the file, type **a:** and press Enter.

The rawrite program transfers the boot image file to the floppy disk in drive A.

> **TIP** Make sure your computer is set up to boot from drive A before it boots from drive C. This is the default setting with most PCs, but your system may have been changed. To check the default boot sequence, restart your system, and press the key (usually Delete) that enables you to view the default BIOS settings. Find the area where you can specify the default boot sequence, and make sure the system boots first from drive A.

Starting Linux for the First Time

To boot your computer in Linux so that you can run the installation software, do the following:

1. **Important:** If your system is equipped with a removable drive, such as a Zip drive, place a disk in the drive.

2. Do one of the following:

    If your computer can boot from a CD-ROM, place this book's CD-ROM in the CD-ROM drive, and restart your computer.

    or

    If you made a boot disk, insert the disk in drive A, and restart your computer.

You'll see a screen explaining the various boot options. To proceed, just press Enter

> **TIP** If you see an error message indicating that the installation failed, it means that the installation software could not detect your hardware. You'll need to restart the installation in expert mode. For more information, see "Using the Expert Mode," later in this chapter.

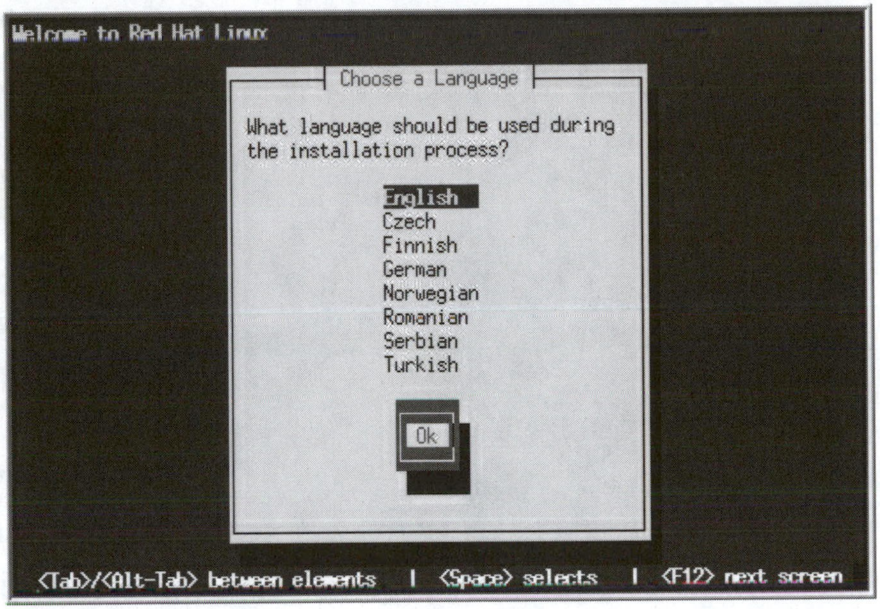

Figure 5.1 Choose a language for the installation.

Starting the Installation

This section walks you through the entire Custom installation process. Should you choose the Workstation- or Server-class installations, you'll see some of the dialog boxes discussed in this section, but not all of them. I strongly recommend that you choose the Custom installation class; this choice will enable you to explore fully the programs and utilities discussed in the rest of this book.

After the initial welcome screen appears, you'll see the window shown in Figure 5.1. Here, you choose a language, but you should take a moment to familiarize yourself with the commands you can use to navigate the installation program's dia-

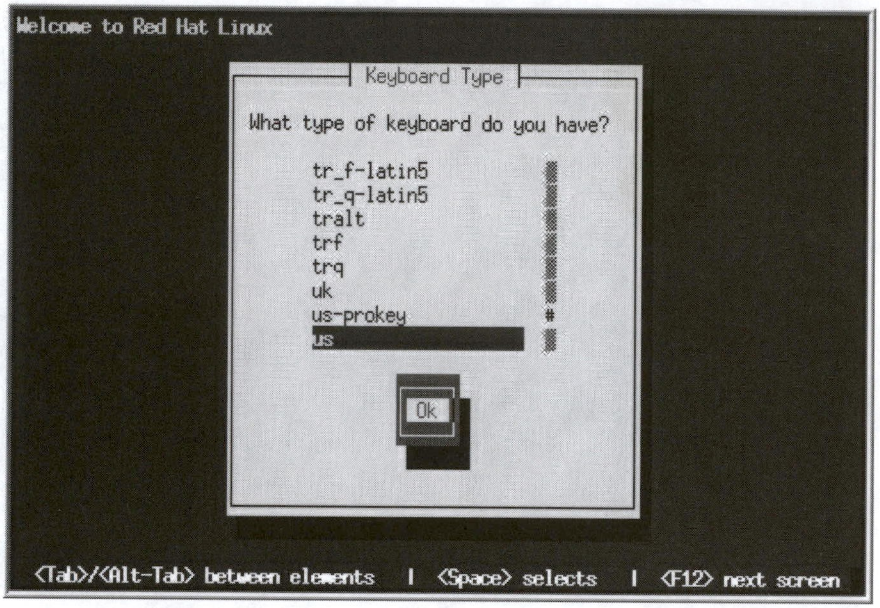

```
Welcome to Red Hat Linux

                        ┤ Keyboard Type ├

               What type of keyboard do you have?

                         tr_f-latin5
                         tr_q-latin5
                         tralt
                         trf
                         trq
                         uk
                         us-prokey                        #
                         us

                              ┌────┐
                              │ Ok │
                              └────┘

 <Tab>/<Alt-Tab> between elements  |  <Space> selects  |  <F12> next screen
```

Figure 5.2 In this dialog box, you choose your keyboard layout.

log boxes (see Table 5.1). Press Tab to select the OK button,
and press Enter to proceed to the next screen.

Table 5.1 lists the keyboard commands you can use during the
installation procedure.

Table 5.1 Installation software navigation commands

To do this:	Press this key:
Move highlight down	Down arrow
Move highlight up	Up arrow
Move to next area	Tab
Move to previous area	Alt + Tab
Press the button	Space
Move to next screen	F12

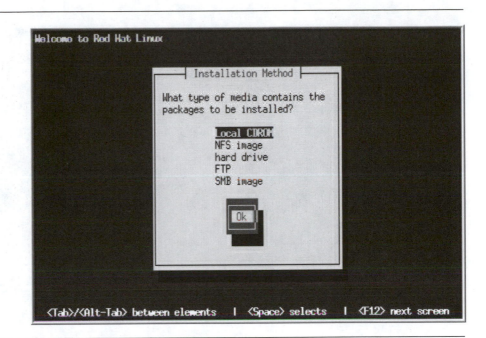

Figure 5.3 Choose CD-ROM to install this book's CD-ROM software.

TIP If you see a scroll bar on the side of the dialog box, you can bring additional options into view. To do so, press the down arrow key, or drag the scroll box with the mouse.

After you select OK, you'll see the dialog box shown in Figure 5.2. From the list, select the keyboard layout you use, and select OK.

Choosing the Installation Method

The next dialog box, shown in Figure 5.3, enables you to choose the type of installation you're going to perform.

To install Red Hat Linux from this book's CD-ROM, select Local CD-ROM, and select OK. Insert the CD-ROM disk, if you haven't already, and select OK in the next dialog box.

Figure 5.4 Choose the Custom installation class for maximum flexibility.

Choosing the Installation Path and Class

In the Installation Path dialog box, select Install and choose OK. (The Upgrade option is only for those who are upgrading from a previous version of Red Hat Linux.) In the next dialog box (see Figure 5.4), you'll be asked to select an installation path. Before choosing any of the options in this dialog box, carefully note the following:

- If you're creating a two-OS installation (see Chapter 4), don't choose the Server-class installation. This installation automatically destroys all existing partitions!
- By choosing the Custom installation class, you can configure the system to meet your precise needs. This is the recommended strategy; I'll walk you through the options.

Select Custom, and choose OK.

SCSI Configuration

If your system is equipped with a SCSI adapter, and the automatic probing software failed to detect it, you'll next see a dialog box asking whether you have any SCSI devices. If so, choose Yes, and do the following:

1. In the Load module dialog box, choose the device's name from the list, and select OK.

TIP If you're installing a Zip Zoom SCSI adapter for an internal Iomega Zip drive, choose Adaptec 152x.

---

2. In the Module options dialog box, select Autoprobe, and choose OK. The installation software will probe your card to determine its settings. If the probe is successful, you'll see a dialog box asking whether you have any additional SCSI cards. Click No to proceed, or click Yes if you have an additional card, and repeat Steps 1 and 2.

TIP If the autoprobe fails to detect your card, you may have changed the IRQ and input/output (IO) settings from the default. In order to configure the card, you'll need to specify module parameters. To do so, go back to Step 1, choose your device's name, and click OK. In Step 2, choose Specify options, and select OK. In the Module Parameters dialog box, type the name of the module, followed by an equal sign, the I/O address, a comma, the card's current IRQ setting, a comma, and the card's current SCSI address. For example, the following sets up the aha152x driver to work with an adapter at I/O 0x340, IRQ 12, and SCSI address 5: aha152x=0x340,12,5.

Running Disk Druid

Disk Druid, part of the installation software you're using, is an easy-to-use program that enables you to partition your hard drive with ease. Before Disk Druid appears, you'll see a dialog box asking which disk partitioning tool you want to use. You can choose between Red Hat's Disk Druid or the older Linux fdisk program. You want Disk Druid.

> **TIP** Don't choose fdisk. This older Linux program requires advanced technical knowledge of disk partitioning. Particularly if you're trying to create a two-OS system, choosing fdisk could leave you with an unbootable system.

Select Disk Druid, and you'll see the Disk Druid window shown in Figure 5.5. Essentially, Disk Druid is a tool that enables you to add, edit, or delete partitions for your Linux installation. You create the partition structure interactively; you can make changes and get thing just right before the software actually writes the partitions to the drive.

Understanding the Disk Druid Window

Take a moment to look at the window before proceeding.

In the Drive Summaries area, you see the hard drive or drives currently installed on your system. The software automatically detects the drive geometry (C = cylinders, H = heads, and S = sectors). You see the total amount of disk space and the amount that's currently used.

Linux doesn't use the "drive C" and "drive D" nomenclature that DOS does. Instead, drives are indicated by the letters "hd" for an IDE drive, and "sd" for a SCSI drive. The first

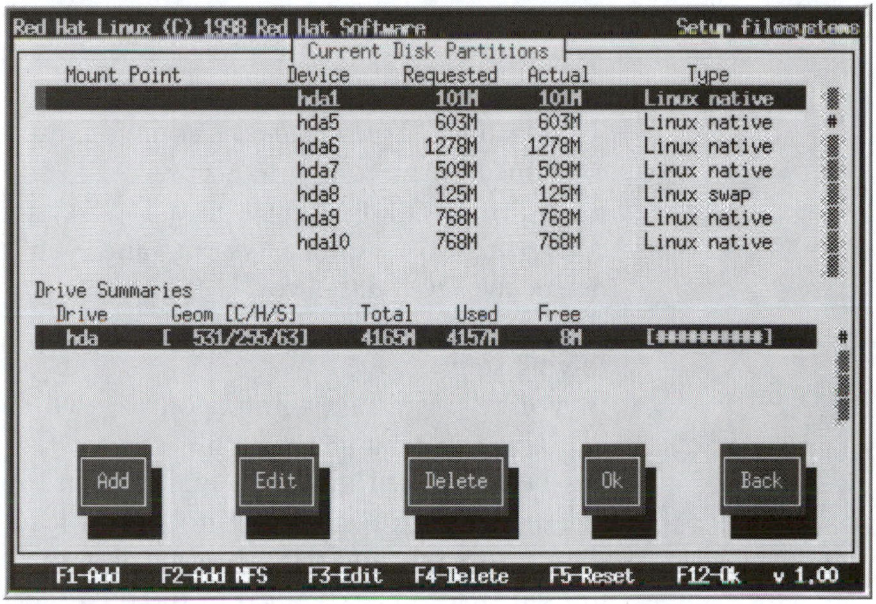

Figure 5.5. The Disk Druid enables you to create Linux partitions.

drive is called "a," so hda is the first IDE drive. If you have a second drive, it's called "b" (as in hdb), and so on.

Partitions are named by adding the partition number to the drive. For example, "hda1" refers to the first partition on the first IDE drive.

TIP If there is no free space on the drive, you must delete unused partitions. Remember, when you delete a partition, you destroy beyond recovery any data stored within it.

In the Current Disk Partitions area, you see the list of current disk partitions. Note the following:

- If you're installing Linux on an unpartitioned disk, this list is empty. You can start adding Linux partitions, as explained in the following steps.
- If you're installing Linux on a DOS system that you're converting to a Linux system, and you didn't already delete the DOS data, you'll see one or more DOS partitions. You'll need to delete them, as explained in the following steps.
- If you're installing Linux on a two-OS system, as explained in Chapter 4, you'll see a DOS partition that has been reduced in size to make room for Linux. Don't delete this partition! If you do, you'll lose all your Windows programs and data. Just add Linux partitions in the unused space, as explained in the next section.

Deleting DOS Partitions

If you didn't delete unwanted DOS partitions before starting the installation software, do so now by following these steps. Do not follow these steps unless you really want to wipe out all the data that these partitions contain.

1. In the Current Disk Partitions list, select the unused DOS partition that you want to delete.

2. Click Delete. You'll be asked to confirm this action since it destroys any data that the partition contains.

3. Repeat steps 1 and 2 to delete additional DOS partitions, if necessary.

Understanding the Partitioning Scheme

In the following instructions, you'll create these partitions:

- **/ (root)** This 200MB partition stores the files Linux needs start your system. It also includes configuration files. 200 MB provides plenty of room for these files; you could reduce the figure to 150MB if you're short on space.
- **/usr** This partition stores the software that is accessible to everyone with an account on your computer. For a workstation-class installation, you need at least 300MB; for a server-class installation, 700MB. If you have plenty of disk space, double these figures (600MB or 1400MB).
- **Swap Partition** Linux uses this partition as an extension of your computer's main (RAM) memory. You should create a swap partition that equals the amount of memory in your computer, up to a maximum of 127MB.
- **/home** In this partition, you'll store your data files, as well as any programs that you want to make available to yourself (but not to other users). You can also create accounts for additional users; their data and programs are stored here. In the procedure to follow, you'll use an option that assigns all the remaining space on the drive to this partition. You'll need plenty of room for the /home partition; you should have a minimum of 250MB (1GB is better).
- **/usr/local** This partition is used to store the non-commercial programs you'll install on your system. It needs its own partition so that you can protect these programs from being overwritten if you reinstall your system software. Ideally, you'll want at least 500MB for this partition—more, if you have the available space.
- **/opt** This partition is used to store commercial programs. Like /usr/local, it needs its own partition so that you can protect it from being overwritten if you reinstall your

system software. Reserve at least 500MB for this partition, if you can.

This partitioning scheme is recommended by experienced Linux users and experts (e.g., Welsh *et al.*, 1992-1998: 44–47; Bailey 1998: 26–27). It's far superior to creating one huge root directory and a swap partition, as many beginning Linux users do. With this partitioning scheme, you can easily upgrade or reinstall Linux without fear of interfering with your installed applications or user directories.

TIP Be sure to write down the list of partitions, as well as their mount points (the place on the file system where the partition appears in the directory tree). If you misconfigure Linux and find that you must reinstall the operating system to recover functionality, you will find that your partitions still exist as you created them, but you must re-type the mount points. In particular, note which partition (i.e., hda5) is assigned to /home; you must be very careful to avoid reformatting this directory when you reinstall or upgrade Linux.

Partitioning Your System with Disk Druid

To configure your system with Disk Druid, follow these steps:

1. Do one of the following:

    If you are creating a Linux-only system and want to overwrite the existing DOS partition, select Delete. Delete the existing DOS partition, and then choose Add.

    or

    If you are creating a two-OS system and want to keep the existing DOS partition, choose Add.

After choosing Add, you'll see the Edit New Partition dialog box.

2. First, create the Linux root partition. This partition contains the Linux kernel and essential files for running Linux. Create a Linux root partition by doing the following:

   In the Mount Point area, type / (a forward slash mark).

   In the Size (Megs): area, type **200**. Leave the Growable box blank.

   In the Type area, select Linux Native.

   In the Allowable Drives area, select the drive on which you want to create this partition (normally hda, unless your system is equipped with two drives and you want to install Linux on the second one).

   Click OK to add the partition to the partition list.

3. Now create a /usr partition for the software that is installed with the Linux operating system. Create a /usr partition by doing the following:

   Click Add to add a new partition.

   In the Mount Point area, type **/usr**.

   In the Size (Megs): area, type a minimum of **300** for a Workstation-class installation or a minimum of **700** for a Server-class installation. Leave the Growable box blank. If you have plenty of disk space, double these numbers (600 for a Workstation-class installation and 1400 for a Server-class installation.)

In the Type area, select Linux Native.

In the Allowable Drives area, select the drive on which you want to create this partition (normally hda, unless your system is equipped with two drives and you want to install Linux on the second one).

Click OK to add the partition to the partition list.

4. Now create /usr/local partition for the noncommercial software you will install. Create a /usr/local partition by doing the following:

   Click Add to add a new partition.

   In the Mount Point area, type **/usr/local**.

   In the Size (Megs): area, specify a size of at least 500MB (more, if you have lots of free space left on your drive).

   In the Type area, select Linux Native.

   In the Allowable Drives area, select the drive on which you want to create this partition (normally hda, unless your system is equipped with two drives and you want to install Linux on the second one).

   Click OK to add the partition to the partition list.

5. Now create an /opt partition for the commercial software that you'll install. Create an /opt partition by doing the following:

   Click Add to add a new partition.

   In the Mount Point area, type **/opt**.

In the Size (Megs): area, specify a size of at least 500MB (more, if you still have lots of drive space left).

In the Type area, select Linux Native.

In the Allowable Drives area, select the drive on which you want to create this partition (normally hda, unless your system is equipped with two drives and you want to install Linux on the second one).

Click OK to add the partition to the partition list.

6. Next create the swap partition. Linux uses this partition to extend your computer's RAM memory onto your hard disk, creating (in effect) a memory up to twice the amount of installed RAM.

TIP Note that the swap partition doesn't need a mount point.

Create a Linux swap partition by doing the following:

In the Size (Megs): area, type a number of megabytes that equals the amount of RAM installed in your computer, up to a maximum of 127. Leave the Growable box blank.

In the Type area, select Linux Swap.

In the Allowable Drives area, select the drive on which you want to create this partition (normally hda, unless your system is equipped with two drives and you want to install Linux on the second one).

Click OK to add the partition to the partition list.

7. Create a Linux /home partition for your files (and those of other users). Create the /home partition by doing the following:

In the Mount Point area, type **/home** (a forward slash mark).

In the Size (Megs) area, type **100**; the exact number doesn't matter, because you'll activate the Growable option. This setting will automatically adjust the partition will take up all the remaining room on the drive.

In the Type area, select Linux Native.

In the Allowable Drives area, select the drive on which you want to create this partition (normally hda, unless your system is equipped with two drives and you want to install Linux on the second one).

Click OK to add the partition to the partition list.

8. When you have finished creating partitions, you can edit a partition (for example, you can change its size). To edit a partition, select it and choose Edit. Adjust the settings, and choose OK.

9. **Important:** If your system is equipped with a removable drive, check the Drive Summaries area to see whether the drive has been detected. Zip drives that use the SCSI adapter will appear as /dev/sda4; Zip drives that use the ATAPI adapter will appear as /dev/hdb4. Identify your drive and assign it to a mount point in the /mnt directory, such as /mnt/zip.

10. If you're creating a two-OS system, and you would like to access your Windows files from within Linux, select the

Windows partition (this is probably /dev/hda1), and press F3. In the Mount Point area, type /mnt/win98, and choose OK.

11. When you're sure you've set up the partitions the way you want, choose OK. The installation software creates the partitions as you've requested.

Initializing the Swap Space

You'll next see the Active Swap Space dialog box, which enables you to activate the swap partition. Select the option that checks for bad sectors. Select OK to continue.

Formatting Your Partitions

Next, you see the Partitions to Format dialog box (see Figure 5.6). **Important:** Select all the non-DOS partitions. If you didn't run Scandisk before starting the installation, select the option that checks for bad sectors. Select OK to continue.

CAUTION If you're performing a two-OS installation, be sure to NOT format the DOS partition—if you do, you'll wipe out all your Windows programs and data!

Selecting Components to Install

Next, you'll see the Components to Install dialog box, shown in Figure 5.7.

CAUTION If you are installing Linux on a computer hooked up to a local area network (LAN), do not install any networking or server utilities (such as Mail/WWW/News Tools, Networked Workstation, and the other networking utilities indicated as security risks in Table 8.5) unless you have first discussed the installation with your networked admnistrator. Many of these utilities install with default configurations that will leave your system—and possibly your organization's entire internal network—wide open to unauthorized computer intrusions, and you could be held liable for any damages such intrusions could cause! Do not install networking utilities unless you are an experienced system or network administrator and fully understand how to operate these utilities safely. For more information, see   Garfinkel and Spafford 1996, Stern 1992: 161-188; Costales and Allman 1997: 327-355; Kabir 1998: 247-342.

You can choose from the following:

- **Printer support** Choose this option if you want to print using your Linux system.
- **X Window System** This is Linux's graphical user interface system. You'll need this to profit from most of the rest of this book.

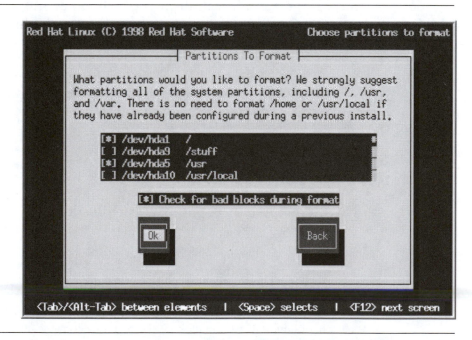

Figure 5.6 Be sure to format all the partitions you created.

Figure 5.8 In this dialog box, you select components to install.

- **GNOME** The GNU Object Model Environment desktop. Choose this option to install GNOME, which is discussed in detail in the rest of this book.
- **KDE** The KDE desktop environment is an alternative to GNOME. Since GNOME can run KDE applications, install this option so you can take advantage of the many KDE-compatible applications that will be installed with this option.
- **Mail/WWW/News Tools** Be sure to choose this option if you would like to access the Internet.
- **DOS/Windows Connectivity** If you would like to access DOS and Windows data from Linux, choose this option.
- **File Managers** Choose this option only if you intend to work with files from the Linux prompt instead of the GNOME file manager.

- **Graphics Manipulation** Choose this option to install some excellent graphics software, including The GIMP (an Adobe Photoshop-like program).
- **X Games** These aren't X-rated games; they're games designed for the X Window System, Linux's graphical user interface.
- **Console games** These games run in the text-only environment.
- **X multimedia support** Choose this option to get the most out of the X Window system.
- **Console multimedia** This option provides multimedia support for those who aren't using X.

CAUTION Do not install the following option (Networked workstation) unless you have first discussed your plans with your network administrator.

- **Networked workstation** Choose this option *only* if you plan to connect your Linux system to a local area network (LAN) *and* you fully understand the security risks of running the Network File System (NFS) and servers such as Apache (a Web server).
- **Dialup workstation** Choose this option if you plan to connect your Linux system to another computer or to the Internet by means of a modem.

CAUTION Do not install the following options (News server, NFS server, SMB connectivity, IPX/Netware connectivity, Anonymous FTP server, Web server, PostGres (SQL) server, and Network management workstation) unless you have first discussed your plans with your network administrator.

- **News server** Choose this option only if you have a permanent Internet address and want to make newsgroups available on this machine.

- **NFS server** Choose this option only if your Linux system is connected to a local area network and you would like to set up a network file system (NFS).
- **SMB (Samba) Connectivity** Choose this option only if your linux system is connected to a local area network and you want to connect with Microsoft Windows 95/98 or Windows NT computers.
- **IPX/Netware connectivity** Choose this option only if your computer is connected to a Netware network.
- **Anonymous FTP server** Choose this option only if your computer has a permanent Internet address and you want to set up an FTP server.
- **Web server** Choose this option only if your computer has a permanent Internet address and you want to set up a Web server.
- **Postgres (SQL) server** Choose this option only if your computer is connected to a local area network and you want to set up a SQL query server for a database.
- **Network management workstation** Choose this option only if your computer is connected to a local area network and you plan to manage the network from this computer.

TIP You'll need the following (TEX document formatting) only if you would like to format documents with TEX; if you're running GNOME, you won't need TEX to view and print documents.

- **TEX document formatting** Choose this option only if you want to format documents with the TEX formatting system.

TIP Most of the following options are of interest only to programmers. However, you may wish to install the GNOME, C, and C++ development tools if you believe you may at some time want to install programs by downloading the source code and compiling them.

- **EMACS** Choose this option only if you want to install the EMACS text editor.
- **EMACS with X windows** Choose this option only if you want to install the X version of EMACS.
- **C development** Choose this option only if you want to install the development environment for C programming.
- **Development libraries** Choose this option only if you want to install the development libraries for C programming.
- **C++ development** Choose this option only if you want to install the development environment for C++ programming.
- **X development** Choose this option only if you want to install the development environment for programming the X Window System.
- **GNOME development** Choose this option only if you want to install the development environment for creating and compiling GNOME applications.
- **Extra documentation** Choose this option to get all the available documentation, including versions in foreign languages.

Recommendations for a Basic Linux Workstation

If you're creating a workstation-class system, install these components:

- **Printer support**
- **GNOME**
- **KDE**
- **X Window System**
- **Mail/WWW/News Tools**
- **DOS/Windows connectivity**
- **Graphics Manipulation**
- **X multimedia support**

Do you plan to connect to the Internet by means of a modem? If so, install the following:

- **Dialup workstation**

Recommendations for Program Development

If you plan to use your Linux system to get started in C, C++, and X Window program development, install the following components in addition to those needed for a workstation-class or server-class computer.

TIP You should also install the following if you believe you may wish to install programs by downloading the source code and compiling the code. Although this method is much tricker than using the Red Hat Package Manager (RPM) to download and install compiled files (binary files), sometimes there's no other way to obtain the software you want. As long as you have sufficient disk space, you should install the following options.

- **EMACS**
- **EMACS with X windows**
- **C development**
- **Development libraries**
- **C++ development**
- **X development**

Recommendations for a Server Installation

Are you using a computer at work? Is the computer hooked up to a local area network? Please read the following carefully.

Unless you possess considerable experience with Linux and have discussed your plans with your network administrator, you should not attempt to install any of the server *daemons* (background programs that respond to incoming requests for information). If you do so, you could unknowingly create an entry point that intruders could use to gain access to your organization's computer network.

The tasks involved in configuring Linux networking for security and safety are very far beyond the scope of this book. If you are interested in exploring the fundamentals of Linux networking, please see this book's companion volume, *Linux Networking Clearly Explained*, also published by Morgan Kaufman Publishers.

Selecting Packages

Now that you've identified the packages you want to install, select them by moving the highlight to the package, and pressing the spacebar, if necessary, so that an asterisk appears between the brackets next to the package's name (see Figure 5.8).

CAUTION As explained in the following, you can activate the Select individual packages option, which enables you to select precisely which packages you wish to install. Unless you know a very great deal about Linux, you should *not* enable this option, or make any changes in the Select Group dialog box. You could inadvertently delete a package that is required by some other package. At the extreme, you could make changes that would result in a completely nonfunctional system. Do not activate this option!

If you would like to select individual packages and you are sure you know what you're doing, activate Select individual packages, and select OK. You'll see the Select Group dialog box. This dialog box organizes the package information in the form of a tree structure. In the left column, a plus sign indicates that you can view the options by selecting this item and pressing Enter. A circle between the brackets indicates that some of the packages within this category are already selected; if there is no circle between the brackets, no packages within this category have been selected. If you see an asterisk between the brackets, all the packages have been selected.

TIP To find out what a package does, select the package, and press F1. You'll see a brief description of the package. Press Enter to return to the Select Group dialog box.

Writing Your File System to the Disk

When you finish choosing components to install, select OK in the Components to Install dialog box (click Done if you decided to select individual packages in the Select Group dialog box). The installation software will begin creating your file system. The installation could consume as much as an hour, but you'll see a progress indicator informing you how the installation is progressing.

From Here

When the installation software finishes writing your Linux file system to your hard drive, you'll have an opportunity to configure your Linux system, as explained in the next chapter.

References and Further Reading

Bailey, Edward C. 1998. *Red Hat Linux 5.2: The Official Red Hat Linux Installation Guide.* Research Triangle Park, NC: Red Hat Software, Inc.

Costales, Bryan, and Eric Allman. 1997. *Sendmail.* Petaluma, CA: O'Reilly & Associates.

Garfinkel, Simon, and Gene Spafford. 1996. *Practical UNIX and Internet Security*. Petaluma, CA: O'Reilly & Associates.

Kabir, Mohammad. 1998. *Apache Server Bible*. Foster City, CA: IDG Books Worldwide.

Koehntopp, Kris. 1997. "Linux Partition HOWTO." Linux Documentation Project. Available online at metalab.unc.edu/LDP/HOWTO/mini/Partition.html.

Raymond, Eric. 1998. "The Linux Installation HOWTO." Linux Documentation Project. Available online at metalab.unc.edu/LD/HOWTO/.

Stern, Hal. 1991. *Managing NFS and NIS*. Petaluma, CA: O'Reilly & Associates.

Welsh, Matt, *et al*. 1992-1998. *Linux Installation and Getting Started*. Linux Documentation Project. Available online at metalab.unc.edu/LDP/LDP/gs/gs.html.

Completing the Installation

Now that you've created the Linux file system and copied the software to your hard disk, you're ready to complete your installation by configuring your system.

The Red Hat installation software automatically takes you to the configuration dialog boxes, so this chapter is, in effect, an extension of Chapter 5.

Configuring Your Mouse

Continuing with the Red Hat installation software, you'll see a dialog box that requests information about your mouse. If your mouse was detected automatically by the installation

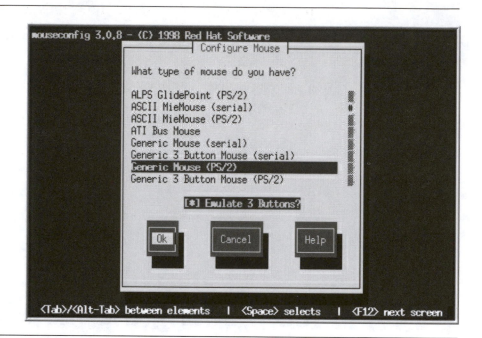

Figure 6.1 Choose your mouse from the list.

software, you'll be asked to confirm the port settings. If the software couldn't detect your mouse automatically, you'll see the Configure Mouse dialog box, shown in Figure 6.1.

TIP If you don't have a three-button mouse, check the Emulate 3 Buttons option. As you'll see later in this book, the X Window System makes use of the third mouse button for some operations. Emulation enables you to use these capabilities by pressing down both mouse buttons at the same time.

If you don't see your mouse on the list, choose one of the following:

- **Generic Mouse (PS/2)** A PS/2-type mouse plugs in to the back of your computer by means of a round plug.

- **Generic Mouse (serial)** A serial mouse plugs into a DB-9 (nine-pin connector) serial port.

When you're finished selecting your mouse, choose OK. If you selected a serial mouse, you'll be asked to identify the port to which it's connected.

TIP If you want to change your mouse settings after you've finished running the installation software, you can do so by running the mouseconfig program. Start your system as the root user (see Chapter 7). Click the Main Menu button, point to AnotherLevel menus, point to Administration, and choose Text-mode tool menu. In the Setup dialog box, select Mouse configuration. You'll see the same utility that ran during the installation.

Configuring Networking

If the installation software detects an Ethernet card in your system, you'll see a dialog box asking you whether you'd like to set up LAN networking. If you plan to connect your Linux computer to a local area network, select Yes. Select No if you plan to connect to the Internet via a modem.

Should the installation software fail to detect your network interface card (NIC) correctly, you'll see the Load Module dialog box. Here, you need to choose a driver that will work with your network card. Look for your network card's brand name and model number. If you don't see your network card, you may be able to choose a driver that works with your card. See the Ethernet HOWTO (Gortmaker 1998). Note that Many "no-name" PCI networking cards are compatible with the NE2000-PCI driver. If you can't find your networking card on the list, try selecting the NE2000-PCI and see whether the installation software can detect it.

After you've selected your network interface card, you'll see the dialog box shown in Figure 6.2. Here, you select the method used to assign an Internet address (also called IP address) to your computer. You'll need to check with your network administrator to find out which option to choose. Here's a quick overview of your choices:

- **Static IP Address** Use this option if your network administrator gave you a fixed IP address for your computer.
- **BOOTP** Use this option if your computer will obtain an IP address dynamically using the BOOTP protocol.
- **DHCP** Use this option if your computer will obtain an IP address dynamically using the DHCP protocol.

If you configure Linux to use a static IP address, you'll see the dialog box shown in Figure 6.3. You won't see this informa-

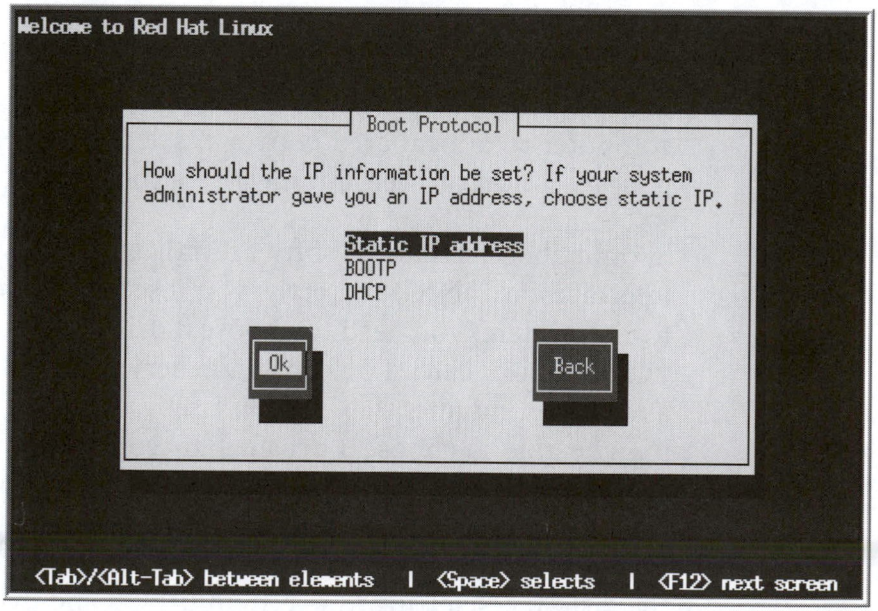

Figure 6.2 Select your network IP addressing method here.

tion if you selected BOOTP or DHCP, because both of these services configure this information automatically. You'll need the following information from your network administrator:

- **IP address** This is the Internet address assigned to your computer's Ethernet port. An IP address has four numbers, separated by dots (a *dotted quad*). Don't leave any spaces between the numbers and the dots.
- **Netmask** This is a number that enables network administrators to configure networks internally. Supply the dotted quad number that your network administrator gives you.
- **Default gateway (IP)** This is the Internet address of the device that provides your LAN with access to the external Internet. Your network administrator will give you this address.

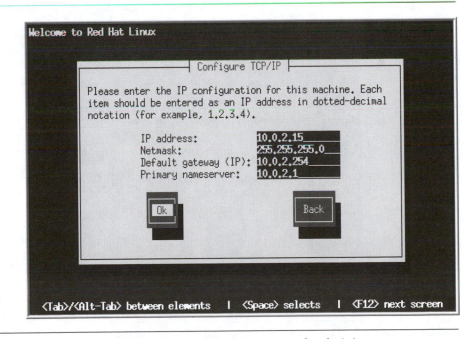

Figure 6.3 Supply the information your network administrator gave you.

- **Primary nameserver** This is the Internet address of the primary domain name server (also called DNS server). Again, your network administrator will supply you with this information.

Choose OK when you've finished entering this information. Next, you'll see the dialog box shown in Figure 6.4. Here, you supply the following information, which you'll need to obtain from your network administrator:

- **Domain name** Here, you supply your network's domain name, such as bigcompany.com. Press Tab after typing this name.
- **Host name** After you press Tab, you'll see the domain name in this area. At the beginning of the line, type the computer name (host name) that your network adminis-

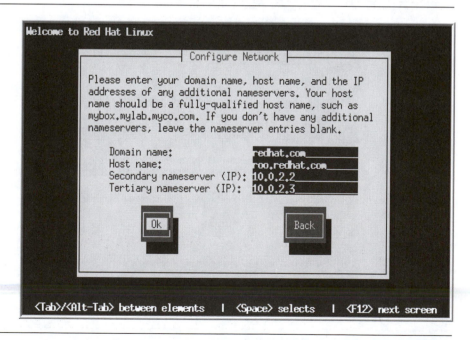

Figure 6.4 Supply the information your network administrator gave you.

trator assigned to your system. The result should be a *fully qualified domain name* (FQDN), a computer name that is recognizable to other Internet computers (such as mymachine.bigcompany.com).

- **Secondary and tertiary nameservers** If your network administrator gave you the Internet addresses of one or more domain name servers (DNS servers), type the addresses here.

When you've finished supplying this information, choose OK.

TIP If you should need to change your networking settings after completing the installation, you can do so by running the LinuxConf utility. For more information on LinuxConf, see Chapter 12.

Configuring the Timezone

You'll next see the Configure Timezones dialog box. If you're creating a dual-OS system, don't check Hardware clock set to GMT. Your Windows programs may not show the time correctly. However, Linux knows how to make this translation. Select your time zone, and choose OK.

TIP Should you need to reset the system time or date, you can do so using the Time Tool, discussed ion Chapter 12.

Choosing Services to Start on Reboot

Next, you'll see a dialog box that asks you which services you'd like to start automatically every time Linux reboots (see Figure 6.5). The default choices are indicated by an asterisk; normally, you should just accept the defaults you see in this list. In case you're curious what these various services do, you'll find a complete list of them here.

CAUTION Unless you are an experienced Linux user and you have discussed your plans with your network administrator, do not enable any of the services marked with "Security Risk" in the following list.

Here's a guide to the services you may see in the list (you don't see services pertaining to packages that you didn't install). Note that options followed by (*) should be enabled on all systems.

- **amd** Mounts devices on demand for the Network File System (NFS). Run this service only if you are planning to use NFS to connect to other Linux or Unix computers on

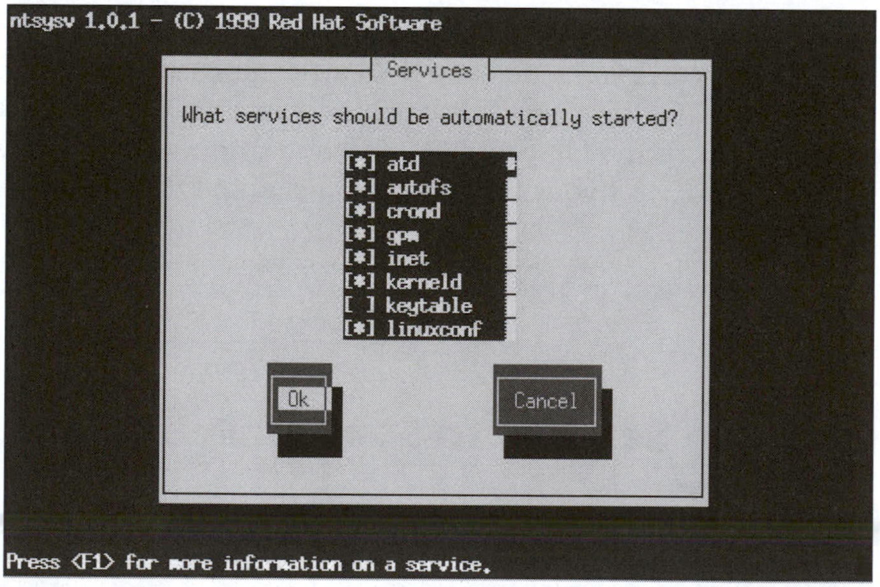

Figure 6.5 Choose the services you want, but be mindful of security risks.

a local area network (LAN). **Security risk:** Enable this option only after discussing your plans with your network administrator.

- **apmd** Monitors battery status and shuts down the system when power is low. Run this service if you're installing Linux on a notebook computer.

- **arpwatch** Keeps track of Ethernet/IP address pairings on a local area network (LAN). Run this service if you plan to connect your computer to a LAN. **Security risk:** Enable this option only after discussing your plans with your network administrator.

- **atd** Runs commands scheduled by the at command at the time specified.

- **autofs** (*) Mounts filesystems automatically when you use them, and unmounts them when they're not in use.

- **bootparamd** An obsolete service that enables older Sun workstations to boot from Linux computers. Enables this option only if your network administrator tells you to do so.

- **crond** Runs user-specified programs at periodic scheduled times. **Security risk:** Enable this option only after discussing your plans with your network administrator.

- **dhcpd** Provides support for the DHCP protocol on local area networks. Ask your network administrator whether you need to enables this service.

- **gated** Provides network routing services. You need to enable this option if you would like your computer to function as a server in a TCP/IP-based network. **Security risk:** Enable this option only after discussing your plans with your network administrator.

- **gpm** (*) Adds mouse support to text-based Linux applications such as Midnight Commander.

- **httpd** Provides support for Web server software. You need to enable this option if you would like to run a Web server on your computer. **Security risk:** Enable this option only after discussing your plans with your network administrator.

- **inetd** (*) Starts Internet services as needed. This service must be enabled in order to access the Internet.
- **innd** A server for Usenet newsgroups. Enable this option if you want to run a Usenet server. **Security risk:** Enable this option only after discussing your plans with your network administrator.
- **kerneld** (*) Automatically loads kernel modules as they are required. This service must be running at all times.
- **keytable** (*) Loads the selected keyboard map. Leave this option enabled.
- **linuxconf** (*) Loads software required by linuxconf, a configuration utility. Make sure this option is enabled.
- **lpd** (*) Provides software support for printing. Make sure this option is enabled if you want to use a printer.
- **mars-nwe** Provides support for NetWare networks. Enable this option if you are connecting your Linux computer to a Novell network. **Security risk:** Enable this option only after discussing your plans with your network administrator.
- **mcserv** Enables remote users to log on to your computer and use the Midnight Commander file manager. **Security risk:** Enable this option only after discussing your plans with your network administrator.
- **named** This is a domain name server (DNS server) that is used to resolve host names to IP addresses on a network. You need to run this service only if you want your computer to function as a DNS server. **Security risk:** Enable this option only after discussing your plans with your network administrator.
- **network** (*) Activates network interfaces. Make sure this service is running.
- **nfs** Provides server support for the Network File System (NFS), which enables you to exchange files with other

users on a TCP/IP network. **Security risk:** Enable this option only after discussing your plans with your network administrator.

- **nfsfs** Mounts Network File System (NFS) directories to your computer. You need to run this service only if you would like to access other Linux or Unix computers on your local area network (LAN). **Security risk:** Enable this option only after discussing your plans with your network administrator.

- **pcmcia** Provides support for PCMCIA devices on laptops. You don't need to enable this option unless you're installing Linux on a notebook or some other computer that uses PCMCIA (PC card) devices.

- **portmap** Manages connections for the Network File System (NFS). You need to run this service only if you would like to access other Linux or Unix computers on your local area network (LAN).

- **postgresql** Provides support for SQL database requests. **Security risk:** Enable this option only after discussing your plans with your network administrator.

- **random** Enables better random number generation for security purposes.

- **routed** Provides Internet addressing services using the RIP protocol. If you're installing Linux on a local area network (LAN), ask your network administrator whether you need this service. **Security risk:** Enable this option only after discussing your plans with your network administrator.

- **rusersd** Enables users on a network to locate other users on any machine on the network. **Security risk:** Enable this option only after discussing your plans with your network administrator.

- **rwalld** Enables users to display messages on all the terminals on a system.

- **rwhod** Enables remote users to obtain a list of all users logged into a machine. **Security risk:** Enable this option only after discussing your plans with your network administrator.

- **sendmail** Enables e-mail transport within a network and allows your computer to function as an e-mail server. You don't need to enable this option unless you want to run an e-mail server on your machine. **Security risk:** Enable this option only after discussing your plans with your network administrator.

- **smb** Enables you to run Samba, a utility that enables Linux to connect to computers running Windows 95, Windows 98, and Windows NT. **Security risk:** Enable this option only after discussing your plans with your network administrator.

- **snmpd** Enables you to set up your Linux computer as a network management workstation. This is needed only by network administrators.

- **sound** (*) Saves and restores sound card settings so these do not have to be entered manually when you restart Linux.

- **squid** Enables local storage (caching) of frequently requested Web pages. You should enable this option only if you are planning to run a Web server and have plenty of disk space.

- **syslog** (*) Enables programs to write data to system log files. Make sure this option is enabled.

- **xntpd** Enables your workstation to function as a network time server. Don't enable this option unless you need this service and have lots of memory. **Security risk:** Enable this option only after discussing your plans with your network administrator.

- **ypbind** Enable this service if your computer will be running within a Network Information Service (NIS) domain.

Ask your network administrator if you need to enable this option.

- **yppasswdd** Enables users to change their passwords on networks running the Network Information Service (NIS). Ask your network administrator if you need to enable this option. **Security risk:** Enable this option only after discussing your plans with your network administrator.

- **ypserv** Enables your computer to function as a Network Information Service (NIS) server. You need to enable this option only if you want to implement NIS on a local area network (LAN). **Security risk:** Enable this option only after discussing your plans with your network administrator.

When you're finished selecting services, select OK.

TIP Should you wish to change the default services after you finish installing Linux, start your system as the root user (see Chapter 7). Click the Main Menu button, point to AnotherLevel menus, point to Administration, and choose Text-mode tool menu. In the Setup dialog box, select Mouse configuration, and choose System services.

Configuring a Printer

Next, you'll be asked whether you want to configure a printer. If you have a printer attached to your computer, or if you're planning to connect your computer to a local area network (LAN) that has a network computer, select Yes.

For best results when printing with Linux, connect a PostScript-compatible printer to your computer. PostScript is a page description language (PDL) that is used by nearly all Linux application programs. Unfortunately, PostScript printers are more expensive than non-PostScript printers because they require their own CPU and memory to decode the programming instructions.

If you don't have a PostScript printer, choose one that's compatible with GhostScript, a PostScript interpreter that takes PostScript output from applications, and translates it into instructions for non-PostScript printers. For a list of GhostScript-compatible printers, see Appendix E.

TIP You can't use any printer that's described as a "Windows printer" or "GDI Printer." These are inexpensive printers that require Windows to run.

Choosing the Printer Connection Method

In the Select Printer Connection dialog box, you choose how the printer is connected to your computer. You have three choices:

- **Local** Choose this option if your printer is connected through a serial or parallel port on your computer.
- **Remote lpd** Choose this option if you would like to print using a network printer on a TCP/IP network.
- **LAN Manager** Choose this option if you would like to print to a network printer on a Novell network.

To set up your system for a local printer, follow these steps:

1. In the Select Printer Connections dialog box, select Local, and choose OK.

2. In the Standard Printer Options dialog box, do one of the following:

   If your computer will connect to just one printer, leave the settings as they are.

   or

   If you plan to connect your computer to more than one printer, type a printer name in the Name of Spool box.

3. Select OK. You'll see the Local Printer Device dialog box, shown in Figure 6.7. Note that the installation software probes your system to detect parallel ports.

4. Select the detected parallel port to which your printer is connected, and choose OK.

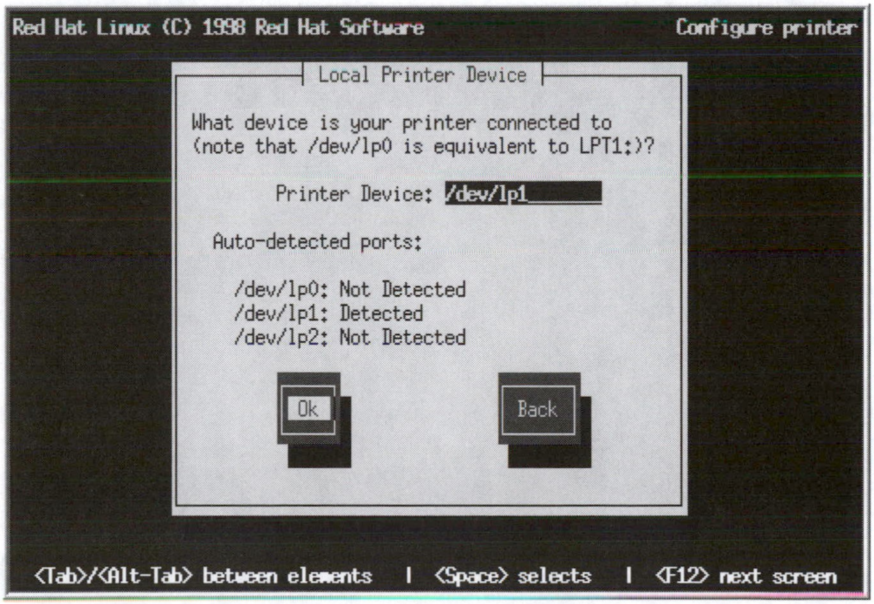

Figure 6.7 Linux can detect your computer's parallel ports.

If you're connecting Linux to a network, and you would like to use a network printer, find out if the network is a TCP/IP network or a NetWare network. Ask your network administrator which kind of network you're using.

To connect your computer to a network printer on a TCP/IP network, do the following:

1. In the Select Network Connections dialog box, select Remote lpd, and choose OK. You'll see the Remote lpd Printer Options dialog box, shown in Figure 6.8.

2. In the Remote Hostname box, type the name of the computer you want to use. Ask your network administrator what to type here.

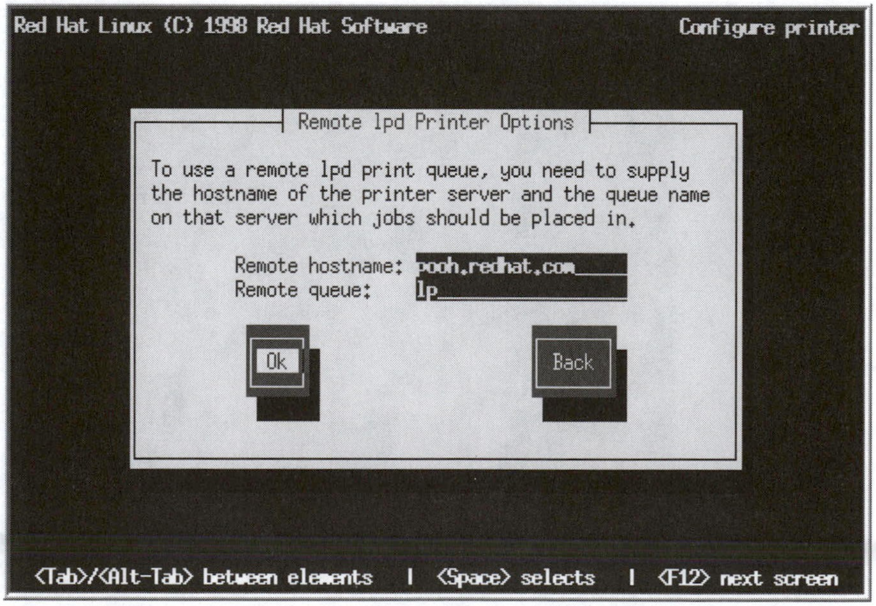

Figure 6.8 Identify your remote (network) printer here.

3. In the Remote Queue box, type the name of the print spooling queue on the network printer. If you're connecting to an HP LaserJet that's equipped with a JetDirect print adapter, type **raw** (this is the name of the print queue for PostScript and PCL print output). If you're not sure what to type here, check the printer manual or ask your network administrator.

4. Choose OK.

To connect your computer to a NetWare network printer, do the following:

1. In the Select Network Connections dialog box, select LAN Manager, and choose OK. You'll see the LAN Manager Printer Options dialog box.

2. Supply the requested information. If you're not sure what to type, ask your network administrator.

3. Choose OK.

Choosing the Printer

After you choose your printer connection method, you'll see the Configure Printer dialog box, and you'll see a list of printers. To choose your printer, do one of the following:

- If your printer is a PostScript printer, select PostScript printer.
- If your printer isn't a PostScript printer, choose the printer name from the list.

TIP What if your printer isn't on the list? Check your printer's manual to find out whether your printer can emulate any of the listed printers. If so, select the type of printer that your printer can emulate.

After you select your printer, choose OK. You'll see the printer configuration dialog box, shown in Figure 6.9. Select the default paper size and resolution you would like to use.

TIP If you see an option called Fix stair-stepping of text, select this option if you plan to print in plain text. (Sometimes it's useful to print the output of Linux text screens.) Most of the printing you'll do will involve the use of PostScript or other binary print output, so stair-stepping won't be a problem.

Click OK to continue. You'll see a dialog box listing your printer configuration choices. To make changes, choose Back. To confirm your choices, choose OK.

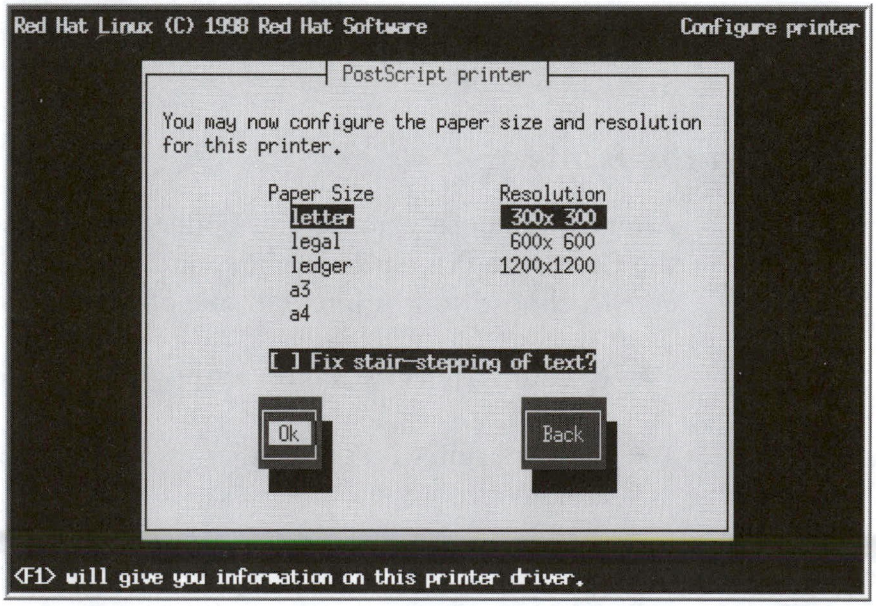

Figure 6.9 Choose configuration options for your printer.

> **TIP** If you want to change printers or adjust any of these settings after you finish installing Linux, start your system as root user (see Chapter 7). Click the Main Menu button, point to System, and choose Control Panel. Click the Printer icon. You'll see the Red Hat Linux Print System Manager. Select the printer you installed, and click Edit. Make the changes, and click OK. From the lpd menu, choose Restart lpd to restart the printing system so that your changes will take effect.

Choosing a Root Password

Next, you'll see the Root Password dialog box. In the Password box, type the password you want to use. In the Password (again) box, type the password again, so that the software can verify that you've typed it correctly.

> **TIP** Be sure to choose a secure password. Use a combination of letters and numbers, and make the password longer than six digits. Don't use a familiar word or name. Be sure to write your password down somewhere so you don't forget it!

Making a Bootdisk

Next, you'll see the Bootdisk dialog box. Don't skip this step! It enables you to make a boot disk that can help you recover from severe system problems, such as configuration error that makes your system unusable.

> **TIP** If you're creating a two-operating system computer, be aware that installing a new version of Windows will probably wipe out the information stored in the master boot record at the beginning of your hard drive. This is where Linux stores LILO, the program that starts Linux and enables you to choose which operating system you want to use. Should this happen, you'll need the boot disk to start Linux and repair the damage. Don't skip making the boot disk!

Choose Yes to make the bootdisk, and insert a blank floppy disk in the disk drive. (Be aware that any data on this disk will be erased, without confirmation.) The installation software creates the bootdisk.

TIP You can change your default LILO configuration by using Linux-Conf. For more information, see Chapter 12.

Installing LILO

After you create your boot disk, you'll choose options for LILO (Linux Loader) in the Lilo Installation dialog box (see Figure 6.10). LILO is the Linux startup program. Normally, you should install LILO in the *master boot record*, the area at

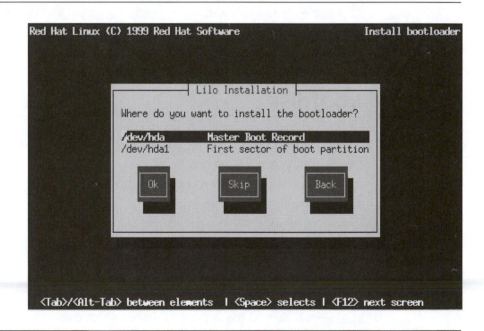

Figure 6.10 Choose Master Boot Record for a two-OS installation.

the beginning of your hard drive that is reserved for programs that enable you to choose which operating system you want to run. You should select First sector of boot partition *only* if you're running a third-party operating system utility, such as Norton Commander. Make your selection, and choose OK.

In the next dialog box, you can supply information that LILO can pass to the kernel. Just leave this blank, unless you're installing a device that needs special configuration information. Don't check Use linear mode unless you've been specifically instructed to do so in order to get a SCSI hard drive working. Select OK to continue.

You'll next see the Bootable Partitions dialog box (Figure 6.11), which lists the available bootable partitions. By default, the installation software selects your Linux root partition (/) as

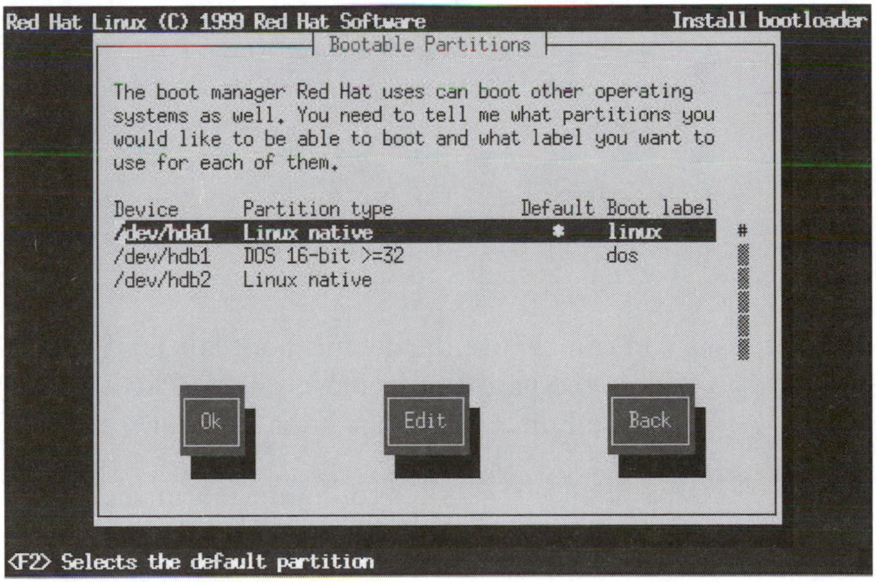

Figure 6.11 Here, you identify the default boot partition.

the default boot partition, and gives it the boot label "Linux." Since this setting is fine, you can just press OK, unless you're creating a two-OS installation.

If you are creating a two-OS installation (Linux and Windows), you'll see an additional partition that has the "dos" boot label. Note the asterisk in the Default column; currently, the default operating system is "linux." To change the default operating system to Windows, select the Windows ("dos") boot partition, and press F2.

With a two-OS installation, you'll have an opportunity to specify which operating system you want to run every time you start or reboot your system. After a start or reboot, watch for the following message:

```
LILO boot:
```

To start the default operating system (Linux, unless you've changed the setting in the Bootable Partitions dialog box), just wait. After a few seconds, the default operating system starts loading.

To start the other operating system, type the boot label. If you accepted the defaults in the Bootable Partitions dialog box, you can type **dos** to start Windows.

You can change the default boot labels, if you wish. To do so, select the partition in the Bootable Partition dialog box, and choose Edit. Change the boot label, and choose OK.

To finalize the LILO configuration in the Bootable Partitions dialog box, choose OK.

Configuring XFree86

After you finish configuring LILO, the installation software probes for your video card. Now it's time to configure XFree86, the X Window System server that provides the foundation for graphical user interfaces (called *window managers*).

To configure XFree86, you will need precise information about your monitor. If the exact brand and model of your monitor is not detected by the automatic probe, you will need to know the horizontal and vertical refresh rates of your monitor. If you have a multisynch monitor, both the horizontal and vertical refresh rates will be expressed as a range, such as 40 to 150 Hz (cycles per second). Consult your monitor's documentation to get this information.

> **CAUTION** If your monitor's brand and model aren't listed, don't use a "similar" monitor's name or try to guess the refresh rates. If you specify a refresh rate that exceeds your monitor's capabilities, you could destroy your monitor!

If the probe detects your video card, you're in luck (Figure 6.12). Otherwise, you'll need to select the video card from a list of supported cards. If your *exact brand and model* is not on this list, choose Unlisted Card. You'll have to select a supported card that matches the chip set on the card you do have.

> **TIP** For information on which driver to select for your video card, see the XFree86 Video Card and X server list (http://www.xfree86.org/ cardlist.html).

Once you've selected your video card, you'll be asked to choose your monitor brand and model. Important: If your

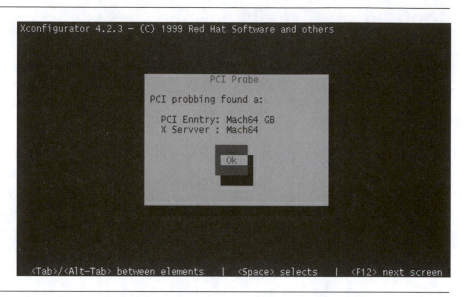

Figure 6.12 If your video card is detected, you're in luck!

monitor isn't on the list, choose Custom; don't try some other monitor's settings.

If you choose Custom, you'll need to specify your monitor's horizontal synch rate by choosing one of the following:

- Standard VGA (640 x 480) at 60 Hz
- Super VGA (800 x 600) at 56 Hz
- 8514 compatible (1024 x 768) at 87 Hz (interlaced)
- Super VGA (1024 x 768) at 87 Hz (interlaced)
- Extended Super VGA (1024 x 786) at 60 Hz
- High Frequency SVGA (1024 x 768) at 70 Hz
- Monitor that can display 1280 x 1024 at 60 Hz
- Monitor that can display 1280 x 1024 at 74 Hz
- Monitor that can display 1280 x 1024 at 76 Hz

You'll also need to specify the vertical and horizontal sync range (50–70, 50–90, 50–100, 40–150).

> **CAUTION** Don't choose a synch rate that's higher than your monitor's capabilities. With some older monitors, doing so could cause your video card to destroy your monitor's electronics.

You may also need to specify the amount of video RAM installed on your video card. Check your video card's documentation if you're not sure.

You may be asked to specify the type of video clockchip in your video card. It's best to choose No Clockchip Setting and let the software probe for the chip. If it's not detected, don't worry; you can still use your monitor with Linux.

After you've provided all the needed information, the software performs a probe to test your video card's capabilities. It's normal for the screen to blink a few times. At the end of the probe, you'll see a screen showing you the recommended default video mode (see Figure 6.13).

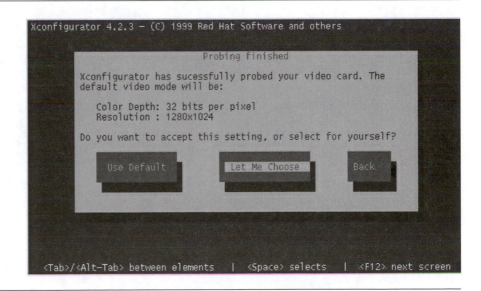

Figure 6.13 The default setting is a good choice for most users.

The easiest choice here is to accept the default video modes. However, you may wish to choose additional video modes; to do so, click Let Me Choose.

If you define more than one video mode, the X Window System enables you to change video modes on the fly by pressing Ctrl + Alt + keypad plus or Ctrl + Alt + keypad minus.

You may be required to select a video mode. If the installation software was unable to come up with a default video mode, you'll have to select one from the Select Video Modes dialog box (see Figure 6.14). Select one or more video modes, and choose OK.

The next dialog box informs you that the installation software will start the X server. Select OK, and watch for a dialog box that enables you to confirm whether the screen looks OK.

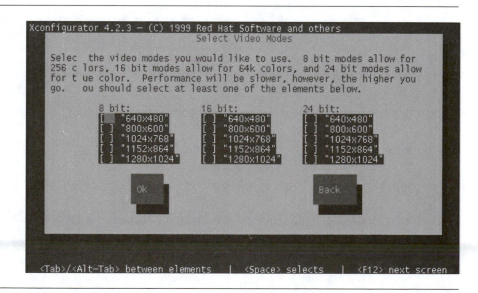

Figure 6.14 Choose at least one video mode here.

CAUTION Be sure to click Yes when you see the confirmation message. If you don't, the installation software will assume that something went wrong with the setup. You have only a few seconds to click Yes, so stay tuned here!

Finally, you'll be asked whether you want to start the X Window System automatically every time your system starts. Choose Yes so that you can take full advantage of the Linux graphical user interface, which includes GNOME. After you choose Yes, you'll see the Done dialog box. Remove the disks from your system, and click OK to reboot. In Chapter 7, you'll get your first taste of Linux on-screen.

Reinstalling Linux

To operate correctly, Linux depends on the integrity of many text-based configuration and script files, which are located in the /etc directory. If you run your system as the root user (see Chapter 7), you could inadvertently modify one of these files, with results that vary from minor inconveniences to a complete system shutdown. If you can't repair the damage, your best bet lies in reinstalling Red Hat Linux by repeating the installation described in this and the previous chapters.

Will you lose your work? No, not if you've followed this book's recommendation to create a separate partition for the /home directory, which contains your data files, mail directories, configuration information, and other essential files. When you reinstall Linux, you'll find that your partitions are still there, but you need to resupply the mount points. Make sure you assign the /home directory's mount point correctly (assign it to the same device to which it was assigned in the previous installation). And be sure to skip reformatting this directory when you're repeating the installation!

After you reinstall Linux, you'll find that your system is functional again.

From Here

You've successfully installed Red Hat Linux on your system. In Part III, you learn how to use GNOME, the new desktop interface system that makes Linux use easy.

References and Further Reading

Gortmaker, Paul. 1998. *Linux HOWTO*. Linux Documentation Project. Available online at http://metalab.unc.edu/LDP.

Short, Geoff. 1998. "The Three-Button Serial Mouse HOWTO," Linux Documentation Project. Available online at http:// metalab.unc.edu/LDP.

Taylor, Grant. 1999. *The Linux Printing HOWTO*. Linux Documentation Project. Available online at http://metalab. unc.edu/LDP.

Wirzenius, Lars. 1993-1997. *Linux System Administrator's Guide*. Linux Documentation Project. Available online at http://metalab.unc.edu/LDP.

Part Three

Running GNOME

System Configuration Essentials

You've successfully installed Linux, and you're rebooting your system. You're about to see Red Hat Linux on-screen for the first time, replete with the beautiful new GNOME desktop system. You'll surely want to explore GNOME, but there's some serious business to take care of first.

When you boot your Linux system for the first time, you must log on as the *root user* (using the login name "root" and the password you created when you installed Red Hat Linux). There's no way around this. However, it's dangerous to run Linux as the root user. As you'll learn in this chapter, you could inadvertently damage your system if you use it while logged in as the root user. Accordingly, this chapter shows you how to create a *user account*, an account that has built-in safe-guards against inadvertent damage to the system configura-tion. For day-to-day work (including initial exploration of the GNOME interface), you should log in with your user account. *Never* do anything as the root user unless you must.

This chapter begins with a quick look at the LILO loader and the boot process; it continues by discussing basic root user concepts, and shows you how to create a user account. Next, you'll learn how to configure Linux so that your disk drives are accessible while you're logged in using your user account. You'll also learn how to activate sound on your Linux system, so that you can take advantage of GNOME's cool sound capa-bilities. Finally, you'll learn how to log out so that you can log in using your user account; you'll also learn how to shut down or reboot Linux.

Booting with LILO

If you created a two-OS installation, you can specify which operating system you want to run when your system starts. After turning on your system, watch for the following mes-sage:

```
LILO boot:
```

Unless you changed the default LILO installation, you need do nothing special to start Linux; after a few seconds, Linux will start. To start Microsoft Windows, type **dos** and press Enter.

Understanding the Boot Process

As Linux starts, you'll see many messages fly by on the screen. You needn't worry about these messages. In case you're curious, here's a brief overview of the boot process with Red Hat Linux:

- **Kernel** The first step involves booting the kernel of the Linux operating system. The kernel loads the *device drivers* for all of your peripherals, including your hard disk and other disk drives. Device drivers tell the kernel how to operate the specific hardware components installed on your system. As each driver is loaded and initialized for peripherals such as sound cards, Ethernet cards, and modems, you'll see confirmation messages, and a green-colored "OK" message (assuming, that is, that everything went well with your installation).
- **init** After the device drivers load, a program called init comes into play. Init runs a variety of programs and scripts that serve to configure your system. Among the programs loaded is getty, which enables you (and other users) to open a terminal device and interact with the Linux kernel.
- **X Window System** Next to load is the X Window System, assuming you followed the last chapter's advice and configured X to start automatically.
- **gdm** Last to load is the GNOME Display Manager (GDM), which starts your GNOME Session and the Enlightenment window manager.

Once the boot process has finished, you'll see the Red Hat logo and a Welcome dialog box. The Welcome dialog box indicates your computer's name, and includes text boxes where you supply your login name and password.

TIP If you're used to Microsoft Windows, you might think you can simply bypass the login process and begin working. But you can't do this with Linux. That's true even if you're using Linux as a single-user workstation. As you'll learn in the following chapter, it's essential that you establish a user account for your day-to-day use. When you log in using your user account, you'll work with Linux in a mode that prevents you from doing any serious damage to your system's configuration.

Logging In

Designed from the beginning as a multi-user system, Linux wants to know who you are when you start your computer. When you installed Red Hat Linux, you configured only one user, called *root*—so that's the login name you'll use. You will also use the password you created when you installed Red Hat Linux.

To start your Linux session, do the following:

1. Move the cursor (a big X) to the Login box, until the cursor changes to an I-beam (text) cursor. Type **root**.

2. Press Tab. (If you prefer, you can click within the Password box.)

3. Carefully type your password. You'll see asterisks on-screen so that nobody can read your password while you're typing it.

TIP Make sure you're not typing with the Caps Lock key depressed. Because Linux user names and passwords are case-sensitive, you will not be able to get into your system if you type your user name and password using a capitalization pattern differing from the one you supplied in Chapter 6.

---

4. If you would like to choose a language other than the default language you chose when you installed Red Hat

Linux, click the Options button, point to Languages, and choose a language from the list. Your language choice will affect the text displayed in terminal windows, GNOME, GNOME applications, and KDE applications.

5. Do one of the following:

Click Login.

or

Press Enter. (When you press Enter, you select the highlighted button; Login is highlighted by default.)

After you select Login, Linux starts the default window manager (called Enlightenment), and displays the GNOME desktop (see Figure 7.1). You'll see an alert box warning you that

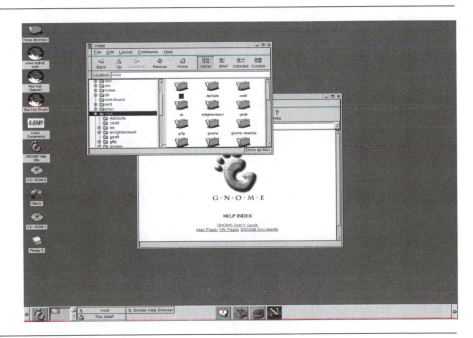

Figure 7.1 After you log in, you'll see the GNOME desktop.

it's not a good idea to run GNOME as root user. For now, just click OK to hide this dialog box. After you click OK, GNOME scans your system for available disk drives; you'll see the GNOME Help System and File Manager on-screen. Along the left of the screen, you'll see icons for the root user's home directory, links to Linux documentation, and icons representing the mountable drives detected on your system.

You'll learn more about the GNOME desktop in Chapter 8. For now, you need to perform some essential system configuration tasks, including creating a user account for yourself.

Understanding the Root User Concept

What's wrong with running Linux as root user? Plenty. The root user has full access to all of your system's files, including configuration files and scripts. Should you inadvertently make a change to one of these files, you could damage your system or even render it completely unusable. (If this happens, follow the instructions in the previous chapter to reinstall Linux.)

In addition, running as root user leaves your system wide open to a variety of external attacks. This isn't a worry if your computer isn't connected to a network or to the Internet, but it becomes a very real concern indeed after you've made the connection. Even if you don't intend to connect your Linux system to a network or to the Internet, there's still reason aplenty to avoid running the system as root user; it's very easy to mess up the underlying configuration, and at this point you don't have enough knowledge to repair the damage.

Despite your lack of knowledge, you'll still need to perform a few relatively risk-free configuration tasks, such as those discussed in this chapter. To do so, you'll need to be logged in as the root user, as you are now. (Configuration tools such as

LinuxConf, to be discussed in the next section, are not available when you log in with your user account.) To avoid doing any damage to your system, follow this chapter's instructions carefully. Do not run any other programs, and try to avoid the temptation to mess around with all the neat stuff you see on-screen. There's plenty of time for that once you've safeguarded your system by creating a user account!

Creating a User Account

I know that you just logged in for the first time; doubtless, you're anxious to explore, but please don't. First, create a user account for yourself. Then, consider configuring your disk drives so that you can access them from your user account, as explained in the following section. Then log out, and log in using your user account, as explained subsequently.

Starting LinuxConf

To create your user account, you'll use the LinuxConf utility, a tool that enables you to perform a wide variety of system configuration tasks. Here, you'll learn how to add a user account for yourself (and anyone else who's going to use your computer).

The version of LinuxConf that you'll use is a GNOME version of a well-seasoned Linux utility. It enables you to perform a variety of system administration functions. There's much to learn about LinuxConf, but you'll use it here to create a user account for yourself.

To start LinuxConf, follow these instructions:

1. Click the GNOME Main Menu button (the one with the four-toed footprint), point to System, and choose Linux-

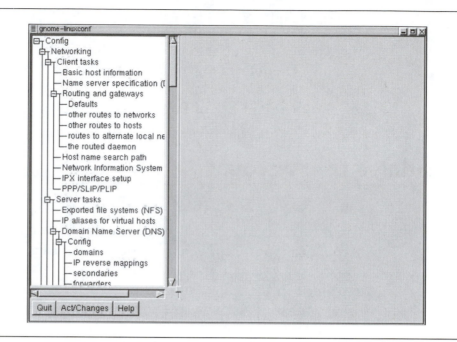

Figure 7.2 LinuxConf enables you to configure your system.

Conf. If you see a Help window, just click the Quit button within this window to start using LinuxConf. You'll see the LinuxConf window, shown in Figure 7.2.

Note that LinuxConf's various configuration modules are organized in a tree structure. If you see a minus sign next to a subject, you are seeing all the subtopics available beneath it. If you see a plus sign, some subtopics are still hidden. You can click the minus or plus signs to hide or show hidden subtopics.

2. Scroll down to Users accounts, and click the plus sign, if necessary, to display the subtopics.

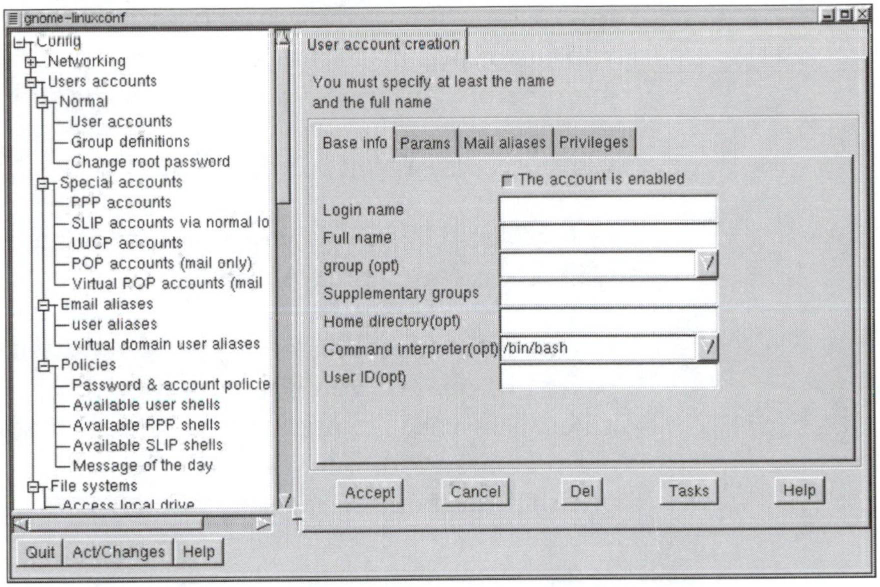

Figure 7.3 Create a user account for yourself before you explore Linux.

3. Under Normal, select User accounts. (If the subtopics under Normal are not visible, click the plus sign next to Normal.)

    You'll see the list of default user accounts, including root. The other user accounts are samples that you can use to configure your system (see Chapter 12 for more information on accounts).

4. Click Add. You'll see the Add page, shown in Figure 7.3.

5. In the Login name, type the login name that you want to use. You can use your first name, if you wish.

6. In the Full Name box, type your full name. This is optional.

7. **Important:** In the Home directory box, type **/home** followed by a forward slash and your login name (the one you just typed in the Login name box). If you choose the login name "suzanne," you would type **/home/suzanne**.

8. Click Accept. You'll see the Changing password page.

9. In the New UNIX password box, type the password you want to use, and click Accept.

   If your password breaks any of several rules concerning password quality, you'll see a notice that you've supplied a bad password. LinuxConf doesn't stop you from creating the password, but you should consider changing it to one that meets basic security standards.

10. Type the password again, and click Accept. If you typed it incorrectly, you'll need to repeat steps 9 and 10.

CAUTION Don't forget to write down your password. If you forget your password, you can still access your files by logging in as the root user, but you'll mess up the file ownership settings in these files.

---

11. Click Quit in the User Accounts area. Without exiting LinuxConf, go on to the next section, in which you'll consider configuring your disk drives so that you can access them when you're logged in using your user account.

Enabling User Access to Disk Drives

As you know, Linux is a multi-user system. On such systems, it's considered bad security policy to give users access to disk drives. Malicious users could do a lot of damage to a system configured in this way.

Chances are these concerns aren't pertinent to your Linux system. You've probably set up your system for your personal use; perhaps others in your family will use it, but you trust these people to refrain from engaging in deliberately destructive actions! If the foregoing describes your use of Linux, by all means provide disk access to users by following the instructions in this section.

After you provide disk access to users, GNOME will automatically create desktop icons for all the available disk drives in your system, including your CD-ROM, floppy disk, and other drives (such as Zip drives). However, these icons will not appear unless you follow these instructions.

To enable user access to disk drives, use LinuxConf, which is already on-screen from the previous section. (If you have not

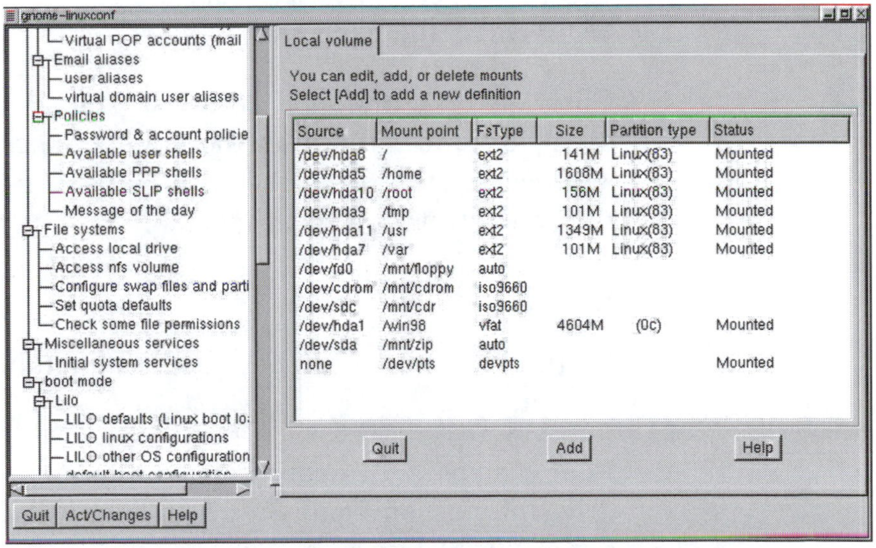

Figure 7.4 This page shows all the storage devices on your system.

yet created a user account, go to the previous section and do so now.)

TIP Before you start LinuxConf, place disk in all the disk drives you want to configure. Note that it's also a good idea to place disks in these drives every time you start Linux. By doing so, you will enable the automatic file-checking utilities to perform routine checks on these drives.

To enable user access to disk drives using LinuxConf, follow these steps:

1. In the LinuxConf tree list, scroll down to File systems.

2. Under File systems, select Access local drive. You'll see the Local volume settings, shown in Figure 7.4.

    Note that the Local volume page lists all the partitions you've created, as well as devices such as floppy disks, CD-ROMs, and Zip drives.

3. Click the disk drive device name (start with the floppy drive, /dev/fd0). You'll see the Volume specification page. The device has already been configured for use; don't disturb the settings on this page.

4. Click the Options tab.

5. In the Options list, click User mountable, and click Accept.

6. Repeat steps 3 through 5 to configure your CD-ROM drive (/dev/cdrom) and any additional disk drives, such as removable SCSI drives.

7. When you are finished activating the User mountable option for your disk drives, click the Quit button in the Local volume area.

8. Click Quit. You'll see a message informing you that your system is "out of sync" with the changes you've made. Don't be alarmed by this; it isn't a horrible thing, and you're about to cure it.

9. Click Activate the changes. LinuxConf runs the initialization scripts needed to restart any services affected by your changes.

   LinuxConf makes the changes you've requested and exits.

TIP After you click Activate the changes, you may see a message informing you that some errors were reported. Chances are good that these are relatively minor; for example, you may have forgotten to insert disks into the disk drives. For now, just click No to skip looking at the error log.

Configuring Your Sound Card

To hear sound on your system, you'll need to run the Sound Configuration Utility, a text-based program that searches for a compatible sound card and enables sound on your system.

Understanding Digital Audio

Computer sounds fall into two general categories: *waveform sounds* and *synthesized sounds*. Waveform sounds are recordings of actual sounds or music. To represent sounds in digital form, digital recording technology takes a "snapshot" of the sound many times per second; this snapshot is called a *sample*. The higher the sampling rate, the better the quality. Audio CDs are recorded with a sampling rate of more than 44,000 samples per second. Digitized waveform sounds are recorded in a variety of file formats, including MP3, the Windows WAV format, the Sun/NeXT format (files with the *.au extension), and SND (a Macintosh sound format); most of these formats offer a variety of sampling rates, as well as the choice of mono or stereo. Although waveform sounds can approach or equal the quality of audio CDs, they require very large files. (An exception is the MP3 format, which uses an advanced compression technique to cut file sizes dramatically.)

Synthesized sounds require very small files that contain text-based instructions that tell the synthesizer what to play. (These instructions are written in a language called MIDI, short for Musical Instrument Digital Interface.) However, synthesized sounds lack the quality of waveform sounds. To play synthesized sounds, you need a sound card equipped with synthesizer circuitry. The oldest (and least satisfactory) type of sound synthesis is called *FM synthesis*. This technique produces the low-quality music you associate with a cheap video game or a child's electronic keyboard. *Wavetable synthesis* relies on actual recordings of real musical instruments to generate sounds, and offers better quality. Most of today's sound cards support wavetable synthesis.

To run the Sound Configuration Utility, follow these steps:

1. Click the Main Menu button, and choose Run Program.

2. In the Run Program dialog box, type **/usr/sbin/sndconfig** and click Run.

    You'll see the text-based Sound Configuration Utility.

3. Press Enter to scan for your soundcard. If the scanning software finds your card, you'll see a message that the probe was successful. If not, you'll be asked to choose your sound card from a list.

4. You'll see messages informing you that configuration files (in the /etc directory) already exist. Just press Enter to overwrite these files.

5. Press Enter to hear a sound sample, and click Yes if you can hear it.

    If you can't hear the sample, check to make sure that your speakers are turned on and plugged in.

6. Press Enter to hear a MIDI sample, and click Yes if you can hear it.

NOTE To hear sound within GNOME, you must open the GNOME Control Center and turn sound on. For more information, see "Enabling Sound," in Chapter 10.

Logging Out

Don't do anything else while you're logged in as root user; log out right now. Subsequently, you'll log in again using your user account.

To log out, do the following:

1. Click the GNOME Main Menu button, and choose Log out. You'll see an alert box with the message, Really log out?

    When you are logged in as root user, you can choose any of the following from this alert box:

    Logout Choose this option to logout of the root user account. You'll see the Welcome screen again, which enables you to log in using your new user account.

Halt Choose this option to shut down your Linux system.

Reboot Choose this option to restart your Linux system.

Note that this alert box also contains an option that enables you to save your system settings, including GNOME applications you've left open. Activate this option if you would like to save your settings.

2. By default, the Logout option is selected. Click Yes to logout.

TIP After you've logged on using your user account, you won't be able to halt or reboot your system using the options in this alert box. (This feature is due to long-standing Unix conventions that prohibit ordinary users from shutting down or rebooting a multi-user system.) To halt or reboot your system from your user account, logout as you did here. In the Welcome dialog box, click the Options button, choose System, and choose Reboot or Halt.

---

3. You'll see the Welcome dialog box. Do one of the following:

    To log in using your user account, type your login name and password, and click Login.

    or

    To halt your computer, click Options, point to System, and choose Halt.

    or

    To reboot your system, click Options, point to System, and choose Reboot.

CAUTION Never quit Linux by skipping the shutdown procedure and shutting down the power. You may scramble the data on your hard drive—so badly, in fact, that you may not be able to restart your system. Always follow the proper shutdown procedure! The reason you might lose data has to do with Linux's disk caching system. This system writes cached data to the disk every few seconds (rather than continuously). This gives better performance, but it also entails the risk of data loss should you switch off the power while the cache software is writing data to the disk. Should you experience a system crash or a failed component (such as a dead keyboard) that prevents you from shutting down properly, wait several minutes before you switch off the power so that the cache software can write cached data to the drive.

From Here

In this chapter, you learned how to configure your system so that you can run GNOME safely. Now that you've created your user account, I'm sure you're eager to explore GNOME; you'll find a guided tour in the next chapter.

8

Exploring GNOME

Now that you've created your user account, you can log in (with your user account, not the root account) and explore to your heart's content. There's lots to learn, starting with some of the peculiarities of the underlying X Window System, which often strike Windows and Mac OS users as somewhat odd or cumbersome. Happily, GNOME eliminates most of X's least-loved quirks.

Most of this chapter presents the essentials of the GNOME and Enlightenment interface. You'll explore GNOME's on-screen appearance, learning the fundamentals of using the GNOME Panel, the GNOME menu, and GNOME desktop features. You'll learn how to get online help, and you'll also learn how to manipulate the application windows created by the Enlightenment window manager.

Since you already have some experience with Microsoft Windows or Mac OS, most of the material in this chapter will be very easy to learn. You can skim the chapter quickly, looking for features that vary from what you're used to. If you've used both Windows and Mac OS, you'll be pleased to find that GNOME combines some of the best features of both interfaces.

CAUTION Do not explore GNOME while you're logged in as root user. Log out and log in using your user account. If you still haven't created a user account, please turn to Chapter 7 and create one now.

Introducing GNOME

Short for the GNU Network Object Model Environment, GNOME is the default desktop interface for Red Hat Linux 6.0. Designed to work with the X Window System, GNOME requires a window manager—preferably, a GNOME-compatible window manager, such as the default window manager, Enlightenment.

Going far beyond the functionality that window managers alone can provide, GNOME provides the desktop functionality that has been available previously only in commercial software (the Common Desktop Environment).

GNOME's Technical Brilliance

GNOME is not merely a nice-looking desktop. It's a technical tour de force that will bring new levels of functionality to computer users (Mason 1999). In addition to providing the desktop functionality missing from X Window System window managers and applications, GNOME provides desktop-level support for the following:

- **GTK+ Toolkit** This application development toolkit, originally developed for The GIMP (a PhotoShop-like graphics application), provides graphics tools that application developers can use so that they do not have to create these tools themselves. A neat capability of GTK+ is its support of *themes*, configuration choices that automatically affect all the applications (including GNOME itself) that rely on the toolkit's support. GTK+ also supports international text display and input, as well as drag-and-drop functionality that supports earlier drag-and-drop protocols as well as the GNOME drag-and-drop standard.
- **CORBA** Short for Common Request Broker Architecture, CORBA enables applications to communicate with each other, regardless of their location on the network or the programming language used to create them. GNOME's implementation of CORBA, called ORBit, will enable the type of interprocess communication that enables Microsoft Windows applications to work with each other
- **GNOME Imaging Architecture** GNOME's imaging support supplies application developers with tools for graphics display, printing, and high quality fonts. Never before available in the X Window environment, these advanced features are enabled by the GNOME canvas (a high-level display system for creating structured graphics), libart (a rendering engine that enables PostScript imaging onscreen), the GNOME print engine, and the GNOME font engine. Of these, the GNOME print and font engines are still under development.
- **EsounD (ESD)** GNOME's sound capabilities are provided by EsounD, a sound daemon that, for the first time,

enables more than one sound source to play simultaneously on X Window systems.

GNOME's technical underpinnings solve many of the most
galling problems of X Window System applications, providing
needed system-wide support for graphics and foreign languages. Yet it is designed to work smoothly with the X Window System, and fully supports older X Window applications.

Learning GNOME

GNOME is easy to learn, but it's important to remember that
GNOME relies on the X Window System for application windowing services. Accordingly, you'll be wise to spend a few
minutes reading about some of the peculiarities of using the X
Window System, as explained in the next section.

Using the X Window System

No matter which window manager and desktop system you're
using, X imposes some common user interface features. If
you're used to Mac OS or Microsoft Windows, some of these
require that you learn some new concepts.

Understanding the Input Focus

To do anything in an on-screen window, you must first move
the *focus* to this window. When you've moved the focus to the
window, it becomes active, and you can type within it. With
most window managers, simply moving the mouse pointer
within the window is sufficient to move the focus to the window, but sometimes you must click within the window. You'll
learn this concept quickly enough, but it can be frustrating at
first; you start typing in a text box, and nothing happens.
There's nothing wrong. You just haven't moved the pointer
within the window.

TIP If you find the default focus behavior annoying, Enlightenment enables you to reconfigure it so that it more closely approximates the way Microsoft Windows and Mac OS work. To change the default focus behavior, click the Main Menu icon in GNOME, point to Settings, and choose Window Manager. Click Run Configuration Tool for Enlightenment, and select Behavior from the list. Activate the following items: All new windows that appear get the keyboard focus, All new pop-up windows get the keyboard focus, and Send the pointer to windows when switching focus with the keyboard.

Using the Keyboard

Because the X Window System is designed for use on a wide variety of computer systems, X uses abstract names for certain keys that have different names on different keyboards. One such name is *meta*. On PC keyboards, meta (abbreviated M) corresponds to the Alt key. If you see a keyboard command such as Meta + F, it means the same thing as Alt + F (hold down the Alt key and press F).

Using a Mouse

In the X Window System world, mice have three buttons. X applications frequently use the third button to implement certain procedures, such as pasting text and graphics from the clipboard. However, most PCs are equipped with mice that have only two buttons. If you selected three-button emulation when you installed Red Hat Linux, you can press both mouse buttons simultaneously to emulate the third mouse button.

In many X applications, the right mouse button reveals a menu that isn't otherwise visible. If you've started an application and can't find a menu bar, right-click the application window's background.

Understanding Terminal Emulators

Should you wish to type commands at the Linux prompt, you can use a *terminal emulator* program. Such a program enables you to work in the text-only mode without having to exit the X Window System.

If you've used Microsoft Windows, you've probably used the MS-DOS window to enter DOS commands directly. Terminal emulators provide much the same function, but with an important difference. Because the X Window System is completely independent of the Linux kernel, the terminal emulator provides a means of communication with the kernel that's established on a session-by-session basis. For this reason, you can have several terminal emulators running at the same time, should you wish to do so. You can also choose which terminal emulator you'd like to run.

In GNOME, you can choose from the following terminal emulators:

- **Regular Xterm** A monochrome, text-only terminal emulator.
- **Color Xterm** Uses colored text against a black background.
- **GNOME terminal** A nifty color terminal emulator that enables you to load a bit-mapped graphic image in the window background.

Understanding Multiple Desktop Areas

Window managers can define a virtual desktop that's larger than the area your monitor can display. For example, Enlightenment's default settings create a virtual desktop that's four times the size of your display screen; you'll find four *desktop areas* (two across and two down). (Enlightenment enables you to define up to 64 desktop areas, eight across and eight down.) When you start Enlightenment, you'll view the top left desktop area.

If you've never used a system with a virtual desktop before, you'll find that the concept takes some getting used to. If you move the mouse pointer to a screen edge that borders on another desktop area, you'll find that the screen jumps to the next desktop area—which can be disconcerting if you don't realize what's happening. (If you dislike this behavior, you can disable edge flipping, as explained later in the section titled "Configuring Enlightenment.")

Chances are you'll grow to like the virtual desktop. Instead of keeping lots of windows all stacked up on one confining screen, try running applications in their own desktop areas. Thanks to GNOME's Pager, part of the GNOME Panel that's discussed in the next section, you can easily move from one desktop area to the next. Each desktop area shows the same background, and each has the GNOME Panel.

Exploring GNOME's On-Screen Features

Now that we've got the fundamentals out of the way, it's time to explore the GNOME desktop. Start by looking at the overall structure of the screen (see Figure 8.1); you'll see the GNOME Panel at the bottom of the screen.

> **TIP** The GNOME desktop is almost infinitely customizable, so bear in mind that that the rather plain-looking screen shots in this chapter show the default GNOME settings. You can add backgrounds, sounds, new custom panels, and much more. You'll learn how in Chapter 10.

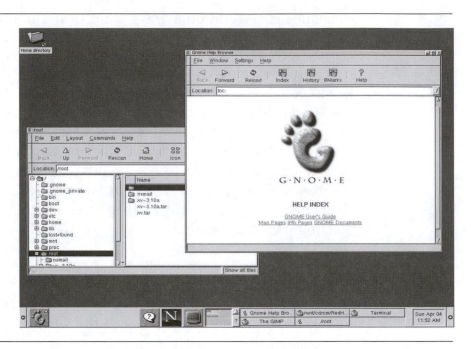

Figure 8.1 At the bottom of the screen you see the GNOME Panel.

Introducing the GNOME Panel

At the bottom of the GNOME screen, you see the GNOME *Panel*, a bar that contains some icons and buttons. It's a big bar, and sometimes it gets in the way—which is why you can hide it. Note the following basic Panel maneuvers:

- To hide the GNOME Panel, click the arrow nearest the edge of the screen.
- To bring the GNOME Panel back, click the arrow again.

The Panel has the following parts (from left to right):

- **Hide Buttons** At each end of the Panel, you'll see buttons that enable you to hide the Panel. Try clicking each of them.

- **Main Menu Button** The big icon (with the GNOME foot-print symbol) is the Main Menu Button. Click the button to see the menu. (We'll explore this menu later, so just click outside the menu, or press Esc, to hide the menu for now.)

- **Application Launchers** You'll see predefined launchers for a couple of applications, including Netscape Communicator and the GNOME Terminal program. You can click on one of these icons to launch the program. Also, you can easily add application launchers, as you'll learn in Chapter 10.

- **Pager** This area (see Figure 8.2) shows where running applications are located on the four default desktops; as you'll learn in a moment, the GNOME desktop is much larger than what you're seeing right now. The pager also shows buttons for running applications. The foreground application (the one that's currently selected on-screen) is highlighted.

Understanding the Pager

Spend a few minutes learning how to use the Pager.

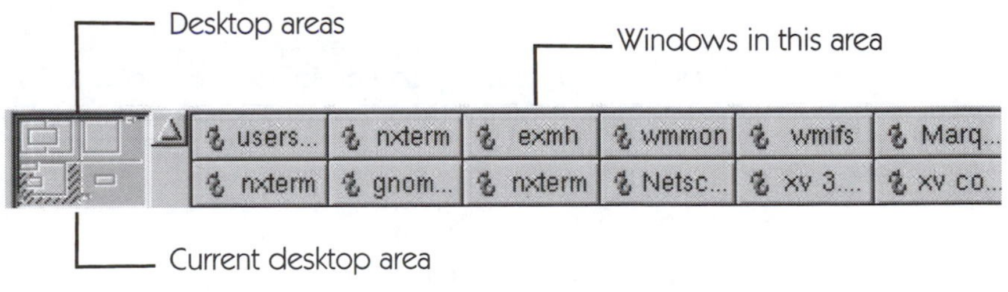

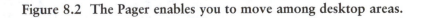

Figure 8.2 The Pager enables you to move among desktop areas.

Try moving the pointer to the right edge of the screen. Suddenly, the windows you were seeing disappear! The Panel is still there, though. Look at the Pager, and you'll see that the highlight has changed to the top-right desktop area.

Now move the pointer down to the bottom edge of the screen, and go past the bottom. You'll see the next desktop area down (the lower right desktop.) Look at the Pager to see how the highlight has changed, showing you which desktop area you're seeing.

To switch to a different desktop area, just click the Pager. Note that the Pager shows the approximate layout of windows in each desktop. Remember, to see a list of windows in each desktop, click the up arrow in the Pager area.

Introducing the GNOME Desktop

On the GNOME desktop, you'll see icons for the following:

- **Home directory** Double-click this icon to view the contents of your home directory.
- **Links to GNOME and Red Hat documentation** Double-click these links to view the documentation.
- **Folders representing mountable drives on your system** To access these drives, just double-click the folder icon.

TIP If the drive icons do not appear, you need to make your disk drive mountable by users. For more information, see Chapter 7.

The GNOME Desktop is fully enabled for drag-and-drop actions. To the desktop, you can drag the following:

- **Applications** From the GNOME File Manager, you can drag an application to the desktop. After you do so, you can start the application by double-clicking its desktop icon.

- **Files** You can also drag files to the desktop. After you do, you can launch the file—and the application that created it—by double-clicking the file.
- **Directories** If you drag a directory to the desktop, you can double-click the directory icon to start the File Manager, which will display the directory's contents.

Getting Help

GNOME brings to Linux all of the essential functionality of desktop interfaces such as Mac OS and Microsoft Windows, including an integrated help utility that applications can also use. To view the GNOME Help Browser, click the Help icon on the Panel (the one with the question mark). You'll see the

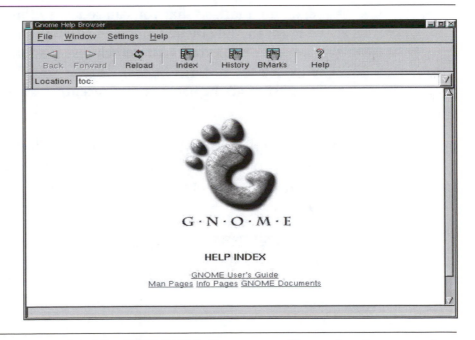

Figure 8.3 The GNOME Help Browser provides ready reference services.

Help Browser on-screen, with the Help Index displayed (see Figure 8.3).

If you've used a Web browser, you already know how to use the Help Browser. To see information about GNOME, for example, just click GNOME User's Guide. You'll see the table of contents for the GNOME User's Guide. To view a subject, just click the subject's title.

While you're using the Help Browser, you can do the following:

- **Redisplay a previously viewed page.** Click the Back button on the toolbar.
- **Return to a page you clicked Back from.** Click the Forward button.
- **Return to the top-level index.** Click the Index button.
- **Set a bookmark so that you can return to this page quickly.** From the File menu, choose Add Bookmark.
- **View your bookmarks list and choose a bookmark you've set.** Click the BMarks button.
- **See a list of all the pages you've recently visited.** Click History.

In addition to the GNOME User's Guide, you'll see links to the help utilities of GNOME-compliant applications, as well as Linux information resources that are available on your system. These include:

- **Info Pages** Extensive documentation for important Linux programs and utilities.
- **MAN Pages** On-screen help for Linux commands that you type at the command prompt.

Using Windows

To anyone who has used Microsoft Windows, the windows you'll see in GNOME (see Figure 8.3) are easy to use. And that's no accident. These windows are generated by the Enlightenment window manager, using a *theme* that's designed to resemble the functionality of Microsoft Windows. (You can choose other themes, if you wish, but you'll be wise to stick with the default themes until you've learned all the basics.)

Although the default Enlightenment theme resembles Microsoft Windows features, you'll also find some nifty features that show the influence of the Finder, the window manager that's built into Mac OS. One example is the window shade/unshade feature, which enables you to "roll up" the window so that only the title bar is visible.

Exploring Window Features

Note the following window features, shown in Figure 8.4:

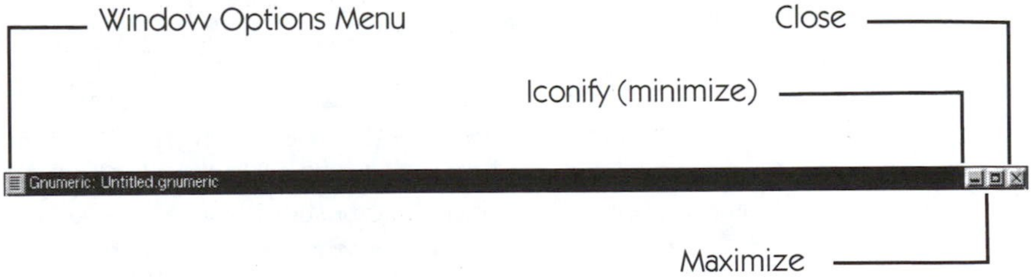

Window Options Menu   Close

Iconify (minimize)

Gnumeric: Untitled.gnumeric

Maximize

Figure 8.4 Window control features on the title bar

- **Title bar** This bar runs across the top of every window. When the window is in the foreground (active), the title bar is highlighted. If you've used a Mac, you can use one of your Mac skills: GNOME windows can "roll up," like a window shade. To shade a window, double-click the title bar. The window is reduced to just the title bar. To unshade the window so that you can see the window contents again, double-click the title bar again.

- **Window Options Menu button** Located at the left edge of the title bar (see Figure 8.4), this icon looks like a box with a row of horizontal lines. If you click this icon, you'll see a menu that provides access to all window features.

- **Iconify button** This button (which looks like a dash or minus sign) minimizes the window. It's located near the right edge of the title bar. After you click this icon, you can bring the window back by clicking the window's button on the Pager.

- **Maximize button** This button (which looks like a square) zooms the window so that it fills the current desktop area.

- **Close button** This button (which looks like an "X") closes the current window.

- **Scroll bar and scroll arrows** If the window contents are larger than the window size, you'll see scroll bars. To scroll the window, click on the scroll arrows or drag the scroll bar.

TIP If you'd like a window to appear in every desktop area, you can make it "sticky." To do so, click the Window Options Menu button, and choose Stick/Unstick. To unstick the window so that it shows up in only one desktop area, repeat this command.

Learning Basic Window Manipulation Tasks

With Microsoft Windows or Mac OS, you can move and size windows, as well as minimize them or zoom them to full size. Thanks to GNOME's default window manager, Enlightenment, you can perform all of these tasks, plus many more. As you'll find when you experiment with on-screen windows, Enlightenment enables several additional cool window maneuvers that you may wish to use frequently:

- **Shade/Unshade** Borrowed from the Mac OS interface, this feature collapses a window (that is, "rolls it up" like a window shade) so that only the title bar is visible. To roll up the shade, just double-click the title bar. To pull down the shade, double-click the title bar again.

- **Stick/Unstick** As you've learned, Enlightenment enables you to define multiple desktop areas. By default, four such areas are defined. If you "stick" a window, it appears in all the desktop areas. You can "unstick" a window so that it appears only in the desktop area where you last placed it. To stick or unstick a window, click the Window Control Menu button, and choose Stick/Unstick.

- **Moving a window to another desktop area** As you grow more comfortable with desktop areas, you'll find that it's convenient to run applications in their own desktop area. You can then switch among applications by clicking a desktop area within the Panel. To move applications to other desktop areas, click the Window Control Menu, point to Desktop, and choose where to move the window.

TIP When you minimize a window with Enlightenment, you're *iconifying* the window, according to Enlightenment's terminology. However, you won't see an icon anywhere on the desktop. Instead, look for a button in the Pager area.

Table 8.1 lists the window maneuvers you can perform.

Table 8.1 Using GNOME Windows

Window actions:	Do this:
Annihilate	To force a window to close, right-click the close button. Alternatively, click the Window Control Menu button, and choose Annihilate. You may need to annihilate a window if the application stops responding.
Close	To close the window, left-click the Close button at the right edge of the title bar. Alternatively, click the Window Options Menu button, and choose Close.
Iconify	Click the Iconify (minimize) button. Alternatively, click the Window Options Menu button, and choose Iconify.
Move	Move the mouse pointer to the window's title bar, hold down the left mouse button, and drag. You can also move the pointer to any of the window borders, hold down the right mouse button, and drag.
	To move a window to a different desktop area, click the Window Options menu, point to Desktop, and choose one of the following options: Move to Area Right, Move to Area Left, Move to Area Above, or Move to Area Below.
Remember State	To tell GNOME to remember the attributes you've chosen for this window, click the Window Control Menu button, and choose one of the following: All Attributes (remembers all window settings), Forget Everything (remembers no window settings), or individual window settings (choose from Border Style, Desktop, Size, Location, Layer Level, Stickyness, or Shaded State).
Shade/Unshade	Double-click the title bar, or click the Window Control Menu button, and choose Shade/Unshade.

Size

Click on a window border or corner, hold down the left mouse button, and drag. Alternatively, click the Window Options Menu button, point to Window Size on the popup menu, and choose one of the following: Height (to adjust the window height), Width (to adjust the window width), or Size (to adjust both height and width).

Stacking

By default, GNOME windows are on top when they're active. To change the stacking level, click the Window Control Menu button, point to Set Stacking, and choose one of the following: Below (beneath all other windows, except when you click within the window and hold down the mouse button), Normal (the default setting, in which windows are above when they're active and below when they're inactive), Above (above other inactive windows even when inactive), or On Top (above all other windows, even active ones).

Stick/Unstick

Click the Window Control Menu button, and choose Stick/Unstick.

TIP To view the previous window you viewed in the current desktop area, hold down the Alt key and press Tab. Press Alt + Tab again to return to the previous window.

TIP Here's another way to show, hide, shade, unshade, close, or annihilate a window: In the Pager, right-click the window's button, and choose one of the following from the popup menu: Show/Hide, Shade/Unshade, Close, or Nuke.

Docking and Undocking Toolbars

If you're viewing a GNOME-compliant application, you can take advantage of fully movable and dockable menu bars and

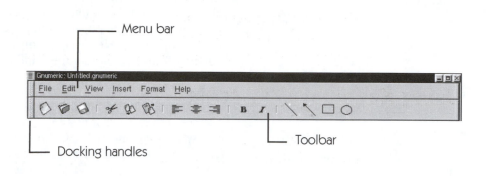

Figure 8.5. Drag the docking handle to move the menu bar or toolbar.

tool bars. To reposition the menu bar or toolbar, drag the docking handles (see Figure 8.5). When you've positioned the toolbar where you want it to appear, release the mouse button.

You can dock the menu bar or toolbar elsewhere within the application window, or on the desktop, if you wish. GNOME remembers your preferences for menu bar or toolbar placement. The next time you start the application, you'll see the menu bar and toolbar where you placed them.

Using Session Management

GNOME implements *session management*, a feature that "remembers" what you were doing when you exited GNOME. To implement session management, activate the Save current setup option when you log out of GNOME. With this option, GNOME will remember which applications were running when you exited—and what's more, where the windows were positioned and which data files you were viewing. However, note the following limitations to session management:

- Session management works only with applications that are fully compliant with GNOME.
- **Important:** Session management does *not* save your data automatically. Before exiting GNOME, make sure that you have saved your work in all applications.

Using Keyboard Shortcuts

Enlightenment comes pre-configured with a bevy of useful keyboard shortcuts, which are listed in Table 8.2. Particularly useful are Ctrl + Alt + r, which enables you to shade or unshade the selected window, Ctrl + Alt + x (closes a window quickly), and Ctrl + Alt + i (iconifies or minimizes a window quickly).

Table 8.2 Enlightenment Keyboard Shortcuts

Press:	To do this:
Ctrl + Alt + up arrow	Raise window one level
Ctrl + Alt + down arrow	Lower window one level
Ctrl + Alt + x	Close window
Ctrl + Alt + k	Kill (annihilate) window
Ctrl + Alt + s	Stick/Unstick window
Ctrl + Alt + i	Iconify (minimize) window
Ctrl + Alt + r	Shade/Unshade window
Alt + Shift + down arrow	Move to next desktop area down
Alt + Shift + up arrow	Move to next desktop area up
Alt + Shift + right arrow	Move to next desktop right
Alt + Shift + left arrow	Move to next desktop left
Ctrl + Alt + Enter	Reset desktop area

Ctrl + Alt + Home	Clean up windows
Ctrl + Alt + Delete	Exit Enlightenment
Ctrl + Alt + End	Restart Enlightenment

TIP If you disable edge flip resistance (as recommended in Chapter 10, "Personalizing GNOME"), use the Alt + Shift + arrow shortcuts to move from one desktop area to another.

From Here

Now that you've learned the fundamentals of the GNOME desktop, you should learn how to manage files using the GNOME File Manager. You'll thoroughly explore this indispensable utility in the next chapter. In Chapter 10, you'll learn how to customize GNOME so that it looks and works just the way you want.

References and Further Reading

Lewis, Todd Graham, and David "Gleef" Zoll. 1999. *GNOME Frequently Asked Questions*. Available online at http://www.gnome.org.

Mason, David. 1999. *GNOME Technologies: A Brief Description of the Technology Behind GNOME*. Available online at http://www.gnome.org.

Mason, David, and David Wheeler. 1999. *GNOME User's Guide*. Available online at http://www.gnome.org.

Managing Files

The GNOME File Manager is the centerpiece of the GNOME desktop, and rightly so. Finally, Linux users can manage files without learning lengthy, convoluted commands. File Manager is a drag-and-drop capable program that presents a simple, familiar interface. Also called GNOME Midnight Commander (GMC), File Manager is a GNOME version of the respected Midnight Commander, a text-mode file management utility (see Chapter 16).

File Manager's apparent simplicity belies a powerhouse of technical innovation. File Manager transforms the wilderness of Linux files into terrain that's both manageable and understandable. For example, thanks to an impressive technical innovation, File Manager can tell which application generated a file, so launching an application is as simple as double-clicking the file's icon. These are capabilities long enjoyed by Mac OS uses (and, to a limited extent, Microsoft Windows users), but they're finally available on the Linux platform as well. Compared to other X file managers, which are typically unfinished projects that lack the functionality users expect, File Manager is a very impressive program. This chapter fully explores the essentials of File Manager use.

Introducing the File Manager

Closely resembling the Windows Explorer in Microsoft Windows 95, 98, and NT, the File Manager displays two panels: a *tree view*, which shows all of the directories on your system, and the *directory window*, which shows the contents of the *current directory*, the directory that's currently selected (see Figure 9.1).

Navigating the Tree View

The Tree View displays a hierarchical map of your system's directories. The *root directory* (/) is at the top of the "tree," and directly beneath the root directory are the directories at the top level (including bin, boot, etc, home, lib, and the other standard Linux directories). If these directories contain subdirectories that aren't displayed, you see a plus sign next to the directory's name. To see the subdirectories (directories within a directory), click the plus sign. When the plus sign changes to a minus, you know that you are viewing all the subdirectories one level below the selected directory.

Within the directory window, you'll see icons representing directories and files. Directories are represented by folder icons. Note that one of these is named .. (two dots). This directory, called the *parent directory*, represents the directory one level above the current directory. For example, suppose the current directory is /home/bryan. If you double-click the parent directory icon, you'll see the contents of /home.

TIP You can also view the parent directory by clicking the Up button.

You can navigate directories by double-clicking their icons within the directory window.

TIP To launch an application, just double-click a file that's associated with a particular type of data, such as a JPEG graphic or a Word-Perfect document. The File Manager will automatically launch the application that's associated with the file.

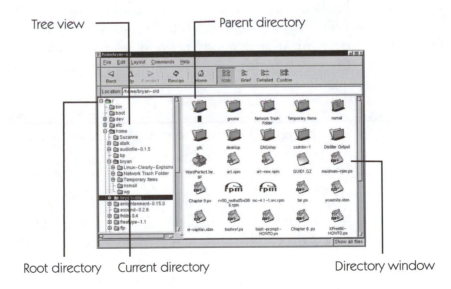

Figure 9.1 The GNOME File Manager makes file management easy.

Using the Navigation Icons

The Back, Up, and Forward buttons enable you to navigate the tree view as if you were using a Web browser. Here's a quick rundown of what these buttons do:

- **Up** To go to the directory one level up from the currently selected directory, click Up.
- **Back** To return to a previously viewed directory, click Back. You can continue clicking Back to visit previously viewed directories, until you return to the current directory.
- **Forward** To redisplay a directory from which you clicked Back, click Forward.

Understanding Your Home Directory

When you log on, you tell Linux your user name. Each user has a default *home directory*, which is the directory where this user stores files. You should be looking at the home directory of your user account now. If you see the root user's home directory (/root), log out and log in again using your user account.

TIP For more information on creating a user account for yourself, see Chapter 7.

You'll use your user home directory to store all your data files. In addition, this directory stores configuration information based on choices you make when you run GNOME, Enlightenment, and applications. When you've connected to the Internet, this directory will also store your mail, Internet bookmarks, and cached Web documents.

Folder Icons in the Directory Window

Within the directory window, you see icons representing sub-directories and files. Table 9.1 shows the icons used for accessible and inaccessible directories.

Table 9.1 Directory icons in the directory window

Icon	Description
	A directory that is closed because you do not have the correct permission settings. All directories are open to the root user. With your user account, you can't access directories other than your own unless the system administrator (root user) has specifically given a user permission to do so.
	An accessible directory. Double-click the folder icon to open the directory and view its contents.

TIP You'll see an icon for a directory named ".." (two periods). If you double-click this directory, you move to the next directory up.

File Icons in the Directory Window

As you'll notice when you examine the directory window (see Figure 9.2), File Manager can determine the contents of many types of files. In the Icons view, many files have distinctive icons that identify the type of data the file contains, such as audio or video data.

To determine the file type, the file name must have an *extension*, consisting of a period followed by one or more characters. The extension must conform to the standard established

by the Multipurpose Internet Mail Extension (MIME) protocol. For example, if a file has the .jpg extension, the File Manager considers the file to contain a JPEG graphic, and uses an
icon that indicates that the file is a JPEG file. For a list of common file icons and the type of data file they signify, see Table
9.2.

Table 9.2 File icons displayed in the Icons View

Icon	Type of file
	Unknown. The File Manager was unable to determine what this file contains. The likely cause is that the file name lacks an extension. If the file has an extension, File Manager has not been configured to associate this type of file with an application (see "Associating File Types with Applications," later in this chapter.
	An audio file. Double-click this icon to hear the sound. File Manager is configured to play a wide variety of sounds, including Sun/NeXT (au) sounds, Apple/Amiga (aiff) sounds, mp3 sounds, Real Audio (ram) sounds, and Windows (wav) sounds.
	A core dump. If a program crashes, this file contains information that a programmer could use to determine what went wrong. You can safely delete these files.
	An executable file. Double-click this icon to launch the program or script.
	A graphic image file. Double-click the icon to view the image in Electric Eyes, the default picture viewer. File Manager can read a very wide variety of graphics files, including JPEG, GIF, and PNG (Portable Network Graphics).

A man (manual) page file. Double-click this icon to view a program's manual page documentation.

A package (file archive). Double-click the archive icon to view the names of the files stored in the archive.

A Red Hat Package Manager (RPM) file. Double-click the icon to install the software contained in this file.

A text file. Double-click this icon to view the file's contents in a text editor.

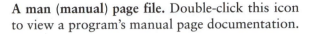

A video or animation. Double-click the icon to view the video or animation on-screen using Xanim. File Manager is set up to read a variety of video and animation files, including MPEG (mpg) and QuickTime (mov) movies, FLI animations, and Windows (avi) videos.

TIP If you install applications, you can associate the new application with one of the file types on your system. For more information, see "Associating File Types with Applications," later in this chapter.

Changing Views in the Directory Window

Within the directory window, you can view a directory's contents in a variety of list formats instead of the default icon view. In addition, you can sort the display so that you can quickly find a file that you're looking for.

Choosing a View

In the directory window, you may choose from the following views:

- **Icons** This is the default view (see Figure 9.2). You see icons representing files and directories. Data files look like documents; in many cases File Manager can tell what type of data the file contains, and the data type is indicated in a small black text box superimposed on the icon. Compressed files and tar archives show up like a cardboard box stuffed with items, while RPM packages appear with an RPM icon.
- **Brief** This view shows just one column, Name.

Figure 9.2 File Manager's icons tell you what type of data is in a file.

- **Detailed** This view (see Figure 9.3) shows three columns: Name, Size, and MTime (date and time of last modification).
- **Custom** This view enables you to choose which columns you display. By default, it displays Name, Size, and Permissions.

TIP If you've performed actions that have changed the contents of a directory, click Rescan to make sure the contents are up to date.

Sorting the File Display

If you've chosen Brief, Detailed, or Custom, you can sort the files by clicking the column header button (note the Name,

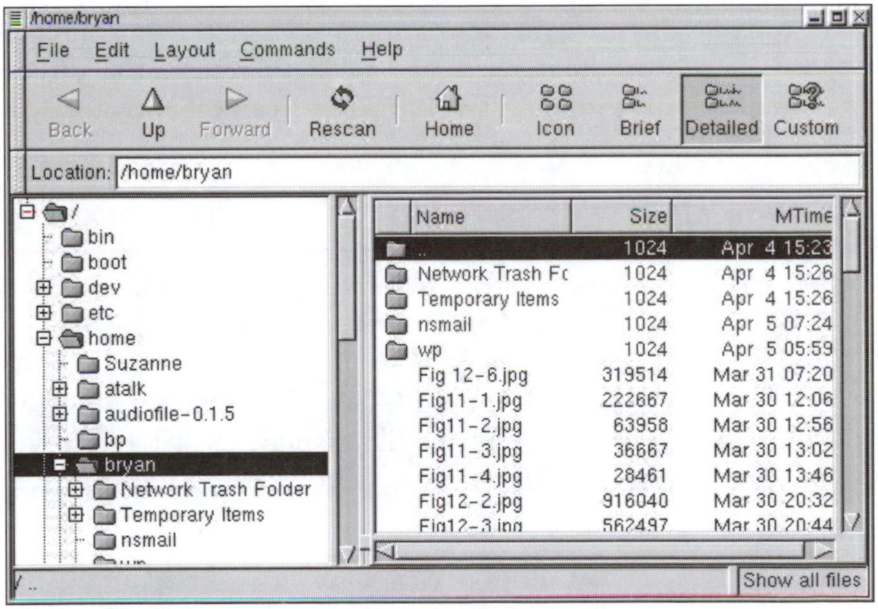

Figure 9.3 The Detailed view shows file sizes and modification dates.

Size, and Mtime buttons in Figure 9.3, which shows the Detail view). Click the button again to sort the files in reverse order.

TIP By default, Linux alphabetizes file names by first listing the files that have names beginning with capital letters; next are listed the files with names beginning with lower-case letters.

You can also sort files clicking Layout on the menu bar, and choose Sort Files. In the Sort By dialog box, you can choose the sort order (Name, File Type, Size, Time Last Accessed, Time Last Modified, or Time Last Changed). You can also ignore case sensitivity, and you can reverse the sort order, if you wish. Choose the sort order you want, and select case sensitivity and sort order options, if desired, and click OK.

Rescanning the Directory

If you've made changes to the directory contents since you last opened it, you may need to rescan the directory to see an up-to-date list of files. To rescan the directory, click the Rescan button on the toolbar.

Filtering Files

Sometimes you're looking at so many files that it's overwhelming to make sense of them. To reduce the number of files displayed, you may wish to use a filter. A filter (such as *.png) shows only those files that have the specified extension (here, .png). To filter the file display, click Layout on the menu bar, choose Filter View, type a filter in the list box, and click OK.

CAUTION Don't forget that you've filtered the view! To restore the display of all files, click Layout on the menu bar, choose Filter View, and choose Show All Files in the list box. Click OK to confirm.

Selecting Files and Directories

To perform actions on files and directories, you begin by selecting them. You can use these techniques in any of File Manager's views (Icons, Brief, Detailed, or Custom).

Here's a quick rundown on the techniques you can use to select files and directories:

- **Selecting a single file or directory.** Point to the name or icon and click the left mouse button.
- **Selecting a group of files or directories.** Click just outside the first file or directory that you want to select, hold down the left mouse button, and drag. You'll see a "rubber band" selection rectangle. Adjust the rectangle's size until you've selected all the files or directories you want, and then release the mouse button.
- **Selecting two or more files or directories that aren't in a group.** If you need to select two or more files or directories that aren't located close together, hold down the Ctrl key and left-click the names or icons of the files or directories that you want to select.
- **Selecting a group of files or directories in a list.** To select a group of files or directories in the Detailed or Custom list, select the first file or directory name in the list. Then move the mouse pointer to the last file or directory name, hold down the Shift key, and click the last file or directory name.
- **Selecting all the files or directories in the Directory View panel.** Press Ctrl + A. You can also click Edit on the menu bar, and choose Select All.

You can also select files using wildcards. To select all the files in a directory with the .jpg extension, for example, click Edit on the menu bar, and choose Select Files. You'll see the Select dialog box (see Figure 9.4). In the text box, type the pattern you want to match. For example, to match all the files that have the jpg extension, type ***.jpg**. Click OK to select the files.

Managing Files and Directories

Once you've selected files, you can move or copy them with drag-and-drop, or you can use the Move or Copy dialog boxes. You can also delete and rename files and directories, and you can create new directories, as the following sections describe.

Moving and Copying with Drag-and-Drop

Be aware that you cannot move or copy files if you do not have the correct file ownership. You can move or copy all you like within your home directory because you own all the files this directory contains. For more information on basic file ownership concepts, see "Understanding File Ownership and Permissions," later in this chapter.

By default, File Manager *moves* files or directories when you use drag-and-drop. To copy files or directories with drag-and-drop, hold down the Shift key.

Figure 9.4 To select a group of files, type a matching pattern here.

TIP If you hold down the Alt key while you're dragging and dropping a file or directory, you'll see a pop-up menu when you release the mouse button. From the menu, you can select Move Here or Copy Here. Note: be sure to click the mouse button *before* you press the Alt key; otherwise, you'll move the whole window when you drag.

You can use drag-and-drop to move or copy files or directories to another folder within your home directory; just drag the selected file or directory to one of the folders in the Tree View. As you drag, you'll see an icon indicating that you're moving or copying something. In the Tree View, you can scroll the panel by moving the pointer to the top or the bottom of the panel. To open a collapsed folder, just position the pointer over the folder; File Manager will expand the display to reveal the hidden directories.

You can also move or copy files or directories between two File Manager windows. To open a new File Manager window, click File on the menu bar and choose Create New Window. After opening the source directory in one window and the destination directory in the other, you can drag the file from the source window to the destination window; drop the file on the folder where you want the copied or moved file to appear.

TIP To make frequently used files more accessible, you can move or copy them to the desktop. Use drag-and-drop to move or copy the file, and release the mouse button where you want the file to appear.

Copying and Moving Directories in the Tree View

You can use drag-and-drop to restructure directories within the Tree View. When you're logged in with your user account, you can perform these actions only within your home directory.

To move a directory in the Tree View panel, select the directory and drag the pointer to the destination folder. To copy a directory in the Tree View panel, hold down the Shift key and drag.

CAUTION Don't copy or move directories that have been placed in your home directory by GNOME, Enlightenment, or application programs. Use the techniques discussed in this section only for directories you have created yourself. For information on creating directories, see "Creating Directories," later in this chapter. If you're using File Manager with the default preference settings, these directories aren't visible; still, you should copy, move, or delete any file or folder that you didn't place there personally.

Moving Files and Directories with the Move Dialog Box

If you'd rather not use drag-and-drop, you can move files and directories with the Move dialog box. This Move dialog box offers more options (including advanced options, discussed later in this chapter). It also offers a very convenient feature: you can select a destination directory from a list of recently accessed directories. This feature comes in very handy when you're doing some serious housecleaning and moving many files around.

To move files or directories with the Move dialog box, follow these steps:

1. Select the files or directories you want to move.

2. Do one of the following:

   Right-click the selection, and choose Move.

or

From the File menu, choose Move.

You'll see the Move dialog box, shown in Figure 9.5.

2. In the text box, type the destination directory, or click Browse to select the directory from the Tree View. If you're moving lots of files and would like the copy operation to run as a background process, check Copy as a background process.

TIP To see a list of directories you've recently accessed, click the down arrow icon.

---

3. Click OK.

If the destination directory already contains a file or directory with the same name, you'll see the File Exists alert

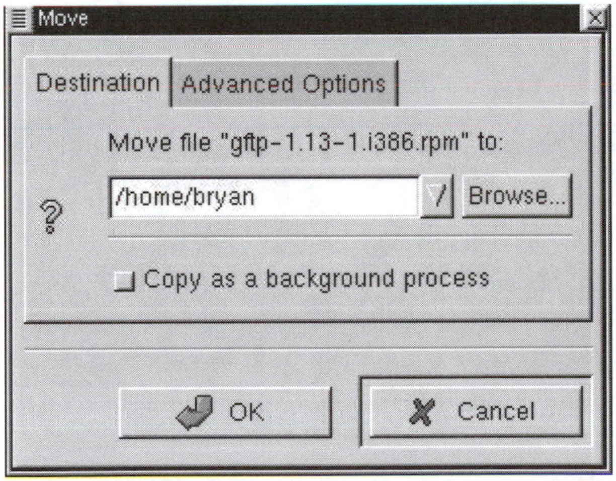

Figure 9.5 In the Move dialog box, you specify the destination directory.

box. To replace the file or directory, click Yes. To skip replacing this file or directory (but continue with additional files or directories, if any), click No. To cancel the copying operation, click Cancel.

Copying Files and Directories with the Copy Dialog Box

As an alternative to drag-and-drop for copying files or directories, you can use the Copy dialog box (see Figure 9.6). Like the Move dialog box, the Copy dialog box offers advanced features and conveniences that aren't available with drag-and-drop.

To copy files or directories with the Copy dialog box, follow these steps:

1. Select the files or directories you want to copy.

2. Do one of the following:

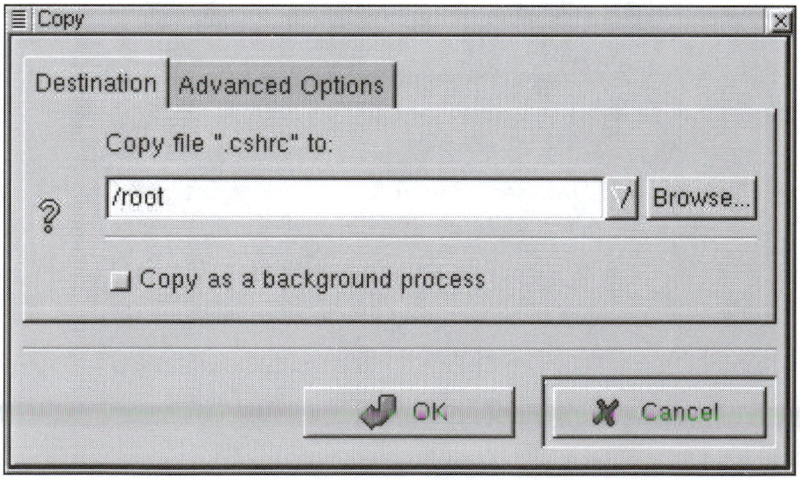

Figure 9.6 In the Copy dialog box, you specify the destination directory.

Right-click the selection, and choose Copy.

or

From the File menu, choose Copy.

You'll see the Copy dialog box, shown in Figure 9.6, on the previous page.

3. In the text box, type the destination directory, or click Browse to select the directory from the Tree View. If you're moving lots of files or directories and would like the copy operation to run as a background process, check Copy as a background process.

TIP To see a list of directories you've recently accessed, click the down arrow icon.

---

4. Click OK.

If the destination directory already contains a file or directory with the same name, you'll see the File Exists alert box. To replace the file, click Yes. To skip replacing this file (but continue with additional files, if any), click No. To cancel the copying operation, click Cancel.

Deleting Files and Directories

You can delete files or directories within your home directory, in which you possess the correct file ownership and permissions. If you try to delete files in most other directories, you'll see an alert box informing you that you are denied permission for this operation.

To delete one or more files or directories, do the following:

1.   In the Directory View, select the files or directories that you want to delete.

2.   Do one of the following:

Right-click the selection, and choose Delete.

or

From the File menu, choose Delete.

or

Press the Delete key.

NOTE In GNOME version 1.0, the Delete key may not function correctly when you use it to delete files. If you select a file and get no response when you press Delete, try logging out and logging in again so that GNOME and Enlightenment restart.

You'll see an alert box asking you to confirm the deletion.

3.   Click Yes to delete the files or directories, or click No to keep it.

CAUTION If you're deleting a directory that contains files or subdirectories, you'll see an alert box. You'll be asked whether you want to delete the directory contents recursively. This means that File Manager will delete all the files and directories within the selected directory. Because this command is very powerful and could do a lot of damage, you should not use it until you're more familiar with Linux and you're sure you know what you're doing.

Renaming Files and Directories

You can use two techniques to rename files or directories. The first technique, familiar to Mac OS and Windows users, enables you to edit the file name directory, but this technique works only in the Icons view. In other views, as well as Icons view, you can use the second technique, which requires you to display and edit the Properties box for the file or directory that you're renaming.

To rename a file or directory in the Icons view, do the following:

1. Select the file or directory that you want to rename.

2. Slowly double-click the file or directory's name. If you double-click too fast, you'll launch the file or open the directory. When you've performed the slow double-click successfully, File Manager will select the text of the name.

    Note that this renaming technique works only in Icons view and only within the Directory View window.

3. Edit the file name.

    CAUTION If the file has an extension (such as .pdf), do not change it. Otherwise, File Manager may not be able to determine which application created the file.

    ---

4. **Important:** When you are finished editing the file name, press Enter to confirm.

You can also rename a file by right-clicking the file and displaying the file's Properties dialog box (see Figure 9.7). Edit the text in the File Name box, and click OK. This technique works in the Brief, Detailed, and Custom views as well as the Icons view.

Creating Directories

To create a directory, follow these steps:

1. In the Tree View, select the directory within which you would like to create a new directory.

2. Click File on the menu bar, point to New, and choose Directory. You'll see the Create a New Directory dialog box.

3. Type a name for the new directory, and click OK.

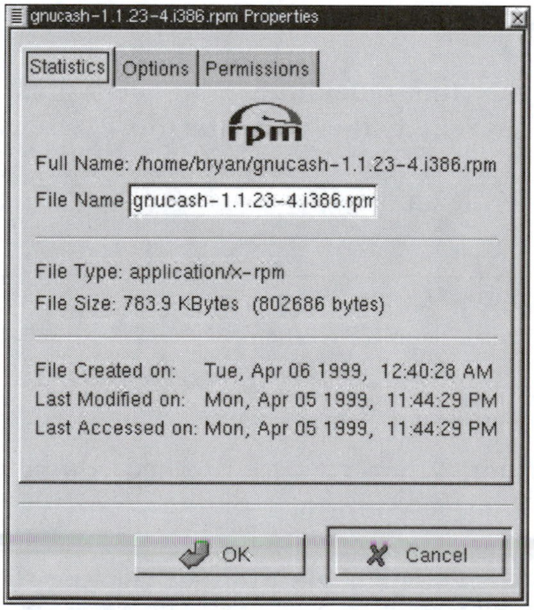

Figure 9.7 You can also rename a file by editing the file's Properties.

Finding Out What's in a File

Thanks to GNOME's ability to tell (in most cases) what kind of data a file contains, you can quickly view or listen to the contents of a file. GNOME will choose the file viewer that is associated by default with the type of data the file contains. To launch the default file viewer for a given type of file, just double-click the file's icon or name.

Listening to Audio Files

GNOME works with the EsounD daemon, which can play a wide variety of audio file formats (see Table 9.3 for a list of these formats). If a sound file is supported, you'll know this fact because the File Manager will display the file using the Audio file icon.

> **NOTE** To enable sound within GNOME, you must install your sound card (see "Configuring Your Sound Card," in Chapter 7), and you must also turn on GNOME by using the GNOME Control Panel (see "Enabling Sounds within GNOME," in Chapter 10).

To listen to an audio file, just double-click the sound file's icon or file name. The sound starts playing.

To gain more control over sounds, you may prefer to play them with a sound player application. Included in your Red Hat 6.0 installation is Xmms (formerly called X11 Amp), a sound player that looks like the popular WinAmp MP3 player (see Figure 9.8). However, Xmms can play just about any type of sound file; it can even play CDs. You can play files one at a time, or create playlists that enable you to listen to hours of beautiful music while you're working with your computer.

Xmms fully implements the popular *skins* feature of the Windows application. This feature enables you to change the look of the player by downloading skin packages from the Internet (for more information, see http://www.xmms.org).

TIP To hear sound on your system, you must install sound support (see "Configuring Sound Card Support," in Chapter 7), and you must also enable sound support within GNOME. To enable GNOME sound support, click the Main Menu button, point to Settings, and choose Multimedia. Click the General tab, if necessary, and activate GNOME sound support. Click OK to confirm.

Adjusting Sound Volume

To adjust sound listening volume, you can make use of the Audio Mixer. This GNOME application (also called gmix), shown in Figure 9.9, enables you to adjust the sound volume from all the sound sources in your system, including sounds from sound files, audio CDs, a microphone, and the sound card's line input. You can adjust the stereo balance, mute sources selectively, and adjust the tone.

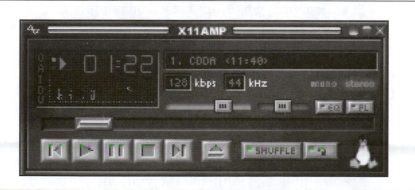

Figure 9.8 Xmms is a sound player for many types of sounds.

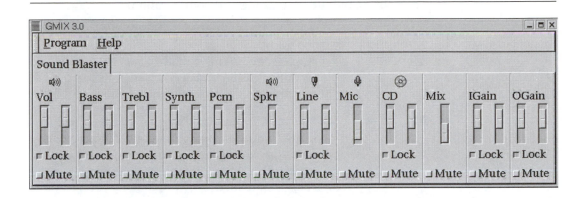

Figure 9.9 You can combine sound inputs with the Audio Mixer.

To use Audio Mixer, click the Main Menu icon, point to Multimedia, and choose Audio Mixer.

Are MP3s illegal?

Contrary to what you may have heard, the MP3 file format is *not* illegal. The notoriety of MP3s lies in the fact that thousands of illegal MP3 *recordings* of copyrighted music are available for downloading on the Internet. Too many Internet users seem to think there's nothing wrong with making MP3 recordings of copyrighted music and distributing these recordings. It is illegal, not to mention unethical, to distribute or download any recording of copyrighted music, whether such recordings are in the MP3 or some other format. Is it legal to make an MP3 recording, intended strictly for your own use on one computer system, of a copyrighted CD that you've lawfully obtained and paid for? Such a recording would appear to be legal under the provisions of the U.S. Audio Home Recording Act (Title 17, Chapter 10, of the U.S. Code), passed by both houses of Congress and signed into law by President Bush in October, 1992, as well as a 1984 U.S. Supreme Court decision that home videotaping does not constitute copyright infringement. Considering that audio CDs are expensive and highly vulnerable to damage due to scratches or heat exposure, consumers ought to be able to exercise their lawful rights to make archival backup copies of recorded music that they have lawfully obtained. For more information, see the home page of the Home Recording Rights Coalition (www.hrcc.org).

Table 9.3 Sound file formats (default configuration)

Format	Description
AIFF	**Apple sounds** This sound format enables sound recordings using a variety of sampling rates; quality varies, but can be very good.
AU	**Sun/NeXT sounds** Originally developed for UNIX workstations, this sound format enables sound recordings using a variety of sampling rates; most often, these are low-quality mono sounds intended for low-fidelity applications (such as providing a brief sample of a higher-quality sound that takes longer to download).
MOD	**Amiga sounds** Like MIDI sounds, MOD files contain a transcription of the notes to be played by a synthesizer. But they also contain samples of the synthesized sounds, so they're larger than MIDI files (but smaller than recorded sounds).
MP3	**MPEG Level 3 sounds** This sound recording format offers exceptionally high quality (CD audio quality) with excellent compression.
RAM	**Real Audio sounds** This sound recording format is generally used to enable real-time (streaming) delivery of low-quality sounds over the Internet.
S3M	**Amiga sounds** This format is a derivative of the Amiga MOV format.
SND	**Macintosh sounds** This sound format closely resembles the AIFF and WAV formats and is used for system and other sounds on Macs.
VOC	**Soundblaster sounds** A sound file recording format created by the makers of the Soundblaster sound cards. Infrequently used.
WAV	**Windows WAV sounds** Like AIFF sounds, this sound file format enables a variety of quality levels for recorded sounds; quality can be excellent, but WAV files are generally very large.

Viewing Compressed Files

The GNOME File Manager is configured to work with two types of compressed files:

- **gzip (gz) files** These compressed files are created with the gzip utility, a mainstay on UNIX and Linux systems. Files compressed with gzip are often stored in *archives* (a single file that contains two or more files) by using the tar utility (such files have the tar.gz extension).
- **WinZip (zip) files** These compressed files are popular in the Windows world. A zipped file may contain one compressed file or an archive containing two or more compressed files.

If you double-click a compressed file within File Manager, you'll see what appears to be a subdirectory, showing you the contents of the file. You can then double-click a file icon to view the contents of the file. Note that File Manager hasn't actually decompressed the file; the "subdirectory" that you're viewing is part of File Manager's *virtual file system (VFS)* capabilities, which enable the program to present certain types of data as if they were seamless extensions of the Linux file system.

To extract the files from a zip or tar archive and store the files in a subdirectory beneath the current directory, right-click the file's icon and choose Extract from the popup menu. If you would like to work with a tar.gz archive, turn to Chapter 12 and read the section titled, "Working with Compressed Files and Archives."

Using the Adobe Acrobat Viewer

The Portable Document Format (PDF), an Adobe-created file format, enables publishers to create documents that can be read on almost any type of computer, without sacrificing fonts or formatting. All that's needed is an PDF viewer. Red Hat Linux 6.0 comes with xpdf, a simple but useful PDF viewer that enables you to view and print PDF documents.

To view a PDF file, just double-click the file's icon. You'll see the xpdf viewer (Figure 9.10). At the bottom of the window, you'll see navigation controls that enable you to page through the document so that you can read it on-screen. To the right are controls that enable you to zoom the magnification, search for text within the file, or initiate printing.

Viewing PostScript Files

Files containing PostScript display instructions are commonly used in the UNIX and Linux worlds to distribute program

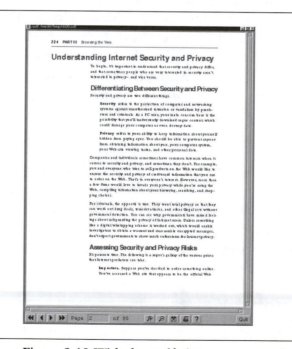

Figure 9.10 With the xpdf viewer, you can view and print Acrobat files.

documentation. Like Adobe Acrobat files, PostScript files contain fonts and layout information that enable you to view and print formatted documents. If you double-click a PostScript file (a file with the ps extension), you'll see gv, the default PostScript viewer (see Figure 9.11). The gv application is quite complex, but it's easy to use it to view or print a PostScript file, such as the "Frequently Asked Questions" document displayed in Figure 9.11. To view the document, just click the page number in the left column, or adjust the slider bar. To print the entire document, click Print All.

Using the Text Viewer

If you right-click a text file and choose View, you'll see the document's text displayed in the default text file viewer (see Figure 9.12). With the text viewer, you can view the contents

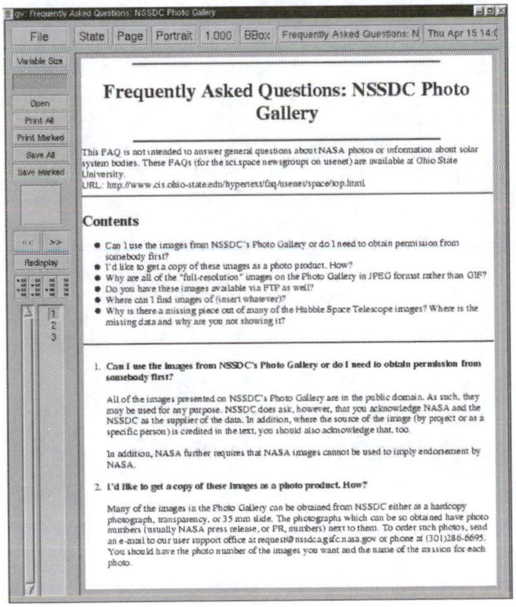

Figure 9.11 The default PostScript viewer enables you to view and print.

of text files—but you can't change the text. That's a good thing if you're viewing a file that turns out to contain crucial configuration settings (such as the one in Figure 9.12); you shouldn't change these settings unless you're sure you know what you're doing.

In the text viewer, you can do the following:

- **Find text** To find text in the file, click Search on the menu bar, and choose Find. (You can also use the F6 keyboard shortcut.) In the Search dialog box, type a word to match, and click OK. To repeat the search, click Search on the menu bar, and choose Find Again. (You can also use the Shift + F6 keyboard shortcut.)
- **Search with regular expressions (regexp)** *Regular expressions* conform to a standard text-matching format that

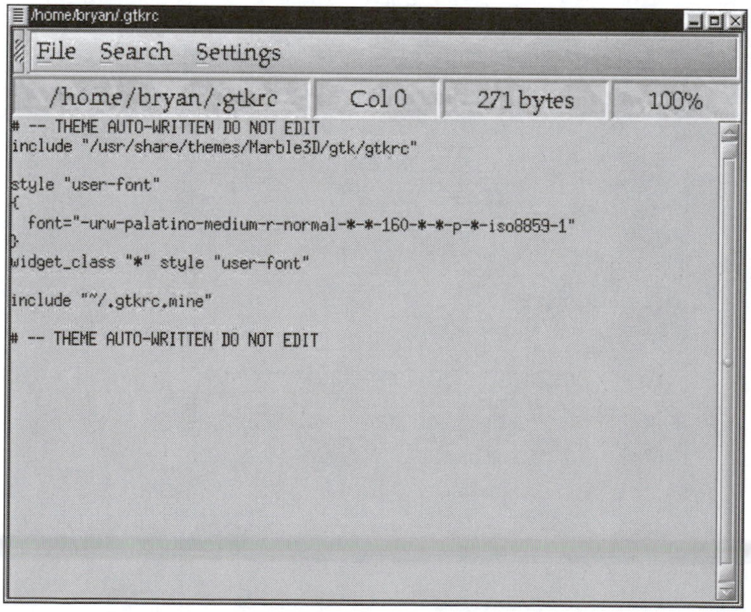

Figure 9.12 The default text editor enables you to view text files.

enables you to use wildcards and other advanced search operators. If you know how to write regular expressions, you can perform more advanced searches than the Find dialog box allows. To perform a regexp search, click Search on the menu bar, and choose Regexp search. In the Enter regexp box, type the regular expression, and choose OK.

- **Change View Options** By default, the text viewer displays text with word wrapping (lengthy lines are shortened and wrapped down to the next line so that you can view all lines lengths within the current window). It also displays text with formatting. You can turn these options off, if you wish. If you're viewing a binary file rather than a text file, you can enable the hex view. To choose view options, click Settings on the menu bar, and check or uncheck the options you want.

TIP To change the default text editor, click the Main Menu button, point to Settings, and choose GNOME Control Center. Select Gnome Edit Properties. In the Gnome Editor list box, click the down arrow to reveal the list of available editors. Choose an editor, and click OK.

Using the Graphics Viewer

To view any file that has a graphics file icon (one that indicates the type of graphics file, such as xbm, jpg, png, or gif), just double-click the file icon. (For a list of the graphics file formats that Electric Eyes can handle, see Table 9.4.) You'll see the Electric Eyes viewer, shown in Figure 9.13. The viewer appears simple on the surface, but there's a great deal of functionality hidden beneath.

To begin exploring Electric Eyes' capabilities, right-click the image background. You'll see a pop-up menu with several

options: File, View, Crop Selection, Save Settings, and Quit.
From the File menu, you can choose Open, Save As, Print, and
Set as Desktop Background. You can also view other graphics
files that you've opened in the list window by clicking Next
image, Previous image, Last image, or First image.

If you click View on the pop-up menu, you'll see options for
displaying the Edit window (which enables you to change the
size or color characteristics of the image), and the List window
(which enables you to open one or more files, including all the
files in a given directory, and view them in a list format with
thumbnail graphics). You can also display a tool bar, or toggle
a display mode with vertical and horizontal scroll bars.

Figure 9.13 Electric Eyes can display many types of graphics files.

Table 9.4 Graphics file formats supported by Electric Eyes

Format	Description
BMP	**Microsoft Windows graphics file format** Good quality, but the files are large.
GIF	**CompuServe Graphics Interchange Format** Limited to 256 colors; includes a patented compression algorithm that requires makers of graphics software to pay royalties.
JPEG	**Joint Photographic Experts Group (JPEG)** Best for complex images; can display millions of colors. Incorporates a significant compression algorithm that reduces file size.
PPM	**Portable Pixmap** A simple graphics format for icons.
PNG	**Portable Network Graphics (PNG)** A bitmap graphics file format intended as a replacement for GIF graphics; the compression algorithm is in the public domain.
RAS	**Sun Rasterfile** A Sun Microsystems bitmap file format.
RGB	**Silicon Graphics RGB** A Silicon Graphics bitmap file format.
TIFF	**Tagged Image File Format (TIFF)** An older bitmap graphics format that includes compression and supports grayscale as well as color.
XBM	**X11 Bitmap** The standard X11 bitmap file format, widely used in the UNIX world.
XPM	**X11 Pixmap** The standard X11 file format for icons.

Viewing Videos

If you double-click a file containing an animation or video, you'll see xanim, the default movie viewer. You view the movie or animation in one window; in another, you can use the VCR-like controls to start viewing, pause, rewind, or adjust the sound volume. The xanim application can work with the video file formats listed in Table 9.5.

Table 9.5 Animation and video formats supported by Xanim

Format	Description
AVI	**Microsoft Windows movies** These movies offer good quality and can include sound, but they take up a lot of storage space.
FLC/FLI	**Autodesk animations** This format does not offer the quality of AVI, MPEG, or QuickTime, but file sizes are relatively small.
GIF89a	**GIF animations** These are a series of bitmap pictures that are displayed fast enough to create the illusion of animation.
IFF	**Interchange File Format** Similar to AVI, but designed for use on UNIX systems.
MPG	**Motion Picture Experts Group (MPEG)** A high quality movie format with good compression. MPEG movies can include sound.
MOV	**Apple QuickTime** Perhaps the best movie file format; offers good compression and can include stereo sound.
SGI	**Silicon Graphics movies** A movie format developed for Silicon Graphics workstations.

Finding Files

Looking for an elusive file? Don't go blind hunting for the file manually. You can use File Manager's Find File command to find a file quickly. If you need more sophisticated search capabilities, you'll find what you're looking for in the GNOME Search Tool.

Finding Files with the Find File Command

To find a file quickly, use the Find File command within the File Manager. Do the following:

1. On the File Manager's menu bar, click Command, and point to Find File. You'll see the Find File dialog box, shown in Figure 9.14. Note that the Start at box contains a period, a symbol for the current directory. Also note that the Filename box contains an asterisk, which matches any file name.

2. In the Start at box, type the name of the directory where you wish to begin the search. By default, the Find File command will search all the subdirectories within this directory.

3. In the Filename box, type the name of the file you're searching for. To search for all the files that conform to a pattern, you can use wildcards. For example, to search for Adobe Acrobat (pdf) files, type *.**pdf**.

4. If you would like Find File to search the content of files for text you specify, type the text in the Content box.

5. Click OK to begin the search. You'll see the dialog box shown in Figure 9.15. If Find File locates one or more

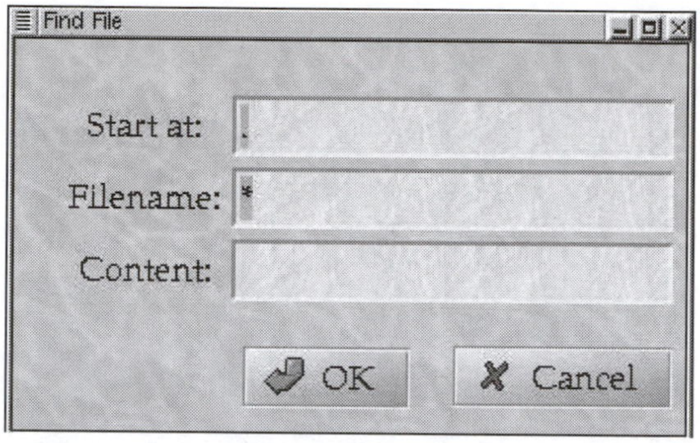

Figure 9.14 Find a file quickly with the Find File command.

matching files, you'll see the file name and location in the list.

6. Do one of the following:

Select a file, and click Change to this directory. You'll see the directory in which the file is contained

or

Click Search again to try the search again, using different matching criteria

or

Click OK to close the Find File dialog box.

Finding Files with the GNOME Search Tool

The GNOME Search Tool provides many more options than the Find File command, although this fact isn't obvious when you first launch the utility. To start the Search Tool, click the Main Menu button, point to Utilities, and choose GNOME Search Tool. You'll see the GNOME Search Tool dialog box

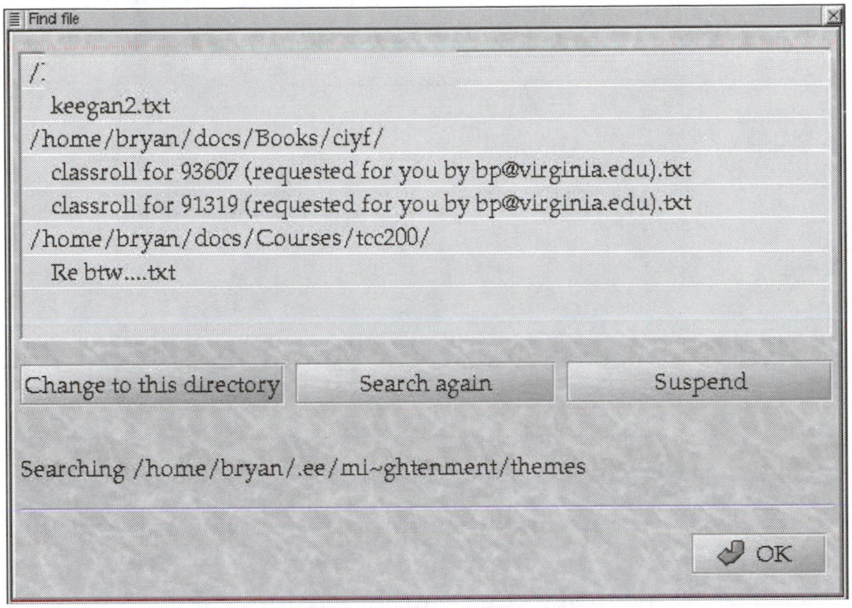

Figure 9.15 If Find File locates a match, you'll see it in this list.

(see Figure 9.16). Like the Find File command within File Manager, the Search Tool enables you to specify the starting directory; by default, it's the current directory (symbolized by the single period). But the Search Tool gives you many ways to refine your search. In the list box at the bottom, you can choose from any of the following search criteria

- **File name** This is the default search criterion. Specify an exact file name or use wildcards to type a matching pattern.
- **Don't search subdirectories** Choose this option to prevent the Search Tool from searching all the subdirectories beneath the directory specified in the Start in directory box.
- **Empty file** Choose this option if you're trying to find a file that contains no data.

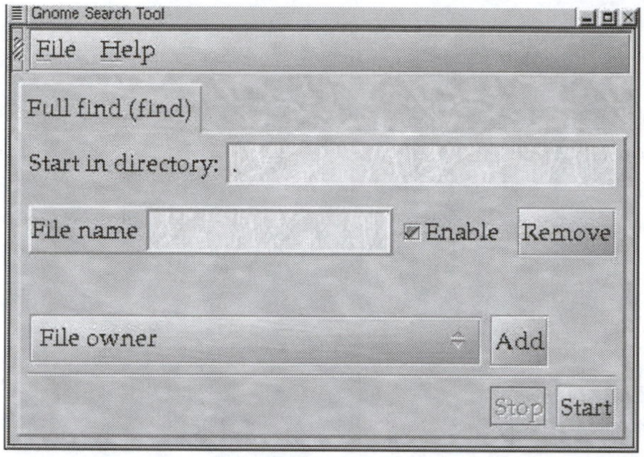

Figure 9.16 The Search Tool looks simple, but it is very powerful.

- **Last modification time** Choose this option to specify the date of last modification.
- **Don't search mounted filesystems** Choose this option to exclude floppy disks, CD-ROM disks, and other filesystems that you have mounted in this session.
- **File owner** Choose this option to specify the user name of the file's owner.
- **Invalid user or group** Choose this option to search for files that have misconfigured file ownership.
- **Filenames except** Choose this option to exclude certain filenames from the search. You can use wildcards.
- **Simple substring search** Choose this option to search for one or more characters within a filename, but without having to use wildcards.
- **Regular expression search and Extended regular expression search** Choose these options only if you know how to write perl *regular expressions* (search expressions using complex search operators).

To add a search criterion, select the criterion in the list box, and click Add. As you click Add, the Search Tool adds search criteria, serving to refine the search (see Figure 9.17). When you've finished choosing criteria, click Start; you'll see the results of the search in the Search Results dialog box. Click Clear to clear the search results and search again, or click Close to stop searching.

Creating Symbolic Links

In Microsoft Windows and Mac OS, you can create *shortcuts* or *aliases* for a file. The shortcut or alias looks like a file, but it is really just a pointer to a file that is present elsewhere on your computer. In Linux, such pointers are called *symbolic links*.

You can create a symbolic link quickly by dragging a file icon to the desktop. (This accomplishes much the same thing as

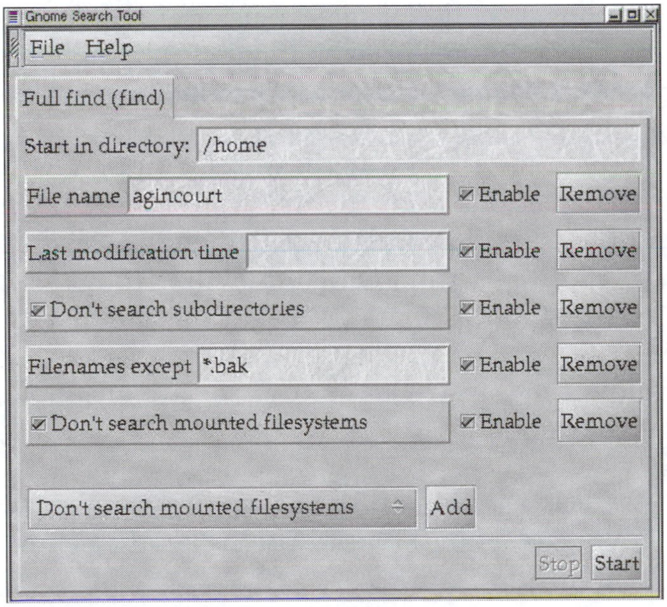

Figure 9.17 You can build complex search expressions with Search Tool.

creating a desktop shortcut in Microsoft Windows.) The original file stays where it is; what's created is a shortcut (a symbolic link).

To create a symbolic link manually, right-click the icon of the file to which you would like to link, and choose Symlink from the pop-up menu. In the Symbolic Link dialog box, you'll see the name of the file that is the destination of the link (the one you selected). In the Symbolic link filename box, type the name of the symbolic link you want to create, and click OK.

Associating File Types with Applications

As you learned earlier in this chapter, File Manager determines the file type by examining the file's extension, the portion of the file name that comes after the period. (Not all files have extensions, however.) When you double-click a file, File Manager consults a list of file extensions, and determines whether an application has been configured to handle this type of file. If so, File Manager launches the application.

After you install new applications, you may wish to associate their extensions with the application. For example, suppose you've installed WordPerfect 8.0, and you would like to associate this application with *.doc files. To do so, use the Mime Type page of the GNOME Control Center (see Figure 9.20).

Follow these instructions to associate an application with a given extension:

1. Click the Main Menu button, point to Settings, and choose Mime Types. You'll see the Mime Types page, shown in Figure 9.18.

2. If the Mime Type list already contains an entry for the type of data this application can handle, skip to step 4. Otherwise, click Add. You'll see the Add Mime Type dialog box.

3. In the Mime Type box, type an identifier for the type of data the file contains. For example, to identify WordPerfect data, type **application/xwp**. In the Extensions box, type the extension the application uses (for example, **.doc**). Don't forget the period. Click OK to confirm.

4. In the Mime Type list, select the application's data type.

5. Click Edit. You'll see the Set Actions for application dialog box.

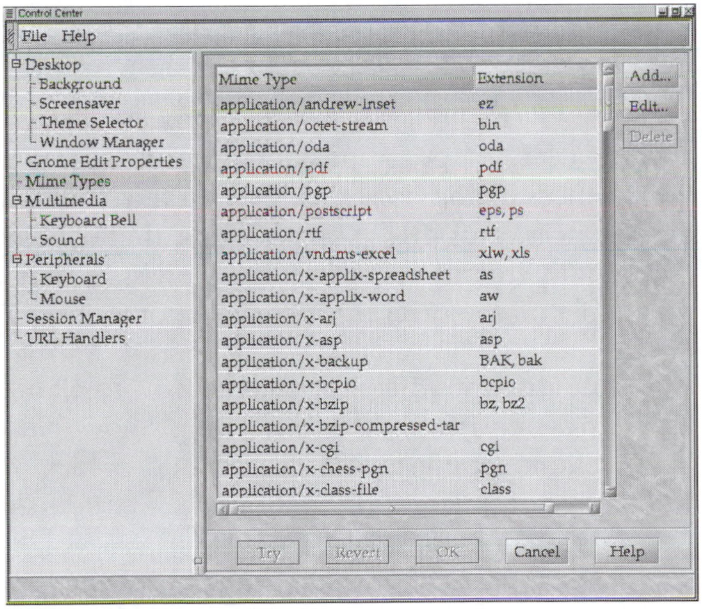

Figure 9.18 Here, you can associate file types with applications.

6. In the Open box, type the exact command you use to launch the application that handles the data (such as xwp for WordPerfect), followed by a space and **%f** (this expression tells the program to open the data file that you double-clicked).

7. In the View box, type the exact command you use to launch an application capable of viewing the data in the file, if you wish.

8. In the Edit box, type the exact command you use to launch a text editor, if you would like to be able to edit the file independently of the application that creates the data. This isn't recommended if the data is something other than plain text.

9. Click OK to confirm.

Choosing File Manager Preferences

File Manager's Preferences dialog box enables you to choose a wide variety of program configuration options. To view the Preferences dialog box, click Edit on the menu bar, and choose Preferences. This dialog box has tabs that enable you to access several different types of settings. Here's a brief guide to what's available on the several pages of options:

- **File display** This page enables you to change default settings for file display, including Show backup files (the default setting is off), Show hidden files (off), Mix files and directories (off), and Use shell patterns instead of regular expressions (on).
- **Confirmation** Here you can choose whether to see confirmation dialog boxes when you perform potentially destructive actions: Confirm when deleting file (on), Con-

firm when overwriting files (on), Confirm when executing files (off), and Show progress while operations are being performed (on).

- **VFS** In this page, you can choose options for virtual file systems, including the time before concluding that a remote service isn't available. You can also specify an anonymous FTP password.

- **Caching** This page controls options for File Manager's disk cache, which helps the program speed file operations. You can choose Fast directory reload (off), Computing totals before copying files (on), and Allow customization of icons in icon view. You can also specify a timeout for the FTP directory cache, in case a connection isn't available.

- **Desktop** Here, you choose options for the desktop display. You can choose Use shaped icons (on), Auto place icons (off), and Snap icons to grid (off).

- **Custom View** In this page, you can choose the columns that you would like to appear when you click the Custom view option. From the Possible Columns list, select a column to display, and click Add. To remove a column, select the column in the Displayed Columns list, and click Remove.

Understanding File Ownership and Permissions

Because Linux is a multi-user operating system, it's important that some files are accessible to every user, while others—particularly configuration and password files—are accessible only to the system administrator. In addition, users need to be given full access to their own files, while such access should be restricted or prevented entirely for other users.

For these reasons, every Linux file is stored with *attributes* (settings) that define the following:

- **File ownership** A file is owned by the person who creates it. When you create a file in your home directory, you are the owner, and you automatically have permission to read and alter this file. However, your rights to read or alter files outside your home directory may be restricted.
- **Permissions** A file's *permissions* specify just who can do what with the file. For a given type of user, permissions specify whether the user can read the file, write to the file (including deleting the file), or execute the file (if it is an executable file).

The following sections explain these concepts in more detail; subsequently, you'll learn how to adjust file ownership and permissions with File Manager.

Types of Files

Linux defines the following categories of file owners:

- **User** The user who owns the file. Normally, this is the person who created the file, but the root user (system administrator) can change file ownership, as explained in Chapter 15.
- **Group** When you create user accounts, you can place two or more users into a *group*. Groups are very useful when two or more people need to work on the same file or within the same directory.
- **Others** This category includes all other users *except* the user and group.

Types of Permissions

For each type of file owner, you can define the following permissions:

- **Read** Determines whether a given category of users can read a file.
- **Write** Determines whether a given category of users can alter a file (including deleting the file).
- **Execute** Determines whether a given category of users can launch (execute) a program or script. Applied to directories, this term is equivalent to directory access.

NOTE Executable (program) files have two additional permission types called *set userid (Set UID)* and *set group userid (Set GUID)*. Of use to system administrators, these permissions specify that the program will start with the permissions available to the owner of the file. This is often a very useful feature (and sometimes it is essential for security reasons). For example, suppose you've installed Word-Perfect for Linux 8.0, and you want to make a public document directory available for all users. So you create a user account called wp. You also create a directory called /home/wp. When users start WordPerfect, the program runs so that everyone has access to the documents in /home/wp.

Examining and Changing Ownership and Permissions

As the owner of all the files within your home directory, you can change the ownership and permissions of any of these files. However, you cannot adjust the ownership or permissions of files outside your home directory, unless you have specifically set up your system to give users this right—which isn't a very good idea. One of the basic reasons for creating user accounts is to prevent users from making a mess of permissions outside their home directories.

To view a file's ownership and permissions, right-click the file icon or name of a file within your home directory, and choose Properties from the pop-up menu. You'll see the Properties dialog box. Click the Permissions tab. You'll see the Permissions page, shown in Figure 9.19. You see the current file permissions and ownership settings in the two areas.

In the Permissions area, you can change the permissions for any owner type, including User (that's you, if you're looking at a file in your home directory), Group, and Other.

In the File ownership area, you see the current file owners. (You can't change the file's owner to anyone but yourself, but you can change the Group owner.)

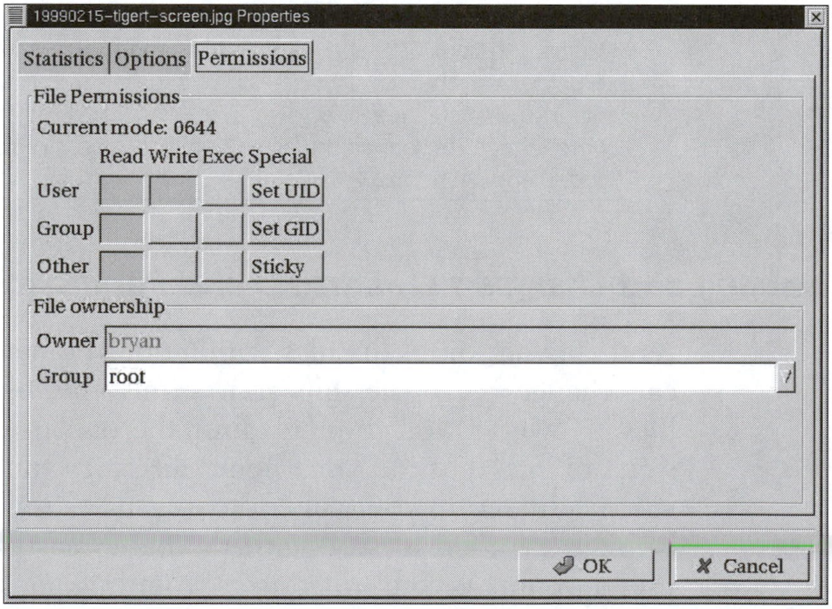

Figure 9.19 The Properties dialog box displays permissions and ownership.

> **TIP** In the Properties dialog box, you will see that the file's permissions are summed up by a number, such as 0644 (this number is found after Current Mode). For more information on what these numbers mean, see "Changing File Ownership and Permissions," in Chapter 15.

Here are some suggestions for ways you can adjust file ownership and permissions within your home directory:

- To prevent anyone but yourself from viewing the files within your home directory, click the home directory (/home) folder within the Tree View. In the Directory View, select your home directory folder icon (mine is /home/bryan). Right-click the icon, choose Properties, and click Permissions. Deactivate all permissions for Group and Other. In the File ownership area, choose None.
- To enable another user to have write access to a file within your home directory, create a group and assign yourself and the other user to this group. (For information on creating groups, see Chapter 12.) Then use the Properties dialog box within File Manager to give write permission to the group. (Make sure that your home directory gives this group permission to read files within the directory; otherwise, the other user won't be able to open your home directory.)

> **TIP** When you log in as root user to perform system maintenance (see Chapter 12), avoid copying or moving any files to your home directory. If you do, you will find that you may not be able to write or execute these files after you logout and login using your user account! If you've messed up the permissions of files within your home directory, log in as root user and use the Properties dialog box to change the file ownership back to your user account.

Switching to Superuser Status

If you've used Unix or Linux previously, you know that it's possible to switch to *superuser* status without logging out of your user account. Superuser status gives you all the privileges of the root user, including the ability to modify file ownership and permissions outside the root directory. Superuser status can come in very handy when you need to make some small change to a configuration file outside your home directory. However, the File Manager does not enable you to switch to superuser status. Such access would leave security holes open that a knowledgeable system intruder could exploit.

To switch to superuser status, you'll need to open a terminal user and use the text-mode commands that give you superuser access. For more information on these commands, see Chapter 15. You can then use text-mode commands (see Chapter 15) or the text-mode version of File Manager, called Midnight Commander (see Chapter 16), to modify files outside your home directory.

You can accomplish the same by logging out of your user account and logging in as the root user. When you're running File Manager as root, you can open and modify files anywhere on your system.

CAUTION Please don't modify files outside your home directory unless you're absolutely sure you know what you're doing. It's quite easy to make some small change to a configuration file that will degrade your system's functionality—or at the extreme, render it so unstable that you will not be able to access your files!

Accessing Disk Drives

If you configured your system so that users can access disk drives (see Chapter 7), you'll see disk drive icons on the left side of your screen. Try right-clicking one of these icons. You'll see a pop-up menu that enables you to do the following:

- **Open** This option mounts the disk, if necessary, and displays the disk's contents in File Manager.
- **Mount** This option mounts the disk, but without opening a File Manager window. If the disk is already mounted, this option is called Unmount.
- **Eject** If the device uses ejectable media (such as a Zip disk or a CD-ROM), you can choose this option to unmount the drive and eject the disk.

TIP If you don't see the disk drive options, right-click the desktop background, and choose Recreate Desktop Shortcuts. If you still don't see them, you need to configure your system so that users can access disk drives, as explained in Chapter 7.

From Here

Now that you've mastered the fundamentals of the GNOME File Manager, you're ready to choose your preferences for the way GNOME works. Find out how in the next chapter.

10

Personalizing GNOME

Windows and Mac OS users enjoy personalizing their systems. They choose a default desktop font, paint their displays with a cool background graphic, and assign sounds to system events, such as the *Star Trek* door sound when they open or close a window. Customization options such as these aren't all fun and games, of course. Anyone with impaired vision will appreciate being able to enlarge the default desktop font, for example. Thanks to GNOME, desktop customization is now available for Linux users. This chapter shows you how to customize the GNOME environment.

> **CAUTION** Please remember that you should not use GNOME as the root user. Customize GNOME's appearance within your user account.

Understanding GNOME Customization

As you've already learned, GNOME enables you to work with more than one window manager. By default, your Red Hat 6.0 installation enables you to work with either of two GNOME-compatible window managers, Window Maker or Enlightenment (the default). Both of these offer some features that duplicate GNOME desktop configuration options, such as the ability to choose a background graphic. Although the ability to define such options in two different ways reflects the Unix philosophy of giving users a choice, it can also prove confusing to new users.

Here's a simple solution: If a customization option is available in both the window manager and GNOME, define it within GNOME. GNOME works best when the window manager is restricted to a limited set of functions (such as defining the appearance of window borders).

To customize GNOME, you can do the following:

- **Customize the GNOME Environment** using the GNOME Control Center. You can choose backgrounds, enable a screen saver, choose a theme, select a window manager, choose a default text editor, specify MIME types, specify the sound of the keyboard bell, assign sounds to specific system events, and choose options for your mouse and keyboard.

- **Customize the GNOME Panels** by adding applets, drawers within panels, additional panels, and application launchers.
- **Customize the GNOME Menus** using the GNOME Menu Editor.
- **Choose additional customization options in your window manager,** such as Enlightenment. You should choose only those options that do not conflict with GNOME's options.

Because there are so many GNOME customization options, the next section surveys the options that most users will want to learn. You can read the rest of the chapter to learn additional ways you can customize GNOME.

Top Customization Options

You'll probably want to perform some or all of the top customization options discussed in this section. In the following, you'll learn how to add a logout button to the Panel so you can log out without choosing Logout from the menu. You'll also learn how to add application launchers and disk drive mount/unmount buttons to the Panel, and how to modify Enlightenment's focus behaviors so that it works more like Mac OS or Microsoft Windows.

Adding a Logout Button

To exit GNOME, you click the Main Menu button and choose Log Out. But there's an easier way. You can add a Log Out button to the Panel by following these steps:

1.   Click the Main Menu button.

2.   Point to Panel.

3.   From the submenu, choose Add log out button.

You'll see the Log Out button on the Panel. Now you can log out by clicking this button.

Adding an Application Launcher

If you would like to run an installed application that is not listed anywhere on the Main Menu, you can click the Main Menu button and choose Run Program. In the Run Program dialog box, you can type the name of the program, or click Browse to look for its exact name and location. You click Run to launch the application.

For applications you'll run frequently, you may want to create an application launcher button, located on the Panel. You'll need to know the exact command you type to start the program. For example, to start WordPerfect 8.0 for Linux, you type **/usr/local/wp8/wpbin/xwp** (assuming WordPerfect is installed in the /usr/local/wp8/wpbin directory).

To do so, follow these steps:

1.   Click the Main Menu button.

2.   Point to Panel.

3.   Choose Add new launcher. You'll see the Create launcher applet dialog box, shown in Figure 10.1.

4.   Click the Basic tab, if necessary.

5.   In the Name box, type the program's name (such as WordPerfect or The Gimp).

6.   In the Comment box, type a comment, if you wish. (This is optional.)

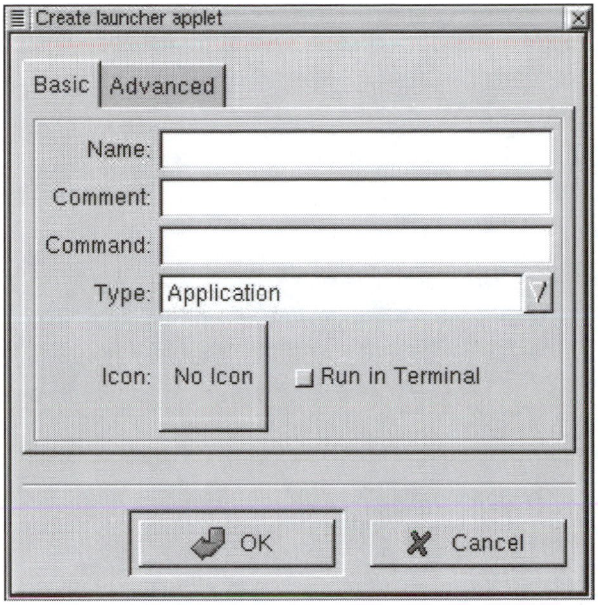

Figure 10.1 Use Create launcher to add an application icon.

7. In the Command box, type the command you use to start
    the program.

8. In the Type list box, leave the Type set to Application.

9. Click the button next to Icon. You'll see the Choose an
    icon dialog box, shown in Figure 10.2.

    By default, you see the icons available in the
    /usr/share/pixmaps directory. Your application may have
    its own icon; click the Browse button see whether your
    application has a directory in /usr/share; if so, look inside
    to see if there's an icon file.

10. Select the icon you want, and click OK.

Figure 10.2 GNOME comes with lots of application icons you can use.

11. Click OK to confirm your choices and exit the Create launcher applet dialog box.

You'll see the new application launcher on the Panel. To launch the application, just click the application's button.

TIP To add an application launcher quickly, use the File Manager to locate the application (look in /usr/bin), and drag the application's icon to the Panel. When you've positioned the pointer where you want the application launcher to appear, release the mouse button. You'll see the Create launcher applet dialog box, with the application's correct name and location already filled in. Locate an icon for the button, and click OK.

Adding Drive Mount Buttons to Panels

GNOME automatically detects mountable disk drives, including floppy drives and CD-ROM drives, and creates folders for these drives on your desktop.

> **TIP** If you don't see the drive folders, your system may not be configured to enable users to access drives. To fix this problem, see Chapter 7.

As explained in Chapter 9, you can open, mount, and unmount disk drives by right-clicking the drive icons on the desktop. However, you may wish to add drive mount buttons to your Panel. Once you've done so, you'll be able to mount and unmount drives without having to display the desktop, which might not be visible if you've opened application windows.

Begin by adding a floppy drive mount button, which is the default disk drive icon. Continue by adding icons for additional drives, such as Zip drives and CD-ROM drives. As you'll see, these icons look like floppy disk icons by default, but you can change the icon (and the drive assigned to the icon) by changing the icon's properties. Let's get started with a floppy disk icon.

To add a floppy disk mount button to the Panel, follow these steps:

1. Click the Main Menu button, point to Panel, point to Add applet, point to Utility, and choose Drive Mount.

    You'll see the floppy disk mount button on the Panel.

2.   To mount the disk, just click the button. Click it again to unmount the disk, and note the difference in the way the button appears.

TIP If you're not sure whether the drive has been mounted, move the pointer to the disk drive mount button.

To add mount buttons for other drives, follow these steps:

1.   Determine the mount point for the disk drive that you're adding.

     To determine the mount point, start File Manager, click the /mnt directory, and look for the directory corresponding to your disk drive. If you're creating a CD-ROM mount button, the correct mount point is probably /mnt/cdrom.

2.   Add an additional floppy disk mount button by following the instructions just given.

3.   On the Panel, right-click the floppy disk mount button you just added, and choose Properties.

     You'll see the Drive Mount Settings dialog box, shown in Figure 10.3.

4.   In the Icon list box, choose an icon. You can choose from Floppy, Cdrom, Zip Drive, or Hard Disk.

5.   In the Mount point box, type the drive's mount point.

6.   Click OK to confirm your choices.

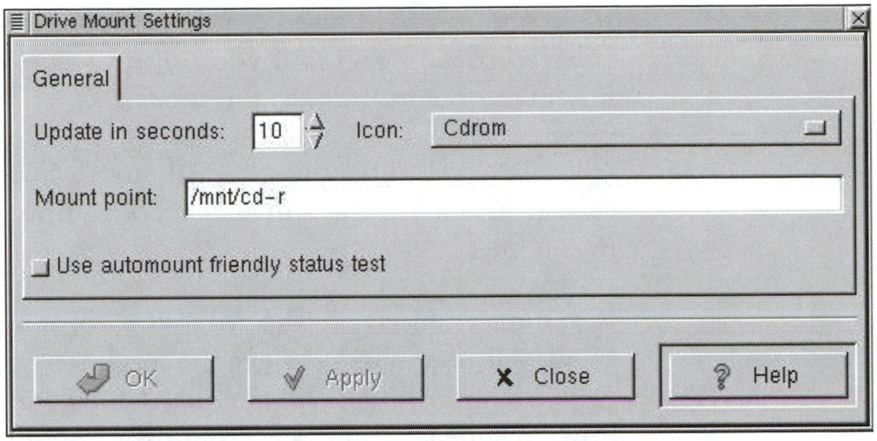

Figure 10.3 In this dialog box, you can define a drive mount button.

Adjusting Window Focus Behaviors

If you're used to the way that Microsoft Windows and Mac OS automatically activate and raise a new window, you may wish to change Enlightenment's default window behavior settings. Without activating these options, you'll have to click within the window before you can type in the window's text box.

To change the default window behavior settings, follow these steps:

1. Click the Main Menu button, point to Settings, point to Desktop, and choose Window Manager. You'll see the GNOME Control Center with the Window Manager page displayed.

2. Click Run Configuration Tool for Enlightenment. You'll see the Enlightenment Configuration Editor.

3. In the list of options, click Basic Options. In the Keyboard
    focus area, click Mouse Pointer. (This will change Enlight-
    enment's defaults so that you do not need to click within
    a window before it takes the focus.)

4. Click Behavior, and click the Advanced Focus tab, if nec-
    essary. You'll see the Advanced Focus options, as shown
    in Figure 10.4.

5. If necessary, activate the following options by clicking
    them: All new windows get the keyboard focus, All new
    popup windows get the keyboard focus, and Raise win-
    dows when switching focus with the keyboard.

6. Click Miscellaneous, and enable Automatic raising of
    windows after X seconds, and adjust the time interval, if

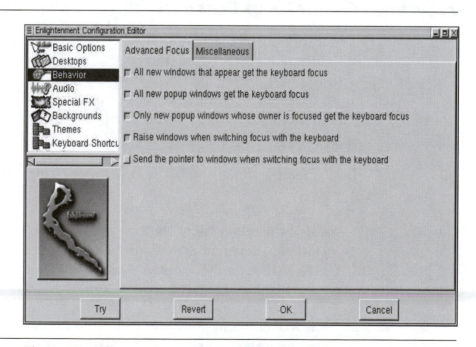

Figure 10.4 These options automatically move the focus to new windows.

you wish. Also enable the option called Switch to where pop-up window appears.

7. Click OK until you see the desktop again.

TIP Are you bothered by the screen switching to another desktop area when the mouse pointer gets close to the window edge? You can disable this feature. To do so, click Desktops within the Enlightenment Configuration Editor, and deactivate the Enable option in the Edge flip resistance area.

Decorating Your Desktop

If you enjoy customizing your computer's on-screen appearance, you'll love GNOME. You can choose background colors and graphics, select from dozens of neat screen savers, assign sounds to system events, and much more. The following sections detail the various ways you can customize GNOME.

Choosing a Background Color

You can paint your desktop with one solid color, or you can choose two different colors and specify a gradient between them (vertical or horizontal).

To choose a background color, follow these steps:

1. Do one of the following:

   Right-click the desktop background, and choose Configure Background Image from the pop-up menu.

   or

Click the Main Menu button, point to Settings, point to Desktop, and choose Background.

or

Click the GNOME configuration tool button on the Panel, and click Background when the Control Center appears.

You'll see Background page of the Control Center, as shown in Figure 10.5.

2. To choose a single, solid color, click the color box next to Color 1, within the Color area. You'll see the Pick a color dialog box, shown in Figure 10.6.

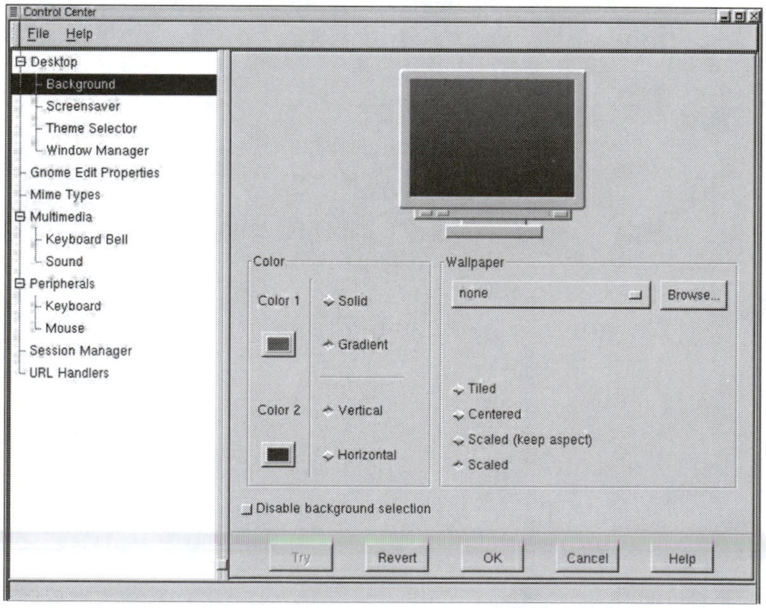

Figure 10.5 You can choose a color or graphic for the desktop.

3. Choose a color by clicking within the color wheel. You can also choose colors by dragging the slider bars or typing values in the text boxes.

4. Click OK to confirm your Color 1 choice.

5. If you would like to choose a second color and enable the gradient option, click Gradient, click the color box next to Color 2, choose a color, and click OK. Select Vertical or Horizontal to control the direction of the gradient.

6. Click OK to confirm your color choice.

Choosing Wallpaper

To add a background graphic (wallpaper) to your desktop, follow these steps:

1. Do one of the following:

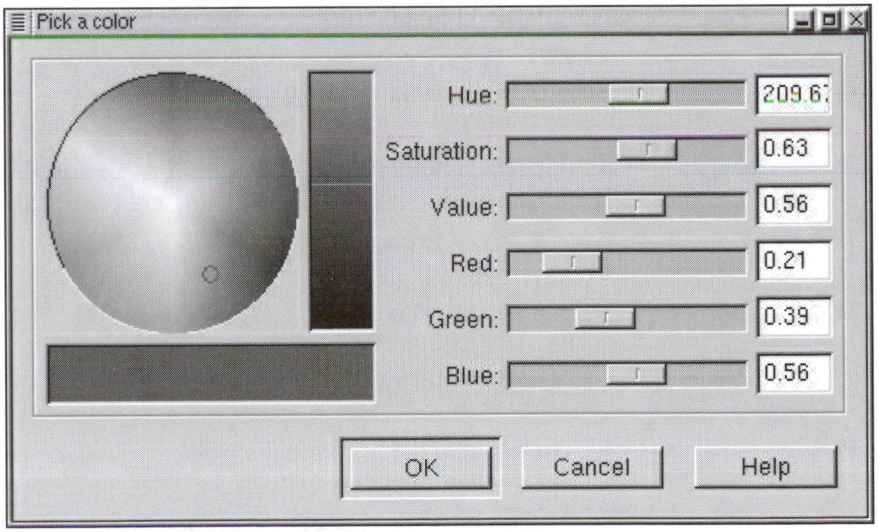

Figure 10.6 Identify your remote (network) printer here.

Right-click the desktop background, and choose Configure Background Image from the pop-up menu.

or

Click the Main Menu button, point to Settings, point to Desktop, and choose Background.

or

Click the GNOME configuration tool button on the Panel, and click Background when the Control Center appears.

You'll see Background page of the Control Center, as shown in Figure 10.5. Enlarge the dialog box, if necessary.

2. In the Wallpaper area, click the Browse button. You'll see the Wallpaper Selection dialog box, shown in Figure 10.7. If necessary, use the Directories list box to display the contents of /usr/share/pixmaps/backgrounds. Figure 10.7 shows the contents of the /usr/share/pixmaps/backgrounds/Propaganda directory.

3. To view a preview of a wallpaper file, click the file's name. If the file can be used as wallpaper, you'll see a preview in the Preview area.

4. Select the file you want to use as wallpaper.

5. Click OK to confirm the file selection.

6. In the Control Center, choose one of the following options within the Wallpaper area: Tiled (repeated across the screen), Centered (centered on the screen),

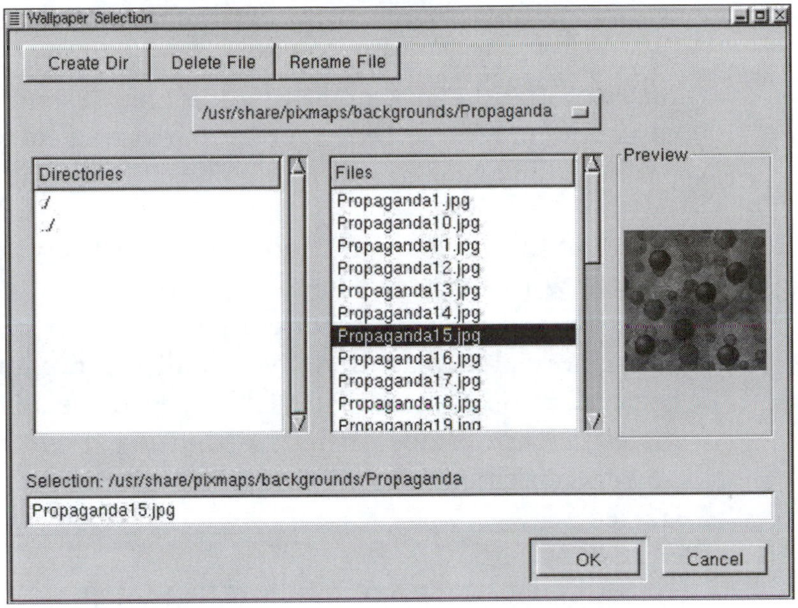

Figure 10.7 Choose a wallpaper from the many patterns provided.

Scaled–Keep Aspect (with the graphic's aspect ratio preserved, or Scaled (expanded to fill the whole screen).

7. Click OK to confirm your wallpaper choice.

TIP You can also choose wallpaper using drag-and-drop. Open the File Manager, and display the directory containing a graphic you would like to use as wallpaper. Then open the Control Center, and click Background, if necessary, to display the background options. Drag the graphic's file to the monitor icon within the Control Center, and release the mouse button.

Enabling a Screen Saver

A screen saver kicks in after you've left your computer alone for a specified number of minutes. The screen saver displays a graphic or video that blanks out the normal screen display. Although screen savers are no longer necessary to prevent monitor damage thanks to improvements in monitor design, they do offer the advantage of additional system security: You can configure the screen saver so that you must type your user password in order to restore the normal display.

With GNOME, you can choose from a variety of nifty screen savers. What's more, you can specify when the screen saver kicks in, and you can require a password for regaining entry to the normal display. If you've installed Linux on a notebook computer, you can configure GNOME to use advanced power management options, including shutting down the monitor's power a specified number of minutes after the screen saver has started.

To turn on a screen saver, follow these steps:

1. Do one of the following:

    Click the Main Menu button, point to Settings, point to Desktop, and choose Screen saver.

    or

    Click the GNOME configuration tool button on the Panel, and click Screen saver when the Control Center appears.

    You'll see the Control Center, with the screen saver options displayed (see Figure 10.8). If necessary, enlarge the dialog box so that you can see all the options.

2. In the Screen Saver list, choose a screen saver name. In the Screen Saver Demo area, you'll see what the screen saver will look like.

3. If the screen saver you've selected has custom options, the settings button will become available. Click the button to adjust the settings to your preference, and click OK.

4. In the Screen Saver Settings area, type the number of minutes of delay after your last mouse movement or keystroke that the screen saver should wait before starting.

5. If you would like to require a password to restore the normal screen display, click Require Password. You'll need to type the password of the account you're using in order to restore the screen display.

6. In the Priority area, choose how much processor capacity the screen saver will use. If you anticipate running lengthy printing jobs or other operations that require CPU power

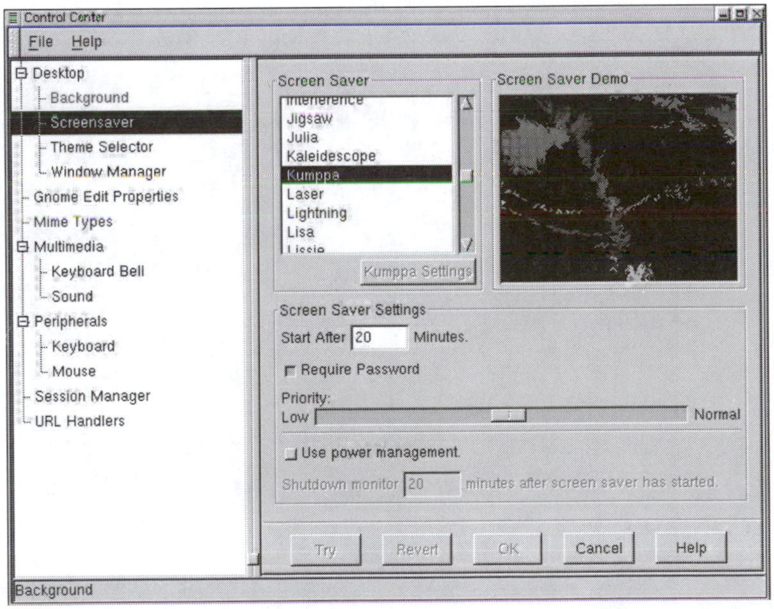

Figure 10.8 You can choose a screen saver in this dialog box.

while the screen saver is running, move the slider toward Low.

7.   If you're using a notebook computer or a monitor that has power management capabilities, check Use power management, and specify the number of minutes to wait before shutting down the monitor's power.

8.   Click OK to confirm your screen saver options.

Selecting a Theme and a Default Desktop Font

In GNOME, a *theme* changes the appearance of windows, menus, and dialog boxes. GNOME comes with several built-in themes, including the Default theme, which you're now using. Figure 10.9 shows the Pixmap theme, which displays dialog boxes and menus with a graphic in the background.

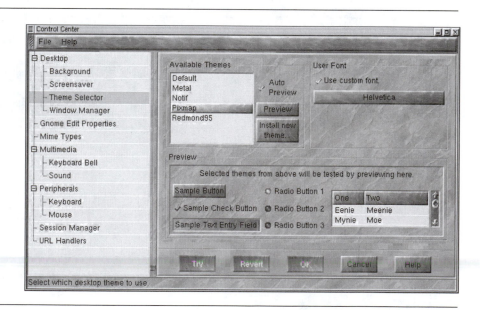

Figure 10.9 The Pixmap theme uses graphics to enliven dialog boxes.

Whether or not you choose a theme, the following procedure also enables you to choose a default desktop font. You can select the font name, the font style (such as bold or italic), and the font size. The font appears in all the dialog boxes, menus, and panels that you see on-screen.

To choose a theme, follow these steps:

1. Do one of the following:

    Click the Main Menu button, point to Settings, point to Desktop, and choose Theme.

    or

    Click the GNOME configuration tool button on the Panel, and click Theme when the Control Center appears.

    You'll see the Control Center, with the Theme options displayed (see Figure 10.9). If necessary, enlarge the dialog box so that you can see all the options.

2. In the Available Themes area, select the theme you would like to apply.

3. To view a preview, click the Preview button, and look in the Preview area.

4. To choose a custom font, activate the Use custom font option, and click the font name button. You'll see the Pick a Font dialog box, shown in Figure 10.10.

5. In the Font list box, choose the font family you want to use. Look in the Preview box for a font sample.

To see more information about the font, click the Font Information tab.

If you'd like to restrict the number of font choices you see, click Filter, and click options that restrict the number of fonts that are displayed. For example, you can restrict the display to just those fonts created by Adobe, or to fonts that use proportional spacing.

6. In the Font Style list box, choose the font style you prefer.

7. In the Size list box, choose the font size you want. If you wish, you can base the measurement on printer's points or screen pixels by clicking Points or Pixels in the Metric area.

8. Click OK to confirm your font choice.

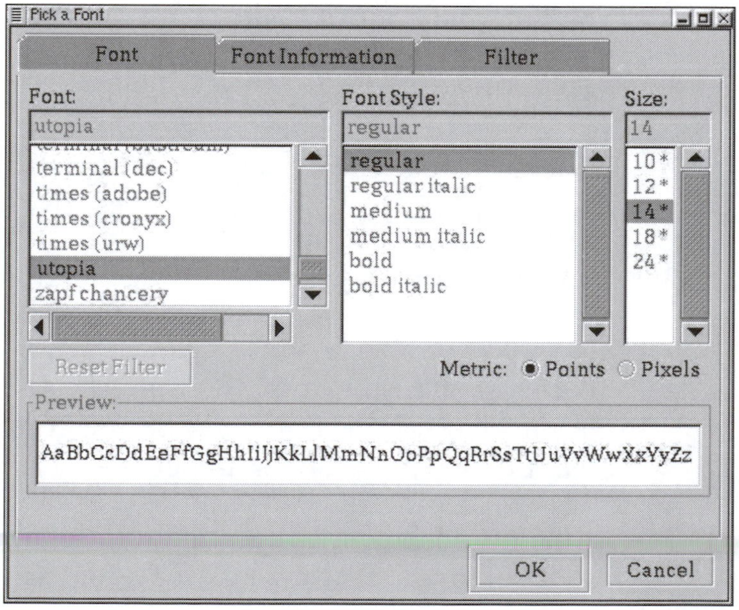

Figure 10.10 Here, you can pick a default font for GNOME.

Enabling Sound within GNOME

If your computer is equipped with a Linux-compatible sound card and speakers, you can make GNOME come alive with sounds that are keyed to system events. You can also listen to audio CDs, play digital sound files

Understanding Sound on Your Linux System

Compared to Windows and Mac OS systems, UNIX and Linux systems have been sound-impaired. In the past, UNIX workstations could play some waveform sound files (recorded sounds), but could not play synthesized (MIDI) sounds. These capabilities were brought to UNIX workstations by the Open Sound System (OSS), a commercial venture; a free version, called Free/OSS, is currently implemented in the Linux kernel. However, Free/OSS did not provide Linux systems with the capabilities any sound-enabled Windows or Mac OS system has, such as the capacity to play more than one sound at a time, and the ability to work with a wide variety of sound files.

Thanks to the Enlightenment Sound Daemon (EsounD), Linux systems now have outstanding sound capabilities. EsounD can play more than one sound at a time. In addition, it works with audiofile, a utility that enables sound applications to work with a wide variety of sound file formats. EsounD and audiofile are integrated with GNOME.

To take advantage of EsounD, GNOME enables you to assign sounds to system events, such as starting up and logging out. In addition, GNOME comes with a variety of ready-to-use sound utilities, including an audio CD player.

In addition to these utilities, you can obtain copies of many additional sound utilities that are EsounD-compatible, such as the following:

- **eMusic** A sound player that can handle just about any digitized waveform file you'll encounter, including MP3, WAV, UAU, and more.
- **x11amp** A Linux version of the popular Windows MP3 player (Winamp).
- **xcdroast** A great application for creating audio or data CD-ROMs using inexpensive CD-R discs.
- **grip** A GNOME-compatible application for reading audio data from CD-ROM discs and transforming this data into WAV or MP3 files.

TIP For the latest information on EsounD, see the EsounD home page at www.tux.org/~ricdude/EsounD.html.

Assigning Sounds to GNOME System Events

Now that you've enabled sound, you can turn on GNOME sound support and assign sounds to events, including the following:

- **GNOME system events** including login, logout, informational messages, warning messages, error messages, question dialogs, and miscellaneous messages.
- **User interface events** including action button click, menu item activation, and check box toggled.
- **Panel** events including expand and collapse panel.

In addition, GNOME-compatible applications can place their own event list within the sound event list. When you install a new GNOME application that enables you to assign sounds to the application's events, the application's name will appear in the sound events list.

GNOME comes preconfigured with sounds for many events. If you wish, you can change the assigned sound to something more to your liking. You can choose from any of the supplied sounds, or use your own. (You can assign any sound stored in the Windows WAV file format.)

TIP Looking for sounds? Try a Web search. You'll find thousands of Web pages that offer free, downloadable WAV sounds, which you can assign to GNOME system events.

To assign sounds to system and application events, follow these steps:

1. Do one of the following:

    On the Panel, click the GNOME configuration tool button, and click Sound on the menu.

    or

    Click the Main Menu button, point to Settings, point to Multimedia, and point to Sound. You'll see the Sound options, with the General page displayed.

2. In the Enable area, activate GNOME sound support, if necessary.

3. Click the Sound Events tab. You'll see the sound events list, shown in Figure 10.11.

4. In the Category area, choose the system component or application, and highlight the event to which you would

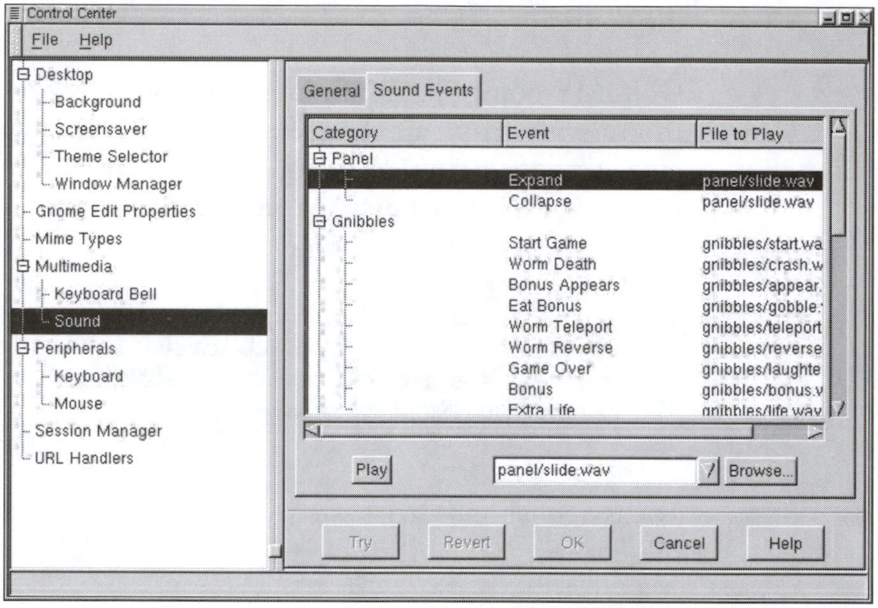

Figure 10.11 You can assign sounds to system and application events.

like to assign a sound. In GNOME, you can assign sounds to Panel actions, to GNOME system events (such as login and logout), and user interface events (such as action button click).

5.   In the list box to the right of the Play button, choose a sound, or click Browse to search for a sound.

6.   Click Play to hear a sample of the sound.

7.   Repeat steps 4 through 6 to assign additional sounds, if you wish.

8.   Click OK to confirm your choices.

TIP So that you'll know what the various sounds mean, listen to the sounds assigned to the various Panel, GNOME, and user interface events. Make sure you're familiar with the sound used for errors

Adjusting Keyboard Bell Properties

Some of GNOME's events sound the keyboard bell, a tone that sounds like a beep. You can control the bell's volume, pitch, and duration. To do so, open the GNOME Control Center, click Keyboard Bell, and adjust the bell properties. Click the Test button to see how the bell sounds. When you're finished, click OK.

Adding Applets to GNOME Panels

The GNOME Panel has plenty of room for *applets*, small applications that fit within the confines of a panel button. Applets you'll want to try include Disk Mount (discussed at the beginning of this chapter), the nifty AfterStep Clock, and Web Search. Most of these will be found on the various panel menus, and more are available for downloading from the GNOME site (http://www.gnome.org).

Exploring the Available Applets

Table 10.1 lists the applets currently available for the GNOME Panel. Most of these are currently available on the various GNOME menus; by the time you get this book, many more will be available.

Table 10.1 Applets you can add to the Panel

Applet name	Description
AfterStep Clock	Displays a nice-looking clock with the date and day of the week.
Another Clock	Displays a clock in the form of an analog watch face.
Battery Charge	Measures the amount of charge remaining in a notebook computer's batteries.

Character Picker	Enables mouse-click entry of accented foreign language characters.
CD Player	Displays a miniature version of the gtcd player. You can start and stop playing the CD, and you can go forward to the next track or backward to the previous one.
Clock/Mailcheck	Displays the time digitally and enables you to click an envelope to access your e-mail.
CPU/MEM Usage	Measures the amount of central processing unit (CPU) and RAM memory usage.
Disk Usage	Graphically displays the amount of free space left on your system's storage devices. Click the applet to see the free space remaining on the next device.
Drive Mount	Displays a drive mount icon.
GNotes	Enables you to write yellow notes that you can stick here and there on the screen.
JBC Binary Clock	Displays a clock that shows the time in time using binary notation. Incomprehensible unless you're a programmer.
Mailcheck	Echoes the LED lights on an external modem's control panel and enables you to connect to the Internet or disconnect.
Mini-Commander	Provides a text box in which you can type commands directly.
Mixer	Displays a volume slider control and a mute button.
MemLoad	Measures the amount of free space left in RAM memory.
Printer Applet	Creates a print icon that enables you to print using drag-and-drop. To print a file, just drag it to this icon.
PPP Dialer	Connects to the Internet via a modem.

SwapLoad	Graphically displays the amount of space left in the system swap file.
Web Control	Provides a text box in which you can type Web addresses and initiate a browser session.
Web Search	Enables you to initiate a search of the Web using your favorite search engine.

Adding an Applet to the Panel

To add an applet to the panel, click the Main Menu button, point to Panel, point to Add Applet, point to one of the applet categories (such as Amusements or Utilities), and select an applet from the submenu.

You'll see the applet on the panel. To move the applet to a different location, see "Moving an Applet," the following section.

After you've added the applet, you may wish to adjust the applet's properties, if any. To do so, right-click the applet button, and choose Properties. What you'll see next depends on which applet you've clicked. Make your selections, and click OK.

Moving an Applet

To move an applet, right-click and choose Move Applet from the pop-up menu. Move the pointer where you want the button to appear, and click the left mouse button.

Deleting an Applet

If you would like to remove an applet that you don't use, right-click it and choose Remove from panel from the pop-up menu.

Adding Drawers to GNOME Panels

Need room for more applets? You can create *drawers* to hold them. A drawer looks like a button. However, when you click it, it "pulls out" the drawer to reveal a new Panel section, at right angles to the existing Panel.

Adding a Drawer

To add a drawer, click the Main Menu button, point to Panel, and choose Add drawer. You'll see the drawer button on the Panel; it's pulled out slightly so you can add applets to it. To close the drawer, click the hide button on the end of the drawer; to open the drawer, click the drawer button (see Figure 10.12).

To add applets to a drawer:

1. Open the drawer by clicking the drawer button.

2. Click the Main Menu button, point to Panel, point to Add Applet, point to one of the applet categories (such as Amusements or Utilities), and select an applet from the submenu.

TIP Chances are you created the drawer because your existing Panel is getting too crowded. To move existing applets to the drawer, open the drawer, right-click the applet button, choose Move applet, and click within the drawer.

If you would like to remove the drawer, right-click the drawer button and choose Remove from panel. Bear in mind that you'll lose the applets you've added to this panel, so you may wish to move the applets to another panel before you remove the drawer.

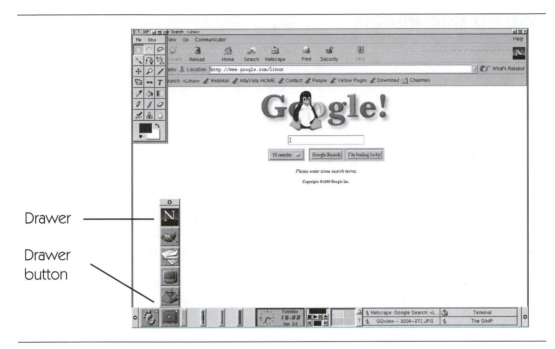

Drawer

Drawer
button

Figure 10.12 Drawers enable you to add more applets to your Panel.

Choosing Edge or Corner Panels

The default GNOME panel spans the bottom of the screen. It's
an *edge panel*, which stretches from one edge of the screen to
the other.

To restrict the panel's length to the size of the applet buttons
you've added, click the Main Menu button, point to Panel,
and choose Convert to corner panel. A *corner panel* is automatically anchored to the southwest, northwest, northeast,
and southeast corners of the screen. These directions refer,
respectively, to the lower left, upper left, upper right, and
lower right corners of the screen.

Positioning Panels

Panels don't have to be positioned at the bottom of the screen. You can choose the following positioning options for panels:

- **Edge panels** You can choose top, right, bottom, or left.
- **Corner panels** You can choose northwest, northeast, southeast, or southwest. You can also choose whether you'd like vertical or horizontal orientation.

To position a panel, follow these steps:

1. Make the panel an edge panel or corner panel, according to your tastes.

2. Click the Main Menu button, point to Panel, and choose This panel properties. You'll see the Panel properties dialog box.

3. In the Position area, click the position you want.

4. Click OK.

Adding More Panels

You can add additional panels, if you wish, although doing so may clutter up your screen too much. If you'd like to try this, click the Main Menu button, point to Panel, point to Add new panel, and choose Edge panel or Corner panel. GNOME adds the new panel on the side opposite the current panel's location. You can now add applets and drawers as you please.

Should you decide to delete the panel, right-click the panel background, and choose Remove this panel. (This option is dimmed if the current panel is the only one on-screen.)

Changing Your Panel's Appearance

You can control a wide variety of panel appearance options. Some apply only to the current panel; others apply to all panels.

Choosing Appearance Options for the Current Panel

For each individual panel, you can choose the following options:

- **Auto hide** Hides the panel until you move the mouse pointer to it. This option is turned off by default.
- **Enable hide buttons** Displays the hide buttons at the ends of the panel. This option is activated by default.
- **Enable hide button arrows** Removes the arrows from the hide buttons so that they take up less space. This option is turned off by default.
- **Background color** You can choose a background color for the panel. The default color is gray.
- **Background graphic** You can add a background graphic to the panel. If the graphic is smaller than the panel area, GNOME tiles the graphic so that it takes up all the available space. You can also scale the graphic to fit the available space.

To choose options for the current panel, do the following:

1. Click the Main Menu button, point to Panel, and choose This panel properties. You'll see the Panel properties dialog box. If necessary, click the Edge panel or Corner panel buttons. (The name of this tab differs depending on whether you're customizing an edge panel or corner panel.)

2. In the Minimize options area, you can choose Auto hide, Enable hide buttons, or Enable hide button arrows.

3. Click Background.

4. Do one of the following:

   To change the background color, click Color in the Background area, and click the Background color button. Choose a color from the color wheel, and click OK to confirm your choice. Click OK again to exit the dialog box, or click Apply to see what the color looks like without exiting the dialog box.

   or

   To use a background graphic, click Pixmap in the Background area. In the Image file area, type the location of the graphic you want to use, or click Browse to locate the file, and click OK to select the file. Click OK to confirm your choice, or click Apply to see what the graphic looks like without exiting the dialog box.

Choosing Pager Options

You can choose options for the Pager. To do so, click the question mark button in the Pager area. You'll see the Gnome Pager Options dialog box. In this dialog box, you can choose the following options:

- **Show pager** This option, switched on by default, enables you to hide the pager (but I recommend you leave it on).
- **Use small pagers** This option, switched off by default, enables you to use a smaller-sized pager.

- **Rows of pagers** This option comes into play only if you choose the Separate Desktops option within the Enlightenment Configuration Editor, discussed in the section titled "Specifying the Number of Desktops," later in this chapter. If you stack more than one desktop on top of each other, you'll get multiple Pagers, which are also stacked on top of each other, enlarging the Panel; you may wish to set this option at 1 so that the Panel remains the height of a normal Panel button.

Customizing the Main Menu

GNOME comes with a full-featured menu editor (see Figure 10.13) that enables you to customize the Main Menu to your heart's content. You can add new submenus, add items to submenus, delete unwanted items, rearranage items, and sort the menu. When you add new items, you can link these items to folders.

Understanding the Main Menu's Organization

The Main Menu is organized into the following categories:

- **User Menus** When you're logged on with your user account, this is the only area of the menu that you can modify. Here, you can create menu items for the applications you like to use.
- **System Menus** These menus are generated automatically when you install new GNOME-compatible software, and they're the same for all the users on your system. You can modify these menus only if you're logged on as the root user.
- **Additional Menus** Just what appears here depends on which options you chose when you installed Red Hat Linux. If you installed KDE, you'll see a KDE menu list-

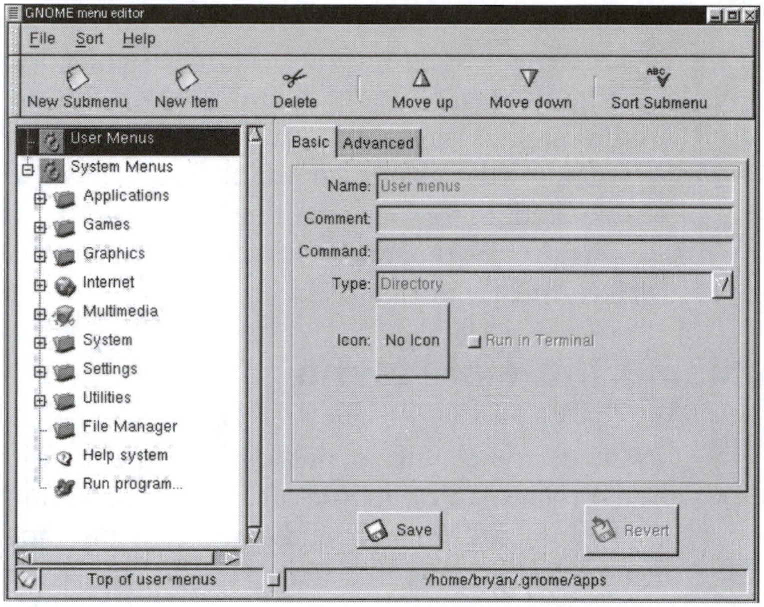

Figure 10.13 You can customize the Main Menu using this editor.

ing all the nifty KDE applications. You'll also see the Another Level menu, which provides access to some important Red Hat utilities.

Adding an Item to the User Menu

To add an application to your user menu, do the following:

1. Click the Main Menu button, point to Settings, and choose Menu Editor. You'll see the Menu Editor on-screen.

2. Click New Item. You'll see a new Untitled item.

3. Click the Basic tab, if necessary. In the Name box, type the name that you want to appear on the menu.

4. In the Command box, type the command that starts the program.

5. In the Type list box, select Application, if necessary.

6. Click the Icon button. You'll see the Choose an icon dialog box.

7. Select an icon.

8. Click OK.

9. Click Save.

Creating a New Submenu

If you plan to add many items to your user menu, you may wish to organize the items into folders. To add a folder, follow these steps:

1. Click the Main Menu button, point to Settings, and choose Menu Editor. You'll see the Menu Editor on-screen.

2. In the menu list within the Menu Editor, select User Menus.

3. Click New Submenu. You'll see a New Folder item in the list.

4. Click the Basic tab, if necessary, and type a name for the folder in the Name box.

5. Click Save.

You can add folders within folders, if you wish. To do so, select a folder, and click New Submenu.

Organizing and Sorting a Submenu

Once you've added items and folders to your menus, you can organize them by moving them up and down, or by sorting them.

To move an item up or down, select the item, and click Move up or Move down.

To sort a submenu, you need to log in as the root user. Log out of your user account, if necessary, and log in as root.

To sort a submenu, select the submenu name (try selecting User Menus), and click Sort Submenu. (You can also use the Ctrl + S keyboard shortcut). This button sorts the submenu in alphabetical order.

TIP If you've created additional submenus within the current submenus, you can sort all of them at the same time. Select the topmost submenu, click Sort on the menu bar, and choose Sort Submenu Recursive. (You can also use the Ctrl + R keyboard shortcut.)

Editing Your Menus

If you would like to delete an item you've added, select it and click Delete. (You can also use the Ctrl + D keyboard shortcut, or just press Del.)

Starting Programs Automatically

When you exit GNOME, you have the option of saving the current setup. (This option is turned off, by default.) If you activate this option, GNOME saves information about the applications you're running, and you'll see these applications on-screen the next time you log in to your account. This capability is called *session management*. As this section explains, session management applies only to GNOME-compatible applications. If you would like other programs to start automatically when you log in to your account, you need to identify these programs using the Session Manager, one of the options in the GNOME Control Center.

Understanding Session Management

Session management is convenient because it enables you to resume working where you left off, with all the open GNOME-compatible applications restored to their on-screen positions. However, it's important to understand that GNOME does *not* save the data you've created with these applications. Before you exit your GNOME session, be sure to save the data you've created with these applications.

Choosing Session Management Options

You can choose from the following session management options:

- **Prompt on Logout** This option asks whether you'd like to save the current session when you log out. (This option is enabled by default.)
- **Automatically save changes to session** This option automatically saves your GNOME session. Although it is not enabled by default, I recommend that you enable it.

To modify these options, click the GNOME Configuration tool icon, select Session Manager, and click the options you want (see Figure 10.14). Click OK to confirm.

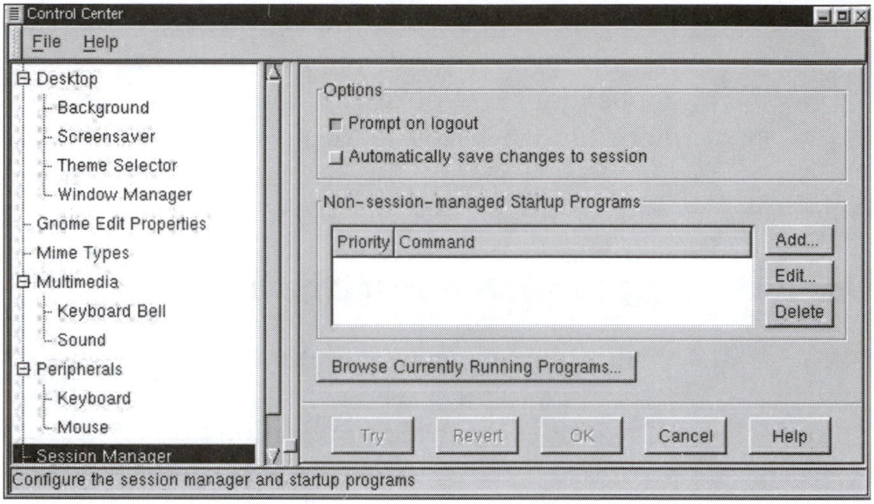

Figure 10.14 You can start programs automatically each time you log in.

Starting Non-GNOME-Compatible Applications

Session management applies only to GNOME-compatible applications. If you would like to start non-GNOME applications automatically at the start of each GNOME session, you need to list these programs using the Session Manager page (one of the pages available in the GNOME Control Center).

To start non-GNOME applications automatically, follow these steps:

1.   Open the GNOME Control Center, if necessary, by clicking the GNOME Configuration tool button.

2.   In the list of items, click Session Manager. You'll see the Session Manager options, shown in Figure 10.14.

3.   Click Add. You'll see the Add Startup Program dialog box, shown in Figure 10.15.

4.   In the Startup Command box, type the command that you use to start the program. If you don't know the command, click Browse to locate the program. (Most programs are stored in /usr/bin, /usr/X11R6/bin, or /usr/local/bin.)

5.   In the Priority area, leave the default setting (50).

6.   Click OK to exit the Add Startup Program dialog box.

7.   Click OK to confirm your startup settings.

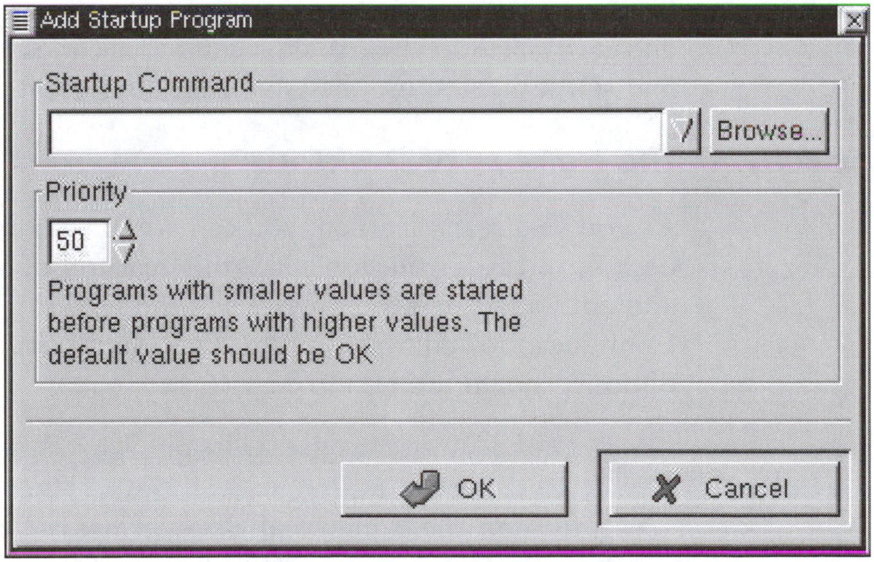

Figure 10.15 Here, you identify the programs that start automatically.

Configuring Enlightenment

As you've already learned, you should choose customization options within GNOME, if they're available. However, some customization options are handled by the window manager. Just which options are available depends on which window manager you're using. By default, Red Hat Linux uses the Enlightenment window manager, so this section briefly discusses some of the Enlightenment options you can use to jazz up your GNOME environment. (Note that some of these options were discussed earlier in this chapter; see the section titled "Adjusting Window Focus Behavior.")

To access the Enlightenment configuration options, click the GNOME Configuration tool button, and choose Window Manager from the list. Click Run Configuration Tool for Enlightenment. You'll see the Enlightenment Configuration Editor, shown in Figure 10.16. Here, you can specify the number of desktops, choose from a variety of neat special effects, and customize keyboard shortcuts. (To choose backgrounds and select themes, use the GNOME Configuration Editor.)

Specifying the Number of Desktops

As you've already learned, you can work with more than one desktop area. If you don't like this feature, or would like to add additional desktop areas, click the Desktop option in the Configuration Editor's option list. You'll see the desktop options, shown in Figure 10.17.

In this area, you can modify desktop areas in two ways:

- **Adjusting the number of desktop areas** Drag the slider bars to increase or decrease the number of desktop areas.

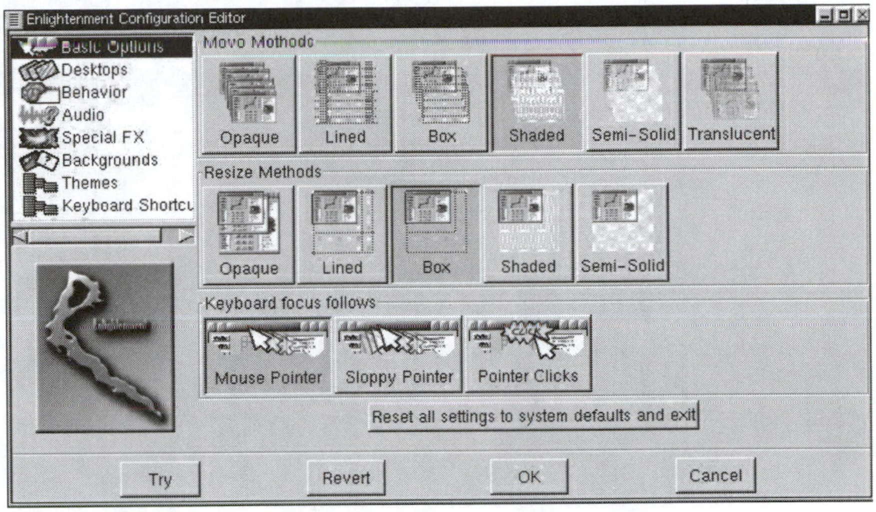

Figure 10.16 The Enlightenment Configuration Editor

- **Creating separate desktops** If you wish, you can "stack" desktops on top of one another. If you move the slider in this area to 2, for example, you get two sets of desktop areas, one on top of the other. To move between them, you use the Alt+Shift+Up or Alt+Shift+Down keyboard shortcuts; you can also select a desktop set from the Pager, which displays a separate Pager panel for each desktop stack.

If you're bothered by the screen flipping to an adjacent desktop area when you move the mouse pointer to the window edge, deactivate the Enable option in the Edge flip resistance area. You can also try increasing the *flip resistance* (the time Enlightenment waits before moving to the next desktop area).

Choosing Special Effects

In the Basic Options and Special FX page of Enlightenment's Configuration Editor, you can choose from a variety of nifty

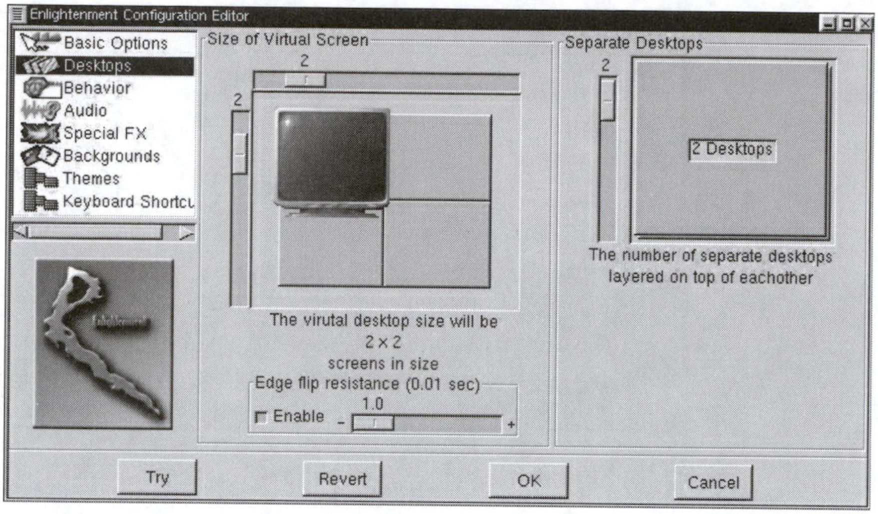

Figure 10.17 You can choose desktop area options here.

special effects. Be forewarned that many of these are distracting or even annoying once the novelty has worn off!

You can choose from the following

- **Move methods** (Basic Options) You can choose from Opaque (the default), Lined, Box, Shaded, Semi-Solid, or Translucent.
- **Resize methods** (Basic Options) You can choose from Opaque, Lined, Box (the default), Shaded, or Semi-Solid.
- **Windows slide in when they appear** (Special FX page) You can control the slide-in rate.
- **Windows slide about during window cleanup** (Special FX page). You can control the slide rate.
- **Desktops slide in when changing desktops** (Special FX page). You can specify the slide rate.

- **Window sliding methods** (Special FX page) You can choose from Opaque (the default), Lined, Box, Shaded, or Semi-Solid.

Just click any of the options you want, and click OK to confirm.

Customizing the Keyboard

If you click the Keyboard Shortcuts option in the Enlightenment Configuration Manager, you'll see the keyboard shortcuts page, shown in Figure 10.17. Here, you can change the existing keyboard shortcuts, or create new ones.

To modify an existing keyboard shortcut, do the following:

1. In the List of keyboard shortcuts, select the keyboard shortcut you want to modify.

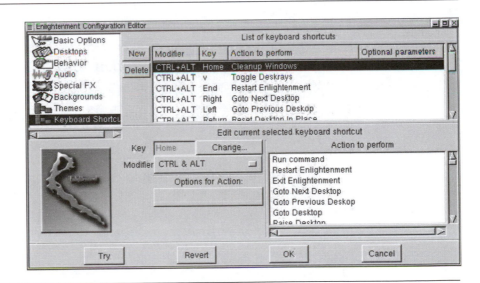

Figure 10.17 You can change Enlightenment's keyboard shortcuts.

2.   In the Edit current selected keyboard shortcut area, click the button to the right of Modifier, and select the new modifier key you want to use.

3.   In the Key area, click Change, and press the key you want to use.

4.   In the Action to perform area, select the action you want to perform.

5.   Click OK to confirm your choice.

TIP If you're accustomed to Microsoft Windows keyboard shortcuts, you can create Enlightenment equivalents of them. For example, you can create a new keyboard shortcut assigned to Ctrl + F4 that closes a window.

To create a new keyboard shortcut, do the following:

1.   Click New.

2.   In the Edit current selected keyboard shortcut area, click the button to the right of Modifier, and select the new modifier key you want to use.

3.   In the Key area, click Change, and press the key you want to use.

4.   In the Action to perform area, select the action you want to perform.

5.   Click OK to confirm your choice.

From Here

You've learned the fundamentals of GNOME, and you've personalized GNOME so that it looks and runs to your tastes. Now it's time to delve beneath the surface of GNOME, and master the fundamentals of system administration. In the following chapter, you'll learn how to modify drive settings so that your disk drives are accessible to users, how to decompress and compress files, how to create file archives, how to install new software, and much more.

References and Further Reading

Lewis, Todd Graham, and David "Gleef" Zoll. 1999. *GNOME Frequently Asked Questions*. Available online at http://www.gnome.org/gnomefaq/html/index.html.

Mason, David A., and David A. Wheeler. 1999. *GNOME User's Guide*. Available online at http://www.gnome.org/users-guide/index.html.

11

Running Applications with GNOME

By now, you've got Linux and GNOME running to your tastes, and it's time to get down to business: running applications. This chapter introduces the wealth of software that's available for personal information management (PIM) and productivity purposes; Chapter 14 discusses Internet software for your Linux system.

Thanks to GNOME's well-conceived design, you're not restricted to running GNOME applications. You can run any of the many applications developed for the KDE desktop environment. You can also run any program designed to work with the X Window System. As you'll learn in this chapter, there is indeed a wealth of software available for your Linux system, and much more is on the way.

This chapter begins by examining some of the GNOME desktop utilities and applications, and continues by briefly examining the much broader slate of KDE software offerings. You'll also learn how to run X Window System applications under GNOME.

Where's GNOME Headed?

As this book has stressed, it's important to understand that GNOME is a work in progress, and the progress is very rapid indeed. Still, at present, some major pieces are missing from the GNOME pie, including GNOME printer support, interprocess communication, modular software resources, and vector graphics support. By the time you read this book, some of these missing pieces may well be in place, so you may wish to check the GNOME site to see whether you can obtain more recent versions of the GNOME applications (and the GNOME desktop itself). You'll find the GNOME home page at www.gnome.org.

Introducing the GNOME Desktop Accessories

GNOME comes with a number of desktop accessories that can help you get organized, including a calendar, address book, time tracker, and calculator. As you'll quickly discover, these aren't throwaway utilities, but full-featured programs that measure up well against the commercial competition. At this writing, however, missing are some important features, not the least of which is printing; GNOME printing support wasn't completed at this writing.

GNOME Calendar

The GNOME Calendar is a full-featured time management program (see Figure 11.1). You can view your schedule in daily, weekly, monthly, and annual views. What's more, you can create recurrent appointments, set alarms, and even send yourself automatic e-mail reminders. Because Calendar's file format conforms to the vCalendar standard, the information you create and save with GNOME Calendar can be used by any other vCalendar application, including intranet scheduling managers that enable team members to share schedules on a network.

GNOME Time Tracker

The GNOME Time Tracker (GTT, shown in Figure 11.2) enables you to define projects, and then to measure the time you spend on one of them. You can use GTT's capabilities to track the time you spend on tasks compensated by the time you spend, but there are other uses. If you'd really like to find

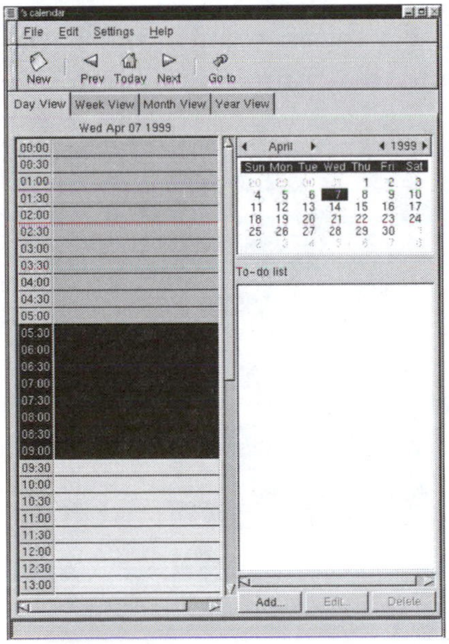

Figure 11.1 The GNOME Calendar helps you organize your schedule.

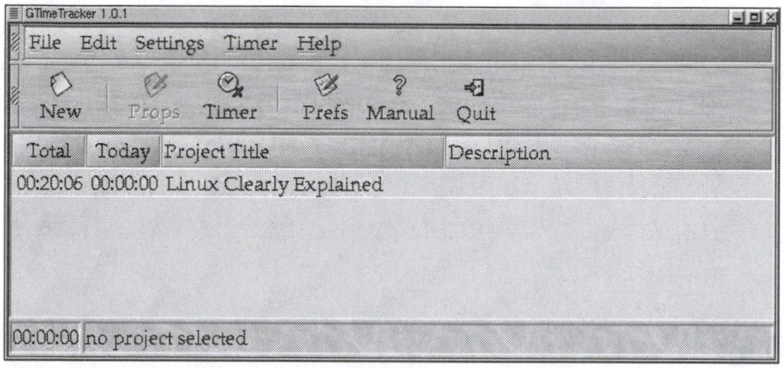

Figure 11.2 This tools enables you to track time spent on projects.

out how much time you spend doing non-productive things
with your computer, use GTT to track activities such as surfing or playing games.

GnomeCard Address Book

Like the GNOME Calendar, the GnomeCard address book
(Figure 11.3) is standards-compliant; it implements the vCard

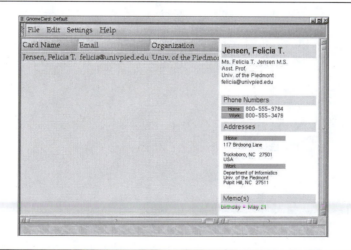

Figure 11.3 GnomeCard adheres to the vCard standard.

format, an Internet address book standard, and will eventually implement every aspect of the vCard standard. Applications compliant with the vCard standard (such as e-mail programs) can make use of the information you store in GnomeCard; what's more, vCard information that your correspondents send to you as an attachment to an e-mail message can be imported into vCard automatically. The e-mail software that can handle such tasks isn't here yet, but it's coming (see Chapter 15).

gNotepad+

A simple HTML editor, gNotepad+ enables you to create HTML code and view the results in a browser window (see Figure 11.4). Not designed to support advanced HTML fea-

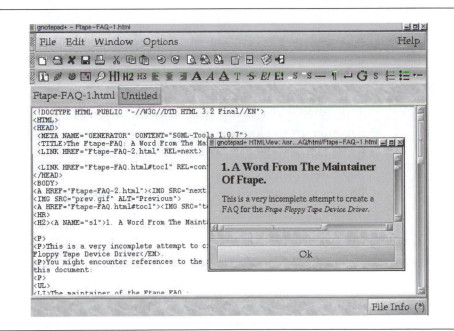

Figure 11.4 gNotepad+ is a simple HTML editor.

tures such as tables and frames, this utility is adequate for creating simple Web pages.

Exploring GNOME Applications

At this writing, GNOME applications are in their infancy; the GNOME project is substantially behind KDE in this respect (see "Exploring KDE Applications," later in this chapter. Now that the GNOME desktop version 1.0 is completed, you can expect to see further development in this area.

The GNU Image Processor (GIMP)

Developed by Peter Mattis and Spencer Kimball, the GNU Image Processor (GIMP) is not only an outstanding program in its own right, but the inspiration for the entire GNOME project. GIMP's developers created the GTK+ interface toolkit, which became the basis for the entire GNOME project. Released under the terms of the GNU General Public License (GPL), The GIMP (as it's affectionately known) is nothing less than a professional-quality program for photo retouching, image composition, and image editing. Graphic artists say that The GIMP rivals the functionality of the pricey commercial product PhotoShop (see Figure 11.5 for a taste of The GIMP in action). Features include a full-suite of painting tools, a plug-in architecture for accessory programs, dozens of supported file formats, multiple levels of undo and redo, and much, much more.

If you're not familiar with PhotoShop-quality image processing software, there's a steep learning curve. Like PhotoShop, GIMP enables artists to create illustrations using independently editable layers, and includes an armada of image manipulation tools. In Figure 11.5, for instance, you see a photograph that's been altered by the addition of painterly effects. For professial applications, GIMP can handle prepress concerns, such as color mapping; these and other professional features require a bit of experience to understand.

TIP GIMP is one of the few open source applications that has decent online documentation. Visit http://manual.gimp.org to access an outstanding, 500-page GIMP manual that comprehensively documents GIMP's many features. For the latest on GIMP, visit http://www.gimp.org.

Scanning in the Linux Environment

Until recently, the words "scanners" and "Linux" rarely appeared in the same sentence. That's no longer the case, thanks to SANE (Scanner Access Now Easy, with headquarters at http://www.mostang.com/sane/). Essentially an interface to scanning and digital

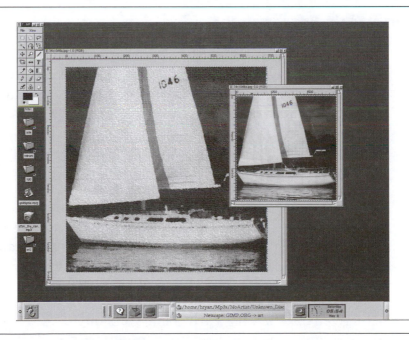

Figure 11.5 The GIMP is an outstanding photo editing program.

camera hardware, SANE is released under the GNU General Public License (GPL) and is true open-source software.

Recently released in a stable version 1.0, SANE provides support for a wide variety of digital cameras and scanners, including scanners made by Agfa, Apple, Canon, Epson, HP, MicroTek, Nikon, Polaroid, Tamarack, Umax, and more (for a complete list, see http://www. mostang.com/sane/sane-backends.html).

In contrast to the TWAIN interface used in Windows and Macintosh scanning, the SANE standard separates the scanning user interface from the underlying code that connects to the scanner. As a result, SANE enables network access to scanners, a cool new development that will ultimately make Linux the preferred environment for scanning purposes. Graphics applications such as GIMP are designed to work directly with SANE. For example, Xsane, a front-end program for Sane, is designed to work as a GIMP plug-in. For more information on Xsane, see http://www.wolfsburg.de/~rauch/ sane/sane-xsane.html.

The Gnumeric Spreadsheet

If The GIMP points the way to the future of GNOME software, it's going to be very bright indeed. Much of this promise is already evident in Gnumeric (see Figure 11.6), a project spearheaded by GNOME leader Miguel de Icaza.

Gnumeric aims for nothing less than feature-to-feature rivalry with the leading commercial spreadsheet packages, but substitutes the basic values of open source software: compliance with recognized standards and freedom from proprietary file formats. Gnumeric stores data in the eXtensible Markup Language (XML), an ASCII-based format that can be used by an XML-compliant application. Gnumeric can also read and write Microsoft Excel files.

Available in very early beta (version 0.25, at this writing), Gnumeric is still a work in progress; there's no support for printing, for example, and chart capabilities await the development of a GNOME-wide vector graphics architecture. Still, it's clear that Gnumeric is following the path laid down by The GIMP; it may become one of the most highly regarded software achievements in personal computing if the Gnumeric team achieves its goals.

To find out the latest information about Gnumeric (and to download the latest version), visit http://www.gnome.org/gnumeric.

GNUCash

Another ambitious project, GNUCash (http:// www.gnucash. org) aims to create a GPL-licensed personal finance and check-writing program, with all the features of the leading commercial products such as Quicken or Microsoft Money.

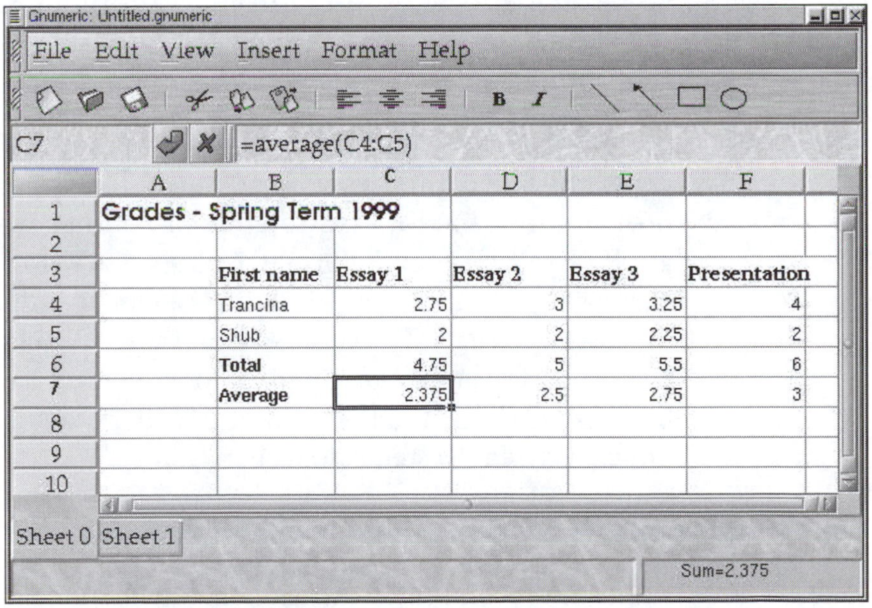

Figure 11.6 Gnumeric may soon rival commercial applications.

Not as far along as Gnumeric, GNUCash (see Figure 11.7) isn't yet available (at this writing) in a stable RPM release. Still, it's possible to see that this project is headed in a promising direction. Capable of reading Quicken (qic) files, GNUCash provides easy-to-use tools for accessing a wide variety of accounts and working with the checking register. Awaiting GNOME-wide vector graphics support are future projects to include charts and graphs.

AbiWord

If you're like most people who use word processing software, you probably work with Microsoft Word files—and not necessarily because you want to. You just don't have any choice. Your coworkers use Word, so you must use Word when you work collaboratively. Perhaps you're working for a publisher that requires Word files. You'd love to make the transition to Linux, but you can't work effectively without a program that can read and write Word files and support the major Word features, such as styles.

A pre-release (0.71) version of AbiWord (http://www.abisuite.com) looks very much like it may solve this problem for Linux users. Capable of reading Word 97 as well as RTF (Rich Text Format) files, AbiWord won't equal Microsoft Word in feature richness, but it will offer most of the features that Word users actually use, including multiple columns. Released on open source principles (AbiWord is licensed with GPL), the program will be available for Windows and Mac systems as well as Linux.

On the Horizon

Many more GNOME projects are well underway, including the GNOME Word Processor (GWP), gfax (a GNOME front end to Linux fax utilities), and the Achtung presentation manager. At this writing, these applications aren't far enough along to try, but keep your eye on the GNOME software list (at http://www.gnome.org) for recent developments.

Running KDE Applications with GNOME

GNOME includes support for KDE applications, so it isn't necessary to switch to the KDE desktop in order to take full advantage of the many KDE applications and utilities. If you installed Red Hat Linux 6.0 as recommended in Part II of this book, you included the KDE software in your installation, and you should see the KDE Menus option in the GNOME Main Menu.

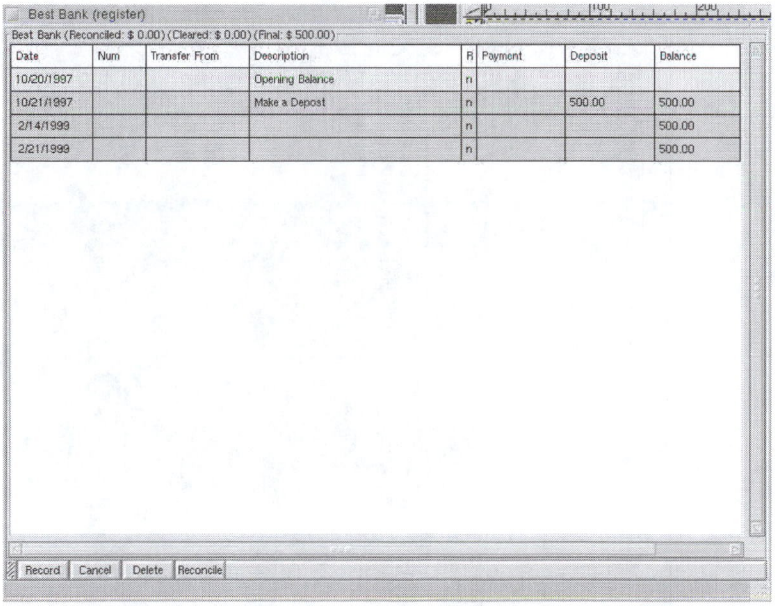

Figure 11.7 GNUCash is a personal financial management program.

Looking at the KDE Applications

Here's a sample of the KDE PIM and productivity applications that you'll find on the KDE menus:

- **Address Book** A simple address book utility.
- **aKtion!** A KDE front end for the xanim movie and animation program.
- **CD Player** Utility for playing audio CDs.
- **KFax** A fax file viewer that enables you to view the fax files created by the UNIX mgetty/sendfax and hylafx utilities, which must be installed and properly configured in order to use Kfax.
- **Media Player** A utility for playing wave sound files.
- **MIDI Player** A utility for playing MIDI sound files.

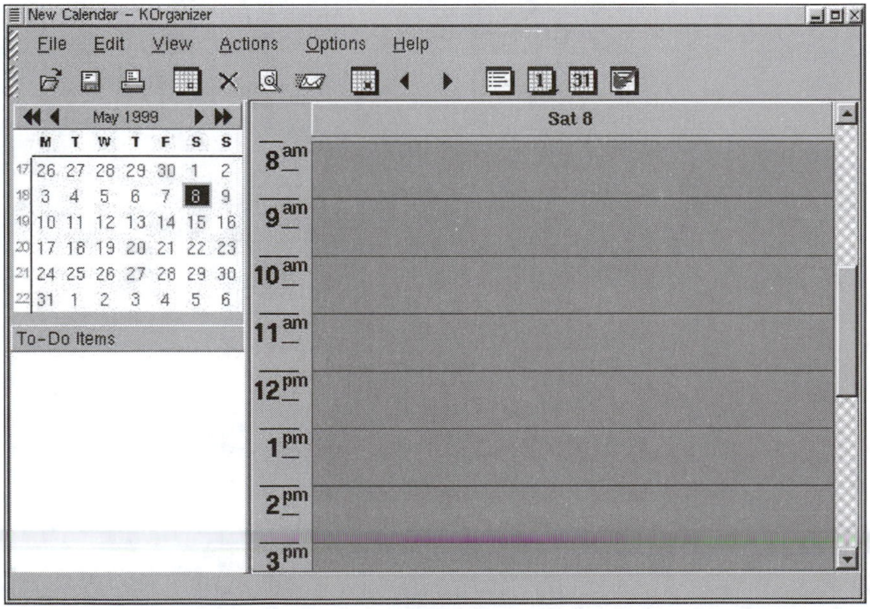

Figure 11.7 The KOrganizer is a useful calendar application.

- **Paint** A bitmapped graphics paint program, similar to the Paint utility in Microsoft Windows.
- **Personal Time Tracker** A time tracking tool.
- **PS Viewer** A PostScript file viewer.
- **Sound Mixer Panel** A utility for adjusting the volume of various sound input sources.

Most of these applications are quite simple, and offer few benefits beyond those already available in their corresponding GNOME utilities. But stay tuned.

The star of the KDE show, the KOffice suite, isn't available (at this writing) in stable binaries, and therefore wasn't included

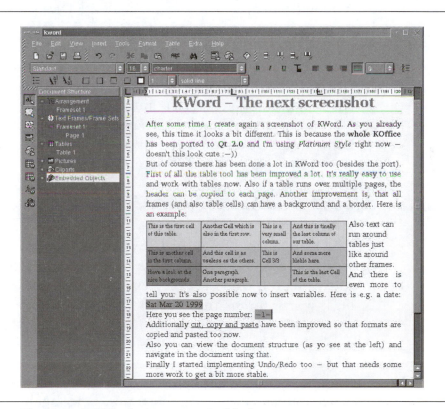

Figure 11.8 KWord sports a navigable document structure.

in the Red Hat 6.0 distribution. However, you'll want to take a look at KOffice once RPM binaries become available. Slated to include a spreadsheet, illustration program, presentation graphics program, a word processing program, and additional utilities, KOffice has the jump on competing GNOME efforts, aside from Gnumeric. Figure 11.8 shows the KWord application, which offers a navigable document structure, frame positioning, tables, autocorrection, and a host of additional features. For the latest information on KOffice availability, see the KDE home page at http://www.kde.org.

Running KDE Applications with GNOME

As you'll discover when you launch a KDE application, KDE programs run just fine under GNOME. You'll be able to make use of GNOME features such as detachable menus. Note, however, that the KDE applications aren't saved along with GNOME's session management information; if you want KDE applications to start automatically when you launch GNOME, select Session Manager in the GNOME Control Center, and click Add to add the program to the list of non-session-managed startup programs.

Running X Applications with GNOME

GNOME runs X Window System applications—and that means you can take advantage of a huge collection of useful software. You won't get the benefit of GNOME's inner workings, which means that you can't detach menus or count on automatic session management. In addition, X applications don't use a consistent set of user interface principles, and not all X application authors are good at designing usable interfaces. That said, there are some real jewels in the X software collection, as this section illustrates. Once again, I'm focusing here on personal information management and productivity applications; Chapter 15 turns to Internet applications, including Netscape Communicator, which is installed by default on your Red Hat Linux 6.0 system.

Among the many available X applications, you'll find a good number of GPL-licensed programs, as well as shareware and commercial programs. Among the commercial offerings are some impressive office suites, some of which are available for free as long as they are used for noncommercial (personal) use.

TIP Looking for Linux software? LinuxBerg (http:// www.linuxberg. com) enables you to search for Linux applications and download them to your computer. For the latest news on Linux applications, visit Freshmeat (http://www.freshmeat.com). You can search a database of more than 4,000 applications at the LInux Software Map (http:// www.linux.org/apps/lsm.html). For GNOME applications, visit the GNOME software map (http://www. gnome.org, and click the link to Software Map).

Looking at an X Application

A nifty program for burning audio and video CDs in a CD-R drive, X-CD-Roast is the work of Thomas Niederreiter, with contributions from Jörg Schilling and Eric Youngdale. It's a well-crafted program that enables you to copy audio and data information compact disks; it also enables you to write such information to CD-R disks, if your system is equipped with a CD-R recorder.

As Figure 11.9 illustrates, X-CD-Roast doesn't look like any other program on-screen; X software authors must create their own user interfaces. This one is well designed and reasonably easy to use, but the variation in user interfaces among X applications does raise the entry bar for beginning computer users.

Office Suites

Several commercial office suites are available for Linux systems. Unless you've a year or more to wait for the open source office suite efforts to bear fruit, you may wish to give one a try. Here's an overview of the two leading contenders:

- **Applixware Suite**(http://www.applix.com) Considered by many to be the best office software suite for Linux, this package includes Applix Words (see Figure 11.10), Applix Graphics (an illustration program), Applix Spreadsheets, Applix Presents, Applix Mail, Applix HTML Author, Applix Data, and Applix Builder (an application development environment). The entire suite is currently $99.
- **StarOffice** (http://www.stardivision.com) Free for non-commercial use, this full-featured office suite is Microsoft

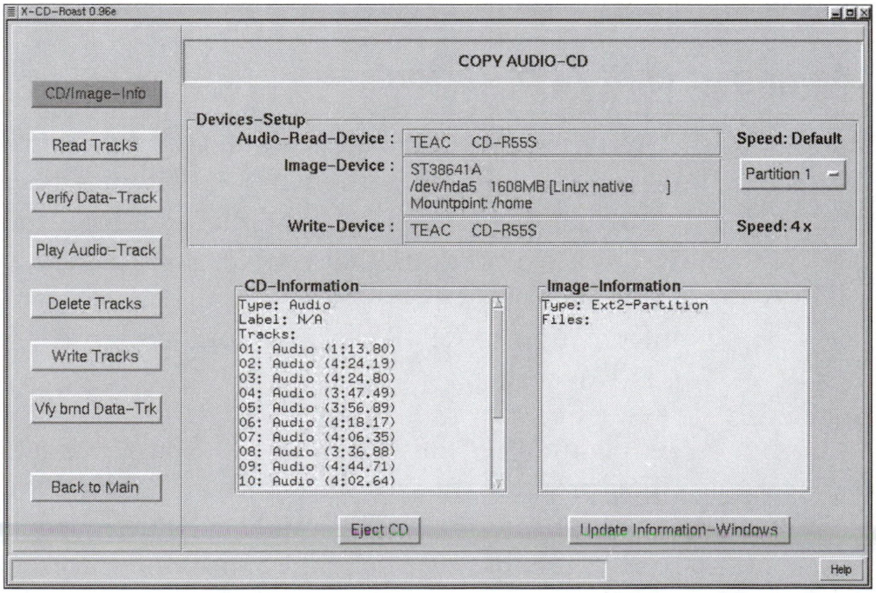

Figure 11.9 X-CD-Roast exemplifies the best in X applications.

Office compatible and features a word processor, spreadsheet, presentation graphics, e-mail, news, charting, and graphics modules.

WordPerfect for Linux 8.0

Currently owned by Corel, WordPerfect was once the most popular word processing program for personal computers, and is still widely used (particularly in the legal profession, where its bevy of special legal features make it close to indispensable). By any standard, it's still one of the best productivity programs available. The good news for Linux users is that Corel is currently making WordPerfect for Linux 8.0 available for free personal use (registration is required if you would like to use the product after the 90-day evaluation period). You'll

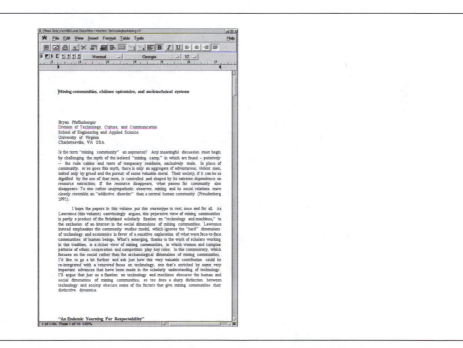

Figure 11.10 Applix Words opens Microsoft Word documents flawlessly.

find a copy of WordPerfect 8.0 for Linux on this book's CD-ROM.

If you're looking for a professional-quality word processing program to replace Microsoft Word for Windows, look no further. WordPerfect 8.0 for Linux (see Figure 11.11) can read and write Word files flawlessly, so you won't be out of touch with Microsoft Office users. WordPerfect's feature list rivals Word's: you'll find built-in grammar correction, charting and drawing, tables, Internet publishing, on-screen real-time spelling correction, and much more.

WordPerfect 8.0 for Linux is a big, complex program, and it's only natural that there's a fairly steep learning curve. You'll find a basic software user's guide included with the software, but you may want to read Corel's excellent WordPerfect Suite

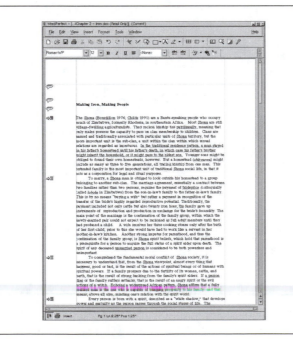

Figure 11.11 WordPerfect 8.0 for Linux is currently free for personal use.

8 Resource Guide (Corel 1999), http://www.corel.com/support/suite8manuals/Resource_Guide/), a complete, book-length manual that's accessible over the Internet, and for free.

According to news reports, Corel plans to make its entire Corel Office 2000 suite available free for personal use on Linux systems. Again, this is good news indeed for Linux users.

Running Windows Software on Linux Systems

After reading this chapter, perhaps you're convinced that you can make the move to Linux, and give up on Windows. But what about the one or two Windows programs that you can't do without? If that's your problem, read on.

Using a technique called *emulation,* it's possible to run software designed for use on one operating system on a computer that's running another operating system. The WINE project(http://www.winehq.com) seeks to create an emulator that will enable Linux users to run Microsoft Windows programs.

Released under the terms of the GNU General Public License, WINE is a work in progress. Currently, WINE can run many Windows applications well, but others do not run smoothly, and some do not run at all. (For an up-to-date list, see http://www.winehq.com/Apps.) For example, as of April 1999 WINE could run Quicken for Windows and the Windows desktop accessories flawlessly, but not Microsoft Internet Explorer, Microsoft Word 97, Paint Shop Pro, or PowerPoint. A major problem: Microsoft has not fully released certain details of the Windows application programming interface (API). In the absence of complete disclosure of these interface details, the WINE project may well be able to attain only sporadic success; still, if WINE can run the one program you need, it will prove its worth to you.

From Here

By now, you've developed a functioning GNOME system and you're ready to do productive work. Before long, you'll create valuable work that you'll want to protect, so it's time to learn some system administration fundamentals (including how to back up your work). You'll learn how to keep your system running smoothly in Chapter 12.

12

Keeping Your System Running Smoothly

Traditionally, large, multi-user Unix systems are run by two kinds of people: users and system administrators. Users rarely venture out of their home directories and do not have root privileges—perish the thought! Users with root privileges could copy sensitive information to disk drives, create havoc among system configuration settings, and even shut down the system maliciously, cutting off computer access for other users. That's why there's such a sharp distinction between users and system administrators. And that's also why Linux defaults to a configuration in which you can't do much damage from your user account.

Sooner or later, though, you'll need to step into the role of system administrator. You'll need to switch to the root user, and perform tasks such as mounting external filesystems (such as disk drives), archiving and compressing files, and performing regular system backups.

In this chapter, you'll learn how to take off your "user hat," and take on the system administrator's role. If that sounds scary, read on. Thanks to GNOME, such tasks are no longer the nightmare they once were. In this chapter, you'll learn how to use GNOME and other easy-to-use tools to perform routine system administration tasks.

Mounting Disks and Filesystems

To use the files on external storage devices, such as CD-ROM drives, ZIP drives, and floppy disks, you must *mount* them. When you mount a disk, Linux adds the disk's contents to the Linux filesystem, using a *mount point* such as /mnt/floppy or /mnt/cdrom.

TIP Remember, Linux requires you to log on as root user in order to mount disk drives. If you haven't already done so, turn to Chapter 7 and follow the instructions for making your disk drives available to users (including yourself).

Mounting Disks with GNOME

When you've configured GNOME (see Chapter 7) so that users can access disk drives, you'll see all the mountable drives represented by folders on the desktop. If the folders aren't there, try right-clicking the desktop background, and choose Recreate Desktop Shortcuts from the pop-up menu.

To mount a disk, follow these instructions:

1. Make sure there is a disk in the drive.

2. Double-click the drive icon. File Manager mounts the drive and opens a File Manager window so you can see the drive's contents.

CAUTION Once you've mounted a disk, do not remove it until you have unmounted it, as explained in the following section. If you've mounted a CD-ROM disk, the drive's Eject button won't work until you have unmounted the disk.

Unmounting Disks with GNOME

To unmount a disk, right-click the disk's desktop icon, and choose Unmount from the pop-up menu.

TIP If you see an error message indicating that the disk could not be unmounted, make sure it is not in use. Close any applications that are using the disk, including File Manager.

After you unmount the disk, it's safe to remove the disk from the drive.

TIP You can add drive mount icons to the Panel. For information, see "Adding Drive Mount Buttons to Panels," in Chapter 10.

Mounting Your Windows Partition

Did you create a two-OS system? If so, you can add your Microsoft Windows partition to the list of mountable drives. You can even configure Linux so that the Windows partition is mounted automatically at the beginning of each Linux session.

TIP You'll need to know the device name (such as /dev/hda1) of the partition on which your Windows filesystem is stored.

To configure Linux to mount your Windows partition, do the following:

1. If necessary, log out and log in again as root user.

2. Click the Main Menu button, point to System, and choose LinuxConf. You'll see the Gnome-LinuxConf dialog box.

3. In the tree list, find File systems, and select Access local drive. You'll see the Local volume list, shown in Figure 12.1.

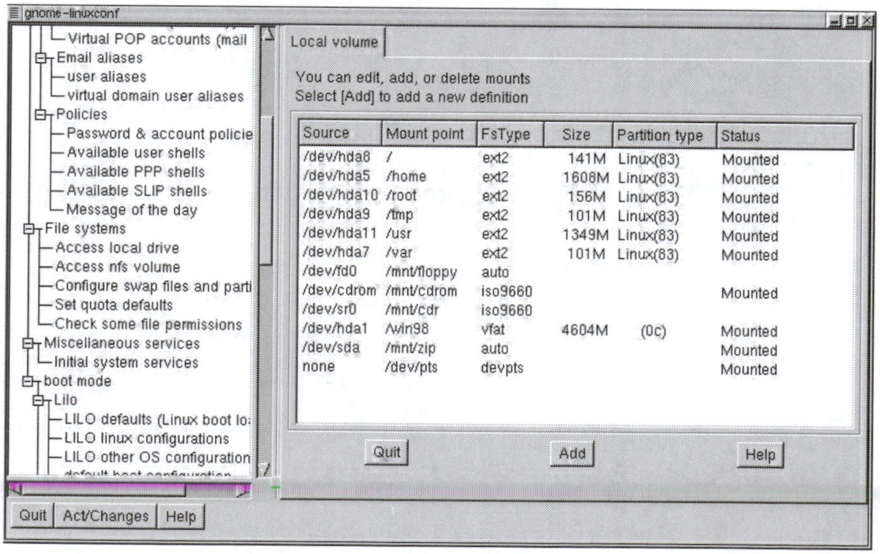

Figure 12.1 You can add a Windows (vfat) filesystem to Linux.

4.   Click Add. You'll see the Volume specification page.

5.   In the Partition box, type the device name of your Windows partition. (This is probably **/dev/hda1**.)

6.   In the Type list box, choose vfat.

7.   In the Mount point box, type **/mnt/win**.

8.   If you would like users to be able to access Windows files, click Options, and activate the User mountable option.

9.   Click Accept.

10. Click Quit.

11. Click Act/Changes.

12. Click Activate the changes.

Formatting a Floppy Disk

Before you can use floppy disks with your Linux system, you must format them. In the Linux world, formatting refers to the process of preparing the disk for use by establishing magnetic patterns on the disk's surface; the term is synonymous with *low-level formatting* in the MS-DOS and Windows worlds. Low-level formatting alone isn't sufficient for disk usage; you must also create the Linux file system on the freshly formatted disk. If you perform this task with Linux command-line options, it's a two-step affair: first you format, and then you create the Linux filesystem.

Thanks to the KDE Floppy Formatter, one of the utilities accessible from the KDE menu, this job is much easier. Formatting a disk and creating the filesystem is as easy as clicking a button. (To use the KDE Floppy Formatter, you must have installed the KDE desktop, utilities, and applications, as explained in Chapter 5.)

CAUTION Be aware that formatting wipes out all the data that may be present on a disk. If a disk contains data, be sure to remove it before formatting the disk.

To format a floppy disk using the KDE Floppy Formatter, follow these steps:

1.   Insert the disk you want to format in the disk drive.

2.   Click the Main Menu button, point to KDE menus, point to Utilities, and choose KFloppy. You'll see the KDE Floppy Formatter window (see Figure 12.2).

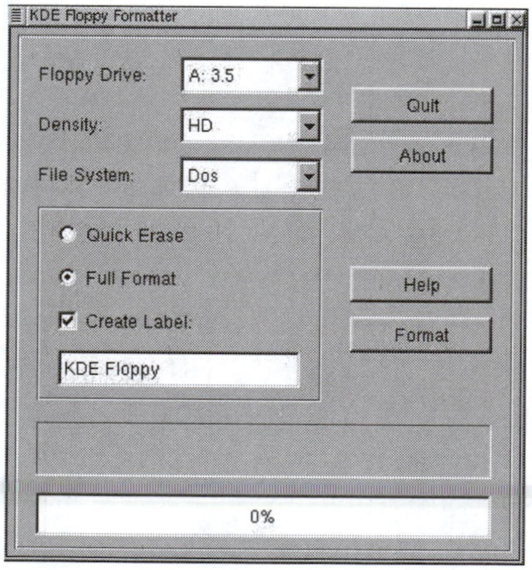

Figure 12.2 It's easy to format disks with the KDE Floppy Formatter.

3. In the Floppy Drive area, choose the name of the drive you want to format. The default is Drive A (/dev/fd0).

4. In the Density area, choose the density. HD (High Density) is the default.

5. In the File System area, choose the filesystem. You can choose from DOS (the default) or ext2 (Linux).

6. In the options list, choose Quick Erase to remove existing files, or Full Format to perform a full, low-level format of the disk. (The default setting is Full Format.)

7. If you would like to label the disk, check Create Label, and type a label in the text box.

8. Click Format to start formatting the floppy disk.

TIP If you didn't install the KDE desktop and utilities, you can use the User Mount Tool to format floppy disks. To use the User Mount Tool, click the Main Menu button, point to System, and choose Disk Management. You'll see the User Mount Tool. Locate the floppy disk entry (/dev/fd0), and click Format. Note: if the disk is mounted, click Unmount before you click Format.

Determining the Amount of Free Disk Space

To find out how much free space is left on any of the mounted storage devices on your system, you can use GNOME Disk-Free or the GNOME System Monitor. Both are shown in Figure 12.3; DiskFree is the utility on the left, with watch-face dials indicating the amount of space that has been consumed on each device. DiskFree is great for a quick view of how much space is left on a drive; the GNOME System Monitor gives you an exact count of the remaining free space.

To open DiskFree, click the Main Menu button, point to Utilities, and choose GNOME DiskFree.

To open the System Monitor, click the Main Menu button, point to Utilities, and choose System Monitor. When System Monitor opens, click the Filesystems (free) tab.

TIP If you're concerned about running out of disk space, you can add the Disk Usage applet to the Panel. To add the applet, click the Main Menu button, point to Panel, point to Add Applet, point to Monitors, and choose Disk Usage. Click the applet background to cycle through all your mounted drives. To choose applet properties, right-click the applet background, and choose Properties.

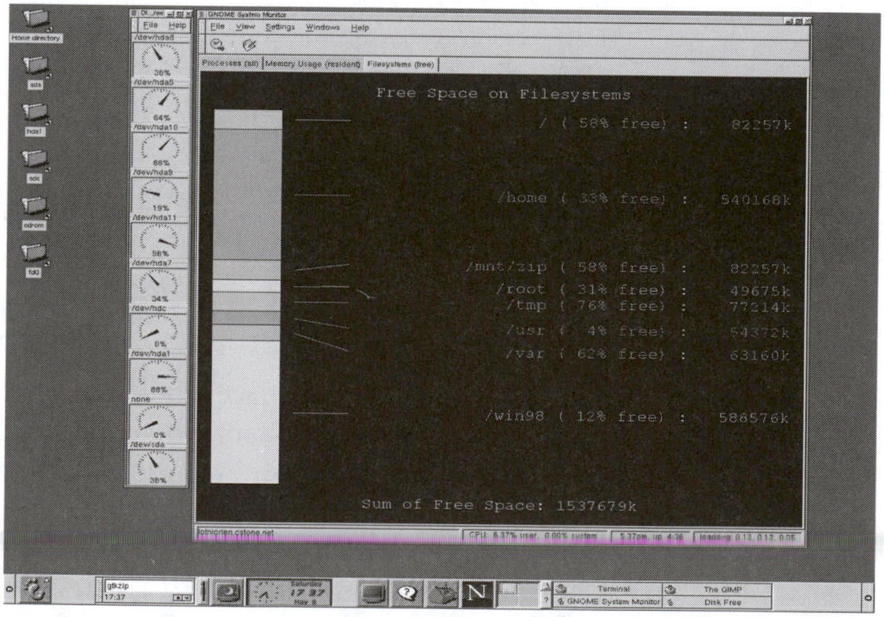

Figure 12.5 These tools check remaining disk space.

A Note on Disk Defragmentation

The term *defragmentation* refers to a process in which pieces of a file become separated from one another during the course of normal storage operations. (This doesn't prevent the files from being used, since the disk utilities keep track of where the various pieces are located.) However, defragmentation slows down a disk drive because the drive head must do more work to find and assemble the various components of a file.

Windows users are accustomed to running defragmentation utilities on their hard drives at regular intervals—as often as once per day, for heavily used systems. But the ext2 filesystem virtually rules out fragmentation, thanks to its advanced design. In ext2, the various portions of a file are automatically kept together as much as possible, so fragmentation seldom becomes an issue.

Installing and Upgrading Software

If Unix-like operating systems have a poor reputation for ease of use, one reason is the difficulty users experience when it comes to installing and upgrading software. Happily, that's changed thanks to Red Hat Software's Red Hat Package Manager (RPM), which provides easy-to-use facilities for installing, uninstalling, and upgrading software provided in rpm packages (files with an *.rpm extension). In the spirit of open source software, Red Hat Software has made the Package Manager available in the form of open source code licensed under the GNU public license (GPL).

You can use RPM by typing commands at the command line, if you wish. And as you'll see, there are some command line options that aren't available if you run the program using friendlier interfaces. For most operations, though, you'll probably prefer to run GnoRPM, the GNOME manager for RPM files. It's a nifty utility, as you'll see—especially when you learn how it's integrated with RPM archives located on the Internet.

Understanding Package Installation

As you'll quickly learn when you begin installing RPM packages, a single program often requires you to install two more separate RPM files. And the order is critical. That's because many packages have *package dependencies*, a term that refers to a package's need to have one or more other packages installed before its own installation becomes possible. If you try to install the packages in the wrong order, you'll get an error message, informing you that a package dependency error has occurred. You'll also see a note informing you which package needs to be installed in order to install the current package.

To make sure you're installing all the packages in the correct order, consult the program's documentation or installation tips prior to installing the RPMs. If the documentation isn't available, you can sometimes work backwards through the error messages to determine the correct order, but this process can get very tedious if the program requires a dozen or more RPMs (which is sometimes the case).

Introducing GnoRPM

GnoRPM is a useful utility that enables you to work with RPM files in a variety of ways. You can do the following with GnoRPM:

- View the list of currently installed packages.
- Find out more information about a given package.
- Verify that all of the software associated with the package is correctly installed.
- Create a desktop launcher for a package.
- Install or upgrade a package on the Red Hat Linux CD-ROM.
- Locate and install an RPM package on the Internet.

TIP You'll need to run GnoRPM as the root user. If you're currently logged in with your user account, log out and log in as root.

To start GnoRPM, click the Main Menu button, point to System, and chose GnoRPM. You'll see the GnoRPM dialog box, shown in Figure 12.4. In the left panel, you see the tree list, which shows the various categories of RPM packages currently installed on your system.

Finding a Package

To find a package, you can hunt manually using the tree navigation tools, but it's faster (and easier) to use the Find command. Follow these instructions to find a package:

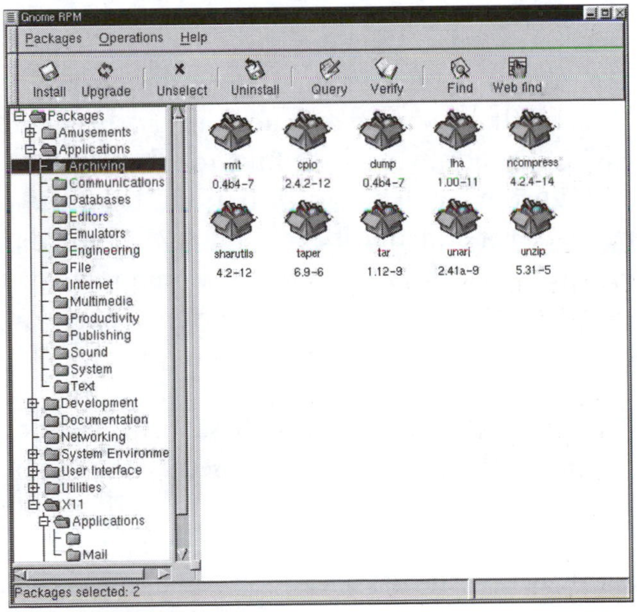

Figure 12.4 GnoRPM makes it easy to install new software.

1. On the GnoRPM menu bar, click Find. You'll see the Find Packages dialog box.

2. In the list box, choose the matching characteristic you want (you can choose from the following options: contain file, are in the group, provide, require, conflict with, match label). To search for a package by name, choose **match label**.

3. In the text box, type text to search for.

4. Click Find.

If GnoRPM finds a match, you'll see a list of matching packages in the window. From here, you can query, uninstall, or verify the package; the following sections discuss these actions.

Querying Packages

To find out what a package does, select the package and click Query. You'll see the Package Info dialog box, shown in Figure 12.5. (If you've examined any other packages in this GnoRPM session, you'll see tabs for those packages, as shown in the figure.) You'll see information about the package's purpose, size, version number, build (creation) date, and install date. You'll also find links to the home page of the program's author. (If you're connected to the Internet, you can click the link to find out more about the program.)

In the scrolling text area, you'll see a brief description of the program. In the list area, you'll see all of the program's files; characters in the D, C, and S columns indicate whether the file is a man page document (D), a configuration file (C), or source code (S). Below the list area, you'll see the Verify and Uninstall buttons.

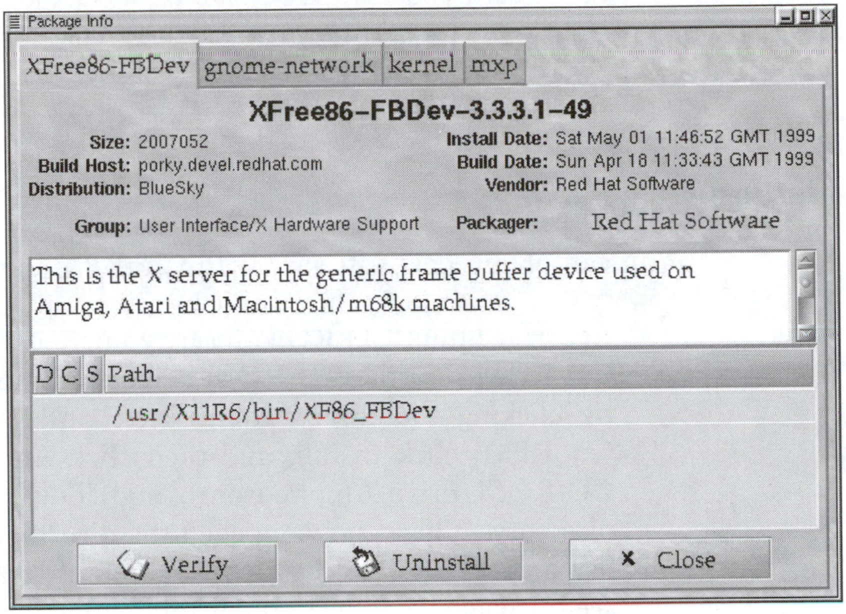

Figure 12.6 When you query a package, you find out what it does.

> **CAUTION** Don't uninstall a package unless you're absolutely sure it's no longer needed. Due to package dependencies, discussed earlier in this chapter, you might uninstall a program that is needed by other packages. GnoRPM will warn you if you try to uninstall a package on which other packages depend, but it's best not to experiment with the Uninstall feature until you've mastered all the fundamentals of Linux.

Verifying a Package

If a package's software isn't running correctly, it's possible that one or more of the files on which it depends has become corrupt or was inadvertently deleted. You can verify the package by selecting the package and clicking Verify. You'll see the Verifying Packages dialog box. If GnoRPM finds any problems, you'll see the file's name and a note indicating the nature of the problem.

TIP If a package doesn't pass verification, it's best to uninstall the package and re-install it. To uninstall the package, select it and click Uninstall. See "Installing a Package," later in this section, for information on locating a fresh copy of the package.

Installing New Packages

You can obtain new software with GnoRPM in two ways:

- **Red Hat Linux CD-ROM** Insert your Red Hat Linux 6.0 CD-ROM into the CD-ROM drive, and mount the drive by clicking the drive's folder icon on the desktop. In GnoRPM, click Install, and then click Add. Open your CD-ROM drive (/mnt/cdrom), and look for an RPMS directory. When you've opened the directory, you'll see a list of packages. Select a package, and click Add; you'll see the package name in the Install dialog box. To find out what it does, click Query. To install the package, click Install.

- **Web Find** If your computer is connected to the Internet, you can make use of a very cool feature called Web Find. This feature makes contact with an Internet-accessible database of thousands of RPM packages, which you can download and install without having to use a Web browser or an FTP tool. To obtain software using Web Find, click the Web Find button; you'll see the Rpmfind dialog box, which displays a tree list of available packages. In the Distribution column, you can tell at a glance whether the package is installed on your system; if it is, you'll see the version number. Click on a package name to learn more about the package (see Figure 12.6). If you already have the package but find a newer version, click Upgrade; if you don't have the package, click Install.

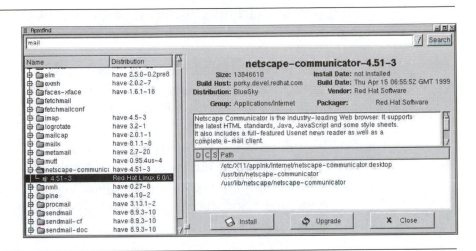

Figure 12.6 GnoRPM can download RPM packages from the Internet.

Installing RPM Packages with File Manager

If you've downloaded an RPM package from a Web site without using GnoRPM, you can install it using File Manager. To do so, just double-click the file; you'll see what appears to be a subdirectory. In reality, this is part of File Manager's *virtual file system (VFS)*, which makes certain types of data appear as if they are part of the Linux filesystem. To get more information about the package, open the INFO folder and read the documentation you'll find. To install the program, double-click Install (for new packages) or Upgrade (for a new version of a package already installed on your system).

Working with Compressed Files and Archives

In the Windows world, file compression programs generally perform archiving tasks as well. (An *archive* is a file—not necessarily compressed—containing two or more files.) Traditionally, UNIX and Linux software keeps these operations separate:

- **Compression** Of the several UNIX and Linux compression programs in common use, gzip is by far the most popular. However, other compression formats are in use, including the zip format (identical to the WinZip/PKzip format in Windows and DOS).
- **Archiving** The archive program of choice for UNIX and Linux is tar, a program originally developed for archiving data to backup tapes (the name "tar" stands for "tape archiver").

A compressed file that contains a tar archive generally has two extensions (.tar.gz). At the command prompt, decompressing the file and extracting the files from the archive is a two-step operation, but that's no longer necessary, thanks to GNOME utilities. An example is gxTar, a GNOME-compatible compression and archiving utility. This program seeks to become nothing less than the WinZip of the Linux world; it seamlessly combines decompression and archive extraction functions. Still in early beta, gxTar will have more capability by the time you read this, so be sure to check the program's Web site and obtain a recent copy.

TIP You can obtain and download a copy of the gxTar RPM at gxtar.netpedia.net. After you've downloaded the RPM, switch to root user, open File Manager, double-click the RPM file, and choose Install.

After you've obtained and installed gxTar, add the program to the GNOME menus by using the Menu Editor (see Chapter 10).

Decompressing and Extracting Files

To open a compressed file, an archived file, or a file that is both an archive and compressed, do the following:

1. Assuming the package installed gxTar in /usr/local/bin, type **/usr/local/bin/gxtar** to start the program. (If this doesn't work, a newer package version may have installed the program elsewhere; use Find File to locate the program, and start it by typing the full path and program name.) You'll see the gxTar dialog box onscreen (see Figure 12.7).

2. Click Open, locate and select the file, and click OK. You'll see the archive's contents in the gxTar file list, as shown in Figure 12.7.

Figure 12.7 gxTar makes it easy to work with file archives.

3. To decompress the file and extract the contents of the archive, select the files (to select all the files, press Ctrl + A), and then click Extract. You'll see the Extract Archives dialog box.

4. Select a location for the extracted files. To create a new directory, click Show Fileops, and click Create Dir.

5. Click OK to decompress and extract the files.

Creating an Archive

To create a file archive with gxTar, do the following:

1. Click New and select a location for the archive.

2. In the text box, type a name for the archive in the text box. To create an archive, use the .tar extension. To create a compressed file, use the .gz extension. To create a compressed archive, use the tar.gz extension.

3. Click OK to create the new archive.

    You'll see the Add Files to Archive dialog box.

4. Locate and select the files you want to add to the archive. You can select more than one file. Click OK to add the files.

5. To close the archive, just click the Close button.

Backing Up Your Work

When you're using Linux, it's very, very important to back up your work. Should the power to your system fail, you could be left with scrambled data. Don't do serious, professional work with Linux without developing a backup routine.

Here are some backup software options:

- **gxTar** If your system is equipped with a Zip or some other removable drive, you can use gxTar to perform backups of your important files. Just create a compressed archive on /mnt/zip, and add the files you want backed up.
- **PerfectBACKUP** This nifty X utility can handle a variety of backup media, including tape drives and Zip disks. You can create schedules and perform a variety of backup operations, including full, incremental, and differential backups.
- **X-CD-Roast** This program can back up data to inexpensive CD-R disks.

TIP It's wise to perform a full backup of your entire hard disk and perform additional backups on changed files. However, it's inconvenient to perform a full hard drive backup unless your computer is equipped with a backup tape drive. For this reason, you may wish to back up only the /home directory. This directory contains all the user configuration files. Should your Linux drive fail, you can rebuild your system by reinstalling Red Hat Linux and restoring your /home directory; you'll have saved all your configuration information and data files.

Changing Your Password

Should you wish to change your password, click the Main Menu button, point to System, and choose Change Password.

In the Input dialog box, type the new password, and click OK. You'll be asked to type the password again for confirmation.

Setting the System Time and Date

If you need to adjust the system time and date, click the Main Menu button, point to System, and choose Time Tool. You'll see the Time Machine, shown in Figure 12.8. To change the date or time, just click on the part of the date or time that you want to change, and click the up or down arrows. Click Set System Clock to change to the new settings. Click Exit Time Machine when you're done.

Figure 12.8 Use the Time Machine to change the system date and time.

From Here

In this chapter, you've learned the fundamentals of system administration for a desktop Linux system, and you've completed your mastery of the GNOME desktop system. In the next part of this book, you learn how to connect your Linux system to the Internet.

References and Further Reading

Biro, Ross. 1995. "Design and Implemenation of the Second Extended Filesystem." Available online at http://ftp.yggdrasil.com/bible/sag-0.2/sag/node66.html.

Hsiao, Aron. 1999. "Let's Mount!" *Mining Co. Focus on Linux* (March 17, 1999). Available online at http://linux.tqn.com/library/weekly/aa072698.htm.

Knaff, Alain. 1999. *Mtools: Accessing MS-DOS Disks*. Available online from http://www.tux.org/pub/tux/knfaff/mtools/mtools.htm.

Sladkey, Rick *et al.* 1999. *Linux Manual Page: mount*. Available online from the Linux Documentation Project.

Weisshaus, Melissa *et al.* 1997. *GNU tar: An Archiver Tool*. Cambridge, Mass: Free Software Foundation. Available online from the Linux Documentation Project.

Part Four

Getting Connected to the Internet

13

Connecting with PPP

In this chapter, you'll learn how to connect your Linux system to the Internet by means of a modem, a telephone line, the Port-to-Port Protocol (PPP) communication standard, and an Internet subscription with an Internet service provider (ISP). Although it's possible to connect to ISPs that still use the older Serial Line Interface Protocol (SLIP), it's much more difficult to configure Linux to use SLIP, which isn't recommended for beginners. Almost all ISPs use PPP nowadays—and if your ISP doesn't, consider switching to one that offers more modern technology. (If you're hoping to connect via cutting-edge technologies such as ISDN, ADSL, or a cable modem, see "Using Other Connection Methods," at the end of this chapter.)

Thanks to user-friendly utilities such as netcfg (discussed in this chapter), this chapter's tasks are much easier to perform than they were in the past, but there's still a chance you'll run into problems—particularly if you're using unsupported equipment. You'll be wise to stop right now if your modem isn't on the list of supported peripherals (see Chapter 3). In particular, you can't use any modem that uses software to emulate compression (such as any modem described as a "winmodem"). Rather than spending days trying to get an unsupported modem to work, wouldn't it be smarter to spend $59 on one that will work instantly?

There's more to success here than mere electronics, though. To connect successfully, you'll need to follow this chapter's instructions carefully. In particular, you need *all* the information discussed in the next section. To obtain it, you'll need to speak to your ISP's technical support representatives. When you do, you might want to think twice about mentioning that you're trying to connect with a Linux system. You'll probably be told, rather icily, "We don't support Linux," and that's that. Instead, focus on getting your specific questions answered (see the next section for a detailed list). Once you've obtained this information, you'll be connected—and surfing—in short order.

> **TIP** If your computer connects to a local area network (LAN) by means of a network interface card, you may already have an Internet connection. Check with your network administrator to find out whether Internet access is available through your LAN.

Getting the Information You'll Need

To connect your Linux system to the Internet, you'll need the information about your modem listed in Table 3.1, in Chapter 4. You'll also need the following information from your ISP:

- **Telephone number** What number do you dial to reach your Internet service provider (ISP)?
- **Authentication information** When you connect to your ISP's computer, what user name do you supply? What is your password?
- **IP address** Does your ISP assign a static (fixed) IP address to your computer? If so, what is this address? Most ISP's use dynamic addressing, but check to make sure. In dynamic addressing, your ISP assigns a temporary IP number to your computer automatically.
- **DNS numbers** What are the IP addresses of the primary and secondary DNS servers?
- **Password authentication** Must you use a password authentication protocol when you log in, such as PAP or CHAP? Or is the initial login accomplished in plain text?
- **Login procedure** Exactly what prompts are presented when your computer first makes a connection, and what must you type to log in?
- **PPP connection startup** Does the PPP connection start automatically after you have supplied your user name and password, or do you have to type a command? If so, what is the command?
- **Mail server** What is the Internet address of the server used for incoming mail (also called the POP server or POP3 server)? What is the Internet address of the server used for outgoing mail (also called the SMTP server)? Sometimes the incoming and outgoing mail servers have the same address; sometimes they're different.
- **E-mail information** What is your e-mail address? What is the password you use to access your e-mail?
- **News server** What is the Internet address of the news server? Is it necessary to supply a user name and password to access the news server? If so, what are these?

With all this information in hand when you begin, you'll have a much better chance of connecting successfully. If you guess at any of these, chances are your connection won't work.

Configuring Your Modem

Provided you're using a Linux-compatible modem (see Chapter 4), it's a simple task to configure your modem to work with Linux. In this section, you use the Linux configuration utility (modemtool) to perform an essential first step: Establishing the link between the Linux device name for your modem (/dev/modem) and the serial port to which your modem is connected. If this sounds difficult, relax: You need to know just one crucial bit of information, namely, the serial port to which your modem is connected.

Determining the Serial Port

In the MS-DOS and Windows world, serial ports are described as COM1, COM2, COM3, or COM4. Chances are good that your modem is connected to COM2, since many systems use COM1 for a mouse. In Chapter 3, you noted the COM port that your modem is currently using. In Table 13.1, you'll learn the nomenclature that Linux uses to describe serial ports.

Table 13.1 Serial port device names

MS-DOS	Port	IRQ	Linux Device name
COM1	0x3f8	4	/dev/cua0 or /dev/tty00
COM2	0x2f8	3	/dev/cua1 or /dev/tty01
COM3	0x3e8	4	/dev/cua2 or /dev/tty02
COM4	0x2e8	3	/dev/cua3 or /dev/tty03

Telling Linux Which Port Your Modem Is Using

Now that you know the Linux nomenclature for serial ports, you can configure your Linux system to access your modem. Here's how:

1. **Important:** Log in as the root user. You can't configure your modem from your user account.

2. Click the Main Menu button, point to System, and choose Control Panel. You'll see the Red Hat Control Panel.

3. Scroll down to the icon showing a telephone (Modem Configuration), and click this icon.

   You'll see the Configure Modem dialog box, shown in Figure 13.1.

4. Select the serial port to which your modem is connected, and click OK.

Testing Your Modem

The steps you just completed should be sufficient to enable your modem to work—that is, respond to commands and dial a number. To make sure your modem is working correctly, try accessing your modem using minicom, a Linux communication program. A communications program enables your computer to connect to non-Internet dialup services, such as bulletin board systems (BBS). Here, you'll use minicom just to see whether your modem will respond to minicom. If it does, you're in business, and you can proceed to the next step (running the netcfg utility).

To run minicom, do the following:

1. Click the Main Menu button, point to AnotherLevel
    menus, point to Network, and choose Minicom.

    The program immediately attempts to access your
    modem. If all goes well, you'll see the characters AT fol-
    lowed by an initialization string (commands that config-
    ure the modem), followed by the modem's OK response
    (see Figure 13.2). If you don't see OK, you have config-
    ured the wrong port setting. Run the modem configura-
    tion utility again, and choose the correct one.

2. Try dialing the number of the line connected to your
    modem. You'll get a busy signal, of course, but this will
    enable you to test whether your modem can obtain a dial
    tone and dial correctly. To dial your number, type **ATDT**
    followed by a space and your telephone number. Press

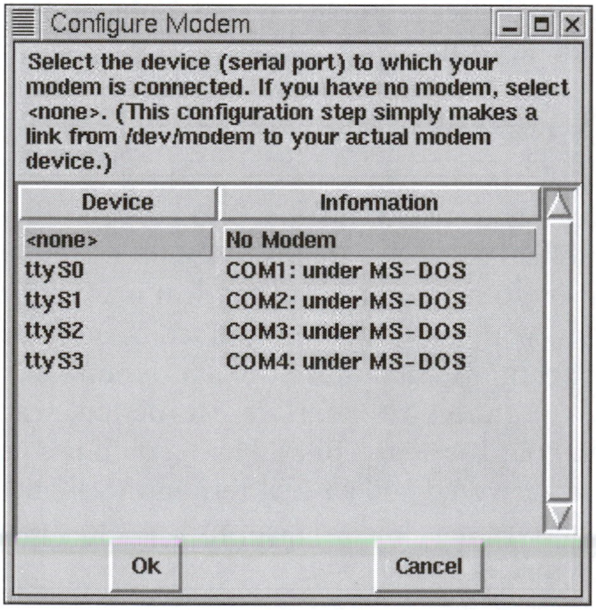

Figure 13.1 In this dialog box, choose your modem's serial port.

Enter to start dialing. Once you've gotten a busy signal, press Ctrl + A, H to hang up.

If you don't get a dial tone, make sure you've connected your modem to a modular telephone outlet, and that both connections (the one on the modem end and the one plugged into the modular phone jack) are securely seated.

3. Now try dialing your ISP. You won't be able to log on (you haven't configured PPP yet) but you'll be able to see exactly which prompts your ISP uses during the login procedure. This information is needed to configure your PPP connection. To connect to your ISP, type **ATDT** followed by a space and your ISP's connection number. Press Enter. You'll see a prompt for your username, which will look something like this:

    ```
    Username:
    ```

Figure 13.2 If you see "OK," you've set up your modem correctly.

Type your username, and press Enter. Next, you'll see a prompt for your password, which will look something like this:

```
password:
```

Type your password, and press Enter. You may see an additional message specifying what to type to establish a PPP connection; if so, write this information down. Most systems will respond by displaying a message such as "Entering PPP mode." If so, your ISP's computers shift into PPP automatically. Since you haven't set up PPP yet, there's no point in staying online, so hang up (press Ctrl + A, H).

4. Press Ctrl + A, Q to shut down your modem and exit minicom.

TIP Write down the exact spelling of the prompts you saw, including any punctuation (such as the colon in the preceding example). Also note whether the computer shifts into PPP automatically or requires you to type something to start PPP. You'll need this information to configure your PPP connection.

Troubleshooting Modem Problems

If you couldn't access your modem with minicom, try the following:

- Make sure your modem is properly seated in the expansion slot and that all the connections are snug.
- Make sure you linked /dev/modem to the correct serial port (normally cua1, but your modem might be installed

in a different port). If you linked /dev/modem to the wrong port, run modemtool again.

- Make sure your modem is set to the correct interrupt (IRQ). To determine the current IRQ assignment for the serial port to which your modem is connected, type **setserial /dev/modem** at the Linux prompt, and press Enter. You'll see the current port assignment and IRQ. Now shut down your system and examine your modem. If your modem has jumpers that enable you to configure the port manually, examine the jumpers to make sure that they match the way you've configured your modem using modemtool. If not, change the jumpers so that they match.

- Restart your system, and press the key that enables you to enter your computer's startup menu (where you can examine the BIOS and other settings). Find the area where serial ports are listed, and make sure that these settings have not been changed from the defaults (COM 1 should be set to 0x3f8 and IRQ 4, while COM 2 should be set to 0x2f8 and IRQ 3. If these settings were changed, try resetting them to the defaults.

If none of these measures work, your modem may not be compatible with Linux—many aren't. See Chapter 4 for an explanation of modem compatibility problems. Many reasonably good, Linux-compatible modems are available for bargain prices; it's better to replace your modem than to spend days in a courageous but possibly unsuccessful attempt to get your current modem working.

Configuring Your PPP Connection

Assuming your modem is working correctly, you're ready to configure your system for Internet access. Thanks to Network Configurator, a user-friendly configuration program, this procedure is considerably easier than it used to be. Still, you'll need to pay very careful attention to the login procedure that your ISP requires, and you may need to do some experimentation in order to connect successfully.

TIP Since you may need to get information from your ISP's technical support personnel, perform this procedure during the hours that your ISP's technical support hotline is available.

Starting the Network Configurator

Check to make sure you have all the information you need (see "Getting All the Information You Need," earlier in this chapter). If you have all the information you need, you're ready to start configuring your Internet settings.

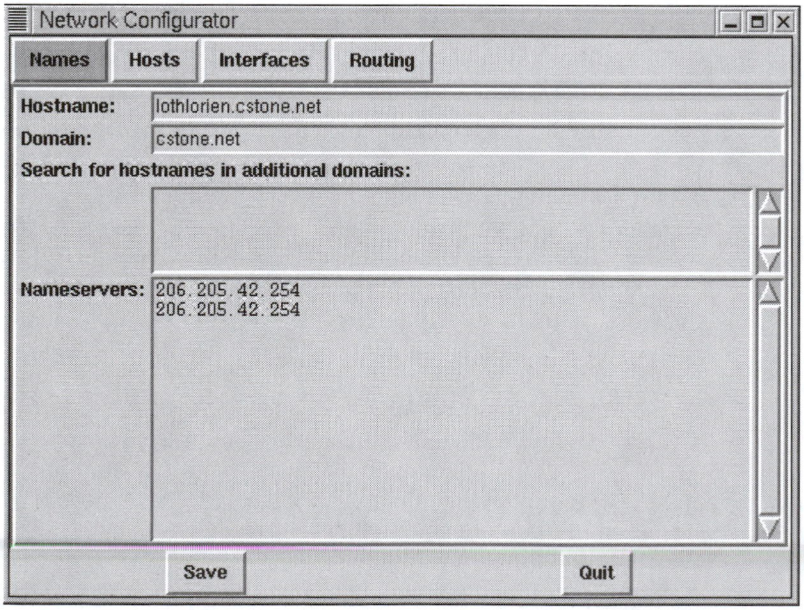

Figure 13.3 The netcfg utility sets up your Internet connection.

To configure these settings, do the following:

1. Click the Main Menu button, point to System, and choose Control Panel. You'll see the Red Hat Control Panel.

2. Click the Network Configuration icon. You'll see the Network Configurator, shown in Figure 13.3.

3. Click the Interfaces tab. You'll see the Interfaces page.

4. Click Add. You'll see a dialog box that enables you to specify the type of connection you're creating.

5. Check PPP, if necessary, and click OK.

    You'll see the Create PPP Interface dialog box, shown in Figure 13.4.

6. Supply the requested information, and double-check your typing. If your ISP uses PAP authentication, activate the check box. **Important:** Do *not* activate this option unless your ISP specifically tells you that PAP is required.

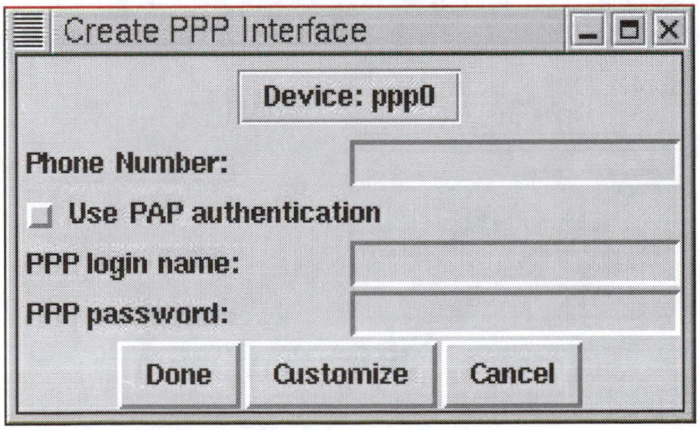

Figure 13.4 Specify your connection information here.

> **TIP** If you must dial an access code or area code to dial the ISP's number, don't forget to add this information. To add a brief delay between numbers, insert a couple of commas (this is particularly useful if you must dial 9 to access an outside line; type 9,, followed by the number). If your line has call waiting, consider prefacing the telephone number with the code that disables call waiting during the duration of the call; with many local telephone companies, this code is *70. (Check with your phone company to make sure.) Be sure to follow this code with a couple of commas, and then type the telephone number, as in this example: *70,,5551212.

7. Click Customize. You'll see the Edit PPP Interface dialog box, shown in Figure 13.5. The default settings here are fine for most users.

8. Click Communication. You'll see the Communication settings, shown in Figure 13.6. Unless you selected PAP authorization in step 6, you must help Network Configurator compose a script that will log in automatically. The program has already entered much of the required infor-

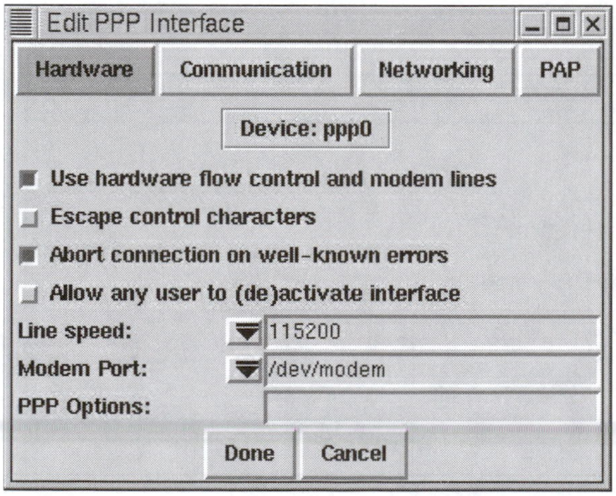

Figure 13.5 The default settings here are fine for most users.

mation for you. If you selected PAP authorization, this page will show your username and password. You can skip to step 9.

TIP Pay particular attention to the settings in this dialog box; if you have a problem connecting, chances are good that it's due to an error here.

The Communication page enables you to set up an automated connection with your ISP's server. To set up this connection, you must tell Network Configurator exactly what text to expect when your ISP prompts for a login name and password, and exactly what to send when these prompts are detected. There are other settings in this dialog box, but tackle the expect/send pairs first.

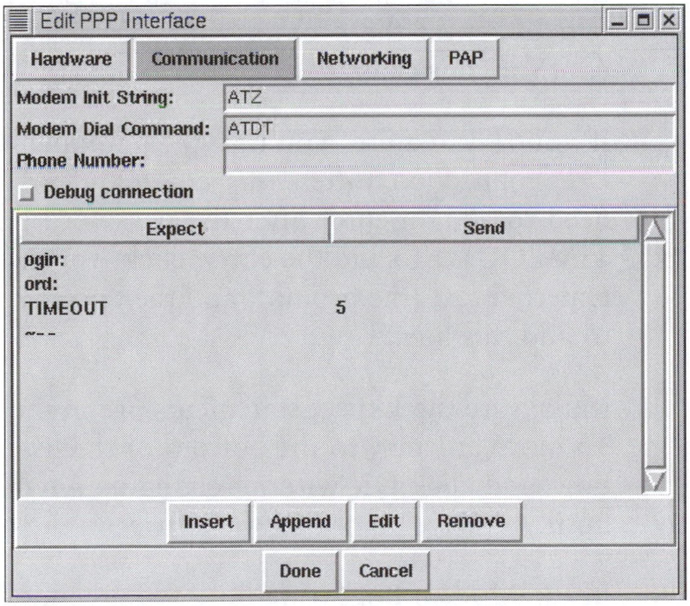

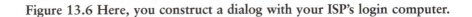

Figure 13.6 Here, you construct a dialog with your ISP's login computer.

In the Expect column, note the entries "ogin:" and "ord:". The "ogin:" entry tells your PPP software to wait until your ISP's computer sends those exact characters; it then responds with your username. Notice that "ogin:" is short for "login:"; it's common to omit the first one or two letters of the expected text, since these are sometimes dropped in transmission. The second Expect entry, "ord:", is short for "password:".

If your ISP's computer presents prompts that match these ("login:" followed by "password:"), then you need not edit these entries. Suppose, however, that your ISP's computer prompts for "username:" instead of "login:", as is often the case. You will need to edit the "ogin:" entry and change it to "name:".

To edit an entry, select the entry and click Edit. You'll see the Edit Chat Entry dialog box. In the Expect line, edit the text to reflect the prompt your ISP uses. Click Done to confirm your change.

If your ISP requires you to type a command to begin the PPP connection (often this command is "PPP"), you'll need to add an entry after the password line (but before TIMEOUT). To add the entry, click Append, and type the expected text (the prompt) and the text to send. Click OK to add this line.

Make sure the Expect statements are in the correct order. To move an entry to the bottom of the list, select it, click Edit, and click OK without changing anything. Continue until you have placed all the entries in the correct order.

9. In the Modem Init String box, type the modem initialization string that your modem requires. You can obtain this information from your modem's documentation.

10. Click Networking. You'll see the Networking page, shown in Figure 13.7. The defaults are fine for most users, except that you may wish to type the maximum values (1500) in the MRU and MTU boxes. Unless your ISP told you that you need to specify a local or remote IP address, leave these settings blank.

    If your ISP told you that you must configure your system to use the Password Authentication Protocol (PAP), click the PAP button. In the Send username box, type your username (login name). Next, click the Append button. In the Expect box, type your username again. In the Send box, type your password, and click OK.

11. Click Done. You'll see a dialog box asking you to confirm saving the configuration.

12. Click Save.

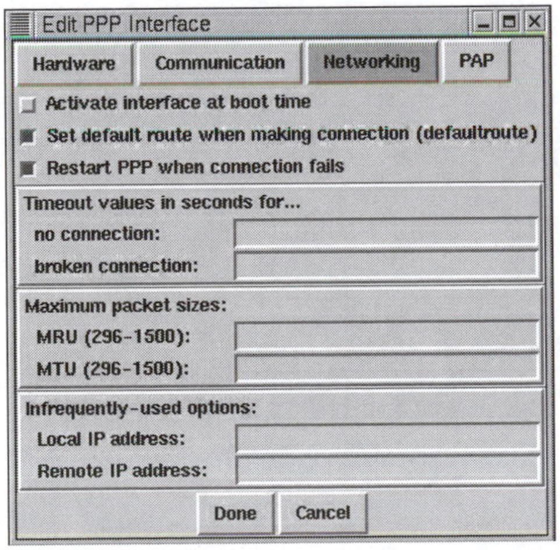

Figure 13.7 In this page, you specify additional connection settings.

13. In the main Network Configurator window, click Names. In the Nameservers box, type the Internet (IP) addresses of your ISP's DNS servers (nameservers). Generally, there are two such servers, a primary server and a secondary server. Type the primary server's address on the first line, and type the secondary server's address on the second line.

    You can leave the other boxes blank.

14. Click Save.

15. Click Interfaces.

16. Select the ppp0 interface that you just defined, and click Activate. Your modem will immediately begin dialing the connection.

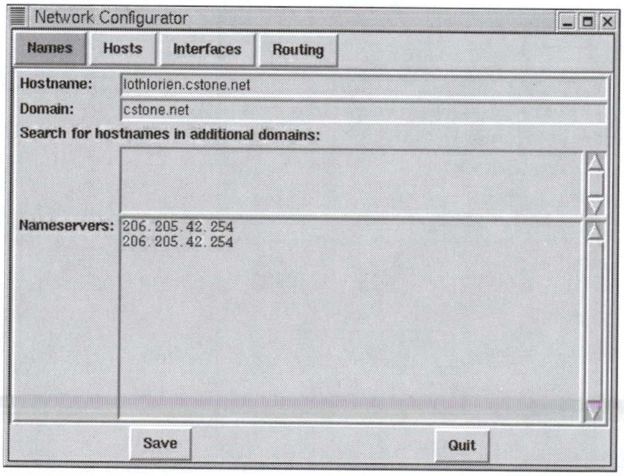

Figure 13.8 Here, you specify the DNS (nameserver) addresses.

Determining Whether Your Connection Is Working

It's an eerie sensation to log on for the first time—you can't tell whether you've succeeded in making the connection, because absolutely nothing happens. To determine whether you're connected, open an xterm window. At the Linux prompt, type **ping** followed by the Internet address of one of your ISP's nameservers (for example, you could type **ping 206.205.42.254**). Press Enter. If you're on the Internet, you'll see responses from the computer you've contacted, indicating that packets have been received. If the transmission fails, something's wrong (see "Troubleshooting Your Connection," below).

Assuming all's well with your connection, open Netscape Communicator by clicking the big green Netscape icon on your Panel. You'll see a Red Hat welcome page that's actually stored on your computer. To access the Internet, click Home, which takes you to Netscape's home page. You're on the Internet!

Activating and Deactivating Connections

Thanks to GNOME, the task of activating and deactivating your connection is quite easy; just install the PPP dialer. To do so, click the Main Menu button, point to Panel, point to Add Applet, point to Network, and choose PPP Dialer. You'll see the PPP dialer applet on the Panel.

To initiate your connection, just click the Start button (the right-facing triangular arrow) on the PPP Dialer applet.

To hang up, click the Stop button (the square one).

Troubleshooting Your Connection

If the modem dials the number, but the connection hangs up soon afterwards, start netcfg and check the following:

- Did you enter the telephone number correctly?
- Did you type your username (login name) and password correctly?
- Did you place the expect/send statements in the correct order?
- Do the expect/send statements match the text that is actually transmitted by the server?
- Did you enter the correct modem initialization string?

If the modem dials the number and seems to connect, but you can't get ping to work, try the following:

- In netcfg, click Names and check the DNS (nameserver) entries. They should consist of four numbers, separated by dots (but no spaces). Did you type them correctly?
- Does your ISP require a command in order to activate PPP? If so, make sure to append a line to the expect/send pairs. (In netcfg, select your PPP connection, click Edit, and click the Communication tab.)

If all else fails, try inserting a blank expect/send pair at the beginning of the expect/send list; sometimes, this produces enough of a delay to eliminate the risk of dropped characters.

Remember that most connection problems are caused by typos that you just didn't see when you proofread your work. One letter or number out of place—in your password, for example, or in the expected text entry—and your connection won't work.

Using Other Connection Methods

Telephone and cable companies are increasingly making high-speed connections available to home and SOHO (small office/home office) users. These services include ISDN (digital telephone service, offering Internet connectivity with speeds up to 128 Kbps), a variety of Digital Subscriber Line services (including ADSL, with Internet connectivity at speeds of up to 1.5 Mbps), and cable modems (with varying speeds, averaging roughly 256 Kbps).

If you'd like to connect your Linux system to one of these services, you're in luck: It's possible, and sometimes it's even easy. That's because ADSL and cable modem services work with Ethernet cards, and you hook up to the service using a standard Ethernet cable. Since Linux is designed to work with Ethernet networks from the get-go, there's no reason (in principle) that you can't connect a Linux box to these advanced, high-speed services.

As usual, the devil is in the details. Many of these high-speed services insist on providing a certain Ethernet card, and most of them are plug-and-play cards—which means that the Linux installation software probably won't recognize the card. To get these cards to work, you need to restart your computer in DOS or Windows, and use the utilities disk provided with the adapter to disable the plug-and-play mode.

Another problem: These services are not nearly as well standardized as PPP; it's one thing to hook up Linux to an Adelphia cable modem, and quite another to do the same with the RoadRunner service.

Although a full discussion of connecting to these services is beyond the scope of this book, the following sections provide an overview of what's required. As long as you're willing to read some online documentation (and scan the newsgroups for specific tips), you should be able to get most of these connections working without too much difficulty.

Connecting with ISDN

Short for Integrated Services Digital Network, ISDN is more popular in Europe and Japan than the United States, thanks to an earlier start (U.S. vendors couldn't agree on an ISDN standard until quite recently). As a result, the ISDN market had only begun to develop when it encountered stiff competition from much faster services, including ADSL and cable modems. If you're looking at ISDN, be aware that you might be able to get much faster connection speeds by skipping ISDN in favor of a Digital Subscriber Line connection or a cable modem.

ISDN can handle voice and data, and makes use of existing telephone wires. Most vendors offer two service levels: a single 56 or 64 Kbps voice/data line, or two 56 or 64 Kbps voice/data lines, for a maximum bandwidth of 128 Kbps. Of the two options, the two-line service is the best, and not only because it's faster: The equipment can automatically detect an incoming or outgoing telephone call, and makes one line available seamlessly. If you're connecting to the Internet at 128 Kbps, you can still make and receive phone calls, and the only thing you'll notice is that your connection speed drops somewhat.

For Linux Systems, the ISDN adapter of choice is one made by SpellCaster (http://www.spellcast.com/products.html), a leader in Linux support. However, you can get Linux to work with just about any "ISDN modem" (the term is technically a misnomer since no digital-analog translation takes place). Such adapters are designed to work just like analog modems, and you should be able to install and configure one by following the instructions in this chapter. You'll run into a challenge getting a two-channel (112 or 128 Kbps) ISDN connection to work; to make use of both channels, you must configure PPP to run in the multilink mode (see PhoneBoy 1998 for instructions).

Connecting with ADSL

Short for Asymmetric Digital Subscriber Line, ADSL is one of a grab-bag of technologies grouped under the Digital Subscriber Line (DSL, or xDSL) rubric. Using ordinary telephone lines, ADSL can deliver Internet data at speeds of up to 1.5 Mbps; uploads are slower, which is why this service is called "asymmetric." ADSL isn't widely available because ADSL signals don't travel more than a couple of miles from the local switching station, so the service is available mainly in upscale urban markets.

A problem with ADSL is lack of standardization, so the vendor will provide you with the equipment you need to connect to the service. This will probably include an Ethernet card, which you may have trouble getting Linux to recognize. Once you solve that problem, configuring Linux to work with ADSL is much like hooking up your system to a local area network. One difficulty you'll encounter is that most of these services require that you configure your computer to work with DHCP; fortunately, it's easy to configure Linux for this service (see Vuksan 1998a).

Connecting with a Cable Modem

Like ADSL, most Internet cable services require you to use an Ethernet card; the challenges you'll face are very much like hooking up to ADSL (getting Linux to recognize your Ethernet card and configuring Linux to work with DHCP). For an excellent overview of cable modems for Linux systems, see

Vuksan 1998b. Some especially enlightened providers are targeting Linux users; Adelphia offers a comprehensive HOWTO (see Sigler 1998) as well as an installation script.

From Here

At this point, you've got a super Linux system for the desktop. You've got sound, a graphical user interface, and an Internet connection. In the next chapter, you'll learn how to configure your Internet applications so that you can make the most out of your Internet connection.

References and Further Reading

Fannin, David. 1998. ADSL HOWTO For Linux Systems. Linux Documentation Project. Available online at http://metalab.unc.edu/LDP.

Hart, Robert. 1997. Linux PPP HOWTO. Linux Documentation Project. Available online at http://metalab.unc.edu/LDP.

Hart, Robert. 1997. PPP Setup Tips. Available online at http://ww1.portal.redhat.com/support/docs/rhl/PPP-Tips/PPP-Tips.html.

Lawyer, David S. 1999. Modem-HOWTO. Linux Documentation Project. Available online at http://metalab.unc.edu/LDP

PhoneBoy. 1998. Primer on Multilink PPP for Linux. Available online at http://www.phoneboy.com/pig/howto/mlppp-linux.html.

Sigler, Clemmit. 1998. "Linux/Adelphia PowerLink Phone-Return Cable Modem mini-HOWTO." Available online at http://home.adelphia.net/~siglercm/files/adelphia_powerlink_ linux_ mini-HOWTO2.txt.

Ts'o, Theodore. 1998. Setserial Manual Page. Linux Documentation Project. Available online at http://metalab. unc.edu/LDP.

Unruh, W.G. 1999. "How to Hook Up PPP in Linux." Available online at http://axion.physics.ubc.ca/ppp-linux.html.

Vuksan, Vladimir. 1998a. "Cable Modem mini-HOWTO." Linux Documentation Project. Available online at http://metalab.unc.edu/LDP.

Vuksan, Vladimir. 1998b. "DHCP mini-HOWTO." Linux Documentation Project. Available online at http://metalab. unc.edu/LDP.

14

Using Internet Applications

Now that you've connected to the Internet (as explained in Chapter 13), you're ready to use Internet applications, such as Netscape Communicator. Chances are you've already browsed the Web with Netscape. As you'll quickly learn, though, you'll need to do some configuration in order to get Netscape to work the way you expect—that is, as well as a browser works on a Windows or Macintosh system. For example, Netscape isn't set up to display multimedia, such as movies and videos. In addition, you'll need to configure Netscape to access your e-mail.

This chapter introduces the Internet applications that are available on your system. It also shows you how to configure these applications, if necessary. The chapter doesn't attempt to teach you all the fundamentals of Internet use; if you're not familiar with the essentials of Web browsing, e-mail, and other Internet services, you should read a good general introduction to the Internet before proceeding with this chapter.

TIP If you're new to Netscape Communicator, check out *Netscape Communicator* (AP Professional), which covers the nearly identical Windows version.

Here's what you'll find in this chapter:

- **Configuring Helper Applications** Learn how to set up your system's default Web browser, Netscape Communicator, so that it can work with animations, movies, and sounds.
- **Configuring Netscape Communicator for E-Mail Access** Set up your Communicator package to access your e-mail account.
- **Configuring Netscape Communicator for Newsgroup Access** Set up your Communicator package to access Usenet newsgroups.
- **Accessing FTP Sites with File Manager** Create virtual file systems for frequently accessed FTP sites; you'll love this feature.
- **Exploring Additional Internet Applications** Introduced are gFTP (a GNOME-compatible FTP client), GNOME-icu (an ICQ "buddy list" program), and X-Chat, a nifty GNOME application for accessing Internet Relay Chat (IRC).

Configuring Netscape Helper Applications

Netscape Communicator is a full-featured suite of Internet applications that includes a browser (Netscape Navigator), e-mail and newsgroups (Netscape Messenger), and Composer, a program that enables you to create Web pages. This section doesn't attempt to teach you how to use Netscape Communicator—that's a subject for a book in itself. Instead, it focuses on configuring the program for Internet use. In this section, you learn how to configure *helper applications*, which Navigator needs in order to display certain types of data.

Understanding Which Applications Navigator Needs

Netscape Navigator needs help to display data types that it doesn't recognize internally. If you configure the program as recommended in this section, Navigator will automatically start the correct helper application when you encounter the specified type of data (such as sound or a video). Table 14.1 lists the data types that you may encounter on the Internet, as well as the applications I recommend that you associate with these data types. For each application, you'll find the recommended startup command (the command that Netscape passes to the application). This includes the command needed to start the application (such as esdplay) followed by recommended options, if any, and %s (a variable that automatically inserts the URL of the remote file you're accessing).

Table 14.1 Data types and recommended application settings

Data Type	Application	Startup Command
AIFF Audio	Esound	esdplay %s
IEF Image	Electric Eyes	ee %s
MPEG Audio	Electric Eyes	mpg123 -b 4096 %s

MPEG Video	xanim	xanim +Zpe +q %s
MPEG2 Video	xanim	xanim +Zpe +q %s
PNG Image	Electric Eyes	ee %s
Portable Doc. Format	xpdf	xpdf %s
PostScript Document	gv	gv %s
PPM Image	Electric Eyes	ee %s
PGM Image	Electric Eyes	ee %s
PBM Image	Electric Eyes	ee %s
RGB Image	Electric Eyes	ee %s
SGI Video	xanim	xanim +Zpe +q %s
TIFF Image	Electric Eyes	ee %s
ULAW Audio	Esound	esdplay %s
WAV Audio	Esound	esdplay %s
Windows bitmap	Electric Eyes	ee %s
QuickTime Video	xanim	xanim +Zpe +q %s
X Pixmap	Electric Eyes	ee %s
X Pixmap	Electric Eyes	**ee %s**

TIP You must make sure that all these applications are correctly installed on your system before Navigator can make use of them. For more information on obtaining and installing software, see Chapter 12.

Note that Table 14.1 does not contain a recommended setting for Real Audio data. At this writing, the Real Audio version 5.0 player for Linux does not work with the Linux 2.2 kernel.

For more information on the availability of a functioning Real Audio player for Linux systems, visit the Real Audio home page at http://www.real.com.

Associating Applications with Data Types

To configure Navigator to work with installed applications on your system, do the following:

1. In Netscape Navigator, click Edit on the menu bar, and choose Preferences. You'll see the Netscape Preferences dialog box.

2. In the Category list, click the arrow next to Navigator, if necessary to reveal the subcategories, and select Applica-

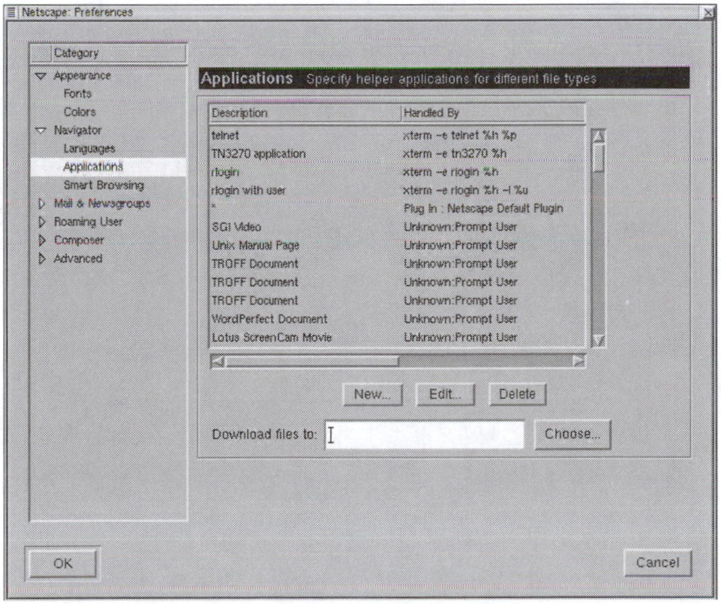

Figure 14.1 You need to tell Navigator which helper applications to use.

tions. You'll see the Applications page, shown in Figure 14.1.

3.   Select the data type you want to change, and click Edit. You'll see the Application dialog box, shown in Figure 14.2.

4.   In the Handled By area, check Application, and type the application's startup command in the text box.

5.   Click OK until you see Netscape Navigator again.

TIP To test your helper application configuration, visit the "Ready-to-Go Solaris Helpers Page" (home1.swipnet.se/ w-10694/helpers. html). You'll find links to small multimedia files throughout; click on these to test your helper applications.

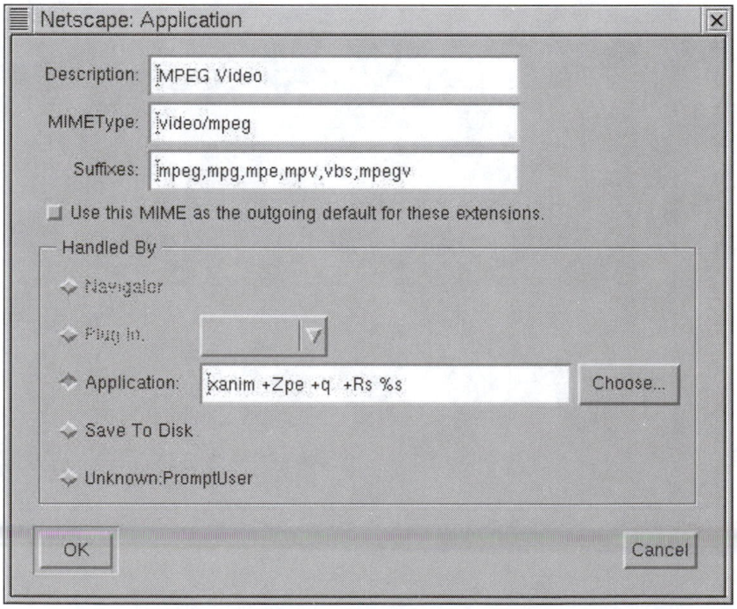

Netscape: Application

Description: MPEG Video

MIMEType: video/mpeg

Suffixes: mpeg,mpg,mpe,mpv,vbs,mpegv

☐ Use this MIME as the outgoing default for these extensions.

Handled By

◆ Navigator

◆ Plug In.

◆ Application: xanim +Zpe +q +Rs %s   Choose...

◆ Save To Disk

◆ Unknown:PromptUser

OK   Cancel

Figure 14.2 In the Application box, type the startup command.

Using Plug-Ins

Helper applications display data in a separate window. In contrast, *plug-ins* enable Netscape Navigator to display certain types of data *inline*—that is, within the Web page. Hundreds of plug-ins exist for the Windows and Macintosh versions of Netscape Navigator, but only a handful are available for Linux. Worse, installing them isn't easy; unless the plug-in is available in an RPM file that's expressly designed for Red Hat Linux, you'll need the command-line skills introduced in Part Five of this book.

Here's a sample of what's available:

- **Adobe Acrobat Reader** (Adobe, www.adobe.com) Displays Portable Document Format (PDF) files within Web pages.
- **Plugger** (Fredrik Hübinette, fredrik.hubbe.net/plugger.html) Organizes sound and video helper applications so that they play inline. Note: The glibc2 RPM version available at this writing installs the needed file, called plugger.so, in an incorrect location (/usr/ local/ lib/ netscape/ plugins/); copy this file to the .netscape directory within your home directory. You'll also need to configure Plugger to work with the various sound and video applications on your system; in order to do this, you'll need to switch to root user and edit the file etc/pluggerrc. Examine the file carefully to see where it mentions specific applications, and replace these application names with the ones installed on your system. Not for the faint of heart!
- **Macromedia Shockwave** (Macromedia, www.macromedia.com) Plays Shockwave animations.

If you'd like to take a stab at obtaining and installing these plug-ins, be sure to read the instructions carefully—and set aside a day or two.

Configuring Netscape Messenger for E-Mail and Newsgroups

Netscape Messenger, the e-mail component of Netscape Communicator, is a full-featured e-mail program that compares favorably with Microsoft Outlook Express and Eudora, the leading packages in the Windows and Mac worlds. You can use Netscape Messenger to access mail from your service provider's POP or IMAP mail server. In the following sections, you'll learn how to add your account information so that Messenger can access your mail.

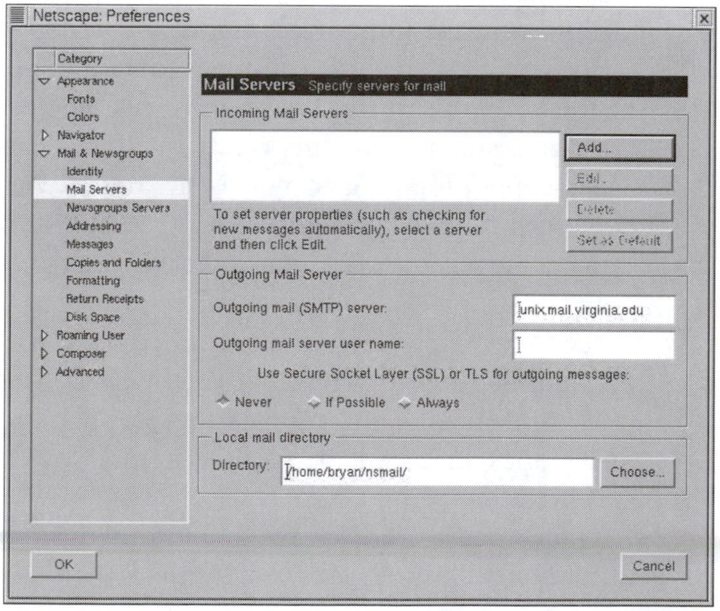

Figure 14.3 Identify your incoming and outgoing mail servers here.

Creating a Signature

You can create a signature (including your name, organizational affiliation, and optional contact information) that Messenger will add automatically to your outgoing messages. To do so, click the Main Menu button, point to Applications, and choose gEdit. Type your signature information, and then click Save. Save the file using the name **.signature** (note the dot in front of the filename), and place this file in the top-level directory of your home directory.

Adding Your Account Information

To add your account information to Messenger, do the following:

1. From the Edit menu in Netscape Communicator, choose Preferences. You'll see the Preferences dialog box.

2. Click the arrow next to Mail & Newsgroups so you can see the subcategories.

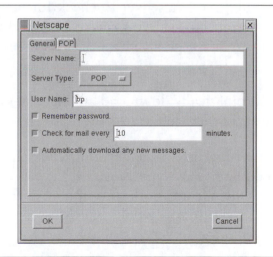

Figure 14.4 Supply your server name and user name here.

3. Select Mail servers. You'll see the Mail Servers page, shown in Figure 14.3.

4. Click Add. You'll see the General page, shown in Figure 14.4.

5. In the Server Name box, type the name of the server that handles your incoming mail (this server is also called the POP server, POP3 server, or IMAP server).

6. In the Server Type box, choose the server type (POP or IMAP).

7. In the User Name box, type the username you supply to log on to your e-mail account. Usually, this is the first part of your e-mail address (the part before the @ sign).

8. If you would like Messenger to remember your password, check this option. Don't check this option if others use your computer.

9. If you would like Messenger to check for new mail automatically at an interval you specify, select the Check for mail option, and type an interval in minutes (the default is 10).

10. Check Automatically download any new messages so that you'll see your new messages automatically.

11. If you're setting up a POP account, click the POP tab. If you would like to leave messages on the server so that you can access them from another computer, check Leave messages on server. If you would like Messenger to delete a message from the server when you delete it locally, check this option.

12. Click OK to confirm your incoming mail server settings. You'll see the Mail Servers page again.

13. In the Outgoing Mail Server text box, type the name of the computer used for outgoing mail (also called SMTP server). Netscape automatically fills in default values for the other options, and these values are fine.

14. In the Category list, select Identity. You'll see the Identity page, shown in Figure 14.5. Supply your name, e-mail address, and organization. State a reply-to address only if your reply address differs from your regular e-mail address.

15. **Important:** In the Category list, click Formatting. You'll see the Formatting page. In the Message formatting area,

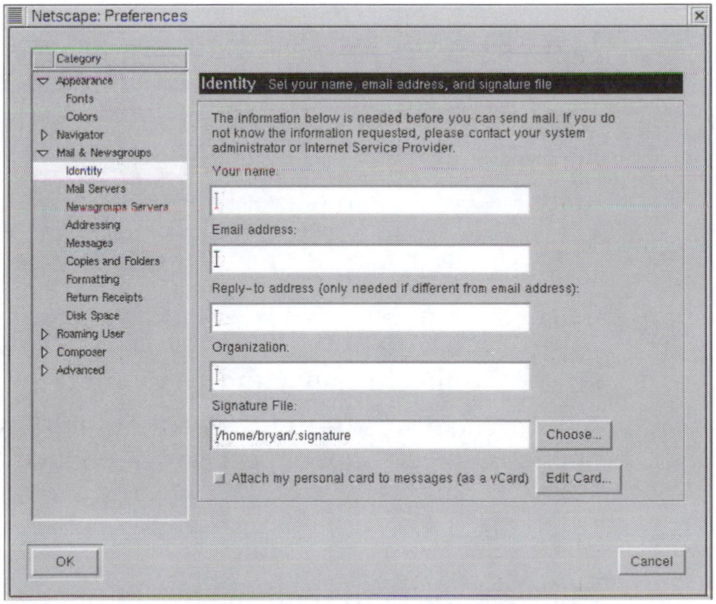

Figure 14.5 Supply information about your identity here.

be sure to check Use the plain text editor to compose messages. Don't use the HTML editor to compose messages; your messages will be unreadable by many recipients. You should send HTML-formatted mail only to those correspondents who have HTML-capable mail programs.

16. Click OK to confirm your mail settings.

To retrieve your mail, click Communicator on the menu bar, choose Messenger, and click the Get Mail button.

Configuring Newsgroups

To configure Messenger to access the newsgroups your ISP makes available, follow these instructions:

1. From the Edit menu in Navigator or Messenger, choose Preferences. You'll see the Preferences dialog box.

2. In the Category list, click the arrow next to Mail & Newsgroups, if necessary to display the subcategories, and select Newsgroups Servers. You'll see the Newsgroups Servers page.

3. Click Add. You'll see a dialog box that enables you to type the server name.

4. In the server text box, type the name of the server. If the server requires a name and password, check Always use name and password. If the server supports encrypted connections, check Support encrypted connections (SSL).

5. Click OK.

6. Click OK again to confirm your settings.

To access newsgroups, click Communicator on the Messenger or Navigator menus, and choose Newsgroups. You'll see the Netscape Message Center. To download the list of newsgroups from your ISP, click Subscribe.

Accessing FTP Sites with File Manager

The File Transfer Protocol (FTP) is another of the Internet's most popular services. By means of *anonymous FTP*, individuals or organizations can make files freely available for public download. Anonymous FTP is one of the chief vehicles for distributing open source software. Other FTP servers require a username and password. If you plan to publish a Web page on your ISP's computers, you will need to learn how to use FTP for uploading files to a password-protected server.

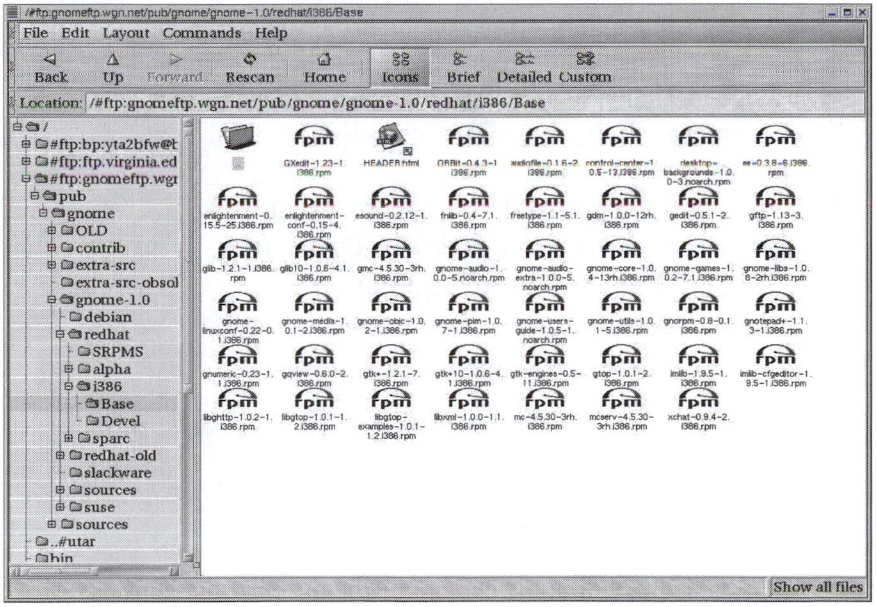

Figure 14.6 The GNOME File Manager can directly access FTP sites.

You can use a separate program (such as gFTP) to access FTP servers, but you can also use the GNOME File Manager (see Figure 14.6). What's so cool about using File Manager for FTP is best understood by trying it; as you'll discover, File Manager's *virtual file system (VFS)* enables you to add the files and directories of a remote FTP server to File Manager's directory list, as if these files and directories were part of your computer system. Once you've opened the FTP server's directory structure, you can use all the File Manager techniques you've already learned to work with files. For example, to download a file, you simply copy it to your home directory.

The following sections show you how to access FTP site's with File Manager's VFS, starting with anonymous FTP servers. You'll go on to learn how to access password-protected sites.

Accessing Anonymous FTP Sites

To access an anonymous FTP site with the GNOME File Manager, do the following:

1. In the directories list, click the root directory symbol (/).

2. In the Location box, type the following URL: **ftp://** followed by the Internet address of the FTP site (such as gnomeftp.wgn.net).

3. Press Enter.

    File Manager attempts to access the site, which may take a while. Once the site has been accessed, you'll see the ftp server's name in the directory window. Click on the server name to see the available files and directories.

Accessing Password-Protected Sites

To access a password protected site, you embed your login name and password into the URL, as follows:

```
ftp://loginname:password@servername
```

For example, suppose you're accessing ftp.september.org; your user name is brenda and your password is 339jqq. You would type the following in File Manager's Location box:

```
ftp://brenda:339jqq@ftp.september.org
```

The connection works the same way. Depending on the permissions established at this server, you may be able to upload files as well as download them.

Exploring Additional Internet Applications

Currently, a number of promising GNOME Internet utilities are under development. Check the GNOME home page frequently (http://www.gnome.org) for news about these and other GNOME-compatible Internet utilities.

Here's an overview of some utilities that were well into their development cycle at this writing:

- **gFTP** You can use File Manager for occasional downloading or uploading from FTP sites. For extensive work with FTP, you'll find it easier to use a utility, such as gFTP, that's designed expressly for FTP usage. Created by Brian Masney, gFTP is a GNU GPL-licensed program that's fully compatible with GNOME. When you access an FTP site with gFTP, you'll see two file panels (see Figure 14.7): on the left, you see your local files and directories; the right panel shows the remote server's files and directories.

Downloading or uploading a file is as simple as selecting the file and clicking the download or upload arrow.

- **GnomeICU** This program is an ICQ-compatible "buddy list" program that's fully integrated with the GNOME desktop. A buddy list program enables you to tell when your friends or contacts are logged on to the Internet (and they, in turn, can tell when you're logged on). When you and a buddy are both online, you can send messages to each other by means of text chatting. You can use Gnome-ICU whether or not you've already signed up for ICQ. If you signed up for ICQ on another computer, jot down your ICQ number, your password, and other identifying information; GnomeICU will reestablish your connection to the ICQ network. If you haven't already signed up, you can use GnomeICU to create a new ICQ membership.

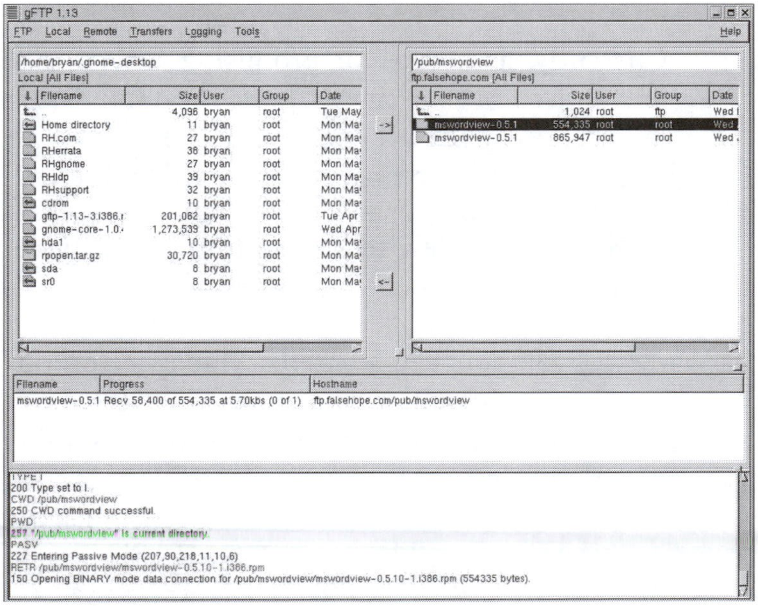

Figure 14.7 gFTP makes FTP usage easy.

- **X-Chat** Internet Relay Chat (IRC) is a popular text-based chatting network, with hundreds of servers (and dozens of networks) in use throughout the world. X-Chat is a GNOME-compatible IRC client that is clearly destined to become one of the best available in any format. It's exceptionally easy to use, and the interface is very well thought out.

On the horizon are a GNOME Web browser, a full-featured e-mail client, and much more. By the time you read this book, these projects may have produced preliminary versions (called *beta versions*) that are far enough along to try out on your system.

From Here

Lurking beneath the attractive surface of GNOME is Linux, a powerful and complex operating system. Sometimes, you'll find that it's actually faster and easier to talk to Linux directly. To do so, you use the text-based, command-line interface, which you can access in any terminal window (including the GNOME Terminal). In Part Five of this book, you'll learn all that's necessary to use the command-line interface.

Part Five

Learning Command Prompt Essentials

15

Using the Shell and File Utilities

If you're shooting for mastery of Linux, it's wise to learn the basics of using Linux with the text-only interface. Sometimes it's more convenient or faster to use this interface for certain operations, and for some operations there's no alternative (yet). In addition, using the text-only interface enables you to take advantage of command options that aren't available with more user-friendly graphical interfaces.

Despite the arrival of GNOME, knowledge of the text-only, command-line interface is part of any Linux user's basic skill set. So be sure to read this chapter and try all of the commands and programs discussed. But don't feel that you must memorize everything in this chapter. For everyday file maintenance chores in the text-only mode, I recommend that you learn how to use Midnight Commander, a file utility that's discussed in Chapter 17. Midnight Commander requires no memorization on your part. Furthermore, for file maintenance purposes, Midnight Commander is much safer to use than the shell commands, some of which provide no confirmation if you're about to overwrite a data file accidentally. What you'll learn in this chapter will give you enough of a foundation so that, should you *need* to use the shell for some purpose, you won't be afraid of it; however, I advise against routine use of the shell for any of the operations discussed in this chapter.

The Bourne-Again Shell (bash)

Most Linux distributions (including Red Hat Linux) default to the Bourne-Again Shell (bash), created by the GNU project. Compliant with the POSIX specification (see Chapter 1), bash is downwardly compatible with the commands defined by the Bourne shell (sh), created by Steve Bourne. However, it includes many useful features from other shells, such as the Korn (ksh) and C (csh) shells. Although you can set up Linux to run a different shell, you should begin by learning bash, which is by far the most widely used shell on Linux systems.

Understanding Shells

A *shell* is a program that enables you to communicate with the heart of Linux, the *kernel,* by typing commands at the keyboard. For this reason, a shell is a *command interpreter*, very much like the MS-DOS program command.com. But Unix shells are much more than mere command interpreters. Most are full-fledged programming languages, which a knowledgeable user can employ to create customized and highly automated systems. Files can contain commands—such a file is known as a *shell script*—and these files can be kicked into action by startup programs, automatically scheduled maintenance routines, and applications. To describe a shell's complexity fully would require an entire book—or better, a series of books.

Happily, most users won't need to delve into the shell's complexities. This chapter teaches the fundamentals of shell usage that every Linux user should know, and these fundamentals suffice for all but the most advanced system administration purposes.

Many shells work with Linux, but most Linux distributions (including Red Hat Linux) install the bash shell by default. The bash shell represents a good compromise among the usability and programming features that distinguish the various shells from one another (Greenfield 1996: 21–22).

Pointers for Shell Usage

To use the shell, you type characters after the Linux prompt. Note the following:

- Shell commands are case-sensitive. The command **Xconfigurator** differs from **xconfigurator.**
- Shell commands have *options*, which are preceded by a hyphen (-). For example, you can use the -i (interactive) or -b (backup) options with the cp (copy) command. Some commands have dozens of options; in practice, you need to learn only two or three of them, on average. They're discussed in this chapter, which you can use as a reference.
- You must carefully follow the *syntax rules* of each command, which specify how the parts of the command are sequenced when you type them. For example, the cp command's syntax requires you to type the command name followed by any options you use, the location and name of the source file, and the location and name of the destination file.

TIP You can customize the prompt, if you like. For more information, see Orr 1999.

Working with the Shell—In and Out of X

You can work with the shell in two ways:

- Within the X Window system, you can work with the shell by opening up xterm or some other X-compatible *terminal emulator* program. A terminal emulator program simulates an old-fashioned computer with no graphical user interface.
- You can also work with the shell directly by exiting your window manager and returning to the text-only shell interface. To exit a window manager, press Ctrl + Alt + Backspace.

TIP To work through this chapter's exercises, open the GNOME terminal emulator. To start this program, just click the computer monitor icon on the Panel. Note that some of the commands discussed in this chapter require root user or superuser status; you shouldn't experiment with these commands unless you're sure you know what you're doing.

Understanding Virtual Consoles

Unlike MS-DOS, Windows 95/98, or Mac OS, Linux is a true multi-user operating system. When you're using the *console* (a keyboard and monitor that are working with Linux), you're only one of many people who could be using the system in the same way. Of course, you probably have only one keyboard and monitor hooked up to your computer right now. But you can still see for yourself what Linux's multi-user capabilities are all about, thanks to *virtual consoles*. Virtual consoles enable you to create two or more separate shell sessions for your own use.

You can't use virtual consoles if you're running GNOME. If you didn't install GNOME, you can exit your window manager by pressing Ctrl + Alt + Backspace. You'll see the text-only shell. Press Alt + F2 to switch to the second virtual console. You'll see a new login prompt! You can log in at this prompt, and create a totally separate Linux session using this virtual console. To switch back to the first virtual console, press Alt + F1.

You may not make much use of virtual consoles—after all, you can only look at one session at a time. Still, switching from one virtual console to another enables you to see how Linux can support several users simultaneously—even dozens or hundreds of them.

Introducing the GNU File Utilities

The bash shell includes some commands that are built into the program. However, many of the commands discussed in this chapter aren't actually part of bash; they're separate programs, called *file utilities*. Standard in Linux distributions are the GNU Project's file utilities, documented in detail by MacKenzie *et al.* (1996) and MacKenzie 1996.

Some Linux books treat the shell commands and file utilities in separate chapters, perhaps to drive home the conceptual distinction between the shell's built-in commands and the separate utility programs. From the user's point of view, it would seem to make more sense to treat related shell commands and file utilities as a unit, as this chapter does.

Creating User Accounts

In Chapter 7, you learned how to set up a user account for yourself using LinuxConf, the GNOME-compatible configuration utility. In this section, you'll learn how to create and manage accounts using the text-mode file utilities.

To create and modify accounts, you'll need to log in as the root user or switch to superuser status. To switch to superuser status, type **su** and supply the root password.

Creating a New Account

The useradd command creates a new user account, including a new home directory for the new user.

At the Linux prompt, type **useradd** followed by a space and the login name of the user you want to add, as in the following example:

```
[root@localhost /root]#useradd suzanne
```

TIP If bash can't find the useradd utility, it's possible that the program's location (/usr/sbin) isn't in the *default path*. The default path is set up by initialization scripts when you log in. To deal with this problem, specify the program's path as well as its name when you start the program. To start useradd, type **/usr/sbin/useradd** followed by the new user's name, and press Enter.

Press Enter to confirm the new user's name. Although you see no confirmation of this, Linux adds the user and creates a home directory for this user.

Choosing a Password

Now you need to create a password for this user.

TIP Be sure to enter a password longer than six characters; avoid common words, and mix letters and numbers. Write down the password so you won't forget! (If you type a password that doesn't meet security standards, you'll see an error message with suggestions about how to improve your password. However, Linux doesn't stop you from creating a bad password, if you really wish to do so.)

At the Linux prompt, type **passwd** followed by the new user's login name, as in this example:

```
#passwd suzanne
```

Press Enter to start creating the password. You'll see the following message:

```
New UNIX password:
```

Type the password, and press Enter. You'll see the following message:

```
Retype new UNIX password:
```

Type the password again. If you made a typing mistake, you'll be asked to repeat the process.

When you see the prompt "New UNIX password," type the password, and press Enter. You'll see a message confirming that the authentication tokens have been updated successfully.

TIP If you've forgotten how to spell a command name ("Is it *password* or *passwd*?"), type the part of the command you know, and then press Tab. You'll see a list of all the commands that start with the letters you typed.

Logging Out and Logging In

To log out of an account and log in as a different user, type **logout** and press Enter. You'll see the login prompt. Type your user login name, and press Enter. When you see the Password prompt, type your password, and press Enter. Try logging in to your user account.

Note that the prompt looks slightly different:

```
[suzanne@localhost suzanne]$
```

When you're logged in with a user account, you see your username instead of root (i.e., suzanne@localhost), and the default directory is your home directory. In addition, the prompt changes from a pound sign (#) to a dollar sign ($).

TIP Always run application programs from your user account; never run them as root. When you run application programs, you will create data files as well as program configuration files. These are saved by default to your home directory, which is within the /home partition that you created when you installed Linux. Should you upgrade Linux to a new version, this directory will not be affected by the reinstallation process. In contrast, the root directory will be overwritten, and you'll lose any configuration or data files that are stored within the root directory.

Switching to Superuser Status

When you're logged in with your user account, you can't do the following:

- Shut down the system
- Modify system configuration files

If you need to shutdown or configure the system, you don't need to go through the whole cycle of logging off as an ordinary user and logging in as root. You can use the superuser command (su) to log in temporarily with root privileges.

To log in as superuser while you're in your user account, type **su** and press Enter. You'll see the Password: prompt. Type the superuser password, and press Enter. You'll see the root prompt, with the pound sign.

Now you can perform whatever operations you need to perform while logged in as root. When you're done, switch back to the shell (that is, exit the window manager, if you're in X); then type **exit** and press Enter. Once again, you're logged in as a user (not as root).

TIP Confused about whether you're logged in under your username or root? Type **whoami,** and press Enter.

Shutting Down and Rebooting

You can shut down or reboot the system only when you're logged in as the root user or superuser. To shut down the system, type **shutdown now** and press Enter. To reboot the system, type **shutdown -r now** and press Enter.

Understanding Linux Directories

The Linux file system is hierarchically organized, like a tree with its trunk and branches. At the top level of the directory tree is the root directory (symbolized by a single forward slash mark, /). Branching off from the root are directories, each of which can contain one or more subdirectories. For example, the /home directory is located on the first branch off the root.

A directory called /home/suzanne is a subdirectory of /home. An expression such as /home/suzanne is called a *pathname*, because it precisely specifies the path that you must take to find the files this directory contains. Among the most important shell commands to learn are those that enable you to navigate the directory tree.

TIP All of the commands discussed in this chapter have many options. Here, you learn only a few of the most useful ones. To see additional options, see the command's *man* page. To view a man page, type **man** followed by a space and the name of the program.

Moving to a Different Directory with CD

To change to a different directory, you use the cd (change directory) command. For example, suppose the shell is currently located in the root directory (/). To change to /usr/bin, type the following:

```
cd /usr/bin
```

The prompt will change to show your current directory location:

```
[suzanne@localhost bin]#
```

You can use shortcuts, such as the following:

- To go up one level in the directory tree, type **cd ..** and press Enter. Note that there's a space between "cd" and the two dots.
- To go to your home directory immediately, just type **cd** and press Enter.

Finding Out Where You Are

If you're not sure which directory you're in, type **pwd** and press Enter. You'll see the directory's full pathname, such as /home/bryan/myfiles.

Displaying Directory Contents

To work with Linux files, you will want to display lists of the files a directory contains. You can perform this task using a variety of commands, including ls and dir, the two discussed in this section.

Listing Directories

You can use the ls command to display a simple list of the files and subdirectories that a directory contains. To do so, type **ls** or **dir** and press Enter. You'll see a display such as the following:

```
yosemite.xbm   soundoff        junk.doc
chapter1.txt   old-stuff       resume
```

One drawback of ls is that you can't tell which of these items is a file and which is a subdirectory. To cure this problem, you can use the -F option (note that you must type a capital "F"). Try typing **ls -F** within the same directory:

```
yosemite.xbm   soundoff*       junk.doc
chapter1.txt   old-stuff/      resume/
```

Note that the subdirectories are marked by a following slash mark. If there are any executable files (programs) in the directory, they're marked with a following asterisk.

Getting More Information

To see all the available information about the files in a directory, type **ls -f** or **vdir** and press Enter. You'll see a display such as the one shown in Figure 15.1.

From left to right, here's what you're seeing:

- **Permissions flags** The odd-looking codes (such as -rw-r--r--) indicate the file's type, as well as just who may read, modify, delete, or run the file. You'll learn more about permissions in Chapter 9.
- **Links** The number (such as 1 or 2) indicates the number of links the file possesses to other files on your system. Links provide a way to access the contents of one file by typing the name of another.
- **Owner name** In the next column, you see the name of the file's owner (here, the owner is the root user). You'll learn more about file owners in Chapter 9.
- **Group name** This column indicates the name of the group to which the user belongs. If the user has not been included within a group, the group name is the same as the owner name. Chapter 9 discusses groups.
- **File size** The file's size is indicated in bytes.
- **Date of creation or last modification** This column shows the date and time when the file was created or last modified.
- **File name** The last column on the right indicates the file's name.

TIP Remember that all the commands discussed in this chapter have many additional command-line options, which you may find convenient to use. To see a list of command-line options, view the command's man page. (To do so, type **man** followed by a space and the command's name, and press Enter.)

```
  nxterm                                                    _ □ ✗
-rw-r--r--    1 root      root            274 Feb 21 08:16 SAVE.fig
-rw-r--r--    1 root      root            318 Feb 21 20:20 Xrootenv.0
-rw-------    1 root      root         528384 Feb 21 19:30 core
-rw-r--r--    1 root      root         119313 Feb 21 09:12 glib-1.1.3-1.i386.
-rw-r--r--    1 root      root         851400 Feb 21 09:05 gtk+-1.0.5-2.i386.
-rw-r--r--    1 root      root         212754 Feb 21 06:27 netatalk-1.4b2+asu
-rw-r--r--    1 root      root             38 Feb 21 06:57 new.xinitrc
drwx------    2 root      root           1024 Feb 21 06:23 nsmail
-rw-r--r--    1 root      root          38210 Feb 21 08:15 unnamed_919602909.
-rw-r--r--    1 root      root         281282 Feb 21 09:00 x11amp-0.9-alpha2-
[root@Lothlorien /root]#
```

Figure 15.1. A complete listing includes file permissions and more.

Finding Files

A variety of commands enable you to search for files, including whereis and find, which are introduced in this section. The following shows you how to perform the basic operations of locating files; for a more detailed introduction, see MacKenzie 1994.

Using the whereis Command

Suppose you want to run a program, such as Xconfigurator. To run a program, you type the program's name, and press Enter. However, you may see the following message:

```
bash: Xconfigurator: command not found
```

If you see this message, check to see that you have typed the program's name correctly (remember, bash is case-sensitive, so you must type the capitalization pattern correctly. To make sure you know the program's correct spelling, type the first few characters of the command that you're sure you know, and press Tab; you'll see a list of all the available programs that match that pattern.

When you're sure that you've typed the program name correctly, and bash still won't start the program, chances are good that the command is located in a directory that's not listed in the current path *environment variable*. An environment variable is a setting that's automatically loaded when Linux starts. The path environment variable tells bash where to look for programs. In order to start the program, you must first find out where the program is located. To do this, use the whereis command. For example, if you type:

```
#whereis mpeg-play
```

you'll see a list of all the files whose names include Xconfigurator, including documentation and other files:

```
/usr/multimedia/mpeg-play
/usr/man/mpeg-play.1x
```

The program is located in the /usr/multimedia directory, so you can start it by switching to /usr/multimedia:

```
#cd /usr/multimedia
```

Now you can start the program by typing its name

Using the find Command

The find command provides a quick way to search your hard drive for a specific file, or for a file that meets a pattern you define by using *wildcards* (characters that stand for any other character).

To use find, you must follow the command's *syntax*. In this context, the term syntax refers to the details of how you type

the command. It boils down to typing the command's compo-
nents in the correct order, and using the correct option names.
In the command's *man* page, you'll see the following under
"Synopsis":

```
find [path ] [expression]
```

In English, this means the following: "To use the find command, you must type **find**, and you may type a path name
followed by an expression." (The brackets indicate optional
command components.) For path, you type the path name of
the directory you want to search. For expression, you've many
options; this section discusses a few of them.

To locate a file named "sunset.jpg," type the following and
press Enter:

```
#find / -iname sunset.jpg
```

The slash mark says, "search the entire file system, starting at
the root," while the option (-iname) tells the command to perform a case-insensitive search for the file named "sunset.jpg."

TIP It's best to perform a case-insensitive search, but you can perform a case-sensitive search by using the -name option.

You can use wildcards to search for files when you're not sure
of the file's exact name, or when you wish to find all the files
that match a certain pattern. If you've used wildcards with
MS-DOS and Microsoft Windows, you already know how to
use the most convenient and popular bash wildcards:

- ? Stands for any single character. The expression sunset?.jpg matches sunset1.jpg, sunset2.jpg, sunsetA.jpg,
  etc.

- * Stands for any single character or any number of characters. The expression sunset*.jpg will match sunset1.jpg and all the others just mentioned. It will also match sunset-beautiful.jpg, sunset-overexposed.jpg, and sunset-oregon-9.jpg.

Here are some examples of find commands that use wildcards. The following command searches your entire hard drive for files with the xpm extension:

```
#find / -iname *.xpm
```

The following command searches the /home directory (including subdirectories) for files matching the pattern tile?.xpm:

```
#find /home -iname tile?.xpm
```

TIP If the search fails to find anything, there's no message; you just return to the Linux prompt. Try again!

Reading Files

As you're working with Linux, you'll find that your system is loaded with documentation; what's more, all of this documentation is stored in text files that you can easily display for on-screen reading. In addition, you will sometimes need to read configuration files, which are also stored in the form of plain text files. To read such files, use the less command. (The name "less" is a pun on "more," the name of its predecessor.)

To read a text file, use the cd command to switch to the directory where the file is stored. Then use the less command.

For example, to read the file "documentation.txt," you would type the following and press Enter:

```
#less documentation.txt
```

Table 15.1 summarizes some of the useful commands you can use while reading files with less.

Table 15.1 Useful less commands

Command	Description
f or space	Display the next page
b	Display the previous page
g	Go to the first line in the file.
G	Go to the last line in the file.
q	Quit less and return to the Linux prompt.
/pattern	Search for the text specified in "pattern" (for example, type /internet to search for the word "internet"

Renaming Files and Directories

Should you need to rename a file or a directory, you can do so with the mv command. This command is also used for moving files, as you'll learn in subsequent sections.

Renaming a File

Use the mv command to rename a file—but bear in mind that it's risky to use, as the following caution explains.

CAUTION The mv command can be dangerous, because it does not warn you before overwriting an existing file. Always use the mv command with the -b option, which automatically backs up any file that would be overwritten by the command, or the -i option, which displays warnings if you are about to overwrite a file.

To rename a file, you type **mv** followed by **-i** (interactive mode), the name of the existing file, and the new file name. For example, the following command renames "sunset-nice.jpg" to "sunset-overexposed.jpg":

```
#mv -i -b sunset-nice.jpg sunset-overexposed.jpg
```

If "sunset-overexposed.jpg" already exists, you will see the message

```
cp: overwrite 'sunset-overexposed.jpg'?
```

To overwrite the file, type **y** or **Y**. To cancel the command, type **n** (or anything other than y or Y).

To see whether the file was indeed renamed, type

```
#ls sunset*.jpg
```

and press Enter, you'll see all the files that start with "sunset" and have the .jpg extension:

```
sunset-overexposed.jpg.
```

Renaming a Directory

You can use the mv command to rename a directory, but the same cautions apply. The following command renames the /home/suzanne/stuff directory with the new name /home/suzanne/junk:

```
#mv -i -b /home/suzanne/stuff /home/suzanne/junk
```

Copying Files

To copy files, use the cp command. Like mv, it's dangerous; by default, the command gives you no confirmation if you're about to overwrite a file. You might accidentally overwrite a file if you specify a destination file name that is the same as an existing file. To avoid overwriting a file accidentally, always use cp with the -b (backup) or -i (interactive) options.

The cp command uses the following syntax:

```
#cp -i source-file destination-file
```

For example, the following command makes a copy of file-1, and names it file-2; the -i option provides confirmation if file-2 already exists and would be overwritten if you proceeded with the command:

```
#cp -i file-1 file-2
```

If you type a directory instead of a destination filename, cp copies the source file to the named directory, as in this example:

```
#cp -i file-1 /home/suzanne/backup
```

You can copy two or more files at a time by using the * wildcard, which stands for any character or any group of characters. The following command copies all the files in /home/mike/docs to /home/mike/backup:

```
#cp -i /home/mike/docs/* /home/mike/backup
```

Deleting Files

To delete files, use the rm command. But bear in mind that this command is dangerous, especially when you're logged in as the root user.

> **CAUTION** Never use rm when you are logged in as the root user. If you are not careful with your use of this command, you could delete configuration files, shell scripts, or other essential files that will cause your Linux system to cease functioning. A well-known Linux disaster involves using rm to erase all the subdirectories that have names beginning with a dot; the disaster-inducing command (rm .*) expands to include the parent directory (..), and wipes out your entire hard drive.

To delete files, log in under your username, if necessary, and always use the interactive mode (the -i option). In the following, you see the dollar sign (ordinary user) prompt instead of the pound sign (root user) prompt; don't use rm if you see the pound sign!

To remove a file called file-1, you would type the following:

```
$rm -i file-1
```

You can name more than one file if you separate the filenames with spaces:

```
$rm -i file-1 file-2 file-3
```

To remove two or more files, you can use wildcards, but be sure to use the -i option; this option confirms each file's deletion. The following command uses the ? wildcard, which stands for any one character:

```
$rm -i file-?
```

You'll see the following prompt:

```
rm: remove 'file-1'?
```

Type **y** or **Y** to delete the file; type anything else to skip deleting this file.

Creating and Removing Directories

You will often need to create directories, so that you can organize your files systematically. Sometimes, you'll need to delete existing directories.

Creating Directories

To create directories, use the cd command to go to the directory where you want to create the new directory. Then use the mkdir command. For example, suppose you want to create a new directory called /home/suzanne/docs, and you are currently viewing the /home directory. You need to type **cd /home/suzanne** before using the mkdir command.

To create the directory, type **mkdir** followed by a space and the name of the new directory you want to create. For example, to create a subdirectory called backup within /home/suzanne, you would type the following:

```
mkdir backup
```

The mkdir command provides no confirmation, so you may wish to type **ls -F** to see that your directory was indeed created.

By default, mkdir creates directories within the current directory. You can use mkdir without any options to create a backup directory within /home/suzanne. However, if the

/home/suzanne directory does not contain a subdirectory called /docs, you cannot use mkdir to create /home/suzanne/docs/backup. To do so, you could first create the docs subdirectory, and then use cd to change to this directory; you would then use mkdir to create the /backup subdirectory. But there's an easier way.

To create more than one subdirectory at a time, use the -p option, as in the following example:

```
mkdir -p /home/suzanne/docs/backup
```

When you use the -p option, you must type the entire path name, from the root on down.

Removing Directories

If you create a directory that you subsequently decide you don't need, you can use the rmdir command to delete it. Note, however, that you must first delete any files and subdirectories that the directory contains; by default, rmdir will not remove a nonempty directory. To remove an empty directory called /home/suzanne/junk, use the cd command to switch to the junk directory's parent directory (the directory one level above, which is /home/suzanne). Then type the following:

```
rmdir junk
```

If the directory contains any file or subdirectory, you will see the message:

```
rmdir: junk: Directory not empty
```

What if you really want to get rid of a directory that's full of unwanted files and subdirectories? There's a way, but it's dangerous. Make sure the directory to be deleted doesn't contain anything valuable. And whatever you do, don't run this command when you're logged in as the root user!

To delete everything within the docs directory, including all files and nonempty subdirectories, use the rm command with the -r (recursive) option, as in the following example:

```
rm -r docs/*
```

Please remember that this command is powerful and could do a great deal of damage. Never use it when you're logged in as root user!

Using Command-Line Editing Shortcuts

Often you will type lengthy commands, only to find out (after you press Enter) that you made a typing mistake. For example, suppose you type the following:

```
#cp wrdmastr1.4-i368 /backup
```

After you press Enter, you see the message:

```
cp: wrdmaster1.4-i368: No such file or directory
```

You should have typed "i386" instead of "i368." Do you have to type the whole line again? Thanks to command-line editing shortcuts, the answer is no. To bring the previous command line back, press Ctrl + p, or press the up arrow key. You'll see the command you just typed, as follows:

```
#cp wrdmastr1.4-i368 /backup
```

The cursor is positioned at the end of the command line. To edit the mistake, press Ctrl + b or the left arrow key to move back within the command line to the area that needs correction, and use the Backspace key (delete previous character) or Ctrl + d (delete current character) to edit the text. Type the correction, and press Enter.

You can make use of many additional command line editing shortcuts, some of which are summarized in Table 15.2 (Displaying command history), Table 15.3 (Moving the cursor), and Table 15.4 (Editing commands). Dozens more exist, but you'll find these to be among the most useful.

Table 15.2 Displaying command history

Command	Description
Ctrl + p or Up arrow	Display the previous command.
Ctrl + l or Down arrow	Display the next command.
Ctrl + <	Go to the start of the command list.

Table 15.3 Moving the cursor

Command	Description
Ctrl + a or Home	Move to the start of the current line.
Ctrl + e or End	Move to the end of the current line.
Ctrl + f or Right arrow	Move forward a character.
Ctrl + b or Left arrow	Move backward a character.
Ctrl + l	Clear the screen.

Table 15.4 Editing commands

Command	Description
Ctrl + d	Delete current character.
Backspace	Delete previous character.
Ctrl + k	Delete to the end of the line.

Running Programs in the Background

In Linux, a running program is called a *process*. Processes can run in the *background*, which means that you do not see any evidence of the running process on-screen (also called the foreground). Some programs are designed to run effectively in the background; for example, a file finding utility can compile a database of all the files on your system while running in the background, thus freeing you to run other programs in the foreground. In practice, you will rarely find it necessary to run programs in the background, but it's wise to understand the essential concepts.

Initiating a Background Process

To start a program and run it in the background, you use the ampersand (&) operator. For example, the following command starts an e-mail program called Pine, and runs it in the background:

```
#pine &
```

You'll see a confirmation, indicating the *job number* (in brackets) and the *process ID (*an identification number):

```
[1] 650
```

Returning a Process to the Foreground

To bring the program into the foreground again, you can use the fg command, followed by a space, a percentage sign, and the job number, as in the following example:

```
#fg %1
```

TIP If you have forgotten a background program's job number, you can see a list of current job numbers by typing **ps** and pressing Enter.

Suspending a Process

In addition to running programs in the background, you can also suspend a running program so that you can do something else, and later return to the program where you left off. To suspend a running program, press Ctrl + z. For example, suppose you are running less to read a lengthy text file, but you would like to pause and do something else at the prompt. Press Ctrl + z within less to suspend the program.

Viewing a List of Processes

To see which programs are running in the background, you can use the ps command. If you type **ps** and press Enter, you'll see a list such as the following:

```
PID TTY STAT TIME COMMAND
484   1 S    0:00 -bash
485   1 T    0:00 pine
486   1 R    0:00 ps
```

In the first column, you see the *process ID* (PID), a unique number that bash assigns to all running processes (including itself). The TTY column indicates which virtual console controls the process. In the STAT column, you see one of the following:

- R   A runnable process
- S   A sleeping (paused) process
- T   A stopped (suspended) process
- Z   A zombie (crashed) process

Killing a Process

If a process is no longer responding, you may need to kill the process in order to resume working with other programs. To do so, use the kill command. Type **kill** followed by a space, a percentage sign, and the name of the process or the job number, as in the following example:

```
kill %1
```

> **TIP** Some processes are designed to run in the background, checking for events that cause them to leap into action. These processes, called daemons, are initiated by shell scripts that load automatically when you start Linux.

Changing File Ownership and Permissions

Chapter 8 introduced the basic concepts of file ownership and permissions, which are concepts of fundamental importance in Linux. (See the section titled "Understanding File Ownership and Permissions.") In this section, you learn how to manipulate file ownership and permissions using the text-mode file utilities.

Changing File Ownership with chown

To change the ownership of files or directories, use the chown command. To use chown, type **chown** followed by a space, the user or group name, and the name of the file or directory. Here's an example:

```
chown bryan mydoc.txt
```

A very neat option is -R, which changes ownership recursively. This option enables you to change file ownership throughout a directory and all the subdirectories it contains. Here's an example:

```
chown -R bryan /home/bryan
```

> **TIP** If you've messed up file ownership in your home directory by saving files there while you're logged in as root user, you can use the recursive (-R) option just mentioned to restore the correct file ownership throughout your home directory. Don't kill these processes; doing so could damage data or bring your system down.

Changing a File's Permissions with chmod

To alter a file's permissions, use the chmod command. To use the chmod command, you need to learn a few abbreviations. Use the following to indicate permission types:

- **r** (**read**) Indicates read-only permission (the file can't be altered or deleted).
- **w** (**write**) Indicates write permission (the file *can* be altered or deleted).
- **x** (**execute**) For program files, indicates execute permissions (the program is available).

Use the following to indicate types of owners:

- **u** (**user**) Normally, this is the user who created the file. Using chown, you can specify a different file owner.
- **g** (**group**) Additional users who are member's of the owner's group.
- **o** (**others**) All other users *except* the user and group.
- **a** (**all**) Any user of the system, including user, group, and others.

When you use chmod, you change the file's current permissions. You can change the current permissions in the following ways:

- **+** (**add**) Adds the specified permission to whatever permissions currently exist for the file. If a file currently has read and write permissions, and you add an execute permission, the file now has read, write, and execute permissions.
- **-** (**remove**) Takes away the specified permission from whatever permissions currently exist for the file. If a file currently has read and write permissions, and you take away an execute permission, the file now has only the read and write permissions.
- **=** (**equals**) Erases all current permissions and assigns the specified permissions for the file. If you specify a read permission for a file that formally had all permissions (read, write, and execute), the file is now restricted to read-only access.

Using chmod

When you use the chmod command to change file permissions, you first type **chmod** and press the space bar. Then you type the user category, the operation, and the permission. Finally, you type the filename or directory name.

Here's an example:

```
chmod +w recipes.txt
```

This command says, in effect, "add the write permission to recipes.txt for all users, no matter what other permissions might exist for the file."

Here are some additional examples:

- **chmod -x /usr/sbin/pppd** "Take away execute permissions for the pppd program from all users except the file owner and members of the file owner's group."
- **chmod +x /home/everyone** "Enable any user to access this directory."
- **chmod =r /usr/docs/minitab.ps** "Erase whatever permissions currently exist for this file, and enable any user to read this file (but not to alter it)."

You can combine user categories and permissions, as the following examples indicate:

- **chmod uo+rwx /usr/sbin/pppd** Sets full permissions (read, write, and execute) for the user and the user's group.
- **chmod u+rwx,o=r /usr/bin/myprogram** Note the use of the comma to separate the two expressions (don't include a space). Sets full permissions for the owner, but limits the owner's group to read-only permission.
- **chmod u+rwx,o= /usr/bin/myprogram** Note that there's nothing after "o=". This specifies that owners have *no* permissions at all. They can't read, write, or execute the file.

Using Numeric Permission Modes

In the previous sections, you've learned how to set permissions using the *symbolic* mode. In this mode, you use symbols for user categories, operations, and permissions. Sometimes, you'll encounter manuals that give you specific chmod commands that use the *numeric* mode. The numeric mode requires a bit of math to understand fully, but there's a quick, easy way to grasp the gist of it.

Here's the trick. Begin with the assumption that the read permission = 4, the write permission = 2, the execute permission = 1, and no permissions = 0. Then use a table such as the following to add up the permissions for each category.

Here's a table that explains chmod 664:

Permission	Owner	Group	Other
Read	4	4	4
Write	2	2	0
Execute	0	0	0
TOTAL	**6**	**6**	**4**

So chmod 664 is the same as chmod ug=rw,o=r.

TIP Although numeric mode permissions are harder to understand, they're easier to type—which is exactly why Linux users love them. In practice, there are a few numeric permissions that get used so frequently that you memorize them (such as chmod 664).

Here's another example, which is often used to set permissions for Web pages:

Permission	Owner	Group	Other
Read	4	4	4
Write	2	0	0
Execute	1	1	1
TOTAL	**7**	**5**	**5**

This is the same as:

```
chmod o=rwx,g=rx,o=rx
```

In other words, this command gives the owner full permission to read and write the page, as well as to execute any active content (such as scripts) that may be present on the page. Members of the owner's group, as well as all other users, are given rights to read the page *and* to execute any content it may contain, but *not* to write (alter) the page.

Here's another example, chmod 711:

Permission	Owner	Group	Other
Read	4	0	0
Write	2	0	0
Execute	1	1	1
TOTAL	**7**	**1**	**1**

This permission gives full privileges to the file owner, but restricts everyone else to executing the file (which is a script or a program). This permission is commonly used when you install a file and want to make it available to everyone in the system.

Using Common Permission Modes

You don't really want to work out a table every time you encounter (or want to use) a numeric file permission. For reference purposes, Table 15.5 lists the ones that are commonly used. Often, you'll type one of these permission modes in response to detailed program configuration instructions; you can refer to this table to see what the numeric file permission means.

Table 15.5 Commonly used numeric file permissions

Permission	Symbolic mode equivalent
600	u=rw,g=,o=
644	u=rw,g=r,o=r
666	u=rw,g=rw,o=rw
700	u=rwx,g=,o=
710	u=rwx,g=x,o=
711	u=rwx,g=x,o=x
750	u=rwx,g=rx,o=x
755	u=rwx,g=rx,o=rx
777	u=rwx,g=rwx,o=rwx

Reading File Permission Information

When you view a file directory with ls -l, you'll see the current permissions for each file expressed in an odd-looking way, such as the following example:

```
r w x r - x - - x
```

Here's how to understand what this means. These are *positional* expressions, in which the location of each character means something. The nine symbols are in groups of three:

```
Owner           Group           Other

r  w  x         r  w  x         r  w  x
```

If any of the permissions has not been granted, you see a hyphen instead of the symbol. For example, consider this example:

```
r w - r w - r - -
```

Here's the table again; note where the hyphens are placed:

```
Owner              Group              Other

r  w  -            r  w  -            r  -  -
```

In other words, the owner and the owner's group have read and write permissions (but not execute), while all others have only read permission.

See Table 15.6 for a guide to the permissions you commonly see in file directories.

Table 15.6 Understanding permissions indicated in directories

Directory listing	Symbolic mode	Numeric mode
r w - - - - - -	u=rw,g=,o=	600
r w - r - - - -	u=rw,g=r,o=r	644
r w - r w - r w -	u=rw,g=rw,o=rw	666
r w x - - - - - -	u=rwx,g=,o=	700
r w x - - x - - -	u=rwx,g=x,o=	710
r w x - - x - - x	u=rwx,g=x,o=x	711
r w x r - x - - x	u=rwx,g=rx,o=x	751
r w x r - x r - x	u=rwx,g=rx,o=rx	755
r w x r w x r w x	u=rwx,g=rwx,o=rwx	777

TIP If you're starting to think that Linux is *not* fun, welcome to the club. Permissions seem unnecessarily difficult to understand and work with. But don't give up on Linux. With Midnight Commander (see Chapter 17) and the GNOME File Manager (see Chapter 9), you can view and set file permissions without having to come back to this chapter, make tables, and calculate sums. It's important to understand the concepts, but there are much easier ways to deal with permissions than to use the command-line utilities.

Understanding Default Permissions

When you create a new file or directory, Linux assigns default permissions to it. If you'd like to find out what these permissions are, type **umask** and press Enter. You'll see a number, such as 022.

To find out what this number means, subtract it from 666 (read/write permissions for owner, group, and other)—but note that this isn't the sort of subtraction you learned in grade school. For each digit, if the subtraction results in a quantity less than zero, put zero. Suppose the umask is 027:

```
  666
- 027
  640
```

The numeric mode value 640 corresponds to read/write permission for the owner, read permission for the owner's group, and no permissions for others. Equivalents are:

```
r w - r - - - -
u=rw,g=r,o=
```

For directories, you subtract the umask value from 777:

```
  777
- 027
  750
```

In symbolic mode, the directory permission 750 is the same as:

```
r w x r - x - - -
u=rwx,g=rx,o=
```

Table 15.7 provides a list of typical umask values and their equivalents.

Table 15.7 Understanding permissions indicated in directories

Umask value	For files	For directories
077	600 (r w - - - - - - -)	700 (r w x - - - - -)
067	600 (r w - - - - - - -)	710 (r w x - - x - -)
066	600 (r w - - - - - - -)	711 (r w x - - x - - x)
027	640 (r w - r - - - - -)	750 (r w x r - x r - x)
022	644 (r w - r - - r - -)	755 (r w x r - x r - x)
000	666 (r w - r w - r w -)	777 (r w x r w x r w x)

Linking Files

As you've learned, Linux files have names—but the name isn't the same thing as the file. In fact, Linux files have their own "real" names, which are internally encoded. As a result, it's quite possible to have two different names that refer to exactly the same file—or, in Linux terminology, a *hard link*. In addition, you can create *symbolic links*, which are like the aliases used in MS-DOS, Windows, or Mac OS: they refer to another file. In this section, you'll learn how to create hard and symbolic links, and you'll learn why you may want to do so.

Creating a Hard Link

As just explained, a *hard link* enables you to define more than one name for a file. Note that this isn't the same as making a *copy* of the file; there's no copy made. Rather, your system has more than one name for a single file.

Why would you want to create more than one name for a file? The reason lies in Linux's heritage as a multi-user operating system. Suppose two users, Michael and Julia, are collaborating on a document called proposal.txt. The original copy of the document is kept in /home/michael. Since Julia doesn't want to bother with typing all that lengthy path information when she opens /home/michael/proposal.txt, she creates a hard link to proposal.txt and calls it big-horrible-job.txt, and places big-horrible-job.txt in her home directory (/home/julia). Now she can open the document as if it were a file in her home directory—but it's exactly the same file that's stored in Michael's home directory. Note that any changes made to either "copy" of the file are reflected in "both files"—and that's because there's really only one file.

> **TIP** When you create more than one name for a file, you must delete *all* the names if you wish to remove the file from your system. Suppose Michael deletes proposal.txt in his directory. That's the "original" file. But big-horrible-job.txt still remains in Julia's directory. The file still exists.

To create a hard link, you use the ln command, followed by the name of the existing file and the name of the new file. In the following example, the command creates a new file (big-horrible-job.txt) that's a hard link to /home/michael/proposal.txt:

```
ln /home/michael/proposal.txt big-horrible-
job.txt
```

After you create the hard link, the file shows up in the current directory (the one that was open when you gave the command) as if it were a "normal" file.

> **TIP** If you want to make sure you don't erase an incredibly valuable file (such as your Ph.D. dissertation), put a bunch of hard links to the file in various directories. The file isn't really deleted unless somebody erases *all* the links.

Note that hard links are subject to the following limitations:

- You can't create hard links to directory names.
- Hard links can't cross partitions. If you set up your hard drive as Chapters 4 and 5 recommend, for example, you can't make a hard link from your home directory (in the /home partition) to a file in the /usr partition.
- Hard links won't work on a network file system.

Creating Symbolic Links

Hard links are useful indeed, but their limitations mean that many times you can't create them. For this reason, Linux enables you to create *symbolic links*, which are nothing but pointers to a file that exists elsewhere.

Symbolic links have some of the advantages of hard links; for example, you can place a symbolic link in your directory, and use it to refer to a file elsewhere on the system or network. In so doing, you save yourself the trouble of typing a lengthy path name.

However, symbolic links don't have the key advantages of hard links. For example, suppose the original file gets deleted. The symbolic link's existence doesn't prevent the deletion. What's more, the symbolic link isn't deleted either, even though it doesn't point to anything anymore. If you try to use a link that points to a deleted file, you'll get an error message, which might not be very informative.

To create a symbolic link, use the ln command with the -s option, followed by the name of the existing file and the name of the new symbolic link:

```
ln -s /home/michael/proposal.txt want-money.txt
```

This command creates a symbolic link called want-money.txt and places it into the current directory.

Exploring Advanced Shell Capabilities

Although this chapter covered the essentials of shell usage, it has barely scratched the surface of the subject. This section briefly introduces some advanced aspects of shell usage, focusing on the ones that may come into play when you are installing and configuring applications. When you obtain a new application for your Linux system, you will also obtain documentation that tells you what to type in order to install your new software. You can simply type these commands without knowing what they're doing; if you'd prefer to understand what's going on, read this section for a short introduction to the essential concepts.

Grouping Commands

The bash shell enables users to type more than one command on a single line. To type more than one command, you separate the commands with semicolons; the shell executes them sequentially, going from left to right. Here's an example:

```
#mkdir backup; cp /home/mike/* backup
```

This command creates a directory called backup, and then copies all the files in /home/mike to the new directory.

Using Pipes

In a *pipe*, the output of one command becomes the input for another. In the following (very useful) example, the output of the ls command is piped to the less command, enabling you to page through a lengthy directory listing:

```
#ls | less
```

Note the vertical bar character (|), the symbol that creates the pipe. Also, notice that this expression is evaluated from left to right; the first command is ls, and its output is piped to less.

Redirecting Output and Input

With a pipeline, you can direct the output of one program to the input of another program. With *output redirection*, in contrast, you can direct the output of a program to a file. With *input redirection*, a file can provide input to the shell.

Here's a simple example of output redirection, signified by the > symbol:

```
ls -l >directory.txt
```

This command tells the ls command to direct its output to a file called directory.txt rather than the display screen.

Here's a simple example of input redirection, signified by the < symbol:

```
ls- l <directory.txt
```

This command starts the ls program, and tells it to receive input from the file called directory.txt.

Shell Scripts

A *shell script* is a plain text file that contains shell commands, including the simple commands you type at the keyboard. You can create a shell script, make it an executable file (see Chapter 9), and run it by typing its name and pressing Enter. All the commands in the file execute, just as if you had typed them.

Shell scripts can be much more complex than a sequence of commands. Because bash incorporates the *control structures* of a full-fledged programming language, shell scripts can act like programs in their own right. (A control structure provides programmers the means to create alternative to simple program sequences; for example, one control structure keeps repeating a procedure until a condition is met.)

To configure your Linux system or one of your applications, a manual may instruct you to locate and edit a shell script. Be careful to make only the specified change. It's a wise practice to make a backup copy of the original script, so that you can restore the original in case you make a change that leads to unwanted consequences.

From Here

In this chapter, you've learned how to use the GNU file utilities and the bash shell. You'll surely find it easier to use the GNOME File Manager (Chapter 9) or the text-mode Midnight Commander (Chapter 17) for most of these operations, but there are times when the text mode comes in handy. You'll learn more about some of the GNU file utilities in the next chapter, which focuses on system administration.

References and Further Reading

Mackenzie, David. 1994. *Finding Files*. Cambridge, MA: Free Software Foundation. Available online at http://www.gnu.org/manual/manual.html.

MacKenzie, David *et al.* 1996. *GNU Fileutils.* Available online at www.gnu.org/manual/manual.html.

Orr, Giles. 1999. *Bash Prompt HOWTO.* Linux Documentation Project. Available online at http://metalab.unc.edu/LDP/ HOWTO/ Bash-Prompt-HOWTO.html

Nelson, Cameron, and Bill Rosenblatt. 1998. *Learning the Bash Shell.* Petaluma, CA: O'Reilly & Associates.

Ramey, Chet, and Brian Fox. 1996. *Bash Reference Manual.* Boston: Free Software Foundation. Available online at http:// www.gnu.org/manuals/

16

Mastering System Administration

In Chapter 12, "Keeping Your System Running Smoothly," you learned to perform some system administration tasks using GNOME and other user-friendly accessories. In this chapter, you learn how to perform many of the same tasks by using the command-line interface. As you'll conclude after reading this chapter, learning this material is a good way to gain more understanding of the Linux operating system that lies underneath GNOME's pretty face. What's more, you may conclude that some tasks—such as decoding tar archives—are actually easier and faster to accomplish by using the shell.

Mounting Disks and Filesystems

To use the files on external storage devices, such as CD-ROM drives, ZIP drives, and floppy disks, you must *mount* them. This section introduces basic mounting concepts, shows you how to use the mount command, and concludes by showing you how to configure Linux to mount storage devices (and other external filesystems) automatically.

TIP By default, Linux requires that users have root access to mount external storage devices and filesystems. To work through the examples in this section, you should log on as the root user. For a single user system, it isn't a security risk to allow regular users (such as yourself on your user account) to mount external storage devices and filesystems, so you should configure Linux to enable users to mount devices. You'll learn how at the end of this section.

Understanding Mounting Concepts

When you install Red Hat Linux, the installation software automatically configures your system to *mount* the various partitions on your hard drive automatically. As a result, the filesystems within these partitions become part of one larger, overarching filesystem. If you installed Red Hat Linux as Part II of this book suggested, you created a /usr partition. It is joined to the rest of the filesystem at a *mount point*. The /usr filesystem is mounted at the root (/).

As you've probably already realized, the various partitions on your hard drive are mounted automatically when Linux starts. That's because Linux is following the instructions found in an important configuration file, called /etc/fstab.

Here's an example of what this file looks like (I've added headers to explain what the columns mean):

```
Device          Mount Point     File system     Settings
/dev/hda6       /               ext2            defaults
/dev/hda7       /home           ext2            defaults
/dev/hda8       /usr            swap            defaults
/dev/fd0        /mnt/floppy     ext2            noauto
/dev/cdrom      /mnt/cdrom      iso9660         noauto
```

Here's an quick explanation of the settings in this file:

- **Device** Instead of drive names, Linux refers to storage and other peripherals using device names (see Table 16.1 for a list of common storage device names).
- **Mount Point** In this column, you see where the external storage device is mounted. For example, the /home partition is mounted at the root (/), while the CD-ROM drive is mounted at /mnt/cdrom.
- **File System** Linux can work with many filesystems, including the native Linux system (ext2). Table 16.2 lists some of the filesystems that Linux can access. As you'll see, Linux can directly access an amazing variety of filesystems.
- **Settings** These settings determine whether Linux mounts the filesystem automatically at the beginning of a session, and they also determine other options. The default setting mounts the filesystem automatically. The noauto setting requires the user to mount the filesystem manually before using it. As you can see the floppy and CD-ROM drives must be mounted before you use them.

Why does Linux require users to mount and unmount external disk drives manually? Simple: There might not be a disk in the drive. When you put in a disk, the mount command forces

Linux to read the disk and add its files to the filesystem. For floppies, there's an additional reason having to do with the disk caching system that Linux uses. If you were to remove a floppy disk from the disk drive without first unmounting it, the disk caching software might not have written changes to the disk, which would scramble its contents.

Table 16.1 Device names for storage peripherals

Device name	Description
/dev/fd0	Floppy drive #1
/dev/fd1	Floppy drive #2
/dev/cdrom	CD-ROM drive

Table 16.2 Filesystems accessible to Linux

File system	Description
ext	Older Linux filesystem
ext2	Today's standard Linux filesystem
hfs	Hierarchical File System (Mac OS)
hpfs	OS/2 filesystem
iso9660	CD-ROM filesystem
msdos	MS-DOS filesystem (no long file names)
nfs	Network File System (NFS)
ntfs	Windows NT
ufs	BSD Unix filesystem
vfat	Windows 95/98 filesystem with long file names

NOTE Filesystem support is built into the Linux kernel, and your kernel may not support all these filesystems without modification. To see which filesystems your kernel supports, type **less /proc/filesystems** and press Enter. Press **q** to exit the list.

Mounting an External Filesystem

To mount an external filesystem, such as the files on a floppy disk, a ZIP disk, or a CD-ROM, you use the mount command. If there's an entry for the device in /etc/fstab, you can use the short version of the mount command, as in the following example:

```
#mount /dev/cdrom
```

After you press Enter, Linux mounts the disk in the CD-ROM drive using the defaults specified in /etc/fstab, such as the iso9660 filesystem (which is the standard filesystem for CD-ROM data).

TIP If the device you're trying to mount is not listed in /etc/fstab, you must use the mount command's options, which (among other things) enable you to specify the filesystem. However, you should not need to do so, since the Red Hat installation software creates entries for these devices automatically.

Once the device is mounted, you can access the files it contains. You do so by going through the mount point (such as /mnt/cdrom). For example, in Midnight Commander (see Chapter 17), you access your floppy drive by selecting the /mnt directory and then choosing the /cdrom directory. To access your floppy drive, you select /mnt and then choose /floppy.

CAUTION After you've mounted a floppy disk, backup tape, ZIP disk, or any other read/write media, don't remove the disk from the drive without first unmounting it! If you do, you could wipe out the data that the device contains. See the next section to learn how to unmount a device.

Unmounting an External File System

Don't pop a disk out of a drive without first unmounting it. To do so, use the umount command, as in the following example:

```
umount /dev/fd0
```

Instead of specifying the device name, you could use the mount point, as in the following example:

```
umount /mnt/floppy
```

Mounting an MS-DOS Disk

By default, the Red Hat installation software configures /etc/fstab so that Linux assumes you're using the ext2 (Linux) filesystem on floppy disks. If you would like to access files on an MS-DOS disk, you need to mount the disk using a command option that specifies the correct filesystem (msdos), as in the following example:

```
#mount -t msdos /dev/fd0 /mnt/floppy
```

Note that you must type all the elements in this command, and you must type them in order: the -t option is followed by a space and the filesystem identifier (msdos); next comes the device name, and finally the mount point.

There's an easier way, thanks to Mtools, a nifty collection of utilities for users of MS-DOS disks (see Knaff 1999). You'll need to know basic MS-DOS commands in order to use Mtools, because the Mtools utilities emulate DOS commands. For example, to see a list of the files on an MS-DOS disk in the floppy drive, just type the following and press Enter:

```
mdir a:
```

Note that you don't need to mount the floppy; this command takes care of everything automatically. You can format MS-DOS disks using mformat, delete files using mdel, copy files (to and from Linux) using mcopy, and even manipulate ZIP disks with the mzip command. See Knaff 1999 for more information on these nifty utilities.

Mounting an MS-DOS Partition Automatically at Start-Up

If you've set up Linux to run on a two-OS system, you may wish to access your MS-DOS or Windows files from within Linux. To do so, first determine which partition contains the MS-DOS or Windows files. To see a list of current partitions, type **cfdisk** at the Linux prompt, and press Enter. You'll see a partition list. Look for the partition with an MS-DOS or Windows FS (filesystem) type, and note the device name. Type **q** to exit this program.

If you have an MS-DOS partition containing Windows, you can add this partition to your Linux filesystem. If your Windows partition is located in /dev/hda1, you would add the following line to your /etc/fstab file:

```
/dev/hda1   /windows   msdos      user,default 0  0
```

This line specifies the following: the device name of the MS-DOS or Windows partition (here, /dev/hda1), the mount point (here, /windows), the filesystem (here, msdos), the settings ("user" enables non-root users to access the Windows files, and "default" specifies several options, including mounting this filesystem automatically when Linux starts).

Configuring Linux to Allow Users to Mount Devices

If you're using Linux on a single-user system, you'll want to configure your /etc/fstab file so that your user—you, that is, after you've logged in using your user account—can mount external devices, such as the floppy and CD-ROM drives. To do so, use Midnight Commander (see Chapter 17) to edit your /etc/fstab file. Find the devices current set to noauto, and change this setting to **user,noauto** for read/write drives or **user,noauto,ro** for read-only drives, as in the following example:

```
/dev/fd0      /mnt/floppy    ext2       user,noauto
/dev/cdrom    /mnt/cdrom     iso9660    user,noauto,ro
```

Save the configuration file. Log on to Linux using your user account (instead of root); you'll be able to access the floppy and CD-ROM drives by using the following commands:

```
mount /dev/cdrom
mount /mnt/cdrom
mount /dev/fd0
mount /mnt/floppy
```

Formatting a Floppy Disk

Before you can use floppy disks with your Linux system, you must format them. In the Linux world, formatting refers to the process of preparing the disk for use by establishing magnetic patterns on the disk's surface; the term is synonymous with *low-level formatting* in the MS-DOS and Windows worlds. Low-level formatting alone isn't sufficient for disk usage; you must also create the Linux filesystem on the freshly formatted disk.

CAUTION Be aware that formatting wipes out all the data that may be present on a disk. If a disk contains data, be sure to remove it before formatting the disk.

To format a floppy disk from the Linux prompt, use the fdformat utility. With this program, you can't use the generic floppy disk identifiers (fd0 or fd1); you must use one of the device names that indicates the disk's capacity, as shown in Table 16.3.

Table 16.3 Floppy disk device names for formatting

Device name	Description
fd0D720	Double-density disk (720K), floppy #1
fd0H1440	High-density disk (1440K), floppy #1
fd1D720	Double-density disk (720K), floppy #2
fd1H1440	High-density disk (1440K), floppy #2

To format a high-density floppy disk in the first floppy drive (/dev/fd0), type the following and press Enter:

```
#fdformat /dev/fd0H1440
```

You'll see a progress indicator that informs you when the disk has been formatted.

Formatting alone isn't sufficient to prepare a Linux disk; you must also create the filesystem using the mkfs command. To do so, type the following and press Enter:

```
#mkfs /dev/fd0
```

This command creates the ext2 filesystem on the first floppy drive (use the /fd1 device name if you're creating a filesystem on a second floppy drive).

Maintaining Disks

To keep floppy disks and ZIP disks running smoothly, you need to know the basics of disk maintenance. In this section, you learn how to check for bad sectors (bad blocks), check the filesystem's integrity, and determine the amount of free space remaining on a disk.

Checking for Bad Sectors

To check a disk for surface errors (called *bad blocks* or *bad sectors*), you can use the badblocks command. The following command checks a 1440K floppy:

```
#badblocks /dev/fd0 1440
```

If all's well, you see the Linux prompt again. Should the program report any bad sectors, move the data off the disk and discard the disk.

Because this command is somewhat dangerous to use, you shouldn't run it on your hard drive. One of the command's options could wipe out all the data on your entire disk!

Checking File System Integrity

You may have noticed that, when you start Linux, a utility called fsck runs automatically. This utility, comparable to the MS-DOS and Windows Scandisk utility, checks the filesystem's integrity and makes needed repairs automatically.

CAUTION Never run fsck manually on your hard drive unless you know what you're doing. This program can be dangerous if you run it on a mounted drive, since the Linux disk caching software might write information to the mounted drive while fsck is running, leading to a scrambled filesystem. Always unmount a device before running fsck on it.

To run fsck on a floppy disk, first unmount the disk. Then type the following (for the first floppy drive, /dev/fd0):

```
fsck -r /dev/fd0
```

If all's well, you'll see a message indicating that the disk's filesystem is clean. Should fsck encounter any errors, you'll be asked to confirm the repairs before they're made.

Determining the Amount of Space Left on a Device

To determine the amount of space left on a device, you can use the df utility, one of the GNU file utilities. If you type **df** at the Linux prompt, you'll see a list of all the currently mounted devices. You'll also see the total amount of available storage for each device (expressed in K, or blocks of 1,024 characters), as well as the amount of used space (expressed both in K and a percentage of used space).

To see how much space is left on a single device (such as a floppy disk), make sure the disk is mounted. Then type **df** followed by the device name, as in the following example:

```
df /dev/fd0
```

Determining the Amount of Space Used by a Directory

If you'd like to know how much storage space is consumed by a specific directory, use the du command. Don't forget the summarize option (abbreviated -s), unless you're content to examine what could be a very lengthy list of files! The following command tells how much space (in kilobytes) has been taken up by the files in the /home/bryan directory:

```
du -s /home/bryan
```

Creating and Extracting Archives

You won't spend long in the Unix and Linux world before you hear of tar, a file archiving utility. Originally designed for backing up data on tapes (the name "tar" stands for "tape archiver"), the program is still widely used for storing a collection of files as a related unit, backing up data to backup disks or tapes, and transferring a collection of files to another computer. In this section, you'll learn basic tar concepts, and then learn how to perform the most frequently used tar operations: creating an archive, listing an archive's contents, and extracting files from an archive. Discussed here is GNU tar (see Weisshaus *et al.* 1997), the most recent and advanced version of this program, and the one that's provided with Red Hat distributions.

Understanding Fundamental tar Concepts

If you're used to using Windows archiving programs such as WinZip, you need to understand that tar doesn't include file compression capabilities; it's strictly an archiving program, which means that it collects one or more files and stores them as a unit. (When stored in an archive, the archived files are called *file members*.) Once you've created the archive, you can compress the archive file using gzip, the GNU compression utility discussed in the next section.

Creating an Archive

To create an archive with tar, you'll make use of three basic command options: --create, --verbose, and --file.

- **Create (--create or -c)** The --create option tells tar to make a new archive file.

- **Verbose (--verbose or -v)** The --verbose option tells tar to give you information about what it's doing.

- **File (--file or -f)** The --file option enables you to specify the name of the file to be created.

In addition, you must also list the files to be archived. You can do so by listing them individually, separated by a space. Alternatively, you can use wildcards. For example, the following command creates an archive containing all the GIF graphics in the current directory:

```
tar -cvf gif-collection.tar *.gif
```

Note that you can use the short form of the option names (-cvf) instead of typing the lengthier versions (--create --verbose --file). When you use the short version, type just one hyphen, not two.

You can create an archive containing all the files in a directory. To do so, follow these steps:

1. Move to the directory above the directory that you want to archive (to do so from the directory to be archived, type cd .. and press Enter).

2. At the Linux prompt, type **tar -cvf** followed by the name of the archive file you want to create, a space, and the name of the subdirectory that you want to archive. For example, to archive all the files in the subdirectory called art, you would type **tar -cvf artfiles.tar art.**

TIP When you archive an entire directory, tar automatically archives all the subdirectories contained in this directory, if any, and preserves the directory structure. This is a feature that makes tar valuable for backup purposes. For example, you should periodically back up the entire /home directory, and all its subdirectories. Should users wipe out their files inadvertently, you'll be able to restore them from the archive.

Listing the Files in an Archive

You can use the text-based tar commands to list the files in an archive; for example, the following command lists the files contained in the archive called art.tar:

```
tar -lt art.tar
```

Rather than using tar to list these files, try using Midnight Commander (see Chapter 17 for an introduction to Midnight Commander). This program can read tar archives directly, and shows you the names of the files contained in the archive.

To view the contents of an archive with Midnight Commander, do the following:

1.   In the file list, select the tar archive that you would like to examine.

2.   Press F3. You'll see a window listing the files in the archive.

TIP To view the actual contents of all the files in the archive, select the archive filename and press F4 (Edit).

Extracting Files from an Archive

If you've created or received an archive, you may wish to extract the files that it contains. To do so, you use the --extract option, as in the following example (note that this example also uses the --verbose option and the required --file option):

```
tar -xvf art.tar
```

By default, this command extracts the entire archive, and places the files in the current directory.

CAUTION Be careful when you're extracting archives. If any file in the current directory has the same name as a file in the tar archive, the program will overwrite the existing file, even if it's more recent than the archived version. Play it safe: Create a new subdirectory, place the tar archive within the new subdirectory, and extract the archive there.

You can extract individual files from an archive. For example, suppose you created a work called great-art.jpg. Subsequently, you archived your entire home directory—and then you accidentally deleted great-art.jpg. To restore this file, place its name at the end of the command you use to extract files from a tar archive. Only the file or files you name will be extracted. The following command extracts only one file, great-art.jpg, from the archive called home.tar:

```
tar -xvf home.tar great-art.jpg
```

Creating a Backup Routine

To safeguard the work you create on your Linux system, you should perform regular backups.

Full Backups and Incremental Backups

A good backup routine begins with a *full backup*, which makes a copy of all your valuable files. If you have a backup tape drive, you can back up your entire hard disk—and that's not a bad idea, unless you're comfortable starting almost from scratch (and reinstalling everything) in the event of a hard disk failure. At the minimum, though, you should make a full backup of your home directory. This directory contains the work you'll do with Linux applications, as well as the configuration files reflecting all the choices you've made as you've set up Linux and the applications you're using.

> **TIP** It's not a bad idea to perform a full backup on your /etc directory, too. This directory contains system-wide configuration files, including settings for the X Window system and the Internet. These files can be a bear to configure sometimes, so it's wise to back them up once you've got them working.

Once you've performed a full backup, you do not need to back up all your files every time you perform a backup operation. You only need to backup the files that have been altered or created since the last backup occurred. Called an *incremental backup*, this procedure is much less time-consuming—which means you're more likely to do it, instead of putting it off (and risking the total loss of all of your work).

Performing the Full Backup

To perform a full backup, use a command such as the following. This command makes an archive of all the files in the /home/bryan directory, and stores them on a ZIP disk (in /dev/sda4):

```
#tar -cvf /dev/sda4 /home/bryan
```

If you suspect that the backup will consume more than one backup tape or disk, you can use the --multi-volume option, abbreviated -M, as in the following example of backing up to floppies:

```
#tar -cvMf /dev/fd0 /home/bryan
```

When you run out of space on the first disk or tape, you'll be prompted to supply the second one. Be sure to number each disk or tape.

Verifying the Backup

Don't skip this step, unless you like taking big risks! In it, you'll run tar with the --compare (-d) option, which verifies that the backup has been bit-perfect. To verify the full backup to a ZIP disk (in /dev/sda4), type the following and press Enter:

```
#tar -dvf /dev/sda4
```

If this utility finds any discrepancies, repeat the backup and check again.

Once you've successfully finished the full backup and verified that the files are correct, make a disk label that says "Full Backup," followed by the date and the directories you've backed up.

Performing an Incremental Backup

Once you've performed a full backup, put the backup disks and tapes away for safekeeping, and perform incremental backups. These backups make copies of only those files that have changed since the last full backup was made.

To perform an incremental backup, use the --newer (-N) option. The following example backs up all the files in the /home/bryan directory created after March 12, 1999, the date of the last full backup:

```
#tar -cvNf '12 Mar 1999' /dev/fd0
```

Be sure to verify the backup:

```
#tar -dvf /dev/fd0
```

When you've successfully completed the incremental backup, make a disk label that says "Incremental Backup of Full Backup," followed by the date of the full backup and this incremental backup.

How often should you perform an incremental backup? If you were running a multi-user Linux system, you'd perform incremental backups every day. On a single-user system, it makes sense to do so only when you've created new files or altered existing ones, and don't want to risk losing this work.

How many incremental backups should you perform before you perform another full backup, and start all over again? It depends on how many backup disks you have, essentially. At some point, you'll conclude that you're ready to start over again and re-use all those disks.

Restoring Files from Backup Devices

Let's say a catastrophe has occurred—you've just wiped out a document (dissertation.doc) that took months of work to create. Fortunately, you made a backup.

To see whether the file you're after is on a given backup disk, use the following command:

```
#tar -lf /dev/fd0 dissertation.doc
```

This command looks for the file called "dissertation.doc" on a floppy disk.

Once you've found the disk containing the file, you can extract it using a command such as the following:

```
#tar -xvf /dev/fd0 dissertation.doc
```

This command uses the --extract option (abbreviated -x), and extracts the file named "dissertation.doc" from the floppy disk. The file is written to its original directory location.

If the ultimate catastrophe has occurred—a hard drive failure—you'll need to get a new hard drive, and re-install Linux. To restore all of your backed-up data, use a command such as the following:

```
#tar -xvf /dev/sda4
```

This command extracts all the archived files from a ZIP disk, and replaces them in their original locations.

File Archiving Horizons

Although you can set up a backup system with tar and protect your data reasonably well, the software does have its limitations. For example, tar doesn't detect when you've changed a file's name, and it also doesn't handle deleted files well; if you've deleted a file that contains unwanted information, it will reappear when you perform a restore operation. In addition, tar doesn't incorporate compression, which means that it eats up backup media quickly. Due to these and other shortcomings, this is an area where commercial software is making inroads.

Compressing and Decompressing Files

As you've just learned, file archiving and compression are two different operations in the Linux world. When you archive a file, you group one or more files together in a single archive file. However, this file is very large—somewhat larger, in fact, than the original files. If you need to make a backup copy to a secondary storage medium (such as a floppy disk) with limited storage space, you may wish to compress the archive after you create it. Additionally, you may wish to compress the archive if you plan to transfer it via the Internet. The same goes for any large file, whether it's an archive or not. A compressed file is smaller than the original file—sometimes 50 percent smaller or more—yet none of the data is lost.

Among the many available compression programs for Linux, the standouts are the gzip (compression) and gunzip (decompression) utilities (see Gailly 1993). Gzip uses the same compression technique found in the popular Windows compression utility called WinZip. A gzipped file has the .gz extension. Gunzip can decompress files that were compressed with gzip or just about any other compression utility in common use in the Linux world.

Compressing Files

To compress a file, type the **gzip** followed by a space, **-v** (the verbose option), another space, and the name of the file you want to compress. The following command compresses art.tar:

```
#gzip -v art.tar
```

Note that the result of a gzip operation is the replacement of the original file; gzip erases art.tar and replaces it with art.tar.gz.

You can also use wildcards. The following example compresses all of the files in a directory:

```
#gzip -v *
```

Decompressing Files

If you need to decompress a file, use gunzip. The following command decompresses art.tar.gz:

```
#gunzip -v art.tar.gz
```

Like gzip, gunzip replaces the file on which it performs operations. After running this command, art.tar.gz is gone; you'll find art.tar in its place.

To decompress all the compressed files in a directory, use this command:

```
#gunzip -v *.gz
```

Managing User Accounts

You've already learned the essentials of creating new users (see "Creating Your User Account" in Chapter 7). Here, you'll learn more about how Linux handles accounts and passwords, and you'll learn more about maintaining accounts with GNOME LinuxConf. This section starts with basic account concepts, and goes on to show you how to manage users with LinuxConf.

Understanding Users and Groups

Linux enables system administrators to provide accounts not only to users, but also to groups of users. On a single-user system, you'll probably have little need for groups. However, if your computer is used by more than one person, you may discover that groups come in very handy. For example, suppose you and another user are working on a project together. By creating a group consisting of the two of you, and assigning permissions to this group, both of you will be able to access each other's home directories, and modify the files contained there.

Understanding How Linux Tracks Passwords

When you create a user, you assign a password. These passwords are stored in /etc/passwd. In older Unix systems, these passwords were stored in plain text, meaning that intruders could obtain them without too much trouble. Later, the passwords were encrypted, but this also presented a security risk, because too many users choose simple or short passwords that can be guessed using brute-force (repeated guessing) techniques. The /etc/passwd file must be accessed by many applications, so there was no way to protect them by restricting the file to only those programs executable by the root user.

To safeguard system security, Red Hat Linux uses *shadow passwords*. These encrypted passwords are stored in a separate file, which can be accessed only by the root user. Applications can still get the information they need from /etc/passwd, but users can't see the passwords at all. However, the system is still at risk if an intruder gains superuser status.

Starting LinuxConf

To modify accounts with LinuxConf, you'll need to log on as the root user. To start LinuxConf, click the Main Menu button, point to System, and choose LinuxConf. You'll see LinuxConf onscreen (see Figure 16.1). In the left panel, you'll see a tree diagram of the various services available. To work with users, scroll down to Users accounts, and click the + sign, if necessary, to expand the listings beneath this heading; select User accounts to see the current list of accounts (shown in Figure 16.2).

Creating Groups

If you would like to be able to assign users to groups, you must first create the groups.

To add a group, do the following:

1. In LinuxConf left panel, locate and click Group definitions. You'll see the filter prefix page.

2. Click Add. You'll see the Group specification page.

3. In the Group name box, type a group name.

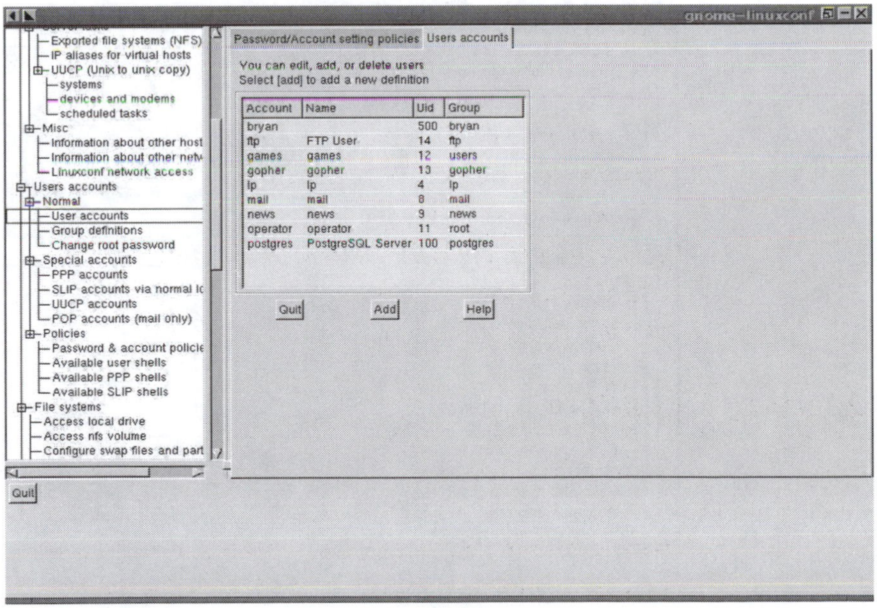

Figure 16.1 With LinuxConf, many system administration tasks are easy.

4. In the Group ID box, accept the nominated numerical ID, or type a new one. Numerical IDs are needed for networking purposes.

5. Click Accept to confirm the group.

Adding Users

To add a user, do the following:

1. In LinuxConf's left panel, click User accounts (under Normal).

2. Click Add. You'll see the User account creation page.

3. In the login name box, type the user's login name.

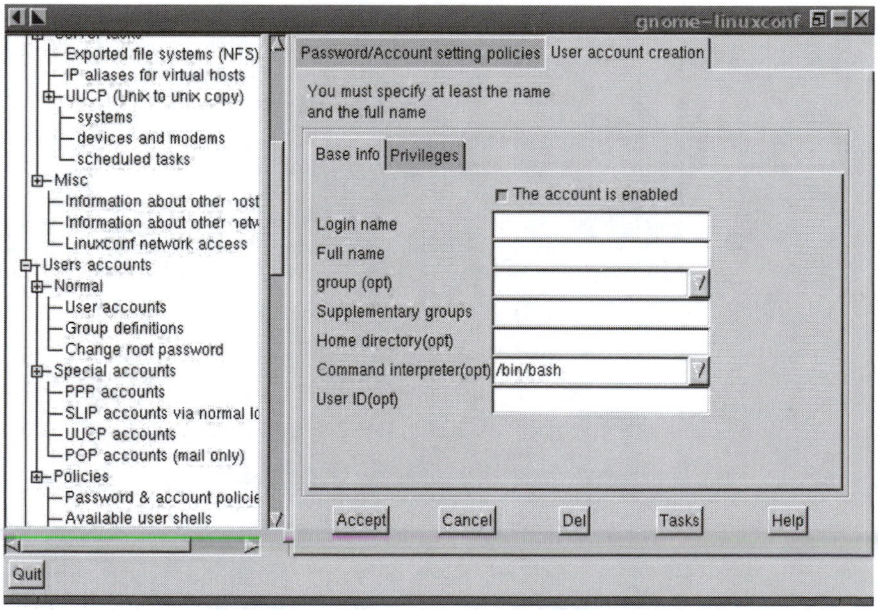

Figure 16.2 You can easily add or modify accounts with LinuxConf.

4. In the Full Name box, type the user's full name.

5. In the group box, you can type a group name, or choose one from the list by clicking the arrow.

6. In the Supplementary group box, type additional group memberships, if you wish.

7. In the Home directory box, type the user's home directory name, if you wish (if you leave this blank, LinuxConf will create a directory called /home/login-name, where "login-name" is the actual login name you defined in the Login name box).

8. In the Command interpreter box, you can select a shell other than the default (bash). If you leave this blank, the user's shell will be the default system shell (again, bash, unless you've changed this).

9. In the User ID box, you can type a numerical user ID. If you leave it blank, LinuxConf will assign a user ID automatically.

10. Click Accept. You'll see the Changing password page.

11. In the Type Unix password box, type the user's password, and click Accept. If you type in a password that violates LinuxConf's password acceptability rules, you'll see a message informing you that the password isn't good, but LinuxConf will still let you create it.

12. In the Retype Unix password box, type the user's password again. This confirms the password.

13. Click Accept and Quit to confirm the new user.

Modifying User Settings

If you need to change user information or privileges, including changing passwords, click User accounts in LinuxConf's left panel, and click the user's name. Make the changes you want, and click Accept and Quit to confirm them.

From Here

In this chapter, you've learned the fundamentals of system administration for a desktop Linux system. There's more to system administration—much more—if you're running a multi-user system, especially one that's connected to the Internet via a permanent, full-time connection. On such systems, security becomes more than a passing concern. Still, you've learned enough to manage a desktop system.

From here, there's just one chapter to go: Chapter 17, which shows you how to use the text-based version of Midnight Commander to perform many system administration tasks.

References and Further Reading

Biro, Ross. 1995. "Design and Implementation of the Second Extended Filesystem." Available online at http://ftp.yggdrasil.com/bible/sag-0.2/sag/node66.html.

Hsiao, Aron. 1999. "Let's Mount!" *Mining Co. Focus on Linux* (March 17, 1999). Available online at http://linux.tqn.com/library/weekly/aa072698.htm.

Knaff, Alain. 1999. *Mtools: Accessing MS-DOS Disks.* Available online from http://www.tux.org/pub/tux/knfaff/mtools/mtools.htm.

Sladkey, Rick *et al.* 1999. *Linux Manual Page: mount.* Available online from the Linux Documentation Project.

Weisshaus, Melissa *et al.* 1997 *GNU tar: An Arhiver Tool.* Cambridge, Mass: Free Software Foundation. Available online from the Linux Documentation Project.

17

Using Midnight Commander

Midnight Commander (MC) is a text-based file management program that you can run at the shell prompt or, within the X Window System, in a terminal emulation window. Either way, it provides easy-to-use tools for performing all of the major file management tasks discussed in Chapter 15—and what's more, with a margin of safety, in that Midnight Commander automatically asks for confirmation before wiping out files.

Why should you bother learning Midnight Commander, when your Red Hat 6.0 system includes the GNOME File Manager? There are two good reasons. First, the GNOME File Manager lacks some of Midnight Commander's advanced features, which aren't yet available with the GNOME File Manager.

Second, the GNOME File Manager doesn't enable you to switch to superuser status when you're logged in using your user account. As a result you cannot modify files outside your home directory unless you logout of your user account and log in as root user. But this isn't very convenient if you need to make just one small change to a configuration file. If you open a terminal window and switch to superuser status, you can start Midnight Commander and perform system modifications without logging out of your user account. Midnight Commander includes a built-in file viewer and editor, so it's convenient to use for editing configuration files.

This chapter introduces all the main features of Midnight Commander. As you'll see when you open the program, Midnight Commander is sufficiently complex to merit book-length treatment in itself, so this chapter can only touch on the highlights.

Running Midnight Commander

To run Midnight Commander, open a terminal emulation window, type **mc**, and press Enter. You'll see Midnight Commander on-screen.

Understanding the MC Interface

The Midnight Commander screen (Figure 17.1) has four parts:

- **Menu Bar** At the top of the screen you'll find the menu bar, from which you can choose any of MC's commands.
- **Directory Panels** By default, this panel is the active one (it contains the highlight).
- **Shell Command Line** This line, the second from the bottom of the screen, enables you to type shell commands

(such as those discussed in the previous chapter) without leaving MC.

- **Function Key Map** This line, the last on the screen, shows what the function keys do in the current context. (The effect of a given function key changes depending on what you're doing.)

Using a Mouse with Midnight Commander

Whether you're running Midnight Commander within the X Window System or at the shell prompt, you can use a mouse with the program. (Support at the shell level depends on the gpm package, which is installed by default with Red Hat Linux.)

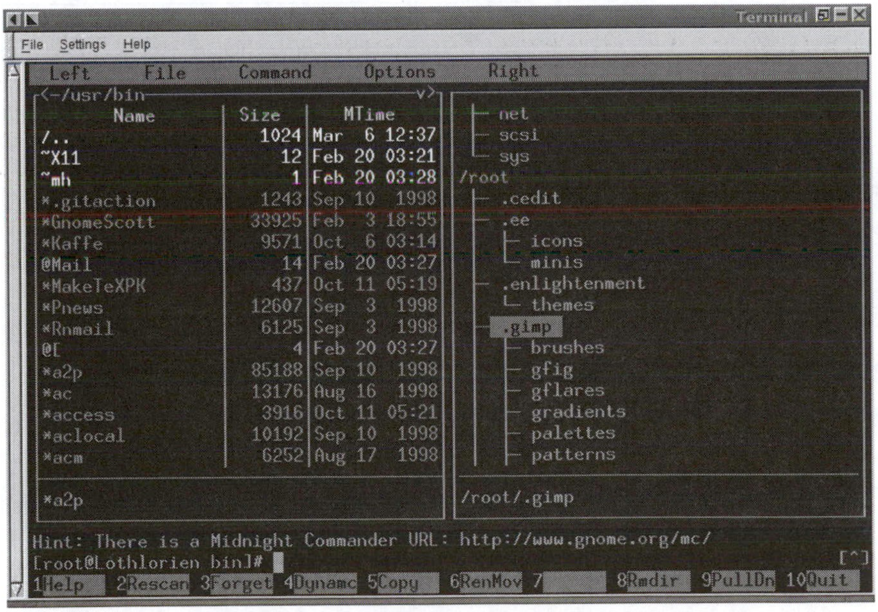

Figure 17.1 Midnight Commander uses a two-panel display.

With the mouse, you can do the following:

- **Select a file** Point to the file's name and click the right mouse button.
- **Mark a file** For certain operations (such as copying or moving more than one file), you will want to mark files. To mark a file, point to the file's name and click the left mouse button.
- **Initiate an action** Double-click a program name to run the program.

TIP To carry out an action assigned to a function key, you can point to the function key on the screen's bottom line, and click the left mouse button.

Midnight Commander's Heritage

If Midnight Commander seems like a classic Unix program, think again. It's inspired by a very influential MS-DOS file manager, first released in 1986: Norton Commander (Bezroukov 1997). Just as Norton Commander made MS-DOS much easier to use, Midnight Commander brings the same benefits to Linux users: It's fast, capable, and designed so that you can perform most operations with very little learning involved.

Navigating Within a Directory

By default, Midnight Commander displays the directory that was current when you started the program. (Both panels show the same directory, but only one of these panels is active.) Within the active panel, you can use the keys listed in Table 17.1 to navigate within the file list.

Table 17.1 Shortcut keys for navigating within the file list

Press this key:	To move:
Down arrow	Down one line
Ctrl + n	Down one line
Up arrow	Up one line
Ctrl + p	Up one line
PgDn	Down one screen
Ctrl + v	Down one screen
PgUp	Up one screen
Alt + v	Up one screen
End	Last item in panel
Alt + >	Last item in panel
Home	First item in panel
Alt + <	First item in panel

TIP In Midnight Commander (as in X Window applications), the Alt key is called the Meta key. Within the program menus, you'll see keyboard shortcuts such as M-p. This means, "Hold down the Meta key and press the p key." This book uses the more familiar Windows and Macintosh keyboard nomenclature, in which Alt + p is the same thing as M-p. (Note that Unix applications use the term "meta" because not all computer keyboards have an Alt key, such as the one found on PC keyboards.)

Changing Directories

To display directories other than the current directory, you can do any of the following:

- **Move to the next directory up** Scroll to the top of the file list, and highlight the /.. (next directory up) symbol. Double-click this line, or press Enter.

Figure 17.2 Use this dialog box to move to a different directory.

- **Move to the next directory down** Scroll to a line that names a subdirectory (you'll see the / symbol in front of the directory's name). Double-click this line, or press Enter.
- **Move to a directory more than one directory up or down from the current directory** From the File menu, choose Quick cd, or use the Alt + c shortcut. You'll see the Quick CD dialog box (see Figure 17.2). Type the path of the directory to which you want to switch, and press Enter.
- **Use the Tree panel** You can display a directory tree in the right or left panel (see Figure 17.3), and use this tree to view the directory structure and move to a directory quickly. For more information, see the next section, "Using Both Panels Effectively."

TIP Once you've used Quick CD to move to a different directory within an MC session, you can make use of this dialog's history list. The next time you use Quick CD, you'll see the history list symbol— brackets surrounding an asterisk—at the end of the text box. To see recently accessed directories, click this symbol. To access a directory from the history list, select the directory using the arrow keys or mouse, and press Enter.

Using Both Panels Effectively

When you run MC for the first time, you see two panels with the same information—the files and directories in the current directory. You will get more out of Midnight Commander if you make full use of both panels. For example, you can display a file list in the left panel while the right panel displays information about the file, or the file's contents.

To activate the other panel, press Tab.

To change what's displayed in a panel, do the following:

1. Click Left or Right on the menu bar, depending on which panel's listing mode you want to change, and choose one of the following options:

   Quick view Displays the contents of the file currently selected in the other panel, if the file contains text.

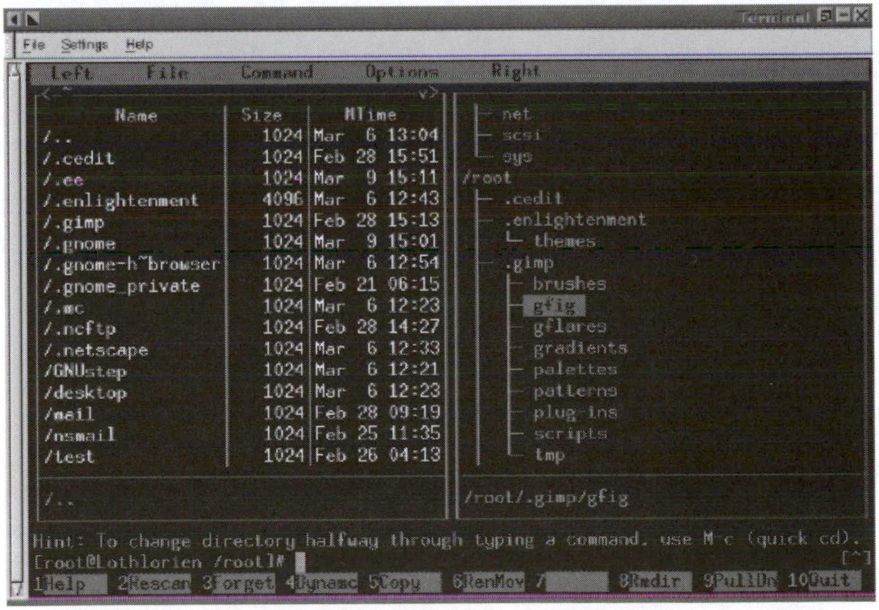

Figure 17.3 You can use the right panel to display a directory tree.

Info Displays information about the file currently selected in the other panel.

Tree Displays a tree diagram of your Linux filesystem, and enables you to move to other directories by clicking a directory name within the tree.

Figure 17.3 displays the Tree mode, which gives you a quick way to navigate your disk's directory structure. To go to a directory, just click its name.

2.   Choose one of the display options, and click OK.

To return to the file list display, click Left or Right, and choose Listing mode. You'll see the Listing Mode dialog box. Choose Full file list (the default listing mode); alternatively, choose Brief file list for an abbreviated format or Full file list for a detailed format. Click OK to confirm your choice.

Sorting and Filtering the File List

Some directories contain dozens or hundreds of files, and are difficult to work with. Instead of slogging through a lengthy directory looking for files, learn how to sort the file list in sort orders other than the default (alphabetical).

For example, if you're looking for a file you created recently, you can sort of files in reverse chronological order, so that the most recent files come first.

You can also use wildcards to create a *filter*, which cuts down the list of displayed files to just the ones that match the filter's pattern. The following sections describe sorting and filtering.

Sorting the File List

To sort the file display, do the following:

1. From the Left or Right menu, choose Sort order.

   You'll see the Sort order dialog box, shown in Figure 17.4.

2. In the left column, choose a sorting method.

3. To sort in reverse order, check Reverse.

4. To perform a case-insensitive sort, uncheck the case sensitive option.

5. Click OK.

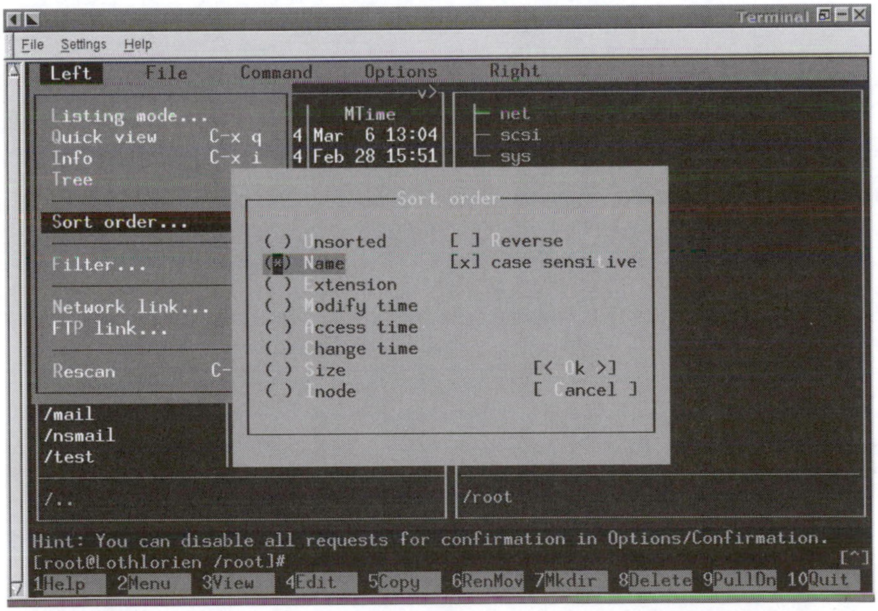

Figure 17.4 You can change the default sort order for displaying files.

Filtering the File Display

You can use wild card filters to cut down a lengthy file display to just the files that match the filter. For example, suppose you're looking for files that contain netscape somewhere in the file name. If you create a filter with asterisk wild cards before and after netscape (*netscape*), Midnight Commander will display only those files with these characters (netscape) somewhere in the filename (such as netscape-communicator or netscape-navigator).

To filter the file display, do the following:

1. From the File menu, choose Filtered view. You can also use the Alt + ! shortcut.

    You'll see the Filtered view dialog box.

2. Type the filter, and click OK.

CAUTION Don't forget that you've filtered the view. In filtered view, the only files that appear are those that match the filter. To cancel filtering, repeat these steps, but delete the filter before clicking OK.

TIP To exit a dialog box and cancel your selections within it, you can click Cancel or press Esc *twice*.

Finding Files

Midnight Commander offers a file-finding utility that makes locating files a snap. You can specify the start directory. If you wish, you can search the entire Linux filesystem, including all the mounted filesystems (such as CD-ROM and floppy drives).

To locate files with Midnight Commander, do the following:

1. From the Command menu, choose Find file. You can also press Alt + ?. You'll see the Find File dialog box, shown in Figure 17.5.

2. In the Start at box, select the directory where you want to start searching. To start searching from the root directory, type /. To select the start directory from a tree diagram of your filesystem, click Tree, select the start directory from the tree diagram, and press Enter.

3. In the Filename box, type the name of the file you're searching for. You can use wildcards (an asterisk stands for zero or more characters, and a question mark stands for any one character).

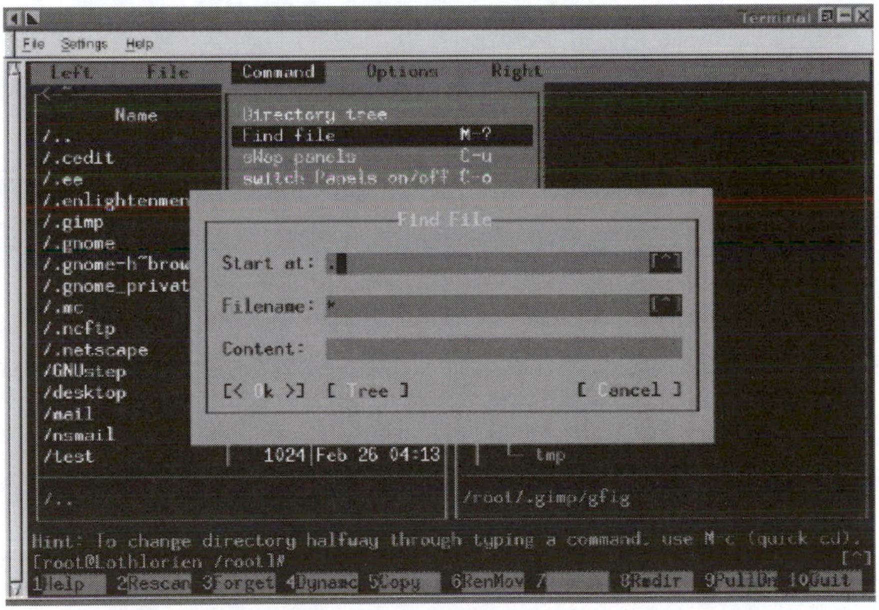

Figure 17.5 You can locate files easily with Midnight Commander.

4. In the Content box, you can type text to match in the body of the file, if you wish.

5. Click OK to begin the search. (If the search is retrieving too many files and you would like it to stop, click Suspend.) When the search is complete, you'll see the results, such as the ones shown in Figure 17.6.

6. If you see more than one file, use the up or down arrow keys (or PgUp and PgDn) to review the list of files retrieved. From here, you can do the following:

    View a file To view a file's contents, select the file and click View. You can also press the letter V or the F3 function key. For more information on using the Midnight

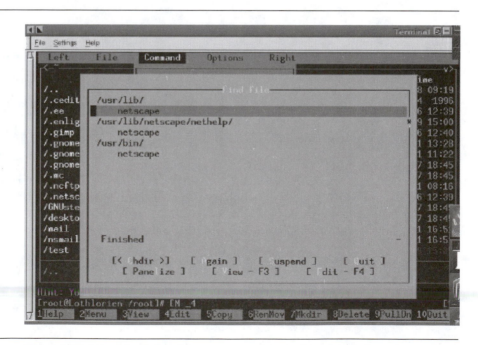

Figure 17.6 In this dialog box, you see the results of your search.

Commander file viewer, see "Viewing Files," later in this chapter.

Edit a file To edit a file, select the file and click Edit. You can also press the letter E or the F4 function key. For more information on editing files with Midnight Commander, see "Editing Files," later in this chapter.

Panelize the retrieved files To view the retrieved file list in a panel, click Panelize or press l.

Change directories To display a directory, select a file, and click ChDir or press C. You'll see the directory in which the selected file is located.

Repeat the search To repeat the search with the option of changing any of the search conditions, click Again, or type A. You'll see the Find File dialog box again.

TIP To view recent search history, click the history symbol (which looks like this: [^]) in any of the text boxes within the Find File dialog box. Note that you do not see the history symbol if you have not previously used a text box in a search.

Viewing Files

Midnight Commander enables you to view the contents of files easily (see Figure 17.7). As you'll learn later, you can also use Midnight Commander to edit files (see "Editing Files," later in this chapter).

The built-in file viewer recognizes several file formats, including plain text, compressed (*.gz) files, HTML, and manual pages. If you're viewing a file with formatting that Midnight Commander recognizes, you'll see the formatting on-screen. If you're viewing a compressed file, the program automatically decompresses it so that you can view the text.

TIP If want to take a peek at an important configuration file, start by viewing the file rather than opening the file in the editor; if you use the editor, you might make a small inadvertent change that could lead to unpredicted consequences.

To view a file, follow these steps:

1. In the file list, select the file you want to view.

2. From the File menu, choose View. You can also use the F3 shortcut. You'll see the document in the file viewer, shown in Figure 17.7.

    You can use any of the keyboard shortcuts described in Table 17.1 to navigate within the displayed document. In addition, Midnight Commander responds to the keys you use to view files with less (see Chapter 15).

    With the viewer on-screen, you can do the following:

    Text wrapping To toggle the viewer between the text wrap mode (lines are wrapped to fit the window) and the unwrapped mode (lines are not wrapped), click Unwrap or Wrap or press F2.

    Hex mode To view the file in hexadecimal mode, click Hex or press F4.

    Go to line To go to a specified line, click Goto Line or press F5, type the line number, and click OK.

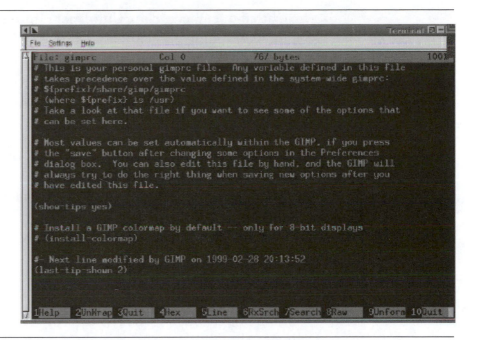

Figure 17.7 View files using Midnight Commander's built-in viewer.

Regular expression search To search with regular expression operators, click RxSearch or press F6.

Text search To search for text within the document, click Search or press F7. In the Search dialog box, type the text you're looking for, and click OK. To go to the next match, press **n**.

Raw/parsed You can set up MC so that the program automatically runs certain files through a filter. If you've done so, you can view the raw (unfiltered) version of the file by clicking Raw. To view the filtered version, click Parse. To toggle between the filtered and unfiltered modes, click F8.

Formatting To view the document with formatting (if available), click Format. To view the unformatted text of a formatted document, click Unformat. To toggle between formatted and unformatted text, press F9.

3.   To quit the file viewer, click Quit, or press F10.

Renaming Files and Directories

If you learned how to maintain files from the command prompt (see Chapter 15), you know that Linux uses the same command—mv— for renaming and moving files. The same is true of Midnight Commander.

Renaming Files

To rename a file, do the following:

1.   From the File menu, choose Rename/Move, or use the F6 keyboard shortcut.

      You'll see the Move dialog box, shown in Figure 17.8. Note that MC has added the current directory's path name to the to: text box.

2.   In the to: text box, type the file's new name. (If you type a new path name, you will move the file to a new location.)

3.   Click OK.

      If a file with the same name exists in the named directory, you'll see the File exists alert box, shown in Figure 17.9. You can choose the following options:

      Overwrite the target file If you intended to overwrite the target file, click Yes.

Cancel the operation Click Abort.

While the file is being copied, you'll see a progress indicator, if only fleetingly for renaming operations. If you're copying or moving many files, you can cancel the operation by clicking Abort in the progress indicator.

Renaming Directories

If you would like to rename a directory, do the following:

1. Click Left or Right on the menu bar, and choose Tree.

2. Select the directory you want to rename.

3. From the File menu, choose Rename/Move, or press F6.

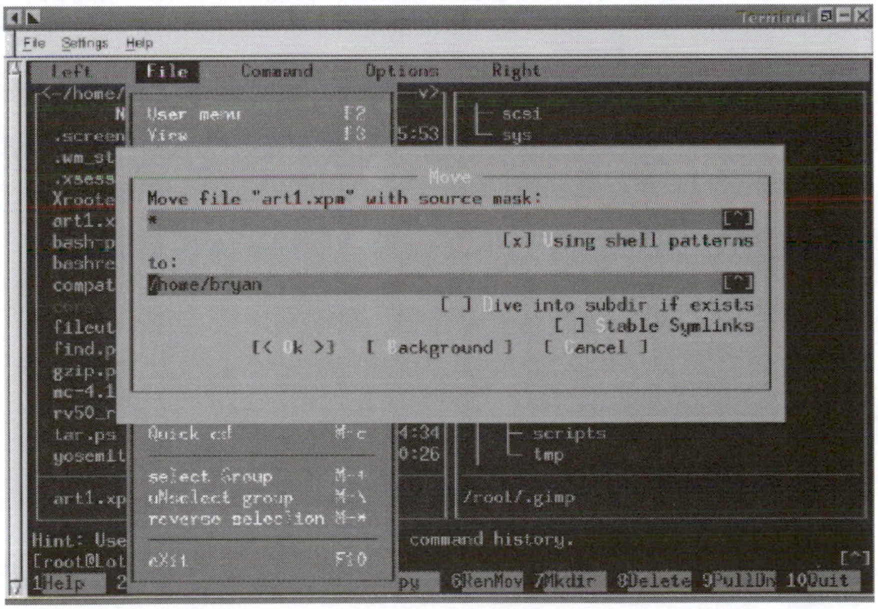

Figure 17.8 To rename a file, you use the Move dialog box, shown here.

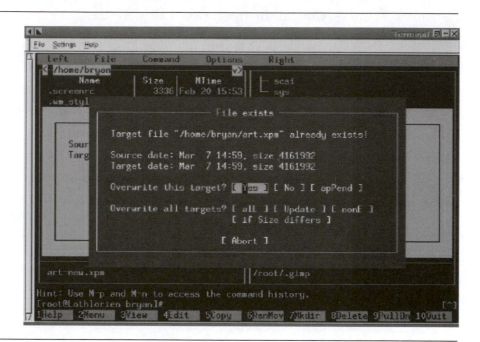

Figure 17.9 If you're about to overwrite a file, you see this alert box.

You'll see the Move dialog box.

4. Type the new directory name, and press OK.

Tagging Files

As you'll learn in the following sections, Midnight Commander enables you to copy, move, and delete files with ease. You can perform file operations on one file at a time, but often you'll need to do so on more than one file. For example, suppose you would like to move all your word processing files (with the *.doc extension) to a backup disk. To make this job easy, you begin by *tagging* (marking or selecting) all the files that have the *.doc extension, and then you use the Copy command.

Tagging Files Individually

If you plan to perform an operation on just one file (such as copying or moving it), you do not need to tag the file. However, you will sometimes need to tag a group of files one by one because they occur here and there within a directory.

To tag files one at a time, point to a file's name and do one of the following:

- Press the Insert key

  or

- Press Ctrl + t

  or

- Right-click the filename.

To untag a file, just repeat one of these commands.

Tagging Two or More Files

If you would like to tag all the files in a directory, press * (asterisk). To untag the files, press * again.

More commonly, you'll want to tag just those files that conform to a pattern, such as all the files with the .txt extension.

To tag multiple files by specifying a pattern , do the following:

1. Display the directory containing the files you want to mark.

2.   Press the plus (+) key on the numeric keypad. You can also press the plus key within the alphanumeric part of the keyboard.

You'll see the Select dialog box.

3.   Type an expression using wildcards that will match all the files you want to mark. For example, to mark all the .doc files in a directory, type *.**doc**.

4.   Click OK to tag the files.

Once you've tagged the files, use the Copy command to copy them to another directory, following the instructions given earlier in this section.

TIP If you have tagged many files and then decide not to copy or move them, you need to untag them. To do so quickly, click File on the menu bar, and choose Unselect Group. In the Unselect dialog box, type the same expression you used to tag the files, and click OK.

Copying Files and Directories

Midnight Commander offers many options for copying files and directories—enough to confuse an inexperienced user. Until you become comfortable with Linux file management tasks, stick to the basics, as described in this section.

Copying One File

To copy a single file, do the following:

1.   In the file list, select the file you want to copy.

2. From the File menu, choose Copy, or press F5. You'll see the Copy dialog box, shown in Figure 17.10. Note that MC has added the current directory path name to the to: box.

3. In the to: box, type new copy's path name. For example, to copy gzip.ps to /home/morgan, type **/home/morgan**.

4. Press Enter or click OK to start copying the file.

Copying Multiple Files

When you want to copy more than one file, you begin by marking the files. Then you copy the marked files.

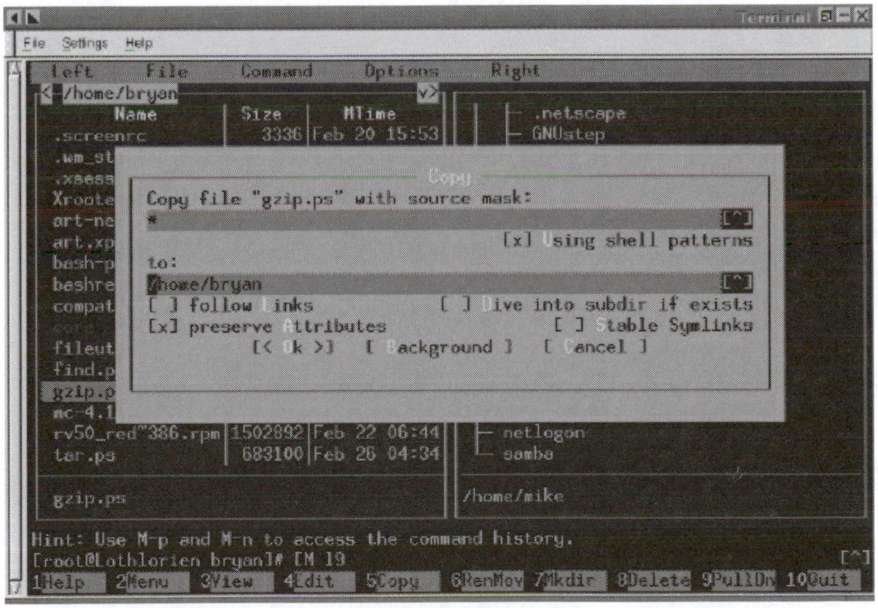

Figure 17.10 Type the new destination directory and click OK.

To copy more than one file, do the following:

1. Tag the files you want to copy (see "Tagging Files," earlier in this chapter). Midnight Commander highlights the file to show that it's marked. Continue until you've marked all the files you want to copy.

   At the bottom of the panel, you see the number of files you've marked, and the number of bytes these files contain.

2. From the File menu, choose Copy, or press F5. You'll see the Copy dialog box.

3. Type the full path name of the directory to which you would like to copy the files, and click OK.

TIP If you change your mind about copying the files, the files remain marked. To unmark the files, select each file, and press Insert to turn the highlight off.

Copying Directories

To copy a directory, follow these steps:

1. Click Left or Right on the menu bar, and choose Tree.

2. Select the directory you want to copy.

3. From the File menu, choose Copy, or press F5.

   You'll see the Copy dialog box.

4. Type the destination directory's full path. For example, suppose you want to copy the /home/mike directory to

/home/mike-backup. Type **/home/mike-backup**, and press OK.

Moving Files and Directories

The procedures you follow to move files and directories closely resemble those you use to copy them. However, Midnight Commander deletes the original file or directory after moving the data to its new location. For this reason, you should be very careful when using the command described in this section. If you're not careful, you could move a directory containing crucial configuration files, which would interfere with Linux's operation. Until you are certain you have learned enough to move files and directories safely, do not experiment with moving data when you're logged in as root user!

CAUTION Do not move files or directories that have names beginning with a period. These files and directories are used by Linux applications. These applications may not work correctly if you move them to a new location.

Moving One File

To move a single file, do the following:

1. In the file list, select the file you want to copy.

2. From the File menu, choose Rename/Move, or press F6. You'll see the Move dialog box. Note that MC has added the current directory path name to the to: box.

3. In the to: box, type the full path name of the directory to which you want to move the file. For example, to move tar.ps to /home/mike, type **/home/mike**.

4.   Press Enter or click OK to start moving the file.

Moving Multiple Files

When you want to move more than one file, you begin by marking the files, just as you do when you're copying multiple files.

To move more than one file, do the following:

1.   Tag the files you want to move (see "Tagging Files," earlier in this chapter).

At the bottom of the panel, you see the number of files you've marked, and the number of bytes these files contain.

2.   From the File menu, choose Rename/Move, or press F6. You'll see the Move dialog box.

3.   Type the full path name of the directory to which you would like to copy the files, and click OK.

Moving Directories

You can move an entire directory, but please note that you should avoid doing so unless you are certain you know what you are doing. For example, suppose you have created subdirectories for your data files. You can safely move one of these subdirectories, as long as they contain no automatically generated configuration files required by an application. Never move a directory that contains one or more files beginning with a period.

To move a directory, follow these steps:

1.   Click Left or Right on the menu bar, and choose Tree.

2.   Select the directory you want to move.

3.   From the File menu, choose Rename/Move, or press F6.

      You'll see the Move dialog box.

4.   Type the destination directory's full path. For example, suppose you want to copy the /home/mike directory to /home/mike-backup. Type **/home/mike-backup**, and press OK.

Deleting Files and Directories

Midnight Commander enables you to delete files with all the features and versatility with which you can copy and move them, but it's best to remember that file deletion can be a dangerous business. Should you inadvertently delete a configuration file, you could lose important configuration information or your applications might not run at all.

TIP To make sure that you do not inadvertently erase configuration files, consider hiding them during the time you're experimenting with deletion commands. To do so, click Options on the menu bar, choose Configuration, and uncheck the Show Hidden Files option. Click OK to confirm this option without saving it. Configuration files will remain hidden during the remainder of your Midnight Commander session, but they will appear again the next time you start the program.

Enabling Safe Delete

To make sure you do not inadvertently delete important files beyond recovery, take advantage of the Safe Delete feature. When you enable this feature, Midnight Commander selects the No option, by default, in the confirmation dialog boxes that appear when you attempt to delete a file or directory.

Deleting One File

To delete a single file, do the following:

1. In the file list, select the file you want to delete.

2. From the File menu, choose Delete, or press F8. You'll see the Delete dialog box, asking you to confirm deletion of the file.

3. To delete the file, click Yes. To cancel deletion, click No.

Deleting Multiple Files

When you want to delete more than one file, you begin by tagging the files, just as you do when you're copying or moving multiple files.

To delete more than one file, do the following:

1. Tag the files you want to delete (see "Tagging Files," earlier in this chapter).

    At the bottom of the panel, you see the number of files you've marked, and the number of bytes these files contain.

2. From the File menu, choose Delete, or press F8. You'll see the Delete dialog box.

3. Choose Yes to delete the files.

Deleting Directories

You can delete an entire directory, but please note that you should avoid doing so unless you are certain you know what you are doing. For example, suppose you have created subdirectories for your data files. You can safely move one of these subdirectories, as long as they contain no automatically generated configuration files required by an application. Never move a directory that contains one or more files beginning with a period.

To move a directory, follow these steps:

1. Click Left or Right on the menu bar, and choose Tree.

2. Select the directory you want to delete.

3. From the File menu, choose Delete, or press F8.

   If the directory isn't empty, you'll see an alert box asking if you would like to delete the directory recursively. Think twice before accepting this option, because it will delete all the subdirectories and all the files within the current directory.

Editing Files

One of Midnight Commander's most useful features is its built-in file editor, which you can use to edit system configuration files (see Chapter 9), a task you'll perform in order to get your Linux system running smoothly. Although seasoned Linux and Unix users may prefer to run some version of emacs, a powerful (but confusing) text editor designed for use by programmers, most users are much happier working with a simple text editor that accomplishes straightforward editing tasks without forcing you to learn complicated commands and procedures. Midnight Commander's text editor fits this requirement very well.

TIP It's easiest to use the internal text editor when you're running Midnight Commander from the Linux command line (rather than in a window manager). You'll be able to use the convenient text-editing shortcuts listed in Table 17.5, which aren't available when you're running Midnight Commander in an X terminal emulation window.

Basics of Text Editing with the Internal Editor

To edit a file with Midnight Commander, do the following

1. In the Midnight Commander file list, select the file.

2. Press F4. You'll see the file in the editing window (see Figure 17.11).

    At the top of the screen, you'll see a status line containing information (including the name of the file and the cursor's location within the file). At the bottom of the screen, you see the function key assignments for the internal editor.

3. Use the mouse or arrow keys to position the cursor where you want to edit the file, and use the Backspace and Delete keys to perform the editing. Type corrected or new text.

4. To save the file, press F2.

5. To quit the editor, press F10.

Advanced Text Editing with the Internal Editor

The internal editor offers many features, including search, search and replace, macros (stored keystroke sequences), a spelling checker, and date/time insertion. You can learn what's available by looking at the editor's menus; to display them, press F9.

Tables 17.2 through 17.5 list the keyboard shortcuts you can use while you're editing files with the internal editor. If you're using Midnight Commander at the Linux prompt rather than running it in from within a window manager, you can use the editing shortcuts listed in Table 17.5.

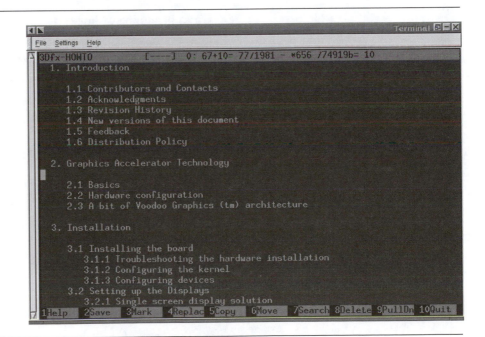

Figure 17.11 Midnight Commander enables you to edit files easily.

TIP If some of the shortcut keys aren't working, quit the editor, click the Options menu within the main Midnight Commander window, and choose Learn Keys. Follow the instructions to teach Midnight Commander which keys to use.

Table 17.2 Internal Editor Shortcut Keys: File Management

Press this key:	To do this:
Ctrl + O	Open a file
Ctrl + N	Create a new file
F2	Save the current file
F12	Save the current file with a new name

Table 17.3 Internal Editor Shortcut Keys: Navigation

Press this key:	To do this:
Home	Go to beginning of line
End	Go to end of line
Ctrl + PgUp	Go to beginning of file
Ctrl + PgDn	Go to end of file
Alt + l	Go to a line you specify

Table 17.4 Internal Editor Shortcut Keys: Editing

Press this key:	To do this:
Ctrl + P	Check spelling
Ctrl + U	Undo last editing change
Ins	Toggle between insert and overwrite mode
F3	Toggle selection on or off
F4	Search and replace
F5	Make a copy of the selected text
F6	Move selected text to the cursor's location

F7	Search for text
F8	Delete the selected text
Shift + F7	Search again

Table 17.5 Internal Editor Shortcut Keys: Editing (Text Mode Only)

Press this key:	To do this:
Ctrl + Ins	Copy selection to clipboard file
Shift + Del	Cut the selection to the clipboard file
Ctrl + Ins	Insert (paste) the clipboard file contents
Shift + arrow key	Select text in direction of arrow key

Setting Permissions

In Chapter 15, you learned the use of the chmod command, which enables you to alter the permissions assigned to a file. You also learned that permissions are difficult to read. Happily, Midnight Commander enables you to work with file permissions easily (see Figure 17.12).

To change file permissions, do the following:

1. In the file list, select the file.

2. From the File menu, choose chmod. You can also press Crtl + x, c.

3. In the Chmod command dialog box, choose the permissions you want for the file.

4. Click Set.

Creating Links

Chapter 15 introduced the important Linux concepts of hard links (two or more names for the same physical file) and symbolic links (alias names for a file). You can easily create either kind of link with Midnight Commander.

To create a hard link, do the following:

1. In the file list, select the name of the file for which you would like to create an additional name (a hard link).

2. From the File menu, choose Link. You can also use the Ctrl + x, l keyboard shortcut.

3. In the Link dialog box, type the new name for the file.

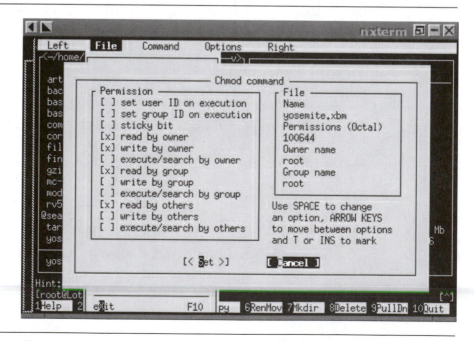

Figure 17.12 You can easily change file permissions.

4.   Click OK.

To create a symbolic link, do the following:

1.   In the file list, select the name of the file for which you would like to create a soft link (an alias).

2.   From the File menu, choose SymLink. You can also use the Ctrl + x, s keyboard shortcut.

3.   In the Symbolic link dialog box, type an alias for the file.

4.   Press Enter to create the symbolic link.

Files that are actually symbolic links are indicated with an "at" sign (@). If you would like to edit the link, select the symbolic link, click File on the menu bar, and choose edit SymLink. In the Edit symlink dialog box, you can change the name of the file to which the link points.

Using Keyboard Shortcuts

As you've noticed here and there throughout this chapter, you can use keyboard shortcuts to access many of Midnight Commander's commands. The function keys perform varying tasks depending on the context you're in; for example, F4 enables you to edit a file when you press this key in the default mode, but the same key starts the find/replace utility when you're viewing the file in the edit mode.

Table 17.6 lists some of the more useful keyboard shortcuts you can use throughout Midnight Commander.

Table 17.6 Midnight Commander keyboard shortcuts (selected)

Press these keys:	To do this:
Alt + plus	Select a group of files
Alt + \	Unselect a group of files
Alt + *	Reverse the current selection pattern
Alt + ?	Find file
Alt + c	Change directory (cd)
Ctrl + r	Refresh file listing
Ctrl + x, c	Change file permissions (chmod)
Ctrl + x, i	Change listing mode to Info view
Ctrl + x, l	Create a hard link
Ctrl + x, q	Change listing mode to Quick view
Ctrl + x, s	Create a symbolic link
Esc, Esc	Cancel current option

From Here

This chapter concludes *Linux Clearly Explained*. You've now learned all the concepts and skills you need to become a proficient user of Red Hat Linux. You've created a credible alternative to the Windows and Mac OS desktops, and you've learned how to manage this sophisticated, powerful operating system. With this solid foundation behind you, you'll be able to take full advantage of the coming deluge of outstanding Linux applications—and you can say goodbye to the constant, oppressive cycle of expensive operating system upgrades. Congratulations!

References and Further Reading

Bezroukav, Nikolai. 1999. *The Orthodox File Manager (OFM) Paradigm.* Available online at http://www.softpanorama.com/OFM/.

Fisk, John M. 1997. "An Introduction to the Midnight Commander," *Linux Gazette* (December, 1997). Available online at http://www.linuxgazette.com.

Midnight Commander Development Team. 1998. *GNU Midnight Commander User's Guide.* Available online at http://www.gnome.org/mc.

Afterword

You've installed Red Hat Linux 6.0, learned how to use the GNOME desktop, and mastered all the fundamentals of Linux system administration. Congratulations!

Now it's time to graduate. As you've learned in this book, Linux isn't just an operating system; it's a powerful, multi-user operating system with advanced networking capabilities built right in. If you're not sure networking is for you, consider this:

- Using the knowledge base you already possess, you can set up a network in your home that will enable every user to access the Internet by means of a single modem.
- Suppose you're running a small business. You don't have the cash to hire a pricey system consultant, but you need to set up a computer network that will enable your employees to share Web access and exchange e-mail. Surprise! It's all built into Linux, and ready to go.
- You want to create a small computer network for your home, a school, or a small business, but you've got just one problem: Some people are using Windows or Mac OS, and they don't want to switch to Linux. Here's some very good news: With Linux networking software, you can easily get the Linux, Windows, and Macintosh boxes to network effectively.

This book's companion volume, *Linux Networking Clearly Explained* (Academic Press, 1999), shows you how to accomplish all of these networking tricks, and many more. With what you've already learned, you'll be ready to start making Linux jump through hoops. Got a couple of disused 386 or 486 computers at home? Connect them, and try it! You'll be amazed at how easy it is to get going with Linux networking, and *Linux Networking Clearly Explained* provides just the information you need.

As you're expanding your knowledge of Linux, don't forget to keep up with Linux and GNOME. There will be new versions of Red Hat Linux, of course, and you'll be wise to upgrade; the new version will sport new features, of course, but it may also include bug fixes, including solutions to security problems that weren't known when the current version was released. (For security reasons, it's always a good idea to keep your system software up to date.) Keep your eye on GNOME, too (see http://www.gnome.org). Under rapid development, GNOME is acquiring new features (and new applications) almost on a daily basis. Without upgrading to a new version of Linux, you can download and install the RPM packages for new GNOME software, ranging from the core GNOME programs to new and upgraded GNOME applications.

Index

/ (root directory): 101, 127, 129
/bin, 101
/boot, 101
/dev, 101
/dev/cdrom: 184
/dev/fd0: 184
/dev/hda1: 133
/dev/hdb4: 132
/dev/modem: 352
/dev/sda4: 132
/etc: 101, 187
/etc/fstab: 436, 441
/etc/passwd: 456
/home: 101, 127, 132, 255

/lib, 101
/mnt, 101
/mnt/cdrom: 437
/mnt/zip: 132
/opt: 127, 129
/proc: 101
/root: 101
/sbin: 101
/tmp: 101
/usr: 101, 127, 129, 436
/usr/doc, 49
/usr/local: 127, 129
/var: 101

AbiWord: 314
Adobe Acrobat Viewer: 235–236, 279
ADSL: 349, 367, 369
aha152x driver: 123
Alt + Tab: 207
Alt key: 195
ampersand (&) operator: 417
anonymous FTP: 385
Apache web server: 44
applet: 283–285
AppleTalk, 43
application
        GNOME–compatible: 209, 296
        installing: 338
        launcher: 262–264
        session management: 295
application programming interface
        (API): 16
Applixware Suite: 320
archive: 339, 342
audio file: 231
Audio Mixer: 233

background color: 269
background graphic: 271–273
background process: 417
BackPack drive, 93
backup: 343, 449–453
bad sector: 444
bash
        command history: 416
        default shell for Linux: 394–395
        editing shortcuts: 415
        grouping commands: 431
        output and input redirection: 432
        pipes: 431–432
        shell script: 432–434
Berkeley Software Distribution (BSD):
        11
beta version: 389
boot disk: 116

boot options: 118
boot process: 174–176
bootable partition: 163
boot disk: 161–162
boot sector virus, 39
bulletin board systems (BBS): 353
bus
        compatible, 89
        incompatible, 95

C (programming language): 6
cable modem: 367, 369–371
        compatible, 92
cached data: 189
cd command: 402
CD-R drive: 111
CD-ROM: 116
        booting: 116
        compatible, 90
        incompatible, 93
        mounting: 326–329, 436–442
cfdisk command: 441
chmod command: 420
chown command: 419
client: 17, 62
clockchip: 167
Color Xterm: 196
command interpreter: 394
Common Desktop Environment (CDE):
        71, 192
compatibility: 88
compiler: 42
components: 133–138
compressed file: 235
compressed file/archive: 339
computer virus, 39
console: 396
Control Center: 248
control structure: 433
Copy dialog box: 226
copyleft: 14

CORBA: 193
corner panel: 287
cp command: 411
CPU compatibility, 89
Ctrl + Alt + Backspace: 397
Ctrl + Alt + Delete: 210
custom installation: 103, 119

DB-9 connector: 145
default gateway: 147
default language: 176
default text file viewer: 237
default video mode: 167
defragmentation: 333
desktop: 64
    background color: 269–271
    wallpaper: 271–273
desktop area: 196–197, 205, 298–299
df command: 445
digital camera: 87, 111
dir command: 403
directory
    changing: 402, 467–468
    copying: 484–485
    creating: 230–231, 413–414
    defined, 97
    deleting: 489–490
    home: 214, 402
    listing: 403
    moving: 486–487
    removing: 414–417
    renaming: 409–410, 479–480
    root: 214, 401
    selecting: 221–222
    window: 215
disk drive
    /dev/fd0: 443
    drive mount buttons: 265–266
    enabling user access: 442
    formatting: 329-331, 442
    free space: 331–333, 445
    mountable: 178
    mounting: 326–329, 436–442
    unmounting: 327
    user access: 183
    ZIP: 443, 450
Disk Druid: 124
distributions, 30
DNS server: 148, 351
documentation: 40, 49
domain name: 148
DOS partitions: 126
drag-and-drop: 200, 222
drawer: 286
driver: 43, 86, 175
du command: 445
DVD drives, 87

e-mail: 380–385
edge flipping: 197
edge panel: 287
Electric Eyes: 239–241
emulation: 323
emulator: 396
eMusic: 280
Enlightenment: 177, 196
    Configuration Editor: 298–302
    iconifying windows: 204
    keyboard shortcuts: 209
    shade/unshade: 203
    stick/unstick: 204, 205
environment variable: 406
EsounD: 193, 279
EsounD daemon: 231
Ethernet: 43, 367
Ethernet card: 369–371
exit command: 401
extended DOS partition: 108
extension: 215, 248

FAQ: 50
fg command: 417
file
    archiving: 446–449
    associating: 248–250
    backup: 449–453
    compressing: 454–455
    copying: 222–223, 223–224,
        226–227, 411, 482–485
    decompressing: 454–455
    deleting: 228, 412–413, 487–489
    editing: 489–493
    finding: 243–247, 405–408,
        472–475
    icons: 216–217
    linking: 247–248, 428, 494–495
    member: 446
    moving: 222–223, 223–224,
        224–226, 478–480, 485–487
    ownership: 252, 254–257, 419-428
    permissions: 252–255, 493
    reading: 408–409, 475–478
    renaming: 229–230, 409–410,
        478–480
    selecting: 221–222
    type: 248–250, 377–378
    tagging: 480–482
    viewing: 235–242
File Manager: 200
    Alt key: 223
    associating files with applications:
        248
    brief view: 218
    column header: 219
    copying files: 222
    custom view: 219
    deleting files: 227–228
    detailed view: 219
    directory window
    filtering files: 220
    finding files: 243–247
    FTP: 386

    home directory: 214
    icon view: 218
    icons: 215, 216–217
    moving files: 222
    navigation icons: 214
    preferences: 250
    Preferences dialog box: 250–251
    renaming files: 229–230
    rescan: 220
    selecting files: 221–222
    Shift key: 222
    Tree View: 212
File Transfer Protocol (FTP): 385–387
filesystem: 96, 438
    /etc/fstab: 439
    /mnt/cdrom: 439
    conceptual orientation: 96
    iso9660: 438, 439
    mounting: 439
    unmounting: 440
    vfat: 438
Filesystem Hierarchy Standard (FHS):
    99–101.
filter: 470
find command: 406–409
Find File command: 243–247
FIPS: 106
FM synthesis: 186
focus: 194
forking: 73
formatting disks: 329–331, 442
Free Software Foundation (FSF): 14
Free/OSS: 279
fsck command: 444
FTP: see File Transfer Protocol (FTP)
full backup: 450–453
FVWM: 67

gdm: 175
General Public License (GPL): 14–15,
    33, 47, 310

gFTP: 387
GhostScript: 156
GIMP: 310–312
GNOME
    applications: 45, 77
    Calendar: 306–307
    Control Center: 260
    defined: 192
    desktop: 177, 197–201
    desktop accessories: 306–310
    desktop icons: 183
    drag-and-drop: 193
    File Manager: 178
    fonts: 278
    GNOME terminal: 196
    GnomeCard address book:
        308–309
    Help System: 178
    imaging architecture: 193
    Main Menu: 291
    Panel: 197–201
    saving the current setup: 294
    sound: 279
    System Monitor: 331
    themes: 193, 203, 277–279
    Time Tracker (GTT): 307–308
    windows: 203
GNOME DiskFree: 332
GNOME Search Tool: 244
GNOME terminal: 196
GnomeCard Address Book: 308–309
GnomeICU: 388
GnoRPM: 333, 334–335
gNotepad+: 309–310
GNU File Utilities: 397–398
GNU Image Processor (GIMP): 310–312
GNUCash: 313–314
Gnumeric: 45, 312–313
GPL: see General Public License (GPL)
graphical user interface (GUI): 21, 59
graphics file formats: 241
grip: 280

group: 457
GTK+ Toolkit: 193
gv: 237
gxTar: 340
gzip: 235

halting the system: 188
hard link: 428, 430, 494–495
hardware compatibility: 89
Help Browser: 201
home directory: 214, 255–257
horizontal synch rate: 166
host name: 148

iconify button: 204
ICQ: 388
IDE adapter compatibility, 89
IDE hard drive compatibility, 89
IMAP: 380–385
incremental backup: 450–453
infrared devices: 112
    compatible, 92
init: 175
input redirection: 432
installation
    Disk Druid: 124
    starting: 119–121
Internet
    Linux IRC channels, 52
interprocess communication: 64
IP address: 146, 351
IRQ: 95–96,123,357
ISDN: 349, 367, 368–369
ISDN adapter compatibility, 90

job number: 417
Joy, Bill: 11
joystick compatibility, 92

K Desktop Environment (KDE): 41, 71
    applications: 45, 74, 316
    KOffice, 45
kernel: 6, 18, 394
keyboard bell: 283
keyboard shortcuts: 301, 495–496
kill command: 419
KOffice: 45

LAN networking: 145
less command: 408
LILO (Linux Loader): 105, 162–164, 174
Linux
    applications: 44
    defined: 29–31
    distribution: 30, 38, 42
    Documentation Project (LDP): 49–50
    features, 35-36
    filesystem: 96–101, 329
    installation: 41, 83, 102–104, 115–142
    logo, 34
    newsgroups: 50
    performance, 35
    reinstallation: 169–170
    reliability: 36–37
    trademark, 53
    system requirements: 85
    user-unfriendliness: 40
LinuxConf: 179–189, 456–457
ln command: 429–431
log in: 400
log out: 400
login name: 176
logout: 187–189, 261
logout command: 400
low-level formatting: 329
ls command: 403

Mac OS: 203, 229
Macromedia Shockwave: 379–380
mailing lists, 43–54
man command: 404
master boot record: 105, 162
maximize button: 204
meta key: 195
Microsoft Windows: 37, 46–47, 104, 105, 323, 327–333, 438
Microsoft Windows NT: 35
    client/server networks: 16
MIDI: 186, 187, 279
Midnight Commander (MC)
    defined: 463
    interface: 464–465
    panels: 468–470
    view file: 475–478
minicom: 353–358
mkdir command: 413
modem
    compatible: 91
    incompatible: 94
    recommended, 87
    testing: 353–356
    troubleshooting: 356–357, 366
monitor: 165
motherboard, 89
    incompatible, 95
mount point: 98, 326, 436
mounting disks: 326–329
mouse
    compatible, 90
    installing, 143-145
    Midnight Commander, 465–466
    three buttons: 195
Move dialog box: 224
MP3 file format: 233
MS-DOS disk: 440
Mtools: 440
multi-user system: 182, 452
Multics: 5

Multipurpose Internet Mail Extension (MIME)
multitasking: 5, 19
    preemptive: 20
mv command: 409

Nation, Robert: 67
Netscape Communicator: 365, 373
    configuring e-mail and news: 380–385
    helper applications: 375–380
    launcher: 199
    plug-in: 379–380
network: 17
network adapter
    compatible, 90
    incompatible, 93
    installing, 145
Network Configurator: 357–364
network interface card (NIC): See network card
network printer: 158
newsgroups: 50, 384–385
nondestructive repartitioning: 106
notebook computer, 82
numeric mode: 422

object code: 42
Open Group: 16, 62
Open Sound System (OSS): 279
open source software: 14, 22–25, 37–38
operating system: 4
ORBit: 193
output redirection: 432
overclocked CPU, 93

package: 140, 335–336
package dependency: 334
Pager: 199–200, 290

options: 290
Panel: 198–199
    add: 288
    adding applets: 283
    appearance: 289
    appearance options: 289
    corner panels: 288
    drawer: 286
    edge panel: 287
    hide buttons: 198–199
    log out button: 261
    position: 288
parent directory: 213
partition: 105, 116
    defined, 97
    Disk Druid: 124
    formatting: 133
    mounting: 98, 129, 441
    relation to directories, 98
    root: 163
passwd command: 399
password: 161, 176, 182, 343, 344, 399, 456
path: 406
pathname: 402
PC card
    compatible, 92
PCMCIA: See PC card
PDF: see Portable Document Format (PDF)
permissions: 251, 253–255, 419–428, 493
ping: 365
pipe: 431–432
plug-and-play: 367
Plugger: 379–380
POP: 380–385
Port-to-Port Protocol (PPP): 357–364
Portable Document Format (PDF): 235–236
PostScript: 155–161, 236–237
PostScript printer: 156

PPP: see Port-to-Port Protocol (PPP)
PPP dialer: 365
printer: 155–161
        recommended, 87
process: 417
process ID: 417, 418
ps command: 418
PS/2: 144
pwd command: 403

radio card compatibility, 92
rawrite program: 117
Real Audio player: 376–380
reboot: 401
rebooting the system: 188
recommended partition scheme:
        127–128
Red Hat Linux
        compatibility levels, 88
        distribution, 30
        hardware compatibility, 89–94
        Web site, 48
Red Hat Package Manager (RPM): 333
        icon
redhat-list: 53
Regular Xterm: 196
Ritchie, Dennis: 6
rm command: 412
rmdir command: 414
root directory: 97, 212
root partition: 129
root password: 161
root user: 39, 102, 173, 176, 178–179,
        187, 326, 353
RPM: see Red Hat Package Manager
        (RPM)

scanner:111, 112, 311
screen saver: 273–276
scroll bar: 204

SCSI: see Small System Computer Inter-
        face (SCSI)
search: 405–408, 472–475
Search Tool: 244–252
security: 139–140, 182
sendmail utility: 44
serial port: 352
server: 17, 62
server-class installation: 103, 119, 139
services: 149–155
session management: 208–209, 295
set group userid (Set GUID): 253
set userid (Set UID): 253
setserial command: 357
shade/unshade: 205
shadow passwords: 456
shell: 8, 18, 40, 394, 431–433
        case sensitivity: 395
        options: 395
        syntax: 395
shell script: 394, 432–434
shut down: 401
shutdown procedure: 189
signature file: 381
single-user system: 452, 455
Small Computer System Interface (SCSI):
        123–124, 132, 163, 184
        controller compatibility, 90
        hard drive compatibility, 89–90
        installing, 123
        recommended adapters, 87

sound card
        compatible, 90
        installing, 185-187
        recommended, 82
Sound Configuration Utility: 186
sound file formats: 234
sound support in GNOME: 279–283
Stallman, Richard: 14
StarOffice: 320
stick/unstick: 205

su (superuser command): 398
superuser: 102, 256, 400–401
swap partition: 127, 131
symbolic link: 247–248, 428, 430,
     494–495
symbolic mode: 422
symmetric multiprocessing (SMP): 36
sync range: 166
syntax: 406
synthesized sounds: 185
system administrator: 325, 455
system crash: 189
system inventory: 94–96
system requirements: 85
     minimum: 85
     recommended: 86

tagging: 480–482
tape drive
     compatible, 90
     incompatible, 93
tar: 340, 446–449
TCP/IP, 12
technical support: 48
terminal emulator: 196, 396
text viewer: 237–239
theme:193, 203, 276–279
Thompson, Ken: 6
Time Tool: 344
Time Tracker: 307–308
time zone: 149
time-sharing: 20
time/date: 344
title bar: 204
toolbar: 207–†210
Torvalds, Linus: 32
Tree View: 212–213
TV tuners: 112
two-drive installation: 110
two-OS installation: 164, 174, 327, 441
two-OS system: 104–105, 115

umask command: 427–428
Universal Serial Bus (USB)
     unsupported, 87
Unix
     defined: 4
     history: 5–17
     philosophy: 6, 7–9
     portability: 20
     scalability: 17
     standardization: 15
     UNIX (trademark): 4
     user-unfriendliness: 10
unmount: 327
unmounting disks: 327
unsupported hardware: 44, 87
     digital cameras: 88
     DVD drives: 87
     overview: 93
     scanners: 88
     Universal Serial Bus (USB): 87
Usenix: 10
user account: 174, 179–182, 398–401,
     455–460
useradd command: 398

vdir command: 404
video: 242
video card: 165
     compatible, 90
     recommended, 87
video file formats: 242
video modes: 168
video RAM: 167
virtual console: 396–397
virtual desktop: 196–197
virtual file system (VFS): 235, 339, 386
virtual memory: 20
virus: 39
volume: 232

wallpaper: 271–273
waveform sounds: 185
wavetable synthesis: 186
wharf: 68
whereis command: 406
wildcard: 406, 472
wildcards: 221, 407
window: 206, 267–269
    annihilate: 206
    close: 206
    focus behaviors: 267–269
    iconify: 206
    move: 206
    remember state: 206
    shade/unshade: 206
    size: 207
    stacking: 207
    stick/unstick: 207
window manager: 64
    AfterStep: 68
    Enlightenment: 69, 76
    GNOME-compatible: 192
    LessTif: 68
window options menu button: 204
windowing: 59
windowing system: 64
WINE: 323
WinZip: 235, 340
WordPerfect for Linux 8.0: 248,
    321–324
workstation-class installation: 103, 119,
    138

X Window System: 41, 44, 60-62, 65-
    67, 165, 175, 194–197
X-CD-Roast: 280, 319, 343
X-Chat: 389
X/Open: 13, 16
X11 Amp: 231
x11amp: 280
xanim: 242

XFree86: 165–169
XML: 312
Xmms: 231
xpdf: 236

Y2K: 56

ZIP drive: 443, 450
    installing, 132